a boo

pay   for

a   ged books.

THE PLEASANT YEARS

By the same author

Novels

SCISSORS
SAILS OF SUNSET
THE LOVE RACK
LITTLE MRS. MANINGTON
SAGUSTO
DAVID AND DIANA
INDIANA JANE
PAMELA'S SPRING SONG
HAVANA BOUND
BARGAIN BASEMENT
SPEARS AGAINST US
PILGRIM COTTAGE
THE GUESTS ARRIVE
VOLCANO
VICTORIA FOUR-THIRTY
THEY WANTED TO LIVE
ONE SMALL CANDLE
SO IMMORTAL A FLOWER
EIGHT FOR ETERNITY
A TERRACE IN THE DARK
THE REMARKABLE YOUNG MAN
LOVE IS LIKE THAT
WIDE IS THE HORIZON
A FLIGHT OF BIRDS
THE PILGRIM COTTAGE OMNIBUS

Miscellaneous

GONE RUSTIC
GONE RAMBLING
GONE AFIELD
GONE SUNWARDS
AND SO TO BATH
AND SO TO AMERICA
AND SO TO ROME
HALF WAY
PORTAL TO PARADISE
ONE YEAR OF LIFE
THE GRAND CRUISE
SELECTED POEMS (1910–1960)
A TALE OF YOUNG LOVERS (POETIC DRAMA)
THE DIARY OF RUSSELL BERESFORD
ALFRED FRIPP: A BIOGRAPHY
A MAN AROSE (CHURCHILL POEM)
THE GROWING BOY: AN AUTOBIOGRAPHY, VOL. I (1892–1908)
THE YEARS OF PROMISE: AN AUTOBIOGRAPHY, VOL. II (1908–1919)
THE BRIGHT TWENTIES: AN AUTOBIOGRAPHY, VOL. III (1920–1929)
SUNSHINE AND SHADOW: AN AUTOBIOGRAPHY, VOL. IV (1930–1946)

The author on his eightieth birthday

THE PLEASANT YEARS

Being the fifth book of an Autobiography

1947–1972

by

CECIL ROBERTS

"What fun to be you!"
Sir Max Beerbohm

HODDER AND STOUGHTON
LONDON SYDNEY AUCKLAND TORONTO

To
CHRISTINA FOYLE
commemorating a friendship of forty-five years

CONTENTS

Chapter		Page
	Foreword	11
1	A Florida Winter	13
2	A Dream Fulfilled	21
3	Alassio and Rome	45
4	Excursion in Spain	69
5	Excursion in Austria	82
6	Life at Palazzo Vairo	99
7	The Fight for Freedom	132
8	Vienna, Geneva, Nassau	178
9	Honorary Citizen	217
10	Shadows in Sicily	236
11	The Grand Cruise	255
12	The Birthday Party	270
13	Irish Excursion	283
14	In England Now	306
15	Turkey and Greece	318
16	Journey's End	341
	Epilogue	349
	Index	353

ILLUSTRATIONS

The author on his eightieth birthday *Frontispiece*

facing page

Alassio from the terrace of Palazzo Vairo 64

The Castello di Conscente 65

The Villino Romano, Alassio 65

Norman Birkett and the author 128

The British Ambassador unveils the Max Beerbohm plaque 129

The condemned cottage 160

Driving to the Feria 161

The Duchess of Alba leaves for the bullfight 161

The author receives the keys of the castle 192

Günther Bauer's wedding at Schloss Orth 192

Eight and eighty. Nicholas Gilliam and the author 193

The Château de la Garoupe, Cap d'Antibes 193

Dr. A. L. Rowse and the author at All Souls College 224

Judith Masefield, the author, and John Masefield 224

Somerset Maugham painted by Sir Gerald Kelly, and Graham
Sutherland[1] 225

Lunch at the Crouching Lion, Honolulu 225

9

The Villa Taranto, Lake Maggiore 288

The Château de l'Echelle, La Roche-sur-Foron 288

Aubrey Cartwright at Eton 289

Sir Max Beerbohm at Villino Chiaro 289

The Lord Mayor of Nottingham presents the Freedom casket[2] 320

Cutting the birthday cake[3] 321

Eighteenth birthday Foyle Literary Lunch 321

Key to acknowledgments

1 The Tate Gallery, London
2 *Nottingham Guardian Journal*
3 Brian Long

FOREWORD

On a bright afternoon in May, 1972, I walked down Park Lane from
the Dorchester Hotel where, at a Foyle Literary Lunch, some four
hundred guests had gathered to celebrate my eightieth birthday and
the publication of *Sunshine and Shadow*, the fourth volume of this
autobiography. I had reached what is termed "a ripe old age". If
you are not over-ripe or "ga ga" you are apt to be regarded as something of a wonder, you have survived so much, and you are still here,
the product of six reigns. You are presumed to have achieved wisdom,
and, with luck, financial security, but you are aware that neither of
these can be of use much longer, for the way is short to the Last
Door.

As I left the Dorchester Hotel I wondered whether I should be
given time and health to complete, with a fifth volume, this autobiography, planned ten years ago. Four volumes of this work, *The
Growing Boy*, *The Years of Promise*, *The Bright Twenties* and *Sunshine
and Shadow*, have recorded an eventful life from 1892 to 1946. And
now the roof to this edifice?

The next morning after the lunch I went to my desk, before a
french window that looked on to a beautiful garden, leafy with plane
trees and bright with roses, and began this, the fifth and final volume.
I call it *The Pleasant Years*, not because they have been any pleasanter
than those that preceded them but because, now, all hopes and
anxieties are futile. One has come to terms with life.

On the day in Rome, my eighty-second birthday, that I ended my
long labour with this book, I walked past the church converted by
Michelangelo out of the ruins of the Baths of Diocletian and read

that a Monsignore would preach there on *L'Importanza di Essere Felice*—the importance of being happy. That would be a fitting subtitle for this volume.

C. R.

CHAPTER ONE

A Florida Winter

I

On the eve of the New Year, 1947, I was a guest in a beautiful villa, "Estella", in Palm Beach, Florida, set between the blue Gulf Stream and palm-fringed Lake Worth. My hostess was Mrs. Beatrice Cartwright, a woman of wealth and beauty, extravagant, wilful, warm-hearted. She had run through two fortunes and four husbands, by American standards not excessive. The issue of her third marriage, with a British naval officer, was a boy, "tall, divinely fair", now at Eton College. So the last toast of the New Year's Eve had been to this absent son, Aubrey.

What had 1947 in store for me? I went into the garden after midnight. The air was warm, the stars bright above the giant palm trees. The long swimming pool, fed with warm water from the Gulf Stream, reflected the gold light in the windows of the villa. In its tower, which commanded views of the Florida peninsula, I had a study. At the side of the pool there was an alfresco chalet-bar. I took a seat there. Such silence, such beauty! I was fortunate to be here, but an undercurrent of uneasiness pervaded my paradise. One should never repine, but one cannot reach middle-age without carrying some debris of misfortune and defeat in the depths of one's being.

How far off seemed that other world of my Pilgrim Cottage in England, where I had written my books, built my career and known the happiest ten years of my life! It had survived the war but it was now imperilled by circumstances that conspired to defeat me. At no time in my life had I been free from anxieties. I could laugh at them now. At fifteen I had been left destitute. I vowed then that at all costs I would be free one day, and independent. By incessant industry, thrift, and some luck I now had an adequate income and some reputation in my profession. But I had experienced shocks concerning the probity of others. I had just spent five strenuous years in the U.S.A., making propaganda for the British Government, and had impaired my health thereby. Having incessantly used me, it had behaved with unbelievable duplicity and ingratitude.* Well, I reflected, I must dismiss all that, I want no fungoid growth in my memory. I had seen so many crippled with the gangrene of resentment.

This year, 1947, would see the publication of *And So To America*. It was the account of my five years' toil, the longest book I had ever written, some three hundred thousand words. Up in the tower of my hostess's villa I was now engaged on my nineteenth novel, *Eight for Eternity*, the story of the embattled monastery of Monte Cassino. During the writing the degree of my exhaustion from war work had revealed itself. I started and stopped, started and stopped, and knew long periods of sterility. Days went by when I could not write a word, devoid of invention. Never in my many years of authorship had I experienced this frustration. Had the well run dry forever?

At this stage, on the verge of despair, a friend descended on me one morning. The telephone rang and the butler's voice said "There is a Mr. Frederick Rivers asking for you, sir." I went downstairs a little incredulous. How could Frederick Rivers be here in Palm Beach? His home was on a Scottish estate in Nairn. He owned a fine house with twelve guest-rooms. He entertained lavishly. He booked sleeping-berths on the Inverness Express for his southern guests. You were commanded, and you went. A house flag flew, the Stars and Stripes if you were an American. He had joined the Roman Catholic Church and liked you to go to Mass with him. At some time in the morning you were gathered up and taken off for lunch on the moor. He opposed the slaughter of birds but had no objection to turtle soup. No one knew where his money came from. There was a rumour, via Oxford friends, that he was the illegitimate son of a Scottish baronet who owned a whisky distillery. He certainly made life a huge frolic. I had wondered what the war had done to him, and here he was, filled with the zest of life. I told him my worry, I had dried up. He laughed scornfully. "Nonsense! You'll never dry up. You'll be writing when you're ninety. Now come along. I'm

* Cf. *Sunshine and Shadow*, Ch. 17, "The British Treasury".

going to take you out in a bath-chair. But I want first to swim in that pool—it looks gorgeous!"

In the dressing-room I extracted a few facts. How had he got the dollars to come here? I was astonished to learn that he had a woollen-weaving mill on his estate. He had come over to get orders, the Treasury had allowed him the money. I gasped. In five years I had not been able to get a pound out of England.

Frederick had arrived overnight on the Florida Express from New York. I enquired how long he would stay. "Oh, I'm going back tonight." He had a suite at eighty dollars a day in the luxurious Plaza Hotel in New York. No, he was not visiting anyone. He had heard I was here, thought he would like to see me after seven years, and to have a look at Palm Beach. We swam. I introduced him to my hostess in the pool. He accepted an invitation to lunch but when we had dressed, a little before noon, he said, "Now, come along! I rode from the station in a bath-chair. I'm going to take you along the promenade in one, it's great fun!"

I had for years seen those "bath-chairs" but had never ridden in one. They were a renowned institution of Palm Beach. They were made of cane. You sat in an open seat and a Negro behind pedalled you along. I had never liked the idea. They suggested slavery. Frederick hailed a double-seater. We got in and were wheeled along the front, by the blue Atlantic Ocean. My friend was almost hilarious with the experience. The sweat ran down the face of the poor Negro. Frederick weighed over two hundred pounds. My conscience was eased with the knowledge that the man would be well tipped. After an hour we arrived back at the villa for lunch. Frederick declined Mrs. Cartwright's invitation to stay the night. He must take the evening train to New York. "I'm here for exports," he explained. Somehow I could not take this seriously. He loved train travel. "Complete isolation. I never sleep so well as on a train." As he stood on the platform he looked at the vermilion flush of evening and the level line of the black, silhouetted jungle. Did the scene suggest his comment?—"How beautiful! And to think we have invented the atomic bomb! My boy, the human race is a mistake. I can't think why it was ever created." The express came in from Miami. He mounted and, from the window of his "drawing-room" in the sleeping car, extracted a promise that I would visit him next summer. Back at the villa, my hostess said, "What a remarkable man! I do wish he had stayed."

I laboured in my tower. Visitors arrived but I was invisible until noon, when I went down to swim in the pool. One morning I saw a young man dive into the water. I wondered who the new guest was. When the swimmer drew near to me, to my amazement I saw it was Lord Sackville threshing the water. He had arrived overnight with Anne, his wife. She had written to me last August—"Our getting out of England this winter looks very remote. I doubt our being allowed even a dollar. But one must close Knole and I must see that my beloved Charles, who will be seventy-seven this year, does not spend the winter in a freezing cold house. It is all so dismal—not allowed to spend what little money one has and all of us being made to look like beggars." So they had made it, somehow. Knole, perhaps the largest private mansion in England, was shut up for the winter.

We went to dine one evening with the Duke and Duchess of Windsor. They had been lent a villa in Palm Beach. We ate on a terrace by moonlight while four musicians played ukeleles, seated in a leafy cabana. The palm trees at the foot of the pool were floodlit. The duchess's white, svelte gown of *peau d'ange* contrasted with her smooth black hair. She was as soignée as ever and a perfect hostess. I was astonished to find the duke dressed in Stuart plaid trousers, with a magenta linen dinner-jacket. He borrowed a ukelele and played it. He looked young and happy. He asked me if I was writing. I told him I was struggling with a novel about the Monte Cassino battle. He said he was thinking of writing his memoirs. I replied that I would be happy to give him any help. "You will? I may take you up on that! It's a frightful job, you know—what *not* to write!" I had last seen him at Baron Eugene de Rothschild's, on Long Island, two years ago. He referred to that visit and the subsequent death of Eugene's wife, the beautiful Kitty. He had taken refuge in their Schloss Enzesfeld, near Vienna, immediately after his abdication in 1936 and he had never forgotten their kindness during those trying days. I wondered what was in store for him now the Bahamas Governorship was ended. He had done a thorough job there, and been very popular, as always. Two years my junior, he was still full of energy.

My hostess told me that this summer she would open "Casa Estella", her villa on the French Riviera coast, at Cap d'Antibes, and hoped I would visit her. She had been caught there by the war breaking out but had lingered on until September, 1940. Then she had made her way across France to Lisbon and the United States.

II

I was back in New York at the end of April. I dined with Mrs. Cartwright at her Fifth Avenue apartment. One of the guests was Mrs. Dorothy Caruso, her cousin. She was very surprised when I recalled that in 1924 she had given me and my travelling companion, Armand de la Rochefoucauld, her box at the Metropolitan Opera House, and we had taken with us the two Mdivani brothers, Prince Serge and Prince Alexis, then in poor lodgings in New York. She had married Caruso a few years before his death. They had one child, Gloria, whom he adored. I said I remembered that she had told me Caruso would not allow any birds to be shot on his Italian estate near Florence, unlike other Italians. "What an incredible memory you have!" she exclaimed, "He loathed 'other singers' being shot."

Soon after my return to New York I was astonished by being called up by Frederick Rivers who had not yet gone home. He told me about a spell-binding cleric, Monsignor Fulton Sheen, who had a great following as a broadcaster and preacher. He was handsome, golden-voiced, with a strong sense of décor. Frederick, entranced, begged me to go with him to St. Patrick's Cathedral on Fifth Avenue to hear him preach. Reluctantly I went, and to his disappointment was not impressed. It was all too rehearsed. The cathedral was crammed. It was the morning of the renowned Easter Sunday parade on Fifth Avenue. We went out into the brilliant sunshine, down an avenue of skyscrapers. A number of top hats and tail coats had survived the war. Lord Beaverbrook, the newspaper tycoon, was there frog-like, diminutive, dapper in black, with cloth-topped button boots.

I finished with a desperate struggle *Eight for Eternity* and sent it to my typist. I was not happy about it, and exhausted. Then one day my despondency vanished with the arrival of a cable from my publisher in London. *And So To America* had been sold out on publication and was reprinting. So I was not forgotten. Within a year it would be reprinted three times. My American publisher gave me lunch, pleased with this news of the book. I began to prepare for my homeward journey. The spring would see me in Pilgrim Cottage, Henley-on-Thames.

When I went to the Cunard office to book a passage on the *Queen Elizabeth* I was astonished by their demand that I should pay in dollars. I was an Englishman with an English bank account, and this was an English company. But they were dollar-avaricious, and didn't want the English on their boat. So I had to borrow dollars to book my passage.

I made a few final visits: to Washington to lunch with our ambassador, Lord Inverchapel; to Glen Cove to stay with Baron Eugene de Rothschild, sad with the loss of his Kitty; to Oyster Bay, the guest of Sir Alexander Cadogan, Permanent Under-Secretary of the Foreign Office, now the U.K. Representative at the United Nations, and soon to receive the Order of Merit. His wife had the delightful name of Theodosia, which reminded one of ambrosia and the food of the gods. There was, as through five years, a notable lunch at Mrs. Murray Crane's, in her apartment overlooking Central Park and its small zoo. Sometimes through the conversation you heard the seals bark in the pool below. You never knew who you would meet at Josephine Crane's table. She was a deft and enterprising collector of people. On this occasion there was the Comte de Paris, the claimant to the French throne, ignoring the upstart Bonapartes. I looked with awe on this father of eleven children. There was a pretty boy of seven, in a kilt, with his mother. He was the third Lord Lyell. His father, a V.C., had been killed in the war. Later, calling on Mrs. Grace Vanderbilt, I found Maggie Teyte, in New York for a recital, and Salvador Dali, the surrealist artist, an exhibition in himself. These were farewell visits; the American phase was over.

I was sad to leave my furnished apartment where I had lived for more than four years. It was only a few yards from the Park and the Metropolitan Museum. It had sunshine, an open fireplace, a bathroom, boxroom and kitchenette. It cost me $80 a month (£20 at the then rate of exchange). It had been my office and from it I had conducted my propaganda campaign which had entailed travelling many thousands of miles, from the Canadian border to the Mexican Gulf, from the Atlantic to the Pacific coast, making hundreds of speeches. In this room one night I had almost died, having collapsed through exhaustion with a duodenal haemorrhage and been rushed to hospital. My apartment had been a refuge, with a kindly landlady. Here I had worked and washed and cooked in desperate economy, my English money blocked, the Government having repeatedly failed to allow me, an honorary worker, to draw on it. But there was an amusing side. I would launder and iron, and then go to someone's box at the Opera, or a gala dinner, or a public meeting at which I spoke. Round the corner there was a delicatessen shop, open all day and night. It was kept by two Sicilian brothers who could sing duets from any known opera, but spoke no intelligible English. There were shelves, ceiling high, crammed with an incredible variety of foodstuffs. Through a curtain of hanging sausages they would address me as "My Lord". Late homeward calls, in evening dress, had produced this. I responded with "Illustrissimi". Their smiles were as expansive as their bellies. One Christmas they gave me a tin of Earl Grey tea. Where they had found it, God only knows. The parting from my landlady was tearful. She was a Pole, with a paralysed husband, both elderly refugees. She had leased this apartment house. Now it had been bought over her head for reconstruction and she would be thrown into the street.

III

At the end of April I went on board the *Queen Elizabeth*, the 83,000-ton luxury liner. Proud, beautiful, she could not know her fate. Within twenty-five years she would be a total wreck, gutted by fire, rusted, at the entrance to Hong Kong harbour, a menace to navigation. Now in the April morning she was astir with excitement. My cabin was filled with flowers and presents, farewell greetings from American friends. Soon after sailing I had a shock. On board, with her elderly husband, was Myra, now a buxom matron, still lovely, who twenty-five years ago had caused me such torment. There was someone else I knew, young Pamela Frankau, the novelist, on the verge of her first success. Poor girl. After a hectic love affair with Humbert Wolfe the poet, she had married in California and lost her baby. And for the second time, crossing the Atlantic, I met the lovely young Marchioness of Hartington, one of the ill-fated Kennedy family. Her husband, the Duke of Devonshire's heir, had been killed in the war. She was now deep in a love affair with the young, rich Lord Fitzwilliam. She was going to join him. Within a year, flying together, they would be killed in an air crash.

I kept to my bed until noon, going over my manuscript. I decided that the ship was too large for comfort. It was a hunt to find anybody. She had been built to regain the blue riband of the Atlantic, challenging the Americans. Like their ships, she proved uneconomic, a folly, and would be sold in the company's slump and go to her disastrous end.

It was a cold spring morning when the ship docked at Southampton. I drove home through the green glory of the English countryside. When I arrived at Pilgrim Cottage the apple trees were not yet in full blossom but the daffodils nodded for me and the forsythia had burst into yellow flame across the sixteenth-century timbers. "Welcome to paradise!" exclaimed my housekeeper, coming up the path to meet me. I went in and opened a pile of letters before a log fire, with the smell of tea and toast filling the low-raftered room. I was home.

CHAPTER TWO

A Dream Fulfilled

I

May, with banners flying, marched over the Chiltern valleys. The beeches on the hills that encompassed me had burst into new leaf. Then one morning a letter from my publisher, Ralph Hodder-Williams, crowned my felicity.

> I took home the manuscript of your novel on the same day that you brought it to us. I read it myself enthralled and without a break. And now I feel my first task must be to congratulate you on giving us your finest novel since *Victoria 4.30*.
>
> I make this comparison deliberately, for in *Eight for Eternity* you have introduced your characters in the same exciting and brilliant way as you did in that earlier best-selling novel. There is the same touch of romance, and a most delightful humour.
>
> Once again I found myself absorbed in each individual character; in Charles Conway, in Frankie and his tragic break with the musician, in Stanislas the Pole, in Chandra the Ghurka and, above all, in Brother Sebastian. Always I found myself looking in suspense for the connecting link between them all.
>
> And there the comparison must end for, in the final chapters of *Eight For Eternity*, I found that connecting link—and with it a depth and power which can, perhaps, only be born in an age in which we have endured and witnessed great sacrifice. I believe that in these final chapters you will bring comfort to thousands of ordinary men and women who, in the midst of war, have felt the tragedy of personal loss but, lacking faith, have never perceived the eternal verities.
>
> I should perhaps add that my nephew John, who was at Cassino with the Eighth Army, has also read the book. Not only does he share my admiration and enthuisasm, but also remains convinced that at some time in your life you too must have visited Monastery Hill.

I sat in my study looking out on a laburnum tree in gold blossom, the letter in my hand. I had worried as never before about a book and it seemed to have come out all right. I heard a blackbird fluting. The world was young and happy. I had anxieties pressing on me but for the time they were dismissed. I liked the reference to the fact that at some time I must have visited Monte Cassino. I had never seen it, or the monastery, being, during the war, five thousand miles away. I had taken a great risk. In New York I had interviewed some eighty British, American, Polish and Gurkha soldiers, who had been in that great battle. I had talked with them in the Service Clubs through which they had passed. I had read confidential Army reports that had been sent to the British Embassy.

There is no reason why one should not write about a place or events one has never seen. Historians are seldom eye-witnesses. The Roman occupation, the Norman Conquest, the Civil War, Waterloo and Trafalgar, had all been described by writers who had never been there. I made three hundred pages of notes before I wrote a line. Six soldiers, newly from the battle of Monte Cassino, had been interviewed by me for a 'press release' by the British Information Services in New York. They had wonderful stories and gave me many details. I knew, however, that the test would come after publication. There is always a reader who is delighted to prove that you are incorrect. There is always someone, somewhere, who knows something better than you do. That is the writer's ever-present challenge. Unlike the doctor whose error is buried away, it is there in print, blatantly.

I had always changed the scenes of my novels. There appeared to me to be three outstanding stories that might be told; the little-known struggle of Austria on two fronts in the First World War; the tremendous conflict waged mostly in the air over Crete; and the costly attempt to break through at Monte Cassino. The first had a titanic Russian background. The second was on classical soil which had seen the birth of the Greek civilisation. The third was dominated by St. Benedict's great monastery on the top of a mountain, a repository of a thousand years of history. So I wrote *Spears Against Us, So Immortal a Flower* and *Eight for Eternity*. The scenes were laid in Austria, Greece and Italy, on battlegrounds contested by various nations—Austrian, Greek, Russian, German, Indian, British,

Italian, Polish, American, New Zealand, Palestinian, French, Algerian, and South African.

And now, having written this novel, what next? Perhaps there would be no next. I wanted a rest, to potter in my garden, entertain my friends. The Henley Regatta was approaching. I went to Nancy Kersley's boathouse, whose balcony overlooked the winning post and down the long course. I had used this scene in the opening chapters of *One Small Candle*. Readers of my books began to arrive from the United States, Australia, New Zealand, South Africa, Canada and elsewhere. It was gratifying but tiring. They were mostly very pleasant. After all, one wrote to be read. But mail, over forty letters a week, was a trial.

One May evening I cut some flowers and motored to the Dorchester Hotel to dine with Emerald, Lady Cunard. That amazing woman was still holding court in her suite on the seventh floor. Birdlike, with quick blue eyes, her mind was as alert as ever, her memory incredible. How did she know so much? She read until four every morning, she said. Perhaps the celebrities were not quite as thick as in the famous Grosvenor Square days but she always had a few Cabinet Ministers, musicians, authors and artists. The Duff Coopers were constant standbys. She had gathered a court of bright young things in the literary world as well as elderly stars. It was thirty years since she had left, anonymously, a suit of dress-clothes at Ezra Pound's lodgings to encourage him to come to her box at Covent Garden, a *rara avis* with massive red hair. She had secretly given money to James Joyce. He found out who his benefactor was many years later when he became famous and called to thank her. "Very charming. And unusual," she remarked to me, "You so often get your hand bitten."

There were eight of us at dinner that evening at the table near the window overlooking Hyde Park. I had not seen her for a year. "So you did not stay to help Lord Inverchapel at the Embassy, as I had hoped," she said, reproachfully. I told her that since the Government had not released any of my money I had withdrawn my offer. It had been her idea. She deplored the exile of the Duke of Windsor. With his abdication all hope had perished of breaking into Buckingham Palace. Its doors were shut against her by Queen Mary, who criticised her "influence on David". Yet what an entrancing little woman she was, even now in old age! Her heart, broken by her wayward *ami*, Sir Thomas Beecham, had not mended. I had seen much of them together in New York. I tactfully did not mention his name, and that I had just seen this erring genius.

On Regatta Saturday young Aubrey Cartwright, seventeen, a blond giant of six-foot-four, cycled from Eton and stayed to lunch, tea and dinner. We went to Phyllis Court, bright, flowery, with a band playing under a huge copper beech, but it all saddened me; there were too many ghosts of the Thirties and of all those dead boys who had rowed the course. My old friend and neighbour, Seddon Cripps (Lord Parmoor) was there, sunk in memories. We shed a few tears together for happier days. There were ghosts in my own garden too, of young Lucien, my heir, killed at twenty-two, of gay Tony Allingham, and his lovely sister, Ann, massacred in Sumatra, twenty-eight and twenty-two respectively; of stalwart Louis, my former secretary, dead at twenty-seven in war-time Paris, of beautiful Nadja Malacrida, killed in a motor accident near my gate. Sometimes I listened for voices that sounded no more. Was it wise to stay on here, living in the past?*

II

It was my housekeeper, named Giulietta Anatrella, an American-born Italian widow, fluent in five languages, almost a hunchback but dynamic, who started me on a new phase of life. I often wrote in bed in the mornings, my desk the three-ply top of a tea-chest. Giulietta came up one morning with my breakfast and a copy of *The Times*. "Look at that!" she said. It was raining and had been raining for almost a week and we were damp and despondent. I looked as commanded. It was the advertisement by a lady who wanted to let her furnished villa at Alassio, on the Italian Riviera. Giulietta, with the light of *O sole mio* in her eyes, passed me the telephone. I rang and learned that the villa had four bedrooms, two sitting-rooms, half an acre of garden with orange, lemon and palm trees, and was on a mountain-side overlooking Alassio and the Mediterranean. Four pounds a week. I explained to the lady that I could not take it for this next winter as I was going to Palm Beach,

* See *Sunshine and Shadow*, Ch. 6.

but the winter after? Yes, she would let it if I took it for six months the winter after. She would send me details.

"You know, it's quite mad to take a place one hasn't seen—it may be ruinous, dark, damp, overrun with rats and cockroaches," I remarked. "At that price you can always walk out," said Giulietta. A month later, I paid a deposit.

Of course, the next winter in Pilgrim Cottage, with me away in Palm Beach, and her only sister living near Florence, may have fostered Giulietta's idea, but was it possible that she knew I was contemplating emigration, an involuntary act into which I was being driven? I owed money to an American who had assisted me during my mission in the U.S.A. This deeply worried me. I had not grown up with the kind of mind that sustains debts cheerfully. Some it never bothered. There was my ebullient friend Matthews, for instance, who had a town house, drove a Rolls-Royce, ordered champagne and oysters, took a stall at Covent Garden and Glyndebourne, and rented a trout-fishing in Austria each August. He had a large bill at his florist's. He had a bill everywhere. He wrote cheques that sometimes bounced. He was always "in the red" at the bank. When I told him that I have never been "in the red", that I would not sleep if I were and always had a balance, he retorted: "You are no good to the bank". Seeing my surprise, he explained. "They make money lending your money to people like me." It did not occur to him that they could not lend him money if there were not people like me. Was he miserable, did he die in want? Not at all. A time came when his arrears of Income Tax made him flee the country. He went to live in Jersey. He died insolvent, sitting in a chair in the hall, a glass of champagne in his hand, directing the removers where to place his furniture.

There was also my friend Adams. He went on living in his manor house long after his wife had died and his business had failed. He spent months looking for a small house to which he could retreat but he never liked any. They looked too mean. I arrived one weekend and learned there was no food in the house. The housekeeper reported that the butcher and the grocer had finally refused to deliver her orders. So I wrote him a cheque for a hundred pounds, and we motored, in his new car, to Oxford, cashed the cheque, paid the butcher and the grocer, and took the food back with us. He opened a bottle of wine at dinner and slept well that night. He suffered from diabetes and had to have injections. He sometimes gave a dinner at the Ritz Hotel, when all the ladies had roses. When I enquired nervously about his bill there, he laughed. "It's enormous, but I keep giving them a little on account. They know they'd lose the whole if they didn't keep me going." He patronised his tailor on these terms. Late one evening, driving home from a Masonic banquet, he ran his powerful car into a stationary lorry in a dark street. He hit it so hard that the fire brigade had to be summoned to lift the lorry off him. When his Will was proved some legacies went unpaid and the solicitor had to cut his bill. Suicide? I don't think so. He loved life and was an optimist. It was probably a diabetic blackout after too good a meal. The church was packed for his service. He was much liked, always cheerful and a splendid host.

It is a gift to be born like this, which I envy. I, severely schooled in economy and thrift, would be a sleepless neurotic if I were "in the red." Because of this my American debt weighed heavily on me. I had incurred it believing I could repay my American friend after the war when the monetary restrictions on sterling would be lifted. But they were not lifted at the end of the war. and they have never been lifted totally. The duplicity of this procedure was revealed when a storm blew up in the House of Commons in November, 1948. The Chancellor of the Exchequer in the Labour Government, Sir Stafford Cripps, had given permission for the National Union of Mineworkers to send £4,000 as a strike "donation" to the French miners. The Exchange Control regulations had been lifted for the transfer of funds "on the understanding that the gift was for charitable purposes". It went, of course, to support the French strikers. Within a fortnight there was another illustration of political chicanery. The Chancellor of the Exchequer had also given permission for the Labour Party to send £5,000 to the French Socialist Party "for the strengthening of its position". In other words, British money was sent to assist a Communistic revolution. It was revealed during the Commons debate that the Treasury had permitted only £500 to be transferred for a war memorial in France to the soldiers of the 49th Division.

In 1947 the travel allowance was fifty pounds, *per gratia* of the Treasury. Travel was the breath of life to me. Thirteen of my eighteen novels had had foreign settings. But one might not travel and spend one's money abroad, not even that which was earned abroad. All earnings must be remitted home, to be taxed and blocked.

The problem that now engaged my thoughts was how to regain my freedom. The Lords of the Treasury when I applied for the release of my money, to cancel my debt, suggested that I should emigrate and that after four years I could retain my foreign earnings, and receive my British income. One of the conditions was that I could not reside or maintain a home in England. I had a lovely home and many friends. I resented being pushed out of my own country. I postponed a decision so difficult to make but my housekeeper, unconsciously, had planted a seed with the advertisement of a villa to let in Italy.

III

At the beginning of September, 1947, I left for Cap d'Antibes to stay with Mrs. Cartwright at her villa "Casa Estella". It was a long, low villa with its own small cove on the coast. The grounds were full of pines. A series of terraces led down to the cove in layers of white rocks. There was a bathing house and a floating platform out in the blue bay. It was one of the most beautifully situated small villas along the Riviera coast. From the top terrace, on to which the rooms opened, there was a magnificent view in the evening when the sun set behind the mountains of the Esterelles. They were mauve by day, towards evening they became pink, and then dramatically black against the sky. My bedroom commanded this lovely vista.

The villa had a literary history. It had belonged originally to Lloyd Osbourne, the stepson and collaborator of Robert Louis Stevenson. George Bernard Shaw had been his guest. There was a photograph in my room which showed him swimming in the cove, a strange bearded figure that looked like ectoplasm floating in the water. On the ground floor, opening to the wide terrace, there was a long salon decorated by Syrie Maugham, entirely in white, my hostess's favourite colour. One end of this salon, with cabinets of blonde-de-chine, was used as a dining-room. There was a curving staircase with a wrought-iron banister with notes of Debussy's

La Mer. The villa was shaded by pine trees, a paradise built above the white rocks. It had weathered the war years, having been placed under the protection of the Finnish Minister, a friend of Mrs. Cartwright. When she arrived back, there was her *maître d'hôtel*, the quiet, smiling Anthime. Unlike other villas it had not suffered in the German occupation. Mrs. Cartwright's elder son, Dallas, has described that return after seven years. "Entering it in 1947 was like walking into the palace of the Sleeping Beauty. Anthime, a little more grey around the temples, appeared beaming at the front door. Then, like a magician, he threw open the door of the salon. Nothing had changed. "In perfect order, Madame", said Anthime. It was the result of his devotion, and genius for "wangling" with the authorities.

The day after my arrival there was a lunch party on the terrace, in the shade of the pines. The Duke and Duchess of Windsor were among the guests. They had taken the near-by Château de la Cröe. The Duke told me that he had begun his memoirs. He was depressed about the state of England and asked me innumerable questions. It was obvious that his heart was still there. Exile had not diminished affection. While we were talking Anthine came and whispered into my ear. There was an Austrian youth in the hall enquiring for me. Bewildered, I asked to be excused and went up to the house. There I found a tall youth in *lederhosen*, grubby, who bowed and asked if I was Cecil Roberts. He said he had hitch-hiked to Cap d'Antibes from Geneva. He told me his name, Günther Bauer, of Salzburg.

In August, 1936, I had arrived late in Salzburg to find all hotels full. The tourist agency sent me to a private house that took in tourists. It was the home of a young Austrian lawyer with a wife and three small boys. They could not have been kinder. I became a friend of the family. My hostess spoke a little English and I gave her one of my books. Nine years later in New York I received a letter from her via the Red Cross. She wrote to say that her eldest son, aged nineteen, a pilot in the Austrian Air Force, was missing. She clung to the hope that he was alive, perhaps a prisoner in England, and asked me to make enquiries. I learned later that he was killed, shot down. Their younger son, Günther, had read in the *Daily Mail* that I was in Cap d'Antibes. He had hitch-hiked to "see the family friend".

I returned to the terrace and explained the situation to my hostess. She immediately insisted on his coming to the table. He asked permission to clean-up. A little later he appeared in white linen shorts and a picturesque Tyrolean jacket. We heard his story. Austria being short of food as a consequence of the war, his parents had despatched him to visit an aunt living in Switzerland to be fed. Without money or a visa he had crossed the French frontier, with no clue to me except " . . . the novelist is at Mrs. Cartwright's villa at Cap d'Antibes", as reported by a *Daily Mail* gossip writer. My kind hostess asked him to stay the night. He stayed three nights, delighting everybody with his good manners, intelligence and looks. On parting he produced a paint box and gave her a beautiful little water-colour he had made of the villa. His subsequent history may be told. He became a leading actor in Vienna, a playwright, a popular broadcaster, and a Professor of Dramatic Art at the "Mozarteum" in Salzburg.

In my second week at the villa my felicity was shattered by a fiendish attack of my old enemy, the duodenal ulcer, the legacy of my work in America. The superb cuisine of the villa was lost on me, being reduced to a milk diet. Young Aubrey brought in a baffled doctor from Cannes. I was a blot on the landscape and proposed leaving but they would not hear of it. One night as I walked my terrace in agony the scene was one of indescribable beauty. A full moon shone over the sea. The lighthouse on the promontory intermittently flashed its beam. The line of the Esterelles lay like a sleeping dromedary on the horizon. The air was warm and pine-scented. I saw the dawn come up, purple and rose and lemon, so much beauty with so much physical misery.

After ten days I mended, the haemorrhage stopped. I began to eat again. One day I went to have tea at the Château de La Crôe. It was well-guarded, I was checked in by two gendarmes who telephoned the house. As I was talking to the duchess on the terrace I saw a youth go by, in a bathing costume, with a towel. He went down the long sloping path to the water. I wondered who the guest was. Twenty minutes later the youth came up the path again. It was the duke, very slim and boyish, with wet, ruffled hair.

The next day there was a touch of comedy. We went to lunch with a Belgian lady at the Villa Diodati, splendidly placed on a sea-washed promontory at Roquebrune. I sat by my hostess, who did not know a word of English. It became rather an ordeal. My inadequate French vocabulary was soon exhausted. As we left and passed through a small salon I was astonished to see eight of my novels, in English, on a shelf. So the lady could read though she could not speak English! I revealed my identity. Astonished, she explained that she had rented the villa from a French friend. Would I autograph one of the books, she was sure her friend would be delighted. I wrote my name. For years when motoring to the Italian border, past the Villa Diodati, I wondered if I was still lodged there and would meet with a welcome if I called. An author never knows where he may be living.

At the end of September I left for Florence and Venice, en route for Rome. I went to my old quarters in Venice, on the Zattere, warm in the October sun, by the broad canal of the Guidecca, fascinating with its liners and merchant ships. Venice is at its best in October. Most of the tourists have gone. The sharp, clear air brings a vista of the Friulian Alps, a massive range that towers over the city and is never seen in the heat-haze of summer.

The proofs of *Eight for Eternity* had arrived. I corrected them in the garden of an old friend, Signora Nobili. She lived near-by on a side canal, in a little studio-house. Her garden had sad memories for me. In it I had first met little Lucien Reid, the boy who became so dear to me, whom I had sent to an English school, had seen row with his crew at Henley Regatta and who now, killed at twenty-two, lay in a soldier's grave in Algeria. In this garden with its fountain and lemon trees, beneath the tall *companile* of San Trovaso, I had written one of my novels *The Guests Arrive*.

By the middle of October I was in Rome. The leaves were yellowing in the Forum as they had yellowed and fallen for two thousand years. There was *The Barber of Seville* at the Argentina Theatre, where it had first been produced. I called on Vera Cacciatore, living in the Keats-Shelley memorial house on the Spanish Steps, of which she was the curator. She gave me tea in a room looking up the Spanish Steps, near to the room where Keats had died. There was some excitement. She had just enlarged the kitchen and in pulling down a wall they found a small wooden box about ten inches long that had been bricked up in it. When opened it contained the skeleton of a parrot, wrapped in a piece of newspaper which gave the date of the interment. This helped to solve the mystery. Axel Munthe, who wrote *The Story of San Michele*, and founded the bird sanctuary at Capri, had lived in the house when a young doctor practising in Rome. Obviously he had interred his pet in the wall.

I had found on arrival in Rome my friend of over twenty-five years, Mrs. Boehm, the widow of my New York doctor. She was the ideal travelling companion. Visiting St. Peter's, we suddenly decided to ascend the cupola, Michelangelo's and Della Porta's masterpiece that dominated the whole of Rome, 400 feet high. Up and up and round and round we went, on narrow stairs where you had to incline yourself to the curve of the dome. My friend never paled. I believe she would have gone up into the great ball surmounted by the cross had it not already held its maximum capacity of sixteen persons. And at fifty-five I was her junior!

We had booked a passage in the *Vulcania*, from Naples to New York, We decided to motor to Naples via Cassino since I wished to ascend the mountain to visit the ruins of the shattered monastery which had crowned it. The chauffeur demurred, the road was in ruins from the bombing. We promised him new tyres if his were lacerated. We left Rome at 7 a.m. We were to sail at 7 p.m. With the utmost difficulty we reached the summit of Monte Cassino. What a scene met our eyes! The vast abbey, founded by St. Benedict in A.D. 529, had been reduced to acres of rubble. Many regarded its destruction by the Allies as a senseless outrage. The Abbey with its famous library was demolished and it was said that the Germans had looted the masterpieces of art in the Abbey. This was not correct. The truth came out in 1951, in *The Times*. A German, Lieutenant-Colonel Schlegel, had approached the old Abbot, aged eighty, suggesting that the paintings and manuscripts should be removed to Rome for safe custody, and in October, 1943, prior to the bombing, German army lorries conveyed many of the treasures to safety in the Vatican. These included paintings by da Vinci, Raphael, Titian, Tintoretto, vases from Pompeii, armour of the Emperor Charles V, and some 80,000 volumes and manuscripts dating from the eighth century. The Abbey's most sacred possessions were also saved; the bones of St. Benedict were reverently packed in a suit case, blessed by the Abbot, and despatched in a lorry. All this was achieved under heavy bombardment of the lorries by Allied bombers. One thing was regarded as a miracle, the tomb of St. Benedict had survived. A monk showed it to me amid a mass of rubble.

When I arrived at the top of the mountain, on a scene of vast desolation, I was moved to find that half a dozen monks, living in a shanty, their habits covered by aprons, were slowly assembling the stones together. Yes, they were rebuilding, they said. I spent two hours there in the cold November day, checking my printed proofs. The monk who escorted me over the rubble was convinced that I had fought there. "But, *signore*, you know your way about!" he exclaimed. "I am English, not German," I said, but he remained unconvinced when I said goodbye.

IV

We sailed on the *Vulcania* from Naples at 7 p.m. that day. As we drew out the rose of sunset filled the upper sky. The bay and the city sparkled with lights. Over Vesuvius there was a crimson glow, not of its internal fire but of the incarnadined clouds burning with the last rays of the sun. A grey spiral of smoke rose from the crater into the serene heaven. As we sailed out into the darkness the town and bay became a jewelled crescent. Swiftly the night descended. I went below to my cabin. It had a small verandah. For me the day had been full of content. I had seen Monte Cassino, for so long only a thing of my imagination.

We made a night call at Gibraltar, its huge rock like a sleeping behemoth filling the sky. After Gibraltar we passed Cape St. Vincent, with its lighthouse on the tip of Portugal. It blinked through the darkness.

The next day I met a fellow passenger, Cardinal McGuigan, the Archbishop of Toronto. My novel was about a famous Catholic monastery. One of my characters had been a monk there, an Englishman. On the outbreak of the war he had broken his vows, discarded his habit, and gone down to the plain and joined the army. He fell on the slopes of Monte Cassino. Actually it was a true story. I am not a Catholic. My story was much concerned with members of that faith. It suddenly occurred to me that here was an opportunity of having my novel authoritatively checked. The Cardinal most affably assented to read my proofs, which I gave him that evening. The next day before noon they were returned with a note which ran— "With gratitude for the great pleasure of reading your book, of extraordinary human interest, of deep spiritual beauty and of great historic worth. May I hope to receive an autographed copy next April?" In the afternoon I met the Cardinal on deck. I thanked him for his message. He said: "Do you know that you kept me awake most of last night? I could not put out my light until I had finished the book at 4 a.m. Do please send me a copy. I want to preach on it in our cathedral."

Some time after publication of *Eight for Eternity* I received a letter from a Mrs. Jean Haydean, of Liverpool. Of all the letters evoked by my novel hers gave me the most pleasure. Moreover, it gave me assurance upon something I had written about and not experienced.

I haven't for years had time for reading. Now my son has gone off to grammar school so I can make my way back to a library. I just didn't know where to start. There was a reader returning a book of yours, a new one. So you had survived the War! I took it out. It was *Eight for Eternity*. I have been wondering ever since how you knew so much about the battle of Monte Cassino. My husband fought there with the O.P. party attached to the 4th Indian Division. We read your descriptions of the battle together, and John says they were very perfect in all details, so that he could live the hours again. He loved the little Gurkhas, his life depended on them at times and he treasures now one of their Kukris that had done battle and was given to him by a Gurkha. He says that, oddly, no matter how many bombing raids were sent to the Abbey it always looked untouched once the dust had settled again.

Later, I received another letter, from a reader in New Zealand, the mother of a soldier. "I see from your book that you must have shared a dugout with my son. You describe an inscription on the wall. I have a photo of him there. Your description is exact. I wonder if you could give me any details of your lives together, and, perhaps, just how he died? They returned his few things, letters, photos, pocket book, etc. In his diary there is an entry. 'R came back with two bottles of wine. It warmed us. A merry evening'. Could you be that R?" Alas, I was not. It was a difficult and sad reply to write. I had been given a photo of the dugout, and a description of it by a returning New Zealand soldier in New York, who must have been a comrade.

In New York I had a room at the University Club on Fifth Avenue, which had always been hospitable to me. My window looked across the busy avenue on to the bright red door of Elizabeth Arden's boutique. I was amused to watch smart women entering it to be made beautiful in order to keep their husbands, and other women to be made beautiful in order to capture them. I gave two lectures which nicely covered my expenses. I could, after seven years of restriction, go out into Fifth Avenue and buy Christmas presents. I sent off four food parcels to England. I had been sending them throughout the war. England was still strictly rationed, long after it was necessary. You could buy pounds of butter and meat in France but were not allowed to bring it in. "You can't know the joy in our house when your ham arrived!" wrote Lady (Norman) Birkett.

Mrs. Cartwright was in New York. I lunched at her apartment facing Central Park and two days later, in the same building, with my old friend Mrs. Murray Crane. As usual she had a party of distinguished guests. Among them was a smooth-faced middle-aged man. Halfway through lunch he asked if I was *the* Cecil Roberts. I was always flattered to be *the*. It was as if I were The Knight of Kerry or The Master of Elibank. When I replied "Yes", he said— "I am one of your most faithful readers. I read you in English and in Czech!" I asked him his name. He was Jan Masaryk, the son of the first president of Czechoslovakia, and its Foreign Minister. When I expressed my pleasure, he said "Not only am I your admiring reader but after our betrayal at Munich you wrote a splendid letter to your Prague publisher, disassociating yourself with the settlement. It was published in our leading newspaper." He said he was returning to Prague in a few days. I told him that I had just received from my Czech publisher a translation of my novel *One Small Candle—Světla Hasnou*. He had not read it. "Then let me give you the copy," I said. His face lit up. "How very kind! I shall be able to read it on the plane going home!" I took the book round to his hotel that evening.

He was in a very difficult position. The Communists were plotting

to take over Czechoslovakia and the Government was being forced
into concessions. His friends pressed him not to return. He wrote a
letter to Dorothy Thompson, the American journalist—"I am
certainly not going down the drain without making a considerable
squawk . . . I must go home as soon as possible, to give my fairly
passionate support to those who are trying to carry on the lovely
Bohemian tradition against cynical and well-organized material
dialectics."

Masaryk flew home. In February, 1948, there was a so-called
revolution engineered by the Russians whose stooges took over the
country. Masaryk kept his post in the Government. He explained
to critical friends his motives. He would not desert Benes, the President, who had faced the Munich betrayal alone. He might be able
to exert some influence on his country's policy. But his hope was
vain. On the morning of March 10, his dead body, clad in pyjamas,
was found in the courtyard of the Czernin Palace, the Foreign
Ministry, in which Masaryk had an apartment on the second floor.
He had been thrown out of the window, "defenestrated". The
Czech Government asserted he had committed suicide. There was
a world-wide controversy over the manner of his death. Was he
murdered or had he committed suicide? At the inquest essential
facts were suppressed. There had been a struggle in his room before
he had "jumped". His body bore marks of violence. Murder by
"defenestration" had been known in Prague since the beginning of
the Thirty Years War in 1618. A police doctor, a famous criminologist,
Dr. Teply, viewed the body. He found bruises on it and a 7.65 bullet
wound in the back of Masaryk's neck, ringed by powder burns.
The hands were marked, as though by a fight. Teply had also
interviewed two Communist ministers, Nosek and Clementis.
Nosek, in charge of State security, was a ruthless Stalinist. Clementis,
also a Communist, took over the Foreign Ministry from Masaryk
but was arrested and executed as a 'Titoist' in a subsequent purge.
Teply had found Masaryk's apartment in complete disarray. Later
he told a confidant, "This is an infamy, a bestial assassination".
Unwisely he talked with an officer of the French Intelligence Service,
SDECE. Later, he suddenly died. An official statement said he had
"mistakenly given himself a wrong injection"! After twenty years
the official Communist newspaper in Prague, *Rude Pravo*, stated

that Masaryk had been murdered by the Soviet Secret Police under the orders of Beria, Stalin's sinister right hand. In 1968 the Czecho-slovakian Government, trying to revive a democratic state, appointed a commission to establish the truth. Nothing conclusive came of it. The Czechs were convinced that it was a Communist murder. So within little more than three months my table companion, whose tribute had given me much pleasure, was dead.

V

The Windsors were in New York, at their apartment in the Waldorf Towers Hotel. They invited me to their Christmas Eve dinner. We were a party of some twenty. I was astonished on entering their suite, which they kept permanently, by its almost regal magni-ficence. There were full-length paintings of George III and George IV in their coronation robes. Others of the duke's ancestors were there, some in the Garter regalia, all illuminated, in the long salon. Two footmen wore liveries. It was a full-dress affair, the ladies decolleté, with jewels. The duchess wore a small tiara on her black, tightly drawn-back hair. A cerise silk gown moulded her svelte figure. The dining-room table shone with silver, cut glass, flowers. The serviettes were embroidered with the royal arms. This did not look like exile.

In the salon after coffee we began to pull crackers and sing carols. After this there were general songs. The duke, in a plum-coloured velvet evening jacket went to the grand piano and began to sing. He had a large repertoire, a good voice and was excellent in some German, Lancashire, Scottish and Irish songs. His à la Harry Lauder "Oh, it's nice to get up in the morning, but it's better to lie in bed" was the chef d'œuvre. The party broke up at three a.m. I learned that we should meet next month in Palm Beach. When I went down into Park Avenue a blizzard was blowing. The Avenue, sidewalks and illuminated Christmas trees down the centre were all blanketed in snow which fell steadily. It was a Christmas card scene, soft, silent and very cold.

On Christmas Day there was another entertainment. Mrs. Grace Vanderbilt opened her new home on Fifth Avenue for her celebrated annual Christmas reception. She had been driven out of the Vanderbilt mansion lower down the Avenue by the encroachment of skyscrapers. The house in which for fifty years they had entertained royalties and statesmen was demolished. It marked the end of an era. Where should she go? Dozens of friends gave advice. She listened to all in a haze of pathetic uncertainty. So we thought, but we were mistaken. As we mounted the marble staircase of the new home, the English ex-Guardsman butler announcing the guests, it was evident that our hostess knew what she wanted, and had achieved it. The morning-room, library, ballroom, drawing-room, with fires blazing and bright with flowers, seemed as before. The huge Turner landscape shone on the wall, the familiar tapestries were all there, the chandeliers glittered from the high ceilings. At the end of the salon a small orchestra played. Mrs. Vanderbilt, wearing her famous *bandeau*, received her guests, standing before the painting of the young Grace Vanderbilt of the Nineties, beautiful, with a petite head of fair curls, and holding a strand of roses. She greeted some two hundred guests. There was a huge Christmas tree, scintillating with coloured globes, and a long buffet. I found myself talking to a young man who came from New Zealand. He was an artist, and thus a friendship started with Felix Kelly. Afterwards I walked down the Avenue to dine with Mrs. Cartwright. Young Aubrey had that morning arrived from England. The *Queen Mary* had docked two days late.

VI

In the last week of January, 1948, I was at "Estella", Palm Beach, in the tower room as before. There was one change. My hostess's late husband, Captain Cartwright, R.N., of a Northamptonshire family, had collected paintings of horses. There were some superb Stubbs and Sartorius pictures. Mrs. Cartwright had now brought them down from New York and hung them. Over the salon fireplace hung the portrait of a young Regency buck, with his horse, and his country house in the background. He was Squire Titmus of Leicestershire. How incredulous he would have been had he been told that one day he would hang in a Florida drawing-room! When the Windsors came to lunch the duke was alarmed on seeing these paintings. "But they'll be ruined in this climate!" he cried. "Not at all, sir," I replied, "Our hostess has built an air-conditioned room where they will be stored in the great heat of summer."

I should have been happy to be back in my lovely room in this winter paradise. In New York I had driven to the station in deep snow. Here at night I had to get up and close my windows, the scent of tuberoses from the garden was sickly and overpowering. I was uneasy in my mind because I was not working. Last winter I had finished *Eight for Eternity* in this room. Now, for nine months I had not written a line. Writing was my life, the thing I lived for. And here I was, lazy, barren, in ideal conditions for work. One day at the Windsors the duke took me into his study. He was working on his memoirs. He showed me a pile of sheets. The handwriting was beautiful, clear, firm, regular, unlike my own untidy, microscopic script. The amateur author was working, I, the professional, was not.

At lunch one day an incredible thing had happened. I had remarked that next winter I should be in Italy, in Alassio, where I had taken a villa. A guest whom I did not know, asked "What's the name of the villa?" I told him it was named Santa Margherita, that I had not seen it but had taken if after reading an advertisement. He smiled. "Then I can show you it. I lived in it for three years. If you'll come home with me I have a colour film of it." He was an Austrian living now in Florida with his American wife. I went home with him, and thus I saw the villa I had taken. It seemed enchanting.

The following morning the mail gave me a shock. I received a copy of the *Times Weekly Edition*. A paragraph in it paralysed me with horror. Ten years ago I had helped a young Austrian who had fled from the Nazis and procured him a post with a Tanganyika mining company. He had been a great success until the war broke out. An Austrian, he was unable to join the King's African Rifles so he hitch-hiked across Africa to Lake Chad, joined the French Foreign Legion, fought, was wounded and decorated. The war ended he returned to his position. Now I read that last month he had been sent with the Chairman's wife and some gold ingots to Dar-es-Salaam. En route, he had murdered the Negro chauffeur and the lady, buried the ingots, and returned, reporting he had been attacked by natives. Police investigations followed. Questioned, he drew a revolver and shot himself. It was all quite inexplicable. But

I had long known that life was inexplicable, that we are pawns moved by the hand of Destiny. I was deeply upset.

Another morning's mail brought me a letter which caused me, a mild-mannered man, to seethe with indignation. I lived near Henley-on-Thames, in a most beautiful small village. To preserve the character of the place, largely seventeenth-century, I bought two old cottages, with others, that had been condemned. There was a demolition order upon them but I felt they should be preserved, being full of character. They stood at an angle of the lane, very picturesque with their old brown tiles and dormer windows. I had bought them on the condition that I should be allowed to repair them. They were twin cottages, occupied at one end by an old couple who kept the house and the garden spotless. At the other end there was a dirty, whining slut. My tenants under the law could not be evicted, indeed I had no desire to do so, but on their deaths I would restore the cottages, converting them into one.

The occupants eventually died and on my return from America after the war I had employed an architect to make plans, with a strict injunction to preserve the character of the property. These plans I submitted to the local authority. I was amazed to be told that the cottages were condemned and must be demolished. It had revoked the undertaking upon which I had bought them. I began a fight to save them. I made appeals to the local council, to the County Council and finally to the Ministry of Housing, under whose law they said they were acting. They were all obdurate. The cottages must be demolished. I was determined they should not. At this stage I had left for Palm Beach. Now came a letter from my solicitor with the incredible news that the authorities had torn out the windows and doors of the cottages. They stood open to the weather and to trespassers.

I left Palm Beach at the end of March, and, after a brief stay in Washington and New York, sailed for England in the *Mauretania*. The solicitor's letter burned in my dossier. When the car that met me at Southampton delivered me at the gate of Pilgrim Cottage, a glaring sight met my eyes. The cottages without windows and doors, like eyeless skeletons, disfigured the end of the lane. I went into action at once. I saw the town clerk, the council surveyor. I saw chairmen and committee men. They all professed to be sympathetic.

They agreed that the cottages were part of the character of the village, but they could not alter the law on condemned property. I got nowhere. I suspended action, there were guests to entertain.

One May day I cut some flowers to take to Lady Cunard, whom I had not seen this year. When I asked for her at the Dorchester Hotel the hall porter said she was ill and not receiving. I left the flowers, with a note. A few days later she wrote thanking me. She was too ill for company but hoped to see me when she was better.

On July 8th there was a Royal Garden Party. Leaving for London, I again took some flowers to her. This time I went up to her room. No one answered when I knocked. I opened the door and took in the the flowers, leaving them with my card. As I left the room I saw that the bedroom door was open. In a Bergère bed lay Emerald. She did not see me, perhaps she was sleeping. Very quietly I left the room. Just as I was outside the door her maid, Gordon, appeared, very distressed. From her I learned that Emerald was dying of cancer.

There was an enormous crowd at the Royal Garden Party. I stayed only a short time, too upset for this sort of thing. I walked round the lake, away from the milling mob. It seemed impossible to believe that such a bright spirit could be quenched. Emerald had always radiated life, her zest insatiable. I had been with her in New York in 1940, when she had suffered the defection of Sir Thomas Beecham, the man she adored. After that mortal blow Emerald had left for London and installed herself in the Dorchester Hotel. The old social life in which she had scintillated, the famous lunch parties thronged with statesmen and celebrities, were dead beyond revival. I had heard there were financial worries. She sold her emeralds, substituting paste. She had made a brave show through the bombing, had furnished her suite with the treasures left after the total destrution of her house in Grosvenor Square, and had entertained, with small lunch and supper parties, where she had revealed her old flair, her marvellous memory. And now the end. All this was in my mind as I walked round the lake at Buckingham Palace.

Three days later a mutual friend called me at my cottage. Emerald has died last evening. Pleurisy had developed on top of cancer. She was seventy-one. Her erratic daughter had come from Paris, too late. Gordon, her maid, had refused to see her. My friend told me a strange story. One night at a dinner party Emerald had startled everyone by raising her glass and saying "To Death!" No one was aware that she had heard her death sentence. A sore throat that afflicted her had been diagnosed as cancer. I remembered, thankfully, that the last time I had talked with her she had expressed her pleasure at what I had written about her in *And so to America*. Knowing her had been an enrichment of my life.

Emerald left her diminished fortune to be divided between her daughter, Lady Diana Cooper and a friend. A small legacy of money, silver plate and clothing, went to Gordon. She expressed a wish that she might be cremated and her ashes buried in Grosvenor Square, only a few yards from the shell of the house where she had given her parties. It seemed an impossible request but Gordon carried it out. Late one night she went into Grosvenor Square and secretly buried the ashes in the lawn. Only she knew the place. On each anniversary, for as long as she lived, Gordon laid a solitary rose on the spot.

VII

I was doing no work, still barren of ideas. Towards the end of July I left for Thun in Switzerland, to join some friends. On the side of the Lake there was a bench with a plaque which recorded that Brahms had walked by the lake, and gained inspiration from it, writing a concerto. I sat on the seat, hopefully, but the lake, grey and stormy, filled me with melancholy. My depression grew so I suddenly departed for Florence, to sunlit Italy and smiling faces. From there I went on to Venice and ran into tragedy. My only brother, over ten years my senior, survivor of five operations, a skeleton, had never been to Italy and longed to go. It was the beginning of the charter-tours. You bought a ticket, and the organiser did all the rest, transport, bus, car, hotels. It was then an enterprise that had not grown into a plague, infecting every beauty spot in the world. I presented him and his wife with the tour, and went to Venice, where they would be for three days, to meet them. The bus journey over the Alps had been exhilarating, too exhilarating. My brother arrived in Venice like a sheet of white paper. Thinking some air would do him good, it was a September day of *sirocco*, I took him out in a gondola on the Grand Canal. There he had a haemorrhage, so bad that I feared he would turn the Canal blood-red. An ambulance was called. It was an open boat, with a bucket into which he could vomit. Unconscious, he was carried up to the first floor of the hospital, after my battle with an idiot-concierge who demanded his passport, and, still unconscious, arrived in a public ward. I chose this rather than a private room. It is the custom for Italians not to trust nurses overnight. So they sleep all night in a camp chair by the side of the ailing relative. My brother, with no language, might have died in isolation.

For three weeks he lay there, desperately ill. The doctors were very attentive. Then one night at 3 a.m. we received a message. He was dying. Unable to find a gondola, his wife and I walked through the silent maze of streets to the hospital. They had put a screen around him. Near by hovered a rotund Benedictine monk in a habit. He was of Maltese origin and spoke English. He hoped to snatch a heretic's soul before it went to Hell. My sister-in-law gave one look at my brother. "He'll live," she said. She had seen him like that on half a dozen occasions. She was right, he lived to be eighty-three and to bury her and a succession of doctors.

After three weeks I moved him to the Luna Hotel and arranged for him to be flown home. There was an amusing scene on leaving the hospital. As he was wheeled down the ward, its twelve male occupants, all in white nightgowns, flapped their arms, crying "*Volo! Volo!*" (Fly! Fly!), excited by the knowledge of his flight to England. My poor brother had seen Venice for only a couple of tragic hours but for years after he recalled the Grand Canal, without reference to how he had crimsoned it.

Exhausted by all this I could not enjoy Venice. I lunched with Duff Cooper and Lady Diana—she always created a ripple as she walked past Florian's—and the next day Aubrey Cartwright and his cousin Giles arrived from Cap d'Antibes. One evening Baron Maurice de Rothschild gave a supper for me at the *Taverna Fenice*. On returning to my hotel a telegram awaited me. Pilgrim Cottage had been broken into. When the three young burglars went upstairs they were astonished to find my housekeeper, Giulietta, in bed. They opened a bottle of wine and took some up to drink with her, calling her a gallant soul. She said she wouldn't drink with scally-wags but would go to see them in gaol. When they left she tried to call the police. They had cut the telephone wire. They were three local lads who thought we had all gone to Venice and the cottage was empty.

It was all very unpleasant, coming on top of my brother's illness, so that when Aubrey suggested that I should join them on their return from Venice to the Riviera I agreed to go as far as Monte Carlo to visit my Australian friend Guido Wertheim who had rented rooms there. En route we passed through Parma, and then Alassio. We found the villa I had taken. It was locked up, nestling on the hillside, with a splendid view of the sea and mountains. It seemed all that I had seen in the film at Palm Beach.

After a short stay in Monte Carlo where Guido had rooms overlooking the trap-shooting of pigeons that plunged into the sea, a thing that set me in a rage against those ghastly "sportsmen", I went on to Rome, bathed in October's gold. The British Ambassador, Sir Victor Mallet, invited me to lunch. The Jews having bombed the British Embassy, he was now housed in the Villa Wolkonsky where a Russian princess, a friend of a Czar, had once lived. It had a vast garden which held some ruins of Nero's aqueduct. The Mallets were very hospitable and a warm friendship ensued. One evening when I dined I found Lady Diana and Duff Cooper there, and also Prince Doria-Pamphili, of the great Roman family. A week later I was a guest in his palazzo on the Corso. The long façade masks the immensity of the palace, built round a large courtyard with palm trees. It is two-thirds the size of St. Peter's, in area little less than that of the Colosseum. It had housed eight hundred persons. It was now occupied by Prince Doria, his Scottish wife, and his daughter, Orietta. I was destined to know that family and palace intimately.

My host, Prince Filippo, had been a resolute opponent of the Fascist regime. When the Germans arrived in Rome the Gestapo sought to arrest him. Late one night a shabby old man in a long black coat, with a false beard, shuffled out of a side door, walked over a Tiber bridge and went into hiding in a poor cobbler's house in Trastevere. There was a reward of a million lire for anyone who supplied a clue to his whereabouts. The cobbler told the Gestapo not to be ridiculous when they asked if the prince was there. Princess Doria and her daughter, afraid of becoming hostages, also went into hiding, disguised. When the liberation came Prince Doria was elected the first mayor of freed Rome. Such was my gentle host, owner of a palace with a thousand rooms. Once when I asked if he had been in them all he shook his head and said quietly, "I don't think so!"

After a month in Rome I left for Alassio. My housekeeper awaited me. I arrived in the evening, went up a long garden path with palm trees to the little pink villa. It had two floors, seven rooms, a small hall and three balconies. Below lay the little town in a plain enclosed by low mountains, a hemisphere, with the Mediterranean beyond. Here I began a new life. It had always been my dream to live in Italy, and now it was fulfilled.

CHAPTER THREE

Alassio and Rome

I

It was almost dark when I arrived the previous evening. Now on rising I found that Giulietta had set my breakfast on the little balcony overlooking the long, walled-in garden. The Villa Santa Margherita had two terraces on the hillside. It had, also, what all Italian gardens should have, a tall, dark cypress. There were also some palm, lemon, orange, tangerine and mimosa trees. The face of the villa blazed with purple bougainvillaea. A rose pergola led down to a gate in the high brick wall over which spread a carob tree. Half of the town below had red tiled roofs, and the other half grey slate ones. Eighty years ago there had been an earthquake which had destroyed many of the roofs, and these had been retiled with slate, hence the two colours.

While I was at breakfast an old woman, wrinkled and gnomish, came out and smiled at me with a mouth of decayed teeth. This, said Giulietta, appearing behind her, was Anna. She was an inseparable part of the villa, where she had spent her life in service. It was in our six-month tenancy agreement that we should take her on, at a wage of £1.50 a month. She looked underfed. By a previous arrangement she had fed herself on a meagre food allowance. She was stone deaf and not one word ever penetrated. The chief drawback was that she never heard any visitor ringing down at the gate or at the villa's door. Giulietta worked with her by sign language. We decided that she should eat the food we ate. In a month she nearly doubled in weight, and I increased her wages, thereby being censured for spoiling the market. In the third week she fell and broke her arm and for a month was almost useless to us.

For some reason, despite my affability, I inspired terror in this

45

deaf gnome. Possibly it was my strange manner of earning a living by making cabalistic signs on a sheet of paper. On any reference to me she would cross her hands on her breast and roll her eyes as if seeking protection from the Virgin Mary. Although in time our our relationship became almost affectionate, I knew she thought I was "strange". *"Il Signor ha qualche cosa!"* she would murmur, tapping her brow significantly—"The Signor has something!" We were told that she was a spinster, but one day as I went down hill into the town, Anna, returning from shopping, was suddenly embraced by a pretty little boy. He sometimes came to the kitchen and was fed with cakes. Then the truth came out. It was her grandson! But how could she have a grandson, never having been married? The explanation was simple. When she was young, Anna explained, she had been *tradita nel bosco*—"betrayed in a wood". This was her married daughter's child.

After breakfast I examined the villa. There was one very large sitting-room, with a bedroom over. These faced east and looked down upon the English church, with the rotunda of its library, and a pergola in a long garden full of roses. The original owner of the villa, it transpired, was a devout spinster and loved bishops and canons of the English Established Church. To entertain them worthily when they came to preach she had built this large addition. An itinerant Bishop of Gibraltar, whose See comprised the whole Mediterranean coast, and other eminent divines had slept in the east wing. Its view was superb, across the bay towards Genoa and southwards to Corsica. The new English church, built by the prosperous British colony, was beautifully designed. But a thousand British residents, largely recruited from retired members of the Indian Civil Service, with India now lost as a recruiting ground, plus the exchange restrictions, had shrunk to about fifty. It had a lovable old clergyman. His always-bewildered wife played the organ. She devoutly believed in the magic Adam's Box. You pricked your finger and sent a smear of blood to a healer near Norwich who consulted the box and prescribed a cure. She beseeched me, with a needle, to let her send a sample of my blood, and be healed of my ulcer. I was obdurate, to her sorrow.

At the villa we found ourselves steeped in an ecclesiastical atmosphere. Beyond the south garden wall the Roman Church was in evidence in the guise of the Convent of Santa Chiara. It received female paying guests in the holiday season, and it took in sewing. The windows on the garden and road side of the nunnery were always tightly shuttered. It appeared dead. But one day there was contact between the Catholic and the Anglican Churches. A canon of St. Paul's, staying at the villa, had played tennis at the English Club so vigorously that he split his white duck trousers. They were sent for mending to the industrious nuns. Towards evening, a gentle little nun appeared at the villa with the canon's trousers, saying she would call for them the next morning as the repairs had not been completed. "Then why not keep them and bring them when they are finished?" she was asked. To this she responded gently, "The rules do not permit us to keep male garments in the convent overnight."

It was in the ecclesiastical wing of our villa that I started work but I found the views, with their ever-changing beauty transforming sea, mountains and town, too distracting. Later something more distracting drove me out of this delightful room—the intense cold when winter came. All through that glorious November there was no sign that anything like winter could visit us. We basked in the sun, we lunched on the balcony, we picked the golden tangerines, persimmons and grapefruit on our trees. There were beds of violets still in flower and blue wistaria and roses on the pergola. Working one morning in the garden, I heard a youth sing to his guitar below me, and the bells jangled in a hillside campanile. The stars at night were brilliant over the cypress. Out in the bay there was a crescent of sparkling lights from the acetylene flares of the fishing fleet. 'Twas very heaven.

And I had begun work at last. During my visit to Rome I learned that 1950 would be the *Anno Santo*, the Holy Year, when the walled-up door in St. Peter's would be broken down and the Pope progress through it with great pageantry. It was a ceremony observed every fifty years that was instituted by Pope Boniface in 1300, the year Dante, in Rome, learned of his exile. In the English library of 10,000 volumes, belonging to the church, there was a splendid collection of books on Roman history. Undeterred by the fact that 2,886 books had been written on Rome, according to the National Library, I decided to add another. I had, as old Anna put it, *qualche cosa*.

In off hours I explored Alassio. The chief shopping street had been christened "The Drain" by the British colony. Probably it had once smelt. It was now a narrow, crowded, kaleidoscopic street of shops. It had, Italian fashion, changed its name several times, having been the Via Roma, the Via Garibaldi, the Via Brennero, the Via Vittorio Veneto. It had emerged from the mists of history. As part of the ancient Via Aurelia, the Roman legions had marched along it, as also Napoleon on his way in 1796 to the conquest of Italy. Now it supplied everything. English was the shopping language. For a hundred years Alassio had been almost an English town, with English-owned villas. But two wars had killed "the gentry". Alassio's goldmine was its beach, a perfect half-moon of golden sand, unlike most of the rocky shore of the French and Italian Rivieras. When summer came there was not a square yard of space between bathing huts and beach chairs.

One night I was awakened in bed by the cold. When I arose the villa was an ice-house. It is an illusion that the winter on the Riviera is always warm and sunny. It can be suddenly arctic. Our hall had a wood-burning stove, but the marble staircase in which we had exulted defeated the stove and made the hall a frigidaire that set the temperature of the house. It became an act of courage to walk upstairs to bed. I made vain attempts to heat the Bishop's room. I bought a large round stove, one of those ancient contraptions that used to heat parish halls and station waiting-rooms. My stove had been Hellenised with a frieze of naked nymphs and youths that reminded one of Keats' "Ode to a Grecian Urn". It had a cavernous interior that swallowed half a tree, to no effect. The fireplaces in the rooms were like dog kennels, with deep interiors that sent all the heat up the chimney. We were soon spending on wood twice the rent of the house, and had to sit frozen, with small electric stoves focused on us. It was during this "freeze" that a guest arrived by car. I had to put him in the Bishop's bedroom, with four blankets on the bed. His toothbrush froze in its glass. When he was told that a week earlier we had lunched on the balcony he thought we were just lying.

They were performing *The Marriage of Figaro* at the Scala in Milan. An opera fan, he proposed that we should see it. We started off by car. We surmounted the barrier of the Ligurian Alps, a snow-covered expanse. A hoar-frost whitened the Piedmont plain. I had always wondered how those Roman legions, coming from semitropical Italy, wearing kilts, had survived our northern clime. I wondered no longer. Italians who can survive the winter of the northern plains, or of the Apennine and Abruzzi mountains, can survive anywhere. The Scala was certainly splendid to look at, with its tiers of gold boxes. But the opera was poor and we came out after the second act. A war-profiteer audience glittered with jewellery, a sight all the more singular since Italy had joined the Germans, and come to disaster. She was now on the verge of a phenomenal wave of prosperity. The second-class hotels would line themselves with marble and move into the de-luxe class. The lira would stand firm while the pound plummeted. Only last March Sir Stafford Cripps, Chancellor of the Exchequer, had avowed that, despite rumours, the pound would not be devalued. I did not believe him, for a year earlier a Zurich banker had told me that the pound was going to be devalued, a prophecy later fulfilled.

I returned from Milan to the villa. Buried in blankets, with a hot-water bottle at my feet, and a portable electric radiator turned on my hands, I stayed in bed until lunch and worked on *And so to Rome*. Then, after three weeks of this, winter departed as suddenly as it had come. The sun blazed, the blue sea sparkled, we basked on the balcony.

By Christmas we had met most of the members of the English colony. There was a prodigious crop of octogenarians, desperately surviving on diminished incomes. You met them at the library exchanging books. Every Sunday I called on Sir Louis Rieu, chairbound, nearing eighty, stone-deaf, with only one eye. He had been secretary to the Bombay Council, and the Governor of a Province. He could speak sixteen Urdu dialects. Balliol-educated, he was a Greek and Latin scholar, son of a Professor of Arabic at Cambridge, of Swiss extraction. Sir Louis had firm opinions. The great Jowett was the Master of Balliol when he was there. "He was a frightful snob and never spoke to a humble undergraduate. He made a bad translation of Plato, which was superseded by Cornford's version. He owed his inflated reputation to a galaxy of toady dons." Sir Louis snorted when I asked him about E. M. Forster's *Passage to India*, then having a boom. "The book is a hotchpotch, a travesty. He knows little about India. Another instance of boosting by a clique," he said.

When Lady Rieu made a trip to England she left him in charge of a friend, Mrs. Bock, who had been trained as a nurse, and who slept in the house. In the middle of one night she heard Sir Louis bellowing and hurried to his bedroom. She switched on the light, and, writing on a pad, the only means of communication, asked what was the matter. He looked very surprised and answered "Nothing". He explained that, sleepless, to amuse himself he had recited, in Greek, the Catalogue of the Ships in Homer's *Iliad*. Being deaf he could not hear the booming of his own voice. Greek was in the family blood. His brother, E. V. Rieu, editor of the Penguin Classics, wrote for it a best-seller, a translation of Homer. When the Athenaeum Club dug underground in Carlton House Gardens, to make a restaurant, a motto in Greek was put over the portal. Rieu selected an appropriate passage in which the sorceress Calypso invites Ulysses to "come in" (*Odyssey*, V. 91). But passers by, mistaking the Greek lettering for Hebrew, remarked "What a strange place to put a Synagogue!"

In December I was faced with a second unpleasant journey in the cold. I had undertaken to lecture to a literary society at Lucca, a town I had never seen. I arrived, in a downpour of rain, and lodged at the *Hotel Universo* that looked on a small piazza. Just before I was called for by the secretary of the society I heard music coming up from the piazza below. From my window I looked down on an astonishing sight. The rain was still falling heavily. In the middle of the shining wet piazza I saw six umbrellas and, under these, six musicians with violins, viola and flute. They were seated on collapsible chairs to which the umbrellas were attached. The music of *La Bohème* rose in the dark night, with not even a cat or dog as an audience. Mystified, I listened until the desk clerk telephoned to say my host was awaiting below. When I got into the car I sought enlightenment upon this extraordinary scene. "Your hotel overlooks the Piazza Puccini, named for Puccini who was born here", he said. "On each anniversary of his birthday the local Puccini Circolo celebrates it by giving a performance of his music in the Piazza. It is sad that it is raining but tradition is strong and they are not deterred, very rightly," he added, as our car turned out of the empty Piazza to the strains of "Un bel giorno".

The next day it was fine though still bitterly cold. I visited the Romanesque cathedral, and then the Picture Gallery in the

Governor's Palace which faced the large Piazza Napoleone in whose centre there was a marble seated statue of Elisa Bonaparte, Napoleon's sister, who married the man she loved, Felice Baciocchi. As Grand-duchess of Tuscany, she firmly governed the Duchy, suppressed brigandage and supported the arts and sciences.

I made a discovery. My chairman's Christian name was Pompeo. In the eighteenth century a kinsman of mine, during the Grand Tour, had his portrait painted in Rome by the fashionable artist of the day, Pompeo Batoni. Hence my interest in the name. Pompeo Batoni had been born in Lucca. I was shown his birthplace, with a bust of the artist outside. But why Pompeo? The great Roman, Pompey, of Shakespeare's "Even at the foot of Pompey's statua, Which all the while ran blood, great Caesar fell", was born here. He, Crassus and Julius Caesar in 60 B.C. formed the first Triumvirate that ruled Rome. So since those days little boys of Lucca had been christened Pompeo.

I returned from Lucca via Lerici on the coast. Just outside that picturesque little port I found, on the panoramic road skirting the bay, San Terenzo. Here, in the Casa Magni, Shelley had lived and sailing home to it in his boat from Leghorn, he had been drowned. His house stood on the beach which a motor road now intersected. The house was much the same but to my surprise I found it was occupied by a Signor Giorgio Popoff, and was a French Consulate! He showed me over the house where the Shelleys had lived until that tragic day. Later, the Marchesa Iris Origo acquired it and founded The Shelley Rooms.

II

The new year of 1949 brought me good news. *Eight for Eternity* had been reprinted three times in England. A week later I heard that in the U.S.A. the book was selling well. Half of this would go in taxes and agents' commissions, and the money would be blocked by the Bank of England and usable only in the sterling area. This caused me to think about my future. A day would come, as I had seen it come to many others, when one's inspiration failed or one's vogue vanished. In old age no author receives a pension from his publisher, his books go out of print, though continually lent out, free, by the libraries that pay him nothing in return. He has no business he can sell. Twice last year I had written cheques for embarrassed authors, desperate in old age. To have the good fortune to earn money and then be taxed, as in no other country, and informed that you cannot spend it where you wish, seemed to me intolerable. My chance of paying off my American debt made me consider again the Treasury's suggestion that I should free myself by emigrating. My philosophy was simple; one's first duty was to be independent, the second, to be happy. The problem worried me. I felt I was climbing a sandhill.

In March, my lease of the Villa Santa Margherita nearing its end and enchanted by the warmth and beauty of the early spring, I wrote to the English owner offering to buy the villa, in sterling, if I could get the Treasury's permission, or to take a lease and put in central heating. The irascible old lady replied that if I did not like her villa I should get out. No one had ever complained of it being cold. I got out. Later she regretted her decision. I left for Rome. I departed with regret. I had been enslaved by the town's beauty and its friendly inhabitants. I did not know that I was destined to return very soon.

In Rome I took a room at the Eden Hotel, with a balcony overlooking the gardens of the Villa Borghese and its cypresses. I was diverted by the nuns of S.S. Trinità, above the Spanish Steps, who every morning went out into their convent garden to collect eggs. The whole of Rome lay below me in the bright morning sunshine as I breakfasted. In the evening, to the west, I saw the glinting of the Mediterranean at Ostia. I was in paradise but how I worked! I was out every morning at eight collecting material for *And So To Rome*. I walked and walked, for you can see Rome only by walking. Often I never reached my chosen destination, sidetracked by some wonder up an alley or in a fountain-courtyard. Before I finished my book I had two hundred pages of notes. Luck was with me. Staying in my hotel was an elderly American, John Basore. He was a retired professor of Latin from Princeton University, a delightful companion. He was able to translate many of the inscriptions I found on ancient buildings and over ferny portals, often in baffling dog-Latin. We became close friends and met year after year.

It was mid-April, the Roman gardens were full of flowers. We lunched on pergola-shaded terraces. In May I went to a reception given by Prince Torlonia for young Princess Margaret of England. The Torlonia palace was on a corner of the Via Condotti, Rome's famous street of de-luxe shops. The palazzo had a large courtyard with a grotto whose cascade fell over emerald frondage into a basin. Prince Torlonia's wife was the Infanta Beatrice of Spain, the late King Alfonso's daughter. There were five salons, in succession, with tapestries, paintings, frescoes, and great vases of flowers on ornamental tables. Two hundred guests were presented to the princess. How tiny she was, frail, dark-eyed, eighteen. It was her first visit to the Eternal City.

Rome was full of delight with hundreds of little shops in the ground floors of old palaces. In these, under a single electric bulb, craftsmen were at work, descended from Renaissance forebears whose skills they had inherited. One day walking down a street near the Fontana di Trevi, beloved of tourists, who throw in coins to ensure their return, I saw a little shop in whose window were engravings of seals, crests, nameplates, etc. Inside, a frail, white-haired old man was at work. It occurred to me that he might be able to make me a book-plate. His family had been engravers to the Popes for four hundred years. I ordered a book-plate. A week later he showed me the sketch. It was delightful. Two weeks later the plate was ready. He asked if I was satisfied. "It has one mistake," I replied. His face fell, his hand trembled. I explained. "When an author writes a book he has name on it. Michelangelo carved his name across the bosom of his famous *Pietà* in St. Peter's. You are an artist, and you have not signed your name on the plate." He was silent for some moments. "Signor, in all my years I have never had such a compliment!" he said. Then he burst into tears. His old wife crossed to him and put her arms around him. "What a compliment, *caro*, what a compliment!" she said. When he added his name at the bottom corner it was microscopical. Later, when Aubrey Cartwright was twenty-one, I gave him a book-plate by the same artist, exquisitely engraved.

On another occasion I took a set of the printed proofs of my novel to be bound at a shop on the corner of the Bocca di Leone. Could they do it? Oh yes. They had bound books for the English poet, Robert Browning. He had had winter quarters down the street. I found a plaque marking his apartment, with his famous tribute carved on it. "Open my heart and you will see 'graved inside of it, 'Italy'." Rome is full of such moments of discovery.

In the middle of May Felix Kelly, the artist, arrived in Rome from Madrid with his companion, Manuel Huidobra, a portrait painter. They lived in a pension near me in a large high room whose window looked across the Villa Borghese park and framed the great dome of St. Peter's on the horizon. The evening scene when the crimson sunset silhouetted the dome, ball and cross, was superlatively beautiful. My friends were gifted and delightful companions. I spent much time in their room and persuaded Kelly to draw a jacket for *And so to Rome*. He had found a sham ruin with Corinthian columns in the Villa Borghese and made a composite picture of famous Roman monuments. Then, impishly, he drew a bust of me and put it on a classical plinth so that I looked like a Roman Emperor. There was a mirthful moment when he tilted a garland over my brow and converted me into one of Nero's bibulous cronies. This was erased.

There was a lot of talent in that room. Huidobra also drew me, simultaneously. He saw me not as a Roman but as an English country squire making the Grand Tour in the eighteenth century. He possessed the extraordinary gift of being able to draw with either hand, and, like Leonardo da Vinci, he could write left-handed, in reverse, so that you had to read the text in a mirror. We made many excursions around Rome in that genial month of May. When in November Kelly held his first exhibition at the Leicester Galleries in London one was not surprised that it was quickly sold out. I bought his painting of "The Appian Way" which is a constant joy.

It was about this time that, for some unknown reason, my books had a great vogue in Spain. When my publisher there suggestsd that I should visit Spain I enquired whether I had enough pesetas to my credit to finance the trip. He replied: "It is of a pleasure to say you they are of mountainous nature." Did he mean mountainous, momentous or mounting? He did not state the exact figure. My London agent reported that the "mountain" was 160,000 pesetas, £4,000, at forty to the pound. But the Bank of England was entitled to these and I might not spend them!

My friends were enthusiastic about Spain and urged me to go. I had finished *And so to Rome* so I was free. Then one day a disconcerting letter arrived from my Henley solicitor, informing me that the

Borough Surveyor had issued a demolition order against my two ancient cottages. It must be obeyed within two months! I instructed my solicitor to inform him that if they touched a brick of my property I would sue them and they would have major publicity over this vandalism. Last year the British Tourist Authority had spent £50,000 advertising "Come to Beautiful Britain" in American magazines. The demolition order seemed a singular contribution to this campaign.

III

In June I had a telephone call that surprised me. It was from a Swiss friend whom I had known in New York during the war, Maurice Sandoz. He was a very rich dilettante who derived his fortune from a pharmaceutical company. He was a tall, reserved, elderly bachelor. He wrote essays and novels, painted, and composed music. I used to meet him at Mrs. Crane's parties in New York. There was always something a little odd about him. One day in 1945 we had got on to the subject of the stigmata. Some of us were sceptical. "You must not scoff. I can show you them!" he said. "When, and where?" asked someone in our company of about ten. "Now, here, if you wish," said Sandoz, and, turning to Mrs. Crane, "That is, if you have no objection?" He asked for the blinds to be drawn, and the door locked to prevent interruption. Then he lay back in a chair and breathed deeply. After a short time he appeared to be in a trance, and on the upturned palms of his hands red lines, bleeding, were visible. Undoubtedly they were marks of the stigmata. Presently they faded and Sandoz came out of his trance. We were all dumbfounded. "It is a matter of inducing it traumatically. You can create it by concentration," he explained.

I often related my experience, and was listened to with so much disbelief that in time I began to wonder if I were the victim of my own imagination. Then one day in 1972 I was the lunch guest at the Caccia Club in Rome of my friend, Sir John Leslie. His other guest was Prince Toumanoff. They were both Knights of Malta and devout Catholics. Owing to a recent film we talked of St. Francis and I told them of that afternoon at Mrs. Crane's, twenty-seven years ago. "Every detail you have told us is quite correct. I was there that

55

afternoon and saw Maurice Sandoz produce the stigmata on his hands," said my host. He went on to explain that traumatically induced stigmata were not the same as those induced by religious ecstasy. "With the latter there are holes through the palms. There is also an incision on the body—of the spear that pierced Christ. The Church has over fifty authenticated cases" he said.

When Maurice Sandoz telephoned me that June morning I did not know that he was in Rome. He surprised me by saying that he had a villa there, near the Baths of Caracalla. I had not seen him for four years. He said that he was going out to the Bagni di Tivoli, having been ordered to take some sulphur baths there. Would I like to go with him and we could go on to Tivoli and lunch at the famous restaurant, La Sybilla, by the waterfall? He would come for me at eleven that morning. When his chauffeur called he led me out to a Rolls-Royce car. It had all its blinds drawn and I found Sandoz inside. He apologised for the darkness. "I can't bear the light. I've had cancer of the eyelids and have had new eyelids grafted on." Was it true or part of his phantasmal life? I found it was true, alas.

After a brief halt at the baths we went on to Tivoli and lunched at the romantically situated restaurant facing the ancient temple and waterfall. We returned to Rome in the late afternoon. He wished to show me his villa, and asked me to dine. Its situation was superb. It had a long, walled terrace that looked down over the vast ruins of the Baths of Caracalla. When in the summer operas were given there, on a gigantic open-air stage, Sandoz could enjoy them from his terrace. He had just published a new book of essays which he gave me. He paid large fees to Salvador Dali for illustrations to some of them, bound de luxe and beautifully printed.

The villa was large, set in a garden with cypresses. There was a long dining-room. I suppressed my surprise when I went into it. Dimly lit, at one end there was a high, black velvet catafalque. On the topmost step lay a skeleton, gilded, with a spotlight on it, macabre but beautiful. We dined under this reminder of mortality. The dinner went through its courses. It would have satisfied Brillat-Savarin, served by a footman in a blue jacket with a white jabot. After dinner we went into a sitting-room opening on to a garden with a semicircular privet alcove and a fountain. By touching a button a jet of water rose some twenty feet.

I knew that Sandoz had a fine collection of Fabergé objets d'art. When I enquired whether he had any new ones he brought out a large egg with a clock face, about eleven inches high. It was of classical design with a shimmering gold surface on an opalescent enamelled shell. On one side there was a white porcelain clock face, with gold hands, rimmed with pearls. The egg stood on a four-sided panelled china pedestal. Sandoz wound up the clock and set the hands near the hour. "Wait!" he said. At the precise moment the lid of the egg opened and out of it appeared a diamond-studded cockerel in gold and enamel. The bird flashed its diamond eyes, flapped its gold, jewelled wings and crowed the hour. This finished, it disappeared into the egg, under a grille which closed down. It did this on each hour. It was a work of fabulous artistry and ingenuity. Sandoz said it had been a present from the Emperor Nicholas II to the Dowager Empress Marie Feodorovna, at Easter, 1903.

"And what next, Maurice?" I said, playfully. He looked at me gravely, then walked to a cabinet, bringing back something wrapped in white silk. He uncovered it and put it on the coffee table. It was a plaster mask. "That's King Ludwig II's death-mask," he said, quietly. "It was made the day after his body had been recovered from Lake Starnberg, in June, 1886. Do you like Haydn's music?" Surprised by the abruptness of the question and its irrelevance I replied, "Well, yes. I have been to Eisenstadt and seen Prince Esterhazy's Schloss where Haydn had been Kapellmeister. And I have seen the composer's grave there."

Sandoz walked over to a wall and unlocked a safe, extracting a small black box. Raising the lid, he took out a skull with empty eye-sockets and broken teeth. "This is Haydn's skull," he said, smoothing the bare cranium as he set it down. He took an envelope from the box. "Here's the history of it. Just before Haydn died in May, 1809, Napoleon occupied Vienna—for the second time. Some of his soldiers made quite a lot of money digging up corpses and sending the skeletons to the Salpêtrière Hospital in Paris. Grave-opening seems to have been an easy thing. One of the corpses dug up was Haydn's, recently buried. His head came into the possession of a French officer, whose descendants sold it to the dealer from whom I have bought it. I shall leave it in my will to the Austrian Government, to be placed in Haydn's grave at Eisenstadt. He lies there now with somebody else's head."

Sandoz picked up the skull and put it in my reluctant hands. "Feel how light it is—like one of his sonatas," he said, gently.

Was it all a phantasy of his? Singular as he was, I regarded him as a truthful person, and a collector of much acumen. My subsequent investigations increased the enigma of Haydn's skull. According to his biographer. H. E. Jacob, *Joseph Haydn: his art, time and glory*, (1950), the story is somewhat different yet not so different as to rule out Sandoz's account.

On May 31st, 1809, in the year Haydn died, Napoleon placed a guard of honour round the composer's house until he was buried in the Hundsthurm Cemetery at the city's gate. Not a single Kapellmeister accompanied the composer on that last journey, but there were a few friends, including two great admirers, Herren Rosenbaum and Peter.

In 1820 peace reigned and H.R.H. the Duke of Cambridge was a guest of Prince Esterhazy at Eisenstadt. The private orchestra performed *The Creation* by Haydn. At a banquet afterwards His Royal Highness cried, addressing the prince, "Happy the man who had Haydn for a friend, and now possesses the body of that immortal!'

This jolted the prince. It had been originally planned that Haydn's body should rest at Eisenstadt. Some ten years had passed and, following the turmoil of the war, the removal of the body from Vienna to Eisenstadt had not been made. The prince now acted. The grave in the Hundsthurm Cemetery was opened. When the exhumed body eventually came to light it was found that the head was missing!

It transpired that Rosenbaum and Peter were fanatical phrenologists. They had bribed the gravedigger the night after the burial to open the coffin and let them take away the composer's skull. The motive was not gain, in the manner of the corpse snatchers, but to study and preserve a skull that had enshrined such musical genius, detectable according to phrenological science.

In the strange circumstances of the day they could not be prosecuted. Prince Esterhazy, frantic, made a foolish move. He offered to buy the skull. The conspirators sold him a false one, and kept Haydn's.

So in the grave at Eisenstadt, Haydn lay with another man's head! In due time, Rosenbaum, dying, bequeathed the genuine skull to the Vienna *Gesellschaft der Musikfreunde* and it was exhibited there in a glass case. It was there, according to H. E. Jacob, that he saw the skull.

The whole story is very strange. Did the original skull go to the mausoleum, via the *Gesellschaft der Musikfreunde*, and did poor Haydn get his own head back? I enquired of the *Gesellschaft*. I was informed "Haydn's skull was in the possession of the famous Dr. Rositansky, whose heirs gave it to the Stadt Wien."

But how did he acquire it and when? Groves *Dictionary of Music and Musicians* has a different version.

"In 1932 the reigning Prince Esterhazy made great efforts to obtain the head for burial with Haydn's body in the mausoleum he had created in the Bergkirche at Eisenstadt, but he was not successful and the skull remained with the *Gesellschaft* until 1954, when it was restored to the body entombed at Eisenstadt."

Did Haydn finally get his own head back? Sandoz's claim has too many corresponding details to be lightly dismissed. How did "Haydn's" skull get to Paris, with its pedigree? Sandoz died in 1960.

After long correspondence I was not able to discover what happened to his bequest. One is still in the dark.

I left the villa that evening quite dizzy with such a bizarre entertainment. I never saw Sandoz again. The sequel was equally singular. In the summer of 1961 I dined with an English friend who had been in a clinic in Switzerland where he had had a very unpleasant experience.

"In the clinic I met Maurice Sandoz, who had become rather mental. He had imagined that someone, an agent of his, had robbed him of all his money. One day he attempted to commit suicide by jumping from the bridge at Berne but was stopped. He was in my clinic for treatment. He often visited me in my room. He was always very interesting to talk with, as you know, and he struck me as quite sane. We dined in our rooms each evening, served with a tray. One evening Sandoz left me about seven o'clock and later one of the nurses asked me if I had seen him. They had taken him his dinner but he was not in his room and could not be found. Later the same evening, they went into his bathroom and there was poor Sandoz, hanging from a bath-rail, dead."

I have known two murderers and ten suicides but Sandoz was the most singular of them all, clever, repressed, kind, most intelligent but mysteriously elusive. He died intestate, so his large fortune went to a brother with whom he had quarrelled, who died soon after. Sandoz had a beautiful villa near Lausanne. In one room there were some steel-shuttered cabinets. On touching a button the shutters rose, revealing an Aladdin's cave of precious stones and objets d'art.

IV

At the end of July, exhausted by intense work in finishing *And so to Rome*, I made a trip to Perugia and Siena, and after being held up by two weeks' illness in Florence, in torrid heat, I went over the Futa Pass to Bologna and Venice. The Futa Pass had not then been "motorized", with tunnels and flyover bridges. You wound up and up, crossed the fiery fields of Pietramala, whose flames probably gave Dante his idea of those flaming pits in Hell, then down and down to the valley of the Po.* One passed through mountain villages, many still in ruins from the fierce fighting on the Pass. In this year of 1949 Italy had not been straddled with those monotonous autostradas that hurry you from one capital to another, ignoring all the picturesque villages. You once ate in small wayside inns that had served travellers through the centuries, and not in steel and glass cafés, ajduncts to petrol stations, where you swallow food to the punch of a cash register, having "done" two hundred miles in three hours, planning another two hundred in the next three, and "We'll make Naples by seven o'clock." We have saved horses much thrashing, turning it on to ourselves.

I arrived in Venice and found many friends at the Hotel Gritti, on the Grand Canal: Mrs. Crane, the Duff Coopers, Lord Robert Cecil and his wife, and a tireless American benefactor of St. Mark's,

* In 1949, at Pietramala, at the height of the Pass, there was an American Soldiers' Cemetery with some three hundred graves, beautifully planned, the American flag flying over it. When I made the same journey in 1956 the cemetery had vanished! All the bodies had been transported for re-burial in the United States.

Mrs. Truxton Beale (her zeal is now marked by a plaque inside the basilica). What fun life was in Venice, what Goldoni-like intrigues, what Guardianesque moments in the pigeon-cluttered Piazza, what strange combinations of people and history! The Robilants gave parties in the salon of their Palazzo Mocenigo on the Grand Canal, where Byron had kept his mistresses and read to Shelley the first Canto of *Don Juan*. One afternoon we went by gondola, with Mrs. Crane and Sir Kenneth and Lady Clark, on the track of a reputed Titian in the studio of Italico Brass. The International PEN, holding a conference, gave a ball at the Palazzo Rezzonico, in the great ballroom with its *trompe d'œil* by Tiepolo, where Robert Browning · had lain in state in 1889, prior to transition to Westminster Abbey.

One day I lunched at the Palladian Villa Malcontenta, with its high-columned portico and the semi-erotic frescoes that my host, restoring the villa, had uncovered. Then one morning I created a sensation at the Accademia Art Gallery. I asked to see the hand of Canova. "The hand of Canova!" exclaimed the attendants. "The hand of Canova—but, *signore*, how could we have such a thing!" Another mad Englishmen out in the noonday sun. I insisted. Finally they brought an assistant curator to talk with me. He looked at me very suspiciously and then drew me aside. Why did I want to see Canova's hand? So they had it! I explained that I was an author interested in Canova, whose birthplace, museum and mausoleum at Possagno I had just visited. He conducted me to the office of the Director, who received me courteously. "We do not show the hand, *signore*," he said. Why did I want to see it? I explained again. "Very well," he said, rising from his desk. I followed him to another room, a lecture room, the headquarters of the Canova Society. The Director opened a safe and took out a box. (Maurice Sandoz all over again!) From the box he extracted a porphyry urn. With a little key he opened its lid, and brought forth a cylindrical glass jar. And there, preserved in alcohol, was the pale hand of Canova, Italy's great sculptor. On his death the hand had been cut off before his burial in the mausoleum he had built for his brother and himself at Possagno. I thanked the Director. The attendant at the entrance watched me depart, open-mouthed.

This was my twenty-first visit to Venice since 1922. There had been changes but many old friends were there. What memories were evoked! For a quarter of a century I had known the Garden of Eden, that island tethered to the Giudecca, with its long sea-wall looking south down the lagoon, and its immense garden of vines, cypresses and roses. It was the home of Princess Aspasia, widow of King Alexander of Greece, killed by a monkey's bite. Dear, sad woman. A ridiculous rumour had grown up that she possessed the evil eye, and suspicious people made the traditional sign with their fingers to ward off the danger in her glance. She was still beautiful, if not with the beauty Compton Mackenzie, seeing her before her marriage, had recorded in his *Greek Memories*. Her home, and this lovely garden, had taken its name from the Englishman, Mr. Eden, who had created it on the Giudecca. It held ghosts for me. Here in the twenties young Derek Mond and my young Lucien Reid and his sister had played with the Princess's little daughter, Alessandra. Both boys had perished in the flower of their youth, in the Second World War. And now at a buffet supper party set out on the patio this moonlit night of September, 1949, I met Derek's mother, Lady Melchett, and we drew apart to talk of him and Lucien.*

It was an evening of enchantment, the Canal under a full moon, zephyr-soft. Mrs. Beale had brought us across in her gondola rowed by Giuseppe, famed for his voice. So while we ate Giuseppe sang to his guitar under the vine pergola. All Venice seemed there, the Windsors, the Duff Coopers, the Melchetts, Mrs. Albert Sidney (later Countess Potocka) Henry May, caricatured in Somerset Maugham's *The Razor's Edge*. ("How could he be so cruel! He swears it isn't me, but of course it is!"), and the Woods Blisses, donors of Dumbarton Oaks, their Washington home in whose Renaissance salon, brought from the Château de Chimerey, Stravinsky had conducted his "Dumbarton Oaks Concerto", composed in honour of their silver wedding.

When I left the Garden of Eden towards midnight I told my gondolier to take me home by the side canals. The moon was high and full, the water flashed silver; this was the peak hour of enchantment. We glided past faded palaces in a velvet silence with only the soft dipping of the oar. A heavy melancholy of beautiful lost things, of faded splendour, lay over everything. The silent palaces towered

* See *Sunshine and Shadow*.

above one, roses trailed over the crumbling brick walls of gardens. The iron grilles of the watergates, dark, with green, slimy steps, seemed to await masked ladies and their gallants. I lay back on the cushions and indulged in reminiscence. Did old Galuppi play in that salon whose lighted windows threw a path of gold across the black water?

> Here you come with your old music, and here's
>   all the good it brings:
> What, they lived once thus at Venice,
>   where the merchants were the kings.

I made the gondolier leave me by the steps of a *calle* and walked the last half mile home, with only a Campo cat stirring; in and out, up and down, by canal and *ponte*, in a silent, horseless, motorless, moonwashed, decaying city.

Two days later there was a world-wide sensation. England had devalued the pound. In March, the previous year, the Labour Chancellor of the Exchequer, the brilliant, fearless Sir Stafford Cripps, had firmly denied any devaluation. Since then he had three times repeated his denial. Now, this September, he ate his words and devalued the pound from $4.03 to $2.80. With this somersault he delivered a shattering blow to the reputation of a Chancellor of the Exchequer. What had happened once could happen again. Churchill accused Cripps of duplicity. For some time the latter would not speak to him. Cripps thought his moral standard was unimpeachable. A vinegary fanatic, he boasted that the Bank of England was now 'controlled'. It was indeed. When a too independent Governor was dismissed, he had foretold that it would become in time the minion of the Treasury. Here was the fulfilment of that prophecy. There was no check any more on Government spending, "Confidence had long been undermined by the over-supply of sterling in relation to the goods it could buy. This superabundance has been partly due to the loose financial policy of His Majesty's Government," observed David Eccles, later a Cabinet Minister, in *The Times*. We had started down a slippery slope. The Bank began to print money like toilet rolls. Within twenty years the paper output was so great that bank customers were requested to accept

dirty notes, replacement having become too expensive. The pound
fell and fell. It went from $4.03 to $2.80 to $2.40. Then it was
"floated" to see if it could swim, and eventually sank to below
$2.30. London, long the world's financial centre, saw the pound now
measured by the dollar.

V

I was back at Pilgrim Cottage in October, to deal with the demolition order on my cottages. The Urban District Council, The County
Council, the Ministry, remained adamant. I had exceeded the time
limit. One day two small boys rapped at my door. They were collecting money to celebrate Guy Fawkes Night on November the fifth.
They were very surprised when I gave them a ten-shilling note, but
they had given me an idea. The following Sunday morning I went
in The Golden Ball, my inn that was a local news exchange, and
said "I hope you boys will be around on Guy Fawkes Night. I am
going to have a bonfire. I'm burning those condemned cottages."
The news travelled very quickly. Two days later the borough
surveyor asked to see me. Surely there was no truth in the rumour?
I assured him there was. I was inviting the Press to be present and
also the Metro-Goldwyn Film Corporation. There would be world-
wide coverage. "I'm informed that there is nothing to prevent me
burning my own property if it constitutes no public danger," I said,
"And it will give pleasure to many, particularly the youngsters. You
tell me you are powerless to keep your promise owing to a Government ruling. A famous lawyer tells me that a loophole can be found
in most Bills. You had better look for it, otherwise the bonfire is on."*
He was a nice little man, he departed sadly. The next day he informed
me that if I would send him new plans his housing committee would
examine them. I asked when the Committee sat. On December the

* The proof of this came in 1972. There was a strike of dockers against
containers. They picketed the docks. An order forbidding obstructionary
picketing was made, and ignored. The three pickets were served writs to
appear in court, which they ignored. They were arrested and sentenced for
contempt of court. A national strike was threatened which frightened the
Government, already defeated by the Coalminers' Union. An obscure
Government solicitor appeared in court and pointed out to the judge a flaw
in the law by which he had ordered the pickets arrested. They were released
from gaol, to a mass demonstration of triumph by the dockers union.

Alassio from the terrace of Palazzo Vairo

The Castello di Conscente

The Villino Romano, Alassio

first. "No good. My deadline is November the fifth. Moreover, I do not propose to change my architect's plans," I replied. Four days later he rang up to say he found that they had read my plans wrongly, and they would agree to my restoration of the cottages! I replied I would proceed with the work but on the condition that there was no limit to what I could spend. I wished to do a first-class job. There was at this time a £1,000 limit on the cost of repairs.

I converted the cottages into one. I had a very good local builder, skilled in period work. We put in central heating and woodblock floors. The exterior shape was carefully preserved. The cottage had not been finished a month when a young married couple bought it for £5,000. It had cost me £2,500 so that I made a nice profit, though this had never been in mind. All I wanted was to preserve the character of the place, and this I had done. It happened that the purchaser worked for a landscape firm. He created a beautiful garden. In the next twenty years the cottage changed hands twice. The last purchaser paid £26,000 for it. Perhaps more than any book I have written, it will be my best memorial.

VI

How gold is the English October! My cottage ensconced in a Chiltern valley was surrounded by beechwoods whose yellow leaves fluttered down, gilding the lanes and exposing the smooth trunks of the noble trees. In the corner of my garden a chestnut tree, glorious with candle-flowers in the spring, stood stripped of her gown, naked to the air. I had seen a thousand birds gather for their flight south. This year I would be copying them, flying not to Florida, but to the French Riviera. In this calm lovely month, the last red apples glowed on the topmost boughs.

I made a round of visits, almost routine now, to the Iliffes at terraced Yattendon, to the Sackvilles at Tudor-chimneyed Knole, to the Birketts in their bow-windowed home commanding the Amersham valley

On the last day of November I left for Monte Carlo. Just before the boat-train drew out of Victoria Station I was astonished to see Frederick Rivers appear. He hated rising early but he had done so and come across London from the Euston Hotel to wish me bon voyage. He was going to Madrid in March so we would meet there if I went, as my publisher suggested. He was boisterously happy as usual. He brought me a cashmere scarf woven in his Scottish mill. There were winter winds even at Monte Carlo, he said. I was touched by his farewell gesture.

My Australian friend Guido Wertheim met me at Monte Carlo, on that open, sea-view station amid the palms and aloes, one of the most romantic in the world. He had found a pied-a-tèrre with his usual genius for a bargain, a suite in an American woman's apartment overlooking the Mediterranean. We had our own kitchen, wherein Guido was adept. Poor fellow, he did not know what he was in for. I fell ill with a frightful attack of the old enemy to which I had now added fibrositis. It sounded like a plant disease. Guido brought in a young Frenchman, Dr. Crimeaux. The usual performance with a black scarf for blood pressure, etc. "I suppose you think I am a complete neurasthenic and would be cured if I worked for a living?" I said, "Well, unlike most people here I do work for a living. Very hard!" "That's your trouble, you've run down the batteries," said Dr. Crimeaux. He prescribed pills, bed and a diet. Guido nursed me devotedly. So all day, from a French Bergère bed, under a crystal chandelier, I looked out over the sunny Mediterranean.

I indulged in an orgy of reading, I devoured the *Letters of Cicero* and the whole eight volumes of Proust. The sunsets over the bay were glorious, followed by a jewelled coastline. I recalled H. G. Wells's caustic description—"a luminous eczema on the fringe of the sea". He had referred to the de-luxe hotels and villas with their ancient occupants getting into "decolletage" and "smoking" for dinner. The impoverished widow of a Russian prince delivered our morning milk and yoghourt. After a month I got up and sat in the sun on the Casino terrace, like a sick horse let out to grass.

VII

In January, this new year of 1950, my Spanish publisher wrote again to my agent. "The royalties due to Mr. Roberts are very elevated. Would he not be interested in spending them on a trip to Spain, as recently did Mr. Somerset Maugham and other writers? Mr. Roberts is the most populous [*sic*] writer of foreign authors in

Spain." I should go, wrote my agent. The letter stirred my discontent. I felt that if I did not get out of Monte Carlo I should die. There was something of a madhouse about this resort. Our genial landlady, a middle-aged divorcée, had a lover, Baron Brassouvie. We called him Baron Brassière, In the early hours of the morning we heard him come in carrying our landlady, dead drunk, over his shoulder. He was a Monégasque, deeply involved in local politics and standing for the Council. He ascribed a black eye one day as due to a "political argument". Monaco was resisting French designs on this tax-haven. Baron Brassière got more and more excited. "They threaten to crush us. If France declares war on us we shall resist. The whole world will cry shame!" We heard this grave news while he prepared breakfast for his mistress, still in bed at noon. I had a vision of the Monégasque army being mobilized—all eighteen of them, and the stone cannon balls on the prince's ramparts being loaded in the antique cannon.

On New Year's Eve I had listened to the singing of hymns at a Watch Night Service in the Anglican Church next-door. The following morning a Cockney valet, who shopped for us, rang our bell. He was in great distress. He had found his employer dead in the kitchen, gassed. He had committed suicide. "It must have taken a long time —the gas here is so poor," complained the tearful valet.

One morning Somerset Maugham rang and invited me to lunch at his Villa Mauresque. Ignoring Guido's protests, I went. Maugham sent his car for me. When I got downstairs I felt so shaky that I was on the point of cancelling the trip. Gradually the lovely bright morning raised my spirits and all along the road the beauty of the scene, the mountains, the indented villa-fringed bays, the pinewoods, the crescent of Beaulieu, the thickly wooded promontory of Cap Ferrat, gave me intense pleasure. When I reached the villa I was in good spirits. "You don't look like a sick man," said Maugham, greeting me in his salon, which was somewhat of a baronial hall with a gothic Arles stone fireplace and a fortune in French paintings on the walls. I had not seen him since we had lunched in New York five years ago. At seventy-six he was still a well-preserved man but, like most millionaires, he was gloomy. He told me he would write no more plays or novels but he was busy on personal prologues to his filmed stories. They proved excellent prologues for he possessed a good speaking-voice. Before lunch we walked round the grounds, the terraces with olive and vine trees, the swimming pool, the rose gardens. He employed four gardeners. The white house was Moorish in character, having been built for a French bishop in retirement from Africa. Over the main door there was carved a sign, like a beehive, a device Maugham used on the covers of all his books. I had assumed it was a charm against the evil eye, brought from Africa. Not at all, he said. It had been his father's sign-manual and he had adopted it.

Three hours passed very pleasantly and the time of the siesta approached. I announced my departure. I declined the car. He was appalled at my intention to walk all the way back to Monte Carlo, about ten miles, but I suddenly felt so well, with the food, the company, the conversation, and free from all pain, that I would have tackled the Matterhorn at that moment. We parted after he had given me some advice on my proposed visit to Spain. I accomplished my walk. The afternoon was lovely and the coast road by Beaulieu was so beautiful that I did not want to miss any part of it. I was well rewarded when at last, in growing fatigue, I rounded Cap d'Ail and suddenly saw, glowing in the last light of the sunset, the rock of Monaco, a wall of rose rising sheer from the purple sea. The high promontory, crowned by the palace-fort, shone like a pilgrim's vision. Then it faded into the blue dusk of evening.

CHAPTER FOUR

Excursion in Spain

I

All through January I debated whether I should go to Spain. My growing resolution was strengthened one morning by a letter from the Spanish Ambassador in London, the Duque de San Lucar. "I entreat you to go. You will have a great welcome." As I observed to the protesting Guido, "The fame of an author is as fragile as the beauty of a flower. It soon wilts and is a thing of dead leaves—like my books will be one day. I'm going!" My Spanish publisher would finance my visit.

I left Monte Carlo from its beautiful Casino station—later demolished for a bus-parking space—on a February evening, taking a couchette to Barcelona, with the rose of sunset fading over the Mediterranean. Guido and our landlady thought they would never see me again. Dr. Crimeaux washed his hands of me. My two companions in the couchette were a Frenchman, M. Diogène, and his Spanish business colleague, Señor Block. Their destinations were Perpignan and Barcelona respectively. After dining together the Spaniard suggested that I should leave the train at Perpignan, have breakfast at his French colleague's house, and go on to Spain in his car, which he was picking up. I accepted the offer.

M. Diogène, despite his name, lived in anything but a tub. His wife, two daughters, a married son and daughter-in-law met the train. There was quite a demonstration. I was astonished to learn he had been away only ten days! We were whirled away to a large house in Perpignan, whereupon mother and daughters went into the kitchen. Rolls and coffee appeared. Afterwards, while the two business men conferred, I went to look at the town. February is no time to judge a place. Long avenues of plane trees must have given shady retreat in the summer heat. The river had been canalized. The great sight was the snow-crowned Mount Canigou, in massive splendour. Kipling paid it a glowing tribute which the French have quoted ever since.

The lunch was formidable. Madame and her daughters had been busy in the kitchen; cold salmon, soup, a great sole, *bonne femme*, two roast ducks, asparagus, new potatoes, a fruit flan, ices, accompanied by four vins-du-pays, then coffee and liqueurs in the salon. At three o'clock we left but before this I had solved two mysteries. What was the business they were engaged in? "Shall we tell him?" asked M. Diogène. The ladies giggled. "We have a concession for France and Italy, of goods made in Barcelona, an elastic concession." He pulled a small object out of his pocket. "We make elastic panties," he explained, holding up a female garment amid general mirth. "And I must tell you how I got my name Diogène. I am one of the Babes in the Wood. Some time after the Revolution a small boy was found destitute, half-wild, in the woods. His clothes, although ragged, suggested that he might have been of aristocratic birth. How he came to be there and what his name was he did not know. He had been sleeping in the forest and was caught one day by a farmer, stealing eggs. They adopted him, and gave him the name Diogène (Diogenes, the philosopher who lived in a tub). I am the great-great-grandson of that rescued child."

I set off with my Spanish friend, Señor Block, by car in the late afternoon, over the Pyrenees by the Col de Perthus, on the route taken by Hannibal invading Italy. It was nine o'clock and dark when we arrived at the Ritz Hotel in Barcelona. There I learned of my misdemeanour. The concierge became very excited when he learned who I was. "But, señor, there has been a deputation at the station to meet you, and another deputation and the Press have waited here over two hours!" Alas, I had informed my publisher, Señor Caralt, that I would arrive at six p.m. They had concluded I has missed the train.

Soon Señor Luis de Caralt appeared and graciously accepted my apology. He reeled off a list of engagements. The next morning eight pressmen arrived, with five photographers. The translator of my novels acted as interpreter. My publisher was the Delegado de Cultura in the Provincial Government. I was taken to call on the

Mayor and the Governor of Catalonia. In the Mayor's office I met the Abbot of Montserrat. I was to visit him on the morrow at the famous mountain abbey. From seven to nine I signed books in a bookshop. Never have I seen so many pretty girls, and had so little time to talk to them, frustrated with the language. It was ten o'clock when I left the bookshop but not too late for a dinner of twenty persons that began at eleven o'clock and went on until half-past two.

The next morning there was a crowd in the hotel lobby, with more books to sign. Then I was taken to the Ramblas, the wide avenue, lined with trees and flower stalls, that runs down to the harbour. Across the avenue hung banners with my name in large letters, proclaiming, in Spanish, "Cecil Roberts is Here". What was I, a film star or an author? I smiled and smiled, and raised my hat to greetings. Then I was rushed away in a powerful car up to the mountains behind Barcelona, to an awesome serrated ridge on which stood the vast monastery of Montserrat. It occupied a mountain three thousand feet high, in a rocky cleft that, legend said, had been created by an earthquake at the time of the Crucifixion, and where, in the Middle Ages, the castle of the Holy Grail was situated. The abbey, a Renaissance basilica, was famous for its choir school. I was received ceremoniously by the Abbot who had the ambulatory chapel, behind the high altar with its revered black wooden Madonna, allegedly carved by St. Luke, opened for me. Forty diminutive choristers, assembled there and formed a half-circle. One little chorister stood in front and conducted, while a benign old monk, their music-master, clasped a Psalter to his paunch. Their voices were like silver trumpets and their little black heads, angel faces, white collars and long black gowns, backed by the rich, stained glass windows of the ambulatory, ablaze in the afternoon sun, composed an unforgettable picture.

The Director of the British Institute had asked me if I would give a lecture. The hall was crowded with students. How could these young Spaniards understand me? I began speaking slowly but their comprehension was so quick that I lapsed into a normal pace. Afterwards for an hour I answered questions. "We have never seen anything like it!" said the Director. "Nor I," I added. Everywhere such Spanish courtesy, such smiling, eager young faces.

On my last night in Barcelona Señor Block gave a dinner for me in his beautiful apartment, high up, overlooking a wide avenue. It went on until 2 a.m. When I left the electricity had failed and the butler escorted us down six flights of stairs, holding a candelabrum. "Why do you laugh?" asked my host, who came down with us. "I feel like a cardinal!" I replied. "Why do you feel like a cardinal?" "Well, the last time I saw a servant carrying a candelabrum was in Rome. One of the guests was a cardinal, and, as is the custom there, when he came and when he departed, he was preceded by a page carrying a lighted candelabrum."

One evening Señor Caralt, my hospitable publisher, took me to his box at the opera house. Accustomed to post-war economy in London. I was staggered by the elegance of the audience, the women heavily jewelled and superbly gowned. The opera was *Die Walküre* with Flagstad singing. A glittering spectacle.

II

When my *wagon-lits* drew into Madrid I was met by Manuel Huidobra who was there for an exhibition of his portraits of Spanish society beauties. He had taken a room for me with a terrace overlooking Madrid, a city on a high plateau, with a view of snowy mountain ranges. It was Barcelona all over again; the Press, book-signing, endless cocktail parties, lunches and dinners. But where was Frederick Rivers who had arranged to meet me here? I enquired in vain until one day I lunched with young David Erskine, newly married, working there for an oil company. He stared at me. "But don't you know? Poor Frederick arrived here a month ago. He had a terrible gastric ulcer attack and flew home for an operation. Dissatisfied with the clinic in which he had his operation, he went home to Nairn too soon. He had a relapse and before they could get a doctor he was dead." Later I learned the whole story. The end was in keeping with his fantastic life. It emerged that he was not a Catholic, and when his estate was wound up he was found to be insolvent. With what élan he had lived! That last gift of a scarf, still worn by me, keeps the memory of him affectionately alive.

Invited to make a broadcast, Manuel thought it would be very appropriate if I made it in Spanish. I wrote out my talk, he then coached me patiently in the Spanish version. It was a great success, and also a disaster. "You are very fluent in Spanish, we heard you on the radio," said my hostess at a dinner party. They thought me perverse when I declared I did not know a word of Spanish. The curator in a museum we went to talked fluently to me and was astonished that I did not comprehend a word. It dogged me throughout my visit.

The Director of the British Institute was Professor Walter Starkie. He was *persona grata* with all Spaniards because of his knowledge of their folk-lore and music. He had written a best-seller *Raggle-Taggle Gipsies*. I lectured for him. Again a wonderful audience with many turned away, so the next evening I spoke to the overflow. There was some irony in all this. Earlier, at the beginning of this Spanish vogue, I suggested to the British Council they should send me to Spain. I was rebuffed. "We make our own arrangements," was the cold reply. They did indeed. All over Europe and the world they sometimes sent out unknown and inarticulate authors. In France, Denmark, Germany, Sweden, Italy, Norway, Holland, Australia, India, South Africa and elsewhere, where my books were well known, I would have found eager audiences. Sometimes these lecturers created astonishment. Here, in Madrid, one of them, Vita Sackville-West, a novelist of aristocratic birth, bizarre, gifted, astonished the Madrileños by tactlessly visiting the brothel-quarter whence her grandmother, a dancer, the mistress of the 2nd Lord Sackville, the English ambassador, had begun her amazing career. All these lecturers had their expenses paid. One day, Manuel coming into my room, found me convulsed with laughter. I showed him a bill and explained. It was for a hundred pesetas for a photograph of me that had been taken for publicity connected with my lecture. A note was attached from Starkie. "I am really ashamed to send you this bill, but we are in the absurd position of having no funds to meet it." The Establishment at work. I did not let this prevent my giving eight lectures in Barcelona, Madrid and Seville.

At the Institute the British Minister and his wife and the Duke of Alba were present, with Starkie in the chair. Our official relations with the Franco Government were somewhat strained and our disapproval was shown by having a Legation and not an Embassy in Madrid, Mr. Hankey being the Minister. The Duke of Alba was undoubtedly the most liked of all Spaniards by the British. A man of wealth, handsome, cultured and of great personal charm, he bore eighty titles that sounded like a roll call of European history. He had been an extremely popular figure when he was the Spanish Ambassador in England, having been educated there. A fervent Royalist, after showing too much independence towards Franco, he resigned and maintained his freedom of action with considerable courage. Neat in person, affable, the more I saw of him in subsequent years the more I liked him. He survived into an era when the smear of communism began to spread across everything that stood for breeding and culture. Dirty clothes and dirty manners became a cult with a new generation that thought it smart to be degenerate, and was happiest near the gutter; a virus that has infected our art, music, literature, the theatre and journalism. Alba did not follow the fashion of apologising for being well-bred. A grandee, landowner, art connoisseur, he was an excellent conversationalist, a perfect host, kindly and modest. He was proud of the treasures he possessed and the historic rôle his ancestors had played. He had some endearing foibles. He was, for instance, not only a descendant of King James II but also of the Duke of Alba whose persecutions in the Netherlands sound a horrifying note throughout Motley's *The Rise of the Dutch Republic*. Jimmie, as everyone called him, thought Motley's book a gross libel. He did not hesitate to go to Oxford and give a lecture there "to defend the good name of one who has not, in my mind, been treated with justice by your historians". Descended from the first Duke of Berwick, a natural son of James II by Arabella, the Duke of Marlborough's sister, he had as much Churchill blood in his veins as Winston.

At the end of my lecture he invited me to lunch. This took place in a modern apartment block. His famous Palacio Liria had been burnt out in the 1936 Revolution. There is a story connected with this. His palace and its great treasures were insured at Lloyd's against fire and enemy action. A Spanish bomb shattered the palace. On a technicality Lloyd's could have claimed it was not destroyed by "enemy action" since the bomb was dropped by one of Franco's aviators, of the party to which Alba belonged. Lloyd's waived the strict legality that absolved them and made a handsome settlement.

The duke now lived in an apartment house until the palace could be rebuilt. He had two apartments in the modern building, the lower converted into a museum. He occupied the upper one. We lunched in this apartment. With us was his only child, the young Duchess of Montoro and her husband. A splendid portrait looked down upon us. I commented on it. "That's the Duke of Berwick, my ancestor. You know, we are all bastards!" said Alba, smiling. After lunch my host took me to the lower floor, the museum. What a display, saved from the bombed palace! There was a large Winterhalter painting of the Empress Eugénie, surrounded by her ladies-in-waiting. She was the sister of my host's grandmother. She had died, aged ninety-four, in his palace. She left him all her family papers and memoirs. The Empress told him that the head of a Chinese Delegation looked at the Winterhalter painting and remarked to the Emperor—"Your first lady is very beautiful but the rest of the harem is much too old!" There was a fine painting by Velasquez of the head of Innocent X. There were other notable portraits, of Bonnie Prince Charlie, of his brother Henry, Cardinal Duke of York, of the Countess of Albany, Charles's wayward wife, a kinswoman of Alba's, letters of Christopher Columbus, a letter from Drake, in most courteous terms addressed to the Duke of Alba, a letter from Titian, dated Venice, October 31st, 1525, a receipt from Lope de Vega to the House of Alba for his pension of 4,000 pesetas, and one from Prince Charles repudiating the Old Pretender's actions.

We met again the next evening when the duke gave a dinner for me at the Nueva Club. It was a quiet affair of some twenty elderly gentlemen. He presided at the centre of a long table. I had on my right Don Antonio Pastor. His English was perfect, learned at Balliol College. He had been a lecturer at Oxford, and a professor at the University of London. He had assisted the Prince of Wales in preparation for his South American tour in 1931. Now he was a banker. He was a fund of information. "This is a most interesting dinner," he said, as he helped himself to *Truites à la gelée*. "You may be interested to know that there are half a dozen Grandees at our table." He enumerated them. Despite resounding titles, they seemed very modest gentlemen. A Grandee of Spain stands in English minds for all that is "pomp and circumstance", and sometimes arrogance· "What do you think you are—a Grandee?" we exclaim in protest. "Four of them are first-class Grandees," said Don Pastor.

"First-class?" I queried. "Yes, there are three classes. Those who speak to the king and receive his reply with heads uncovered; those who speak to him uncovered but put on their hats to hear the answer; those who await the permission of the king before covering themselves. Well, there's no king now. Nobody obeys any rules, but it hasn't made things easier," said my neighbour. "You may wonder how it all got like that but Spain has no monopoly of absurdity. Your own court officials walk backwards in the Royal Presence, contrary to Nature. And in Russia they've substituted Lenin for Jesus Christ."

III

One day Spain's leading publisher, Señor M. Aguilar, motored me out to the Escorial, the colossal monastery-palace-pantheon-cathedral. It had a sinister air with its grey stone façades and slate tiles, its senseless acres of galleries. It is devoid of any beauty, backed by the barren mountainside from which the building material was quarried. It is designed in the form of a gridiron, on which St. Laurence is reputed to have been roasted, and built as a memorial to him. Roasted in the summer heat, it is bitten by icy winter winds that whistle through countless corridors. There are sixteen courtyards, nine towers, fifteen cloisters, eighty-six staircases, three hundred cells, twelve hundred doors and two thousand six hundred and seventy three windows. In all, including the Hapsburg palace esconced in it, I did not see one room I would care to live in.

In the octagonal pantheon lie the Spanish kings, tier upon tier, Charles V, and his descendants. There is only one vacant space left lugubriously open, awaiting the last king to complete the mausoleum. This cavity is reserved for Alfonso XIII. He died in Rome, in the Grand Hotel, and he remains in the Spanish Church of Montserrat there. One day I asked Princess Torlonia, the Infanta Beatrice, daughter of King Alfonso, whether Franco had refused permission for her father's interment. "Oh no!" she replied, "We have not asked him. My father will go there one day in his own right!'

Before I left the Escorial cathedral there was a mercenary tourist-touch. In a gallery above the nave of the church stood a life-sized, white, marble figure of Christ, on a black marble cross. A beautiful

statue, it was the work of Benvenuto Cellini. The Medici Grand
Duke Francesco bought it in 1565. In 1576 he gave it to Phillip II
who placed it in the Escorial. As I lingered to look at it a verger came
up, smiling. A little yellow silk apron hung from the waist. "You will
observe, señor," said the verger, lifting it, "the statue is perfect in
every detail!" A tip expected.

We lunched, after a long march through the Escorial, in the
delightful summer villa owned by my host, with windows framing
the monastery which was seen through boughs of apple blossom.
After lunch we went by car, climbing over the high Guadarrama
range to Segovia, with its fairy-tale castle high on a rock, and thence
to La Granja, the first royal seat built by a Bourbon in Spain,
Philip V who, remembering his birth at Versailles, sought to surpass
it.

IV

At the end of March, fatigued with hospitality, I flew to Seville.
What a flight! We started nearly two hours late, which in Spain is
nothing to wonder at. We took two runs to get up off the aerodrome.
The plane looked very ancient. It was crammed with passengers,
and crates of hens. The pretty stewardess flirted with us and ended
with her arm round the pilot's neck. We swooped and fluttered
over a barren landscape, and circumnavigated Toledo, granite-grey
on its rocks, bound by the deep ravine of the Tagus and spanned by
the spidery Alcantara bridge. In colour and pattern it was like
El Greco's famous painting of the city. It was a mad flight, I expected
the plane to disintegrate at any moment but we made a perfect
landing in a rough field, for the aerodrome was in course of construc-
tion. We had to wait for a bus bringing in passengers, and then went
bumping over potholes into Seville. I arrived at the Hotel Madrid,
with its great patio, palms, parrots, and balconies. There I found my
friend Mrs. Boehm awaiting me. She had just come up from Gibraltar,
having left the *Caronia*, which was making a world cruise.

The day after my arrival the Director of the British Institute gave
a dinner for me at the Hotel Angleterre, facing a square full of orange
and rose trees in full bloom. Some fifty guests were present. With immense patience someone had made a table decoration of flower petals

in the form of a large Union Jack. When I lectured the next evening at the crowded Institute all the pretty señoritas of Seville seemed to be present, and again I signed books, endlessly. The next day in brilliant sunshine we motored to Jerez de la Frontera, the centre of the sherry industry. I had seen the name so often on sherry bottles that it seemed like coming home. Many of the *bodegas* are owned by Anglo-Spanish families, settled there and intermarried. The boys are sent to Catholic schools in England and the men order their suits in Savile Row. Domecq, Sandeman, Byass, Humbert and Williams, are all long established there.

We were royally entertained by Guy Williams of Humbert and Williams, lunching in his home. A handsome young son-in-law was a renowned amateur matador. We toured the *bodegas*. They were dim, immense in height like cathedrals. We walked down long avenues and sampled sherry from vats laid down by the Queen of Spain, and by the Prince of Wales and the Duke of York on their visits in 1927. I was introduced to a Señorita Domecq. The name recalled John Ruskin. His father had made an immense fortune as the London agent, trading as Ruskin, Telford and Domecq. There was a plan, when a Señorita Domecq came on a visit to the Ruskins, to marry her to John. Happily for her that went awry, for his mother was alarmed by the prospect of his marrying a Catholic, and he became the impotent husband of the unfortunate Effie Gray. In Williams's garden fighting cocks were strutting around, a legacy from the time of Wellington's Army. There was also a tame heron, and, high up on a chimney stack, some storks. Our host told us an astonishing story. Some joker placed a goose's egg in the nest. This was duly hatched. When the other storks saw the gosling they took it down to the ground and held a solemn council over it. The verdict reached, they despatched the gosling and then went off and killed the "mother" for adultery.

In the first days of April I was in the midst of the hysteria of Holy Week. Towards dusk the heavily decorated Madonnas, carried aloft on draped floats, borne by invisible sweating stevedores, start their long procession to the cathedral, from which they return after midnight. Ablaze with candles and jewels, each Madonna is escorted by a Fraternity in monks' habits, with tall conical cowls that have slits for eyes, suggesting the horrors of the Inquisition. The costumes

78

of the Madonnas are fabulously rich. The Duke of Alba's daughter had decorated the favourite Madonna, the Macarena, with seven million pesetas' worth of pearls, and had given the signal to start her progress. During these processions there came fanatical wails, *saeta*, from the attendants, which went back to the days of the Moorish occupation of Spain, weird, fanatical.

After a few days of swaying Madonnas we went on to beautiful Granada and stayed at a converted convent, the *Parador* San Francisco, inside the grounds of the fairytale Alhambra of the Moors. It was an enchanting setting. From a terrace gay with pink peach blossom we looked across a valley to the high gardens of the Generalife. Beyond a ravine rose the Albaicin, a hillside honeycombed with gypsy earth-dwellings whose whitewashed façades gleamed in the evening light. A murmur of voices and music drifted faintly across to us from this human anthill. The Mayor arranged for me to see the famous gypsy dances in a cave. It was intolerably hot and noisy, a vivid demonstration of tremendous gusto, with magnificent heads, flashing eyes, exuberant breasts, quick feet and cascades of flounced dresses, all to the snapping of castanets and the thrumming of guitars. The next day I was taken to pay a special call on the greatest of all dancers, Lola Medina, now middle-aged. A widow, she had married a Spanish flying officer who had had to resign his commission. She lived in a luxurious cave dug out of the hillside which had a forecourt with an iron grille. She had been a great friend of Garcia Lorca, who had written a poem on her whitewashed wall.

I lunched one day with the British Consul, Mr. Davenhill. Don Guillermo, as he was called, had been Consul in Granada for some forty years. His father had held this honorary post before him. He lived with two sisters and a brother in a villa that once had a magnificent view. Behind the villa rose the wooded Alhambra Hill. In the distance was the snow-covered range of the Sierra Nevada, and far below lay the great valley where the Cross and the Crescent had come into bloody conflict. Alas, the view of the valley had been blocked out by the Alhambra Grand Hotel. Once upon a time the villa had been a casino devoted to gambling and gypsy dances. Here Edward VII had found entertainment when Prince of Wales. In 1906 Queen Alexandra visited it, not to gamble but to honour the

Consul. When I signed the Visitors Book a signature struck a note of sadness. It was that of the Duke of Wellington, not the Iron Duke, but that of the young sixth duke, a soldier destined to die in battle in Sicily within a short time of signing the book. He had been visiting the Spanish estate given to his ancestor with the Dukedom of Ciudad Rodrigo. "Should I not have signed 'Ciudad Rodrigo and Wellington'?" he asked shyly, as he blotted his name.

Davenhill had a story concerning Queen Alexandra and his mother. Both ladies were extremely deaf and had bellowed to each other. As the Queen left she said to her host "What a charming lady your mother is! What a pity she is so deaf. Cannot something be done about it?" Near the Davenhill villa was the house where Manuel De Falla had lived. It had a long, terraced garden overlooking the great plain, with a bust of the composer. The man who gave the world the music of *The Three-Cornered Hat*, made famous by Massine and the Diaghilev Ballet, and many other compositions, such as *The Fire Dance*, never dined before 2 a.m. and never went to bed but always slept in a chair. He might have died in this villa but he was driven out by a neighbour who played gramophone records. He died in Argentina in 1946.

At the *San Francisco* a New York friend, Lucrezia Bori, arrived. She had been famous for many years at the Metropolitan Opera House, but had had the sense to retire while at the height of her reputation. Lucrezia was now very concerned about the fate of the famous Lippizaner horses, exiled from the Riding School at Vienna. She had had a scheme for exporting them to the United States. This came to nothing. The horses returned to the School.

I was back in Madrid in mid-April. One evening I went to a cocktail party given by Mr. Hankey, our Chargé d'Affaires, at the British Embassy, for ex-King Peter of Yugoslavia. I had a particular interest in him but was quite unaware that he knew it. When I was introduced he said "I've wanted to meet you for a long time. I'm your 'Prince Sixpenny' in *Victoria Four-Thirty*, aren't I?" In that novel I had written one chapter around the assassination of Peter's father and the taking of the little Crown Prince from his preparatory school in England back to Yugoslavia. I had nicknamed my character "Prince Sixpenny" because the little boy, when asked how much pocket money he had, replied to his schoolfellows—"I am allowed sixpence a week." I confessed to the authorship. "Well," said ex-King Peter, "you made me a much nicer little boy that I ever was. But that's not why I am indebted to you. You know, you were the cause of my meeting my wife!"

I was dumb with astonishment but before I could ask for an explanation our host brought up other guests and my chance was lost. I did not see him again, for he left Madrid the next morning. Later, I discovered that he had married Alessandra, the daughter of Princess Aspasia. But in what manner had I brought about their marriage? It was five months before I found the explanation.

CHAPTER FIVE

Excursion in Austria

I

Early in May I returned to England. I found Pilgrim Cottage smothered in white roses, the chestnut tree in flower and the apple trees heavy with blossom. Giulietta said she was in heaven. *And so to Rome* came out and my publisher gave me the good news that it was reprinting. What next? For the time, I gave myself up to the pleasure of life in my cottage, with spring's delights, and friends to entertain. Young Aubrey Cartwright came for the week-end. On leaving Eton he had spent a year training in the Army as a cadet officer at Eaton Hall. Fatherless, by some mishap he had not been entered at a university. His schoolfriend, the Hon. Simon Stuart, was going up to Cambridge next term, on his return from a year of military service abroad. There was tremendous pressure for places. Feeling something must be done, I took a bold step. I wrote to Dr. George Macaulay Trevelyan, O.M., the Master of Trinity College, Cambridge. He was the great-nephew of Macaulay and the son of the famous historian, Sir George Otto Trevelyan, O.M. Thinking that this link with literature might aid an author's appeal, I wrote to him, a stranger, on behalf of a boy whose father had died in his country's service. The reply was immediate and gracious. He could not hold out much hope. There were no vacancies. However, Aubrey should see the Senior Tutor and be interviewed in case a last-minute vacancy occurred.

The week-end after Aubrey's visit I made a frightful gaffe. The Sutherlands invited me to their week-end house party at Sutton Place, near Godalming. I was to arrive for lunch on Saturday. This is one of the most beautiful Tudor mansions in England, built wholly of mellow brick. The manor was settled by Henry VII on his mother after the Battle of Bosworth Field in 1485. Henry VIII inherited it and gave it to Sir Richard Weston, "my well beloved Privy Councillor". Sir Richard built the present house in 1523. He had an only son and heir, Francis. When Anne Boleyn came up for trial young Francis was arrested on the suspicion of being the Queen's lover. Her execution could be more easily justified if infidelity could be added to the charges against her. Francis Weston provided the required justification. Two days before Anne Boleyn went to the block young Weston was executed. That he was the only son of Henry VIII's "trusted friend and minister" availed him nothing. Fear of that ruthless monarch is revealed by the fact that Sir Richard remained on amicable terms with his son's slayer for the rest of his life. And here, after the tragedy, heirless Sir Richard entertained King Henry and had "a grete carpete to lay under the Kynge's feet", as the record runs.

There was a week-end party of twenty guests who assembled for lunch that Saturday. They included the Chilean Ambassador and wife, the Persian Ambassador and wife, young Lord and Lady Duncannon, the young Earl of Westmorland, young Sir Edward and Lady Paston-Bedingfield. It was a case of youth at the prow. To my astonishment there were a dozen menservants in livery, presided over by a grave old butler. I had thought all this had vanished with the war, taxes, and the servant shortage.

The great lawn shimmered with heat. Some of us took refuge after lunch under a giant copper-beech until tea-time in an old pantiled summerhouse adjoining a swimming pool. At dinner that evening, behind the long table gleaming with silver and flowers, above the shaded candles, I noticed a portrait of Henry VIII on the oak-panelled wall. When we rose from the table I discovered the name of the magical artist. The oval portrait of the King was by Holbein, as vivid as on the day it had been painted from life. There were other paintings that caught my attention. In the Great Hall hung a study of Robert Devereux, Earl of Essex, son of Queen Elizabeth the First's lover. There was a fine Romney of handsome young George Granville, 2nd Marquis of Stafford, and a portrait of his sister, Caroline. By the same artist there was an enormous canvas of a group of the Leveson-Gower family. The tragic Earl of Strafford looked down at us, and also a work of Reynolds, the proud Earl

Ligonier, sitting on his charger. After tea I browsed in the long library, housed in a wing. When I had been here, fifteen years before, on a grey November day, the great room then had a ghostly air and chilled my spirit. Today, in sunshine, it was different. In a table cabinet in the centre of the room was a cambric ruff that had adorned the neck of Sir Thomas More when he laid his head on the block on Tower Hill. It was stained with his blood.

There were youth and romance downstairs. Handsome young Lord Westmorland seemed very engrossed in a young lady whose hand he held from time to time. I learned they were just engaged. They would have sons and in due time one of them would be a page to our Queen Elizabeth. Unlike his ancestor in 1782, Westmorland did not have to elope with his bride to Gretna Green, as had the former, on capturing Sarah Child, the rich banker's daughter who had defied her father. After dinner that evening there was a film for us in the hall, with the house staff seated on the wide staircase behind.

Sunday was another blazing June day. It was too hot even to practise archery on the long lawn. Guests kept arriving. In all thirty-eight sat down to lunch, including a polo team that had come over from Henley, to play on the new polo ground the duke had laid down. After tea the house valet came up to me and asked if I wished him to pack for me. Rather surprised I said "No", as I was staying until Monday morning. That evening, coming down to dinner, I found myself alone in the drawing-room. There was a strange quietness over the house. The duke and duchess came in. When we went in to dinner we were only three at a small table! The old butler, alone, waited on us. Something told me I had made a blunder. Dinner finished, I asked my host if he had expected me to leave after tea. "Well, yes, but it doesn't matter!" he said, laughing, "You see, we can't staff this place for a full week-end. All those servants you saw were formerly employed by us. They now have jobs in town. But they like to come back and earn a little money, so I have them collected in a charabanc on Saturday morning, and they go back to London after tea on Sunday." So that was it! In this new post-war era a week-end did not mean Saturday to Monday morning, as formerly. Having been abroad so long I was ignorant of the change. If only the duchess when inviting me had told me! That night I walked down a long corridor where open bedroom doors revealed the beds dismantled. I breakfasted alone with the duke next morning, and left. He and the duchess were motoring to Devon that noon. It took some time for me to recover from my gaffe.

II

That June I raised a hornet's nest about my ears. Christina Foyle gave one of her famous Literary Lunches at the Dorchester Hotel to celebrate the publication of the Gowers Report on the preservation of the historic houses of England. Heavy taxation was threatening them with extinction. A committee of enquiry had been instituted to discover what could be done about meeting this threat. Its able chairman was Sir Ernest Gowers. It produced a proposal for alleviation of taxation if the houses were opened to the public. Christina asked me to propose the toast at this luncheon, with Sir John Anderson, an ex-Chancellor of the Exchequer, in the chair. She had collected a number of peers, reprieved owners of historic houses, including Lord Warwick, Lord Esher, etc., for the high table. I likened these owners of historic houses to birds allowed a little Government seed to enable them to sing in their beautiful cages. I went on to say that the man who had contributed to this parlous state was the Socialist Chancellor of the Exchequer, Sir Stafford Cripps, "the unburnt Savonarola of British politics". There was much laughter and applause. The newspapers headlined the epithet, and all the Leftish papers were out for my blood.

Before I rose to speak there had been an amusing incident. Sitting next to me was Lady (Utica) Beecham. I pleasantly remarked that I had seen much of Sir Thomas Beecham in New York. "Oh, my bigamist husband!" she said, referring to the Reno divorce he had obtained in order to marry the pianist, Betty Humby. It was stupid of me to have raised that bogy.

As a result of the excitement of all this my ulcer kicked up. My devoted doctor, Fergusson Hannay, motored down from Harley Street the next Sunday on the pretext of coming for lunch, but to read me a lesson. So bread and milk, bread and milk again. In bed, I had a battle to get Giulietta to bring me my writing board. "You've branded Savonarola Cripps for life," said Norman Birkett on the telephone.

In July I left for Casa Estella, Mrs. Cartwright's guest again at Cap d'Antibes. Aubrey met me on a blazing morning. I was given a room overlooking the bay, the promonotory with its lighthouse, and the great camel-like lump of the Esterelles on the horizon. In the Train Bleu I had discovered Lady Norman, who was going to her famous Château de La Garoupe on a 100-acre peninsula that her father, Lord Aberconway, had developed, building a large mansion. He had planned magnificently, creating three houses on the promonotory, a sea-wall, orchards and terraced gardens. Lady Norman, known as "Fay", was formidably efficient. Taking over this great property, she ran it like a business—"The stingy Treasury won't let us have any money out," she complained. When she let the Château she moved into The Clos, on the internal bay, and when she let that she moved into a little garden house, the Pavillon du Parc. Her directorial eye never missed a detail. Later I was often her guest and never ceased to be astonished by her business sense, and her forceful character. She terrified some people. She was forth-right, a C.B.E., a J.P., a trustee of the Imperial War Museum, and was decorated with a star and two medals for war work in France in 1914.

I had been at Casa Estella three days when Mrs. Cartwright and I went over to lunch with Fay. She was living in the little Pavillon, having let all her other houses. After lunch we went to the Château to call on Mrs. Randolph Churchill, who had taken it. She had half a dozen persons in her house-party, including Lord and Lady Beatty, Lord Stanley and Peter Rodd. While Lady Norman and Mrs. Churchill discussed a change of curtains in the salon, I went outside and sat on the terrace. A little boy of about ten came up to me. "Look what I've been given!" he said, showing me a small pocket-radio. He chatted away, a bright little fellow. I asked him his name. "Winston Churchill", he replied. I looked at the small boy in wonder. What a name to carry through life! What a grandfather to have! In one sense the name was a rather frightening asset, whatever he was destined to accomplish.

After a week at Casa Estella Aubrey and I left for a motor tour to Florence, Siena, and on, over the Grossglockner, to Salzburg. Four days before starting I went down with a frightful attack of the old enemy but insisted on departing on the morning fixed, at 6 a.m. Poor Aubrey expected to be transporting a corpse. We breakfasted in Alassio where I pointed out the Villa Santa Margherita. We were in Florence for dinner, where I went to bed for three days. I got up and told Aubrey we would go on to Siena. He was alarmed. I said that at the worst I could die of a haemorrhage, but if I gave way to this repeated threat I would become a useless invalid, something I refused to be. So we got out the car and went on to Siena.

I had booked rooms at the Pension Chiusarelli where I had been before. Its back rooms overlooked the Hippodrome, and early each morning the jockeys came to train their horses for the Palio race. Thud, thud, thud, round they went in the early dawn. Siena was already excited and crammed with visitors for one of Italy's finest spectacles. The boys in the streets were practising throwing their flags in the air, and catching them, the traditional *sbandierata*. Two years earlier I had had an inside view of the Palio. A Sienese friend, Benvenuto, a tall youth with a classical head of black curls, who might have passed for Giuliano de Medici, was the captain of his *contrada, Drago*. He wore the traditional suit of armour, greaves, helmet with visor, and carried a great sword. In the *Drago*'s clubroom I had watched the young squires, flag-bearers and pages, put on their skin-tight hose, their fancy leather shoes, their slashed doublets and gay embroidered bonnets. For more than three hundred years successive youths of the seventeen *contrade* had worn these costumes, traditional since 1230 when the Florentines had besieged Siena, catapulting dead donkeys and excrement over its walls to start a plague.

In the year when *Drago* had won the race, Benevenuto and I had walked in the rejoicing *contrada*. The streets were hung with green and red banners, and torches flared in sconces on the walls of palaces. We went to the clubroom, decorated with flowers, where the ancient green and red costumes hung in cabinets. Former Palio flags decorated the walls. There was free wine for all. Nearby we saw a small room with a grille, lit up. Within, munching a great bale of hay with which it had been rewarded, stood *Drago*'s winning horse. There was a coronal of flowers on its head and gay ribbons woven in its tail.

On the day after our arrival in Siena, while I was writing in my room, Aubrey came in, waving a piece of paper, his face radiant. "I'm in! I'm in!" he cried. "I go up to Trinity next term!" So my letter had not been in vain. The following day we saw the Palio, the great horse race in the Piazza. All round, built up against façades of shops and palaces, were tiers of seats filled with some forty thousand spectators. The Podestà's Palazzo was ablaze with flags and armorial shields. High over all, in the great slim bell-tower, 286 feet high, the famous Mangia bell tolled, sending waves of sound over the many-hilled city. The race began when the sun fell low enough to throw a shadow over the Campo. Suddenly there was cheering as mounted carabinieri, twelve abreast, rode round the course. There followed six mace-bearers, then flag-bearers of the communes, on horseback, with grooms, four centurions, twelve trumpeters and twelve musicians playing the Palio march. Next came the six flag-bearers representing the estates and castles of the ancient Republic of Siena. Then followed the Captain of the People, bearing the State sword, and the commander of the Sienese troops, on horseback, led by a groom. All were in fifteenth-century costumes. After this came each *contrada*, with its captain, whirling flags, a jockey on a caparisoned parade horse, and a groom with each racehorse. One looked across a sea of flags, green, blue, crimson, mauve, gold, cerise, purple, each marking a cohort in slashed doublets and parti-coloured hose. Vivid, slender, handsome, the Romeos of the Renaissance were here, as Pinturicchio shows them on his frescoes in the Piccolomini library of the cathedral.

At the end of the procession a dozen small pages, in crimson tights, carried on their shoulders a long green rope of laurel leaves. They seemed to have stepped down from a Della Robbia panel. And now, finally the *Carroccio*, the great mediaeval war-chariot, drawn by four milk-white yoked oxen, carrying the Palio itself, the embroidered flag bearing the image of the Madonna and Child, and the coat of arms of the town.

The race began. Ten horses strained at the starting rope. A cannon sounded. They were off, riding madly three times round the piazza, to a delirium of cheering. The winning horse was immediately surrounded by carabinieri, for frenzied partisanship had sometimes expressed itself in an attack on horse and jockey.

The morning following the race we made a side excursion to Castello Brolio, the fortress-home of Baron Ricasoli, finely situated on a crest of the Chianti hills, from whose vine-yards the famous Brolio chianti was drawn. My host, Baron Ricasoli, came of a distinguished Florentine house. They were the sole barons of Tuscany. The bastions of the old fortress dated back to the ninth century. In 1141 it became the property of the Ricasoli family. It had withstood many sieges, In 1529 the Sienese took the castle, driving out the family, and burned it to its foundations. The castle was rebuilt in 1861 by the statesman, Baron Bettino Ricasoli, who became Prime Minister of a United Italy in that year, following Cavour.

We arrived at a massive gate in the great bastion walls, sixty feet high and almost a mile in circumference. The portal swung back and we drove up a curving ramp to the inner courtyard where we were greeted by the baron. He had given me much help when writing about Tuscany and had placed his rich archives at my disposal. There was a note of surprise. A guest was at that moment leaving, Lady Cartwright of Aynho, born Chigi of Siena, who had married the English diplomat, Sir Fairfax Cartwright, a kinsman of Aubrey.

We drank the famous wine in the great dining-hall whose walls were decorated with cartoons of the House of Ricasoli, and then went out on to the terrace built along the ramparts. It had a stupendous view of the Chianti country spread below us. Lastly, we went into the family chapel built in 1348. On leaving we drove down through the cypress woods to the valley where the great cantines housed the grapes brought in from the surrounding vineyards.

III

After our return to Florence, Aubrey's Eton friend, Simon Stuart, arrived. My two escorts were six foot four and six foot three. Each of them had done a year's military service after leaving Eton. Now they were going up to Trinity College, Cambridge. I found it difficult to believe that Simon, a lieutenant in the Scots Guards, had recently been standing up to the waist in the foetid swamps of Malaya, engaged in jungle warfare.

We began our journey to Salzburg on a torrid August day, going via Mantua, Trento, and up the Brennero highway as far as Cavalese, heading for Austria, over the Pordoi and Falzarego Passes in the Dolomites, and on to Cortina. It was all very familiar to me, the scene of my novel *Spears Against Us*.

We stayed at small inns. Arriving late in the evining at Lienz, in the Tyrol, we found all the hotels booked up. We were seized by a youth who said he could take us to a good lodging. We suspected that he was a tout. He jumped on to the runningboard and insisted on guiding us to a housing settlement. Before one house our guide stopped and led us up a staircase to the first floor. A quiet little woman of about forty opened the door and we stepped into a large kitchen. We were shown a double and a single bedroom, very clean. We moved in our things and went out to dine. In the morning we had a good breakfast in the kitchen. On the wall there was a photograph of a bridal couple taken over twenty years ago. Here was a tragedy such as had visited thousands of these homes. Our guide of the previous evening was the landlady's married son. She had slept out in her son's house in order to free a room. Yes, that was a photograph taken on her wedding day. She was a widow, possibly. Possibly? Yes, her husband had been sent to fight in Russia, now perhaps dead, perhaps a prisoner. She tried not to give up hope—he might return one day. So here she was, alone in her little house, ekeing out a living by dressmaking, washing, letting rooms to summer visitors, helped a little by her son. Waiting, hoping, for eight years now.

We strolled about the town in the morning. An amusing incident evoked our mirth. We were walking along the street when two elderly ladies passed and we heard an unmistakable American voice say—"I guess those are three aristocratic young Englishmen." A damn for the "aristocratic" but gratitude for the "young". I suspect I was well masked by my companions. Both of them had American mothers!

We left the next morning and climbed the great glacier-riven Grossglockner range by the most spectacular mountain road in Europe, and so came at nightfall to Zell-am-Zee on its beautiful lake. We found lodgings, three beds in one room, in the house of a shoemaker. It had a garden full of sunflowers, zinnias and coloured glass-witchballs on sticks. Aubrey and I occupied twin beds, Simon somehow accommodated himself on a short truckle bed. I woke about seven in the morning. Aubrey on my left and Simon on my right were still asleep, so I took up Belloc's *Napoleon*, and began to read. Presently Simon woke, fished for a book in a knapsack, and extracted Wordsworth's *Excursion*. Aubrey now woke and joined the reading club, with Adam Smith's *Wealth of Nations*. In half an hour an apple-cheeked, pigtailed urchin appeared with two cans of hot water, the sign to get up.

We had a clear morning for our run through rolling country but in the car I was in such pain that at Hallein we had to stop, the jolting being too much. I lay on a grass bank for an hour, then we pushed on to Salzburg, bustling with visitors to the Music Festival. My friend Mrs. Boehm was there, awaiting me. We drew up at her hotel. Aubrey went in to announce that I was in the car, half-dead. Luckily there was a vacant bed in the hotel. I occupied it at once while my worried companions went to search for lodgings. Well, I had made it.

I had a good guide in Salzburg. Young Günther Bauer, a native, the hiker who had sought me at Casa Estella, called on me. He was playing in *Jedermann*, on the open stage before the cathedral. He brought his younger brother, six foot five to his six foot two, whom I introduced to my English companions, six foot three, and six foot four. No wonder people turned, when I, only six foot, walked out with these giants.

One day I paid a sad pilgrimage up the Kapuzinerberg to a large, rambling house with a tower. It was locked up and looked desolate. Here in the thirties I had been the guest of Stefan Zweig, the author. Driven out of Salzburg by Nazi hooligans, he had finally settled in Brazil, where, in 1942, depressed by the state of the world, he had committed suicide.

A week later I left with Mrs. Boehm for Bad Gastein, the alpine kurstadt with radium baths. Aubrey and Simon drove us to the station through a downpour of rain. I parted from my two companions with real regret. One of them I knew well, the other but slightly. There was a great disparity between a much-travelled man of fifty-eight and two youngsters of twenty. We had motored, eaten and sight-seen together in unbroken harmony. I left them, with affection for their consideration towards me, their good manners, cheerfulness, and their eagerness, under my tutelage, to examine the many facets of this wonderful world. Eton had moulded them and my admiration of that venerable place was increased.

It was dusk when we got to our hotel in Bad Gastein. My room had a loggia facing south, with arcades, somewhat like the setting of a Fra Angelico *Annunciation*, flower-filled. I looked out on the horsehoe curve of the mountain, revealing the town jewelled with lights. The murmur of the waterfall that cleaves it in half pervaded the air. I walked every morning on the Kaiser Wilhelm Promenade. It had known kings, princes, grand dukes, the Emperor Franz-Joseph, Kaiser Wilhelm and King Edward VII, but those days were over. Two wars had shattered their world, but prosperity was flowing back with the growing tourist vogue. I soon ran into acquaintances, first Yehudi Menuhin on the Promenade. I had last seen him four years previously, at a dinner-party in New York, when he had just come back from a visit to Russia, where he had been well received. Yehudi means "Jew". He told me how he got it. Just before he was born his parents, Russian Jews, emigrated to New York, where they experienced considerable trouble in finding hotel accommodation owing to the ban on Jews in good-class hotels. Incensed, they made a vow never to compromise about their race, so they deliberately called their baby son Yehudi.

Also on the Promenade, where one of the diversions was feeding the innumerable squirrels—you bought a bag of nuts for them at a kiosk—was Daniele Varé, the Italian author-diplomat who wrote that fantasia *The Maker of Heavenly Trousers*, based on his life in Pekin, and *The Laughing Diplomat*. He said he was staying in an hotel where Mozart's mother had stayed, also that Bad Gastein once had goldmines, worked by the Romans.

In the seventh century the Church seized them and by the fourteenth the Prince-Archbishops of Salzburg were masters of the domain. From the great wealth derived from these mines they minted a currency, built the magnificent fortress-palace which dominates Salzburg, and such trifles as the Mirabell Schloss and the Monats Schloss for their mistresses. The mines received a deathblow from the discovery of gold in Klondyke. The small deposits in the rifts made it no longer worth the labour.

The real gold for Bad Gastein is now the radium-charged water, but one has to be careful. There is the story of a Prince-Archbishop seeking rejuvenation who sat in the water with a secretary, playing chess. "It's the Bishop's move," said the secretary. But the archbishop made no move. He could not, he had collapsed and was dead from too much radium. My doctor would not let me take the baths. The air, charged with radium, is the real tonic of the place.

My army friend, John Smyth, joined me so I had a good walking companion. After two weeks I went on to Venice. Through the Tauern tunnel one comes out on the southern side of the great watershed. Below lies the Mediterranean, and Venice. "*Kennst Du das Land?*" I do indeed. Near midnight a gondola bore me down the Grand Canal. It was like coming home. Two days later I lunched with the gay Robilants in their palace on the Canal, and met many old Venetian friends. Among these was Princess Aspasia of Greece, of the Garden of Eden on the Giudecca. When I went to dine there next evening a beautiful young woman came forward to greet me. She said her mother would be down soon. It was the former little Alessandra, who had played in the garden with my Lucien and his sister Bevis. Fourteen years had passed since I had seen her. "I have a question to ask you," I said. "Last April in Madrid I met King Peter and he said my novel had been the cause of his marriage. In what way have I had anything to do with it?" She laughed and told me. "You gave my mother a copy of your novel *Victoria Four-Thirty*. I read it and fell in love with your 'Prince Sixpenny', who was Peter. I wasn't happy until I had met him. We fell in love and married. So you see it was through you!"

I was silent a while, somewhat overwhelmed. It had grown dark on the lagoon. Other guests arrived and assembled on the terrace with my hostess. Before we went towards them I said to Alessandra, "There are fairy tales we never write. I couldn't make this one credible."

The next week I left for Montecatini. Too much lunching and dining and chasing about unwisely in the heat had undone me. In the Hotel *La Pace* I asked for a doctor. A tall, handsome man came, Dr. Pisani, a professor in the University of Florence. He had so much charm that I felt doubtful about him. He looked too much like the fashionable Spa doctor. He had treated the Duke of Windsor, I was told. But the thoroughness of his examination gave me confidence, and he did not, for a change, suggest an operation. He kept me in bed for two weeks, after which I got up, to leave for Rome. When I asked him for his bill, which I expected would be heavy, he said, "I have no bill for an author." Poor man, he was killed in a motor accident soon afterwards.

IV

I went back to my old room at the Eden Hotel in Rome. The next morning when I opened the shutters the whole city lay below me, the gardens of the Villa Medici, the Villa Borghese with its pine trees, Mount Soracte rising on the horizon, the great dome of St Peter's, the façade of the Vatican, the Janiculan Hill and the Roman campagna, with the Mediterranean sea at Ostia. There was endless excitement in Rome, this being the Holy Year. I encountered the incredible savant who had hypnotised me so often at Mrs. Crane's evenings in New York, Edgar Wind, now Professor of the History of Art at Oxford. They had had to take a theatre to house his enthralled audiences. His knowledge of Renaissance art was unfathomable. Dining with him and his wife in the Piazza Navona, I found him in his old form. He astonished me by saying there was a legend that the Ark had settled on the Janiculan Hill. A Dominican monk had written a book in which he propounded the theory that Noah was, in Hebrew, Jajin, wine-bibber. From Jajin came the Roman Janus, the two-faced god, who looked in opposite directions, which supported the story that Noah looked both ways during the subsidence of the flood. So where he landed was now called the Janiculan! Instead of burning him for heresy the Pope rewarded the monk.

The great day of the Anno Santo arrived. I declined a ticket for the tribune in St. Peter's for the ceremony of the Dogma of the Assumption of the Virgin Mary. I had seen two Beatifications there, magnificent but wearisome. I preferred therefore the open Piazza, though warned that if I did not get there at 5 a.m., I should be frustrated by a quarter of a million spectators. I arrived at eight o'clock, and saw the Pope, Pius XII, in his high, pontifical chair borne on the shoulders of his attendants.

The outdoor ceremony was performed in six languages, and at the recital of prayers the crowd made responses from little books, in different languages that had been distributed. Then came the great moment of the promulgation of the Dogma, with the austere Pope, standing with arms uplifted in the sunshine, proclaiming the Latin formula. After his Address and a prayer, five hundred pigeons were released from the colonnades. They wheeled shining in the sun before disappearing in the distance.

I was back in England in November. In Rome I had begun work at last on a new novel. For some time I had brooded over the theme. It took birth from that experience during my stay in Monte Carlo last January, when, after hearing the Watch Night Service in the English Church next door, the tenant below us committed suicide. I had heard also the sad story of a gifted artist called to the Palace to paint a portrait who had been unable to finish it owing to arthritis. My story, which I called *A Terrace in the Sun*, was about a small boy who became a famous artist. He had been a miner's son in Nottingham. When a boy I had lived on the edge of a colliery district in the days when miners were regarded as sub-human, brawling drunkards living in hovels. I knew this background. The first article I wrote, aged fourteen, had been printed in my school magazine after I had been down the mine at Clifton Colliery on the bank of the River Trent. Now, more than forty years later, I went back to that colliery to check my data for the story. I could not recognise the place, it had so much changed for the better. The squalor had gone. The miners had radios and cars. It was no longer possible to send pinched boys of thirteen down to the coal-face, sons of miners who worked ten hours a day for twenty-five shillings a week.

While in Nottingham I visited my invalid brother, happy in the garden of the house I had bought him. Nearly seventy, he had survived five operations. He was always content and tranquil. He had no idea why I wanted to write books. He thought I led a crazy life. "You work much too hard, and isn't it a nuisance being famous?" he asked. "It might be worse if I was infamous," I replied.

V

November 1950 was a golden month. My cottage was alluring with its log-fires, its windows misting at sunset. I finished my novel. I made visits. I dined with Norman and Billy Birkett in their London pied-à-terre. We had many memories. We had crossed to New York in 1946 on the maiden trip of the *Queen Elizabeth*, shortly after he had returned from being one of the judges at the Nuremberg Trials. He was now a Lord Justice of Appeal. It was amusing to see him, home from the Law Courts, in the kitchen helping his wife. We were both ulcer addicts so she contrived a special menu.

I went again to glorious Knole, visiting Charles and Anne Sackville. No other mansion in England, not even Windsor Castle, seems to me more beautifully placed, more essentially English. This vast house, that covered four acres, had seven quadrangles, fifty-two staircases and three hundred and sixty-five rooms, was now open to the public. Charles and Anne lived in a wing. He had just celebrated his eightieth birthday, still alert and handsome. He now rounded off his career as a soldier by waging a war with the Treasury to preserve Knole. In the dining-room that evening I looked at the portraits of Sackvilles who had lived there since the time of Thomas, who had been given Knole by his cousin, Queen Elizabeth, in 1586. She made him her Lord Treasurer.

Four hundred windows destroyed by war bombs had been replaced but something had been destroyed that was not replaceable, a mode of life. There were now only two servants in this vast mansion which had housed two hundred and fifty souls in its great days. When the cook fell ill the Sackvilles called a taxi and went out to eat in a Sevenoaks hotel. This happened on my second evening there. Anne, who owned part of Marie Antoinette's famous Cardinal's necklace, now incorporated in her peeress's coronet, washed up in the pantry, and his lordship went down to the cellar to get a bottle of wine. I carried fire-logs in from an outhouse, two courts away. When I left my host accompanied me to the postern gate. As we stood there, looking across the misty park, he astonished me by saying "There's my Jap!" I was a little startled. Japanese spies at Knole, or a Japanese page in place of a ghostly Chinese one, Hwang-a-Tung, whose portrait by Sir Joshua Reynolds hung in Black Boy's Passage? "A Jap?" I queried, looking round. "There!" said my host, pointing to a stag that stood not ten yards away, watching us. "That's a Japanese stag. One of my family brought some Japanese deer over with him after leaving a diplomatic post in Tokyo. They've bred here ever since."

I was in Glasgow a few days later to lecture at The Athenaeum Theatre in the Celebrities Series, run by a Nonconformist Minister, the Rev. H. S. McClelland. Used as I was to all manner of audiences throughout England and the United States, I cannnot recall one that had such gusto. Compton Mackenzie had lectured there. "I came off that platform like a drunken sailor. It was a sort of Revival Meeting!" he said to me.

The creator of this series was a man whose life-story was fact that sounded wholly like fiction. The Rev. H. McClelland was the Minister of the Claremont St. Trinity Congregational Church. He had originally been an actor but gave up the stage for the pulpit, in which he was a dynamic preacher. He had been a tremendous traveller as a missionary whose work took him all over the world. On one occasion, in Transjordania, he was captured by Bedouins and spent a week in their tents. Wishing to examine and write about the "down-and-outs" of London, he became a tramp and lived among the destitute, spending nights dossing in rescue huts, and on the Embankment. Later, he accepted the ministry of Trinity Church. Here he created a Literary Society that had a thousand members. He ran a a series of lectures and drew to his platform many of the most famous authors of the day.

It was to give a lecture in this series that I went to Glasgow. He had offered to put me up at his home in Kelvinside, or at the Central Hotel. Foolishly, playing for independence, I stayed at the hotel—a mistake. I missed meeting a very remarkable family for he had married a widow with three beautiful daughters and lived in great comfort. He sometimes drew failures. Great names did not guarantee great performances. One lecturer almost had to be carried on the platform. He had been too busy with the bottle in the hotel, and had run-up quite a bill. I saw the point in McClelland offering home hospitality! The worst fiasco of all seems to have been A. S. M. Hutchinson, then famous with his world best-seller, *If Winter Comes*. He read from his novel and was utterly inaudible in a hall renowned for its splendid acoustics.

Three days after my lecture McClelland wrote suggesting a future date. "You saw for yourself at the close of your address how enthusiastic your audience was. We had great anticipations of your visit and you fulfilled them all. All I can say is Glasgow seemed to me a much colder place when I bade you goodbye. You carry the sunshine with you wherever you go." McClelland certainly had a way with him. I made a return visit as he wished.

One December morning in my newspaper there was the picture of a chubby little boy standing with his governess on the deck of a steamer coming into Weymouth from Jersey. The caption-story said that he had been on holiday for six weeks. "His governess has denied that she stated that threats were made to kidnap the little prince." I was glad to learn he was safe for he was little Alexander, the son of ex-King Peter.

Four days later I sailed for New York. I celebrated the New Year seated in the library of Mrs. Cartwright's apartment on Fifth Avenue, whose windows overlooked snow-mantled Central Park, where the skyscraper buildings, lit up, seemed like a cascade of diamonds. Just before midnight, while the bells rang, coming in to us by radio, a bottle of champagne was opened and our small company toasted the New Year, 1951.

Brolio Castle, Chianti Hills.

CHAPTER SIX

Life at Palazzo Vairo

I

Early in the New Year I went to visit John Basore, the retired Latin professor. He shared a house with another bachelor, also a Latinist, David Magie, Professor Emeritus of Classics, retired from Princeton University, who had devoted his whole life to writing an immense volume on *Roman Rule in Asia Minor*. It became the established authority on that phase of Roman history up to the end of the third century after Christ. Travelling in Asia Minor twenty years later, I had proof of his comprehensive and meticulous scholarship.

The Basore–Magie home, standing back in a large garden at Princeton, was carefully divided. There was a central entrance hall, and on each side a study. The two scholars kept strictly separate quarters, downstairs and upstairs. They were punctilious in their conduct towards one another. John politely knocked on David's study door, and David politely knocked on John's study door. When they received jointly it was in the drawing-room, held in common. They reminded me of Edward Lear's lines—

> Two old Bachelors were living in one house;
> One caught a Muffin and the other caught a Mouse.

They had an Italian manservant whose wife was the cook. Even the fat Spaniel dog was shared. He spent the morning in John's study, the afternoon in David's, the evening in the kitchen. He joined them in the dining-room at lunch and dinner, retiring to a special window cushion. Let it be said that the conversation of these two elderly scholars was not grave, sometimes it was almost hilarious. They had lived together in the utmost felicity for thirty years. They entertained freely and were popular with everybody. When I went up to bed each called to enquire if I had all I wanted. There were piles of books at the bedside, a chaise-longue, a special reading lamp, and a table full of drinks, though they were themselves most abstemious. With all this and so many books to devour, my light did not go out until 2 a.m.

At a lunch one day in February, with New York under a mantle of snow, I met Lucrezia Bori and Harold Acton. The pleasure of this was dashed when, after leaving, I learned that Marie Mercati, brightest of hostesses, turned eighty, had died that morning. It was in her salon that I used to talk with Charles Jerome Bonaparte Patterson, the legitimate Bonaparte heir to the French throne. His great-grandfather was Napoleon's brother, Prince Jerome, who had married Elizabeth Patterson in Baltimore. It was a marriage Napoleon refused to recognise and the Pope refused to annul, so that Jerome's subsequent marriage to Princess Catherine of Württemberg was bigamous, and their children illegitimate.

A few evenings later Lucrezia Bori gave a dinner party and put on a record of her greatest role, in *Manon*. Her guests included Sir Kenneth and Lady Clark. Sir Kenneth had a delightful story about the fabulous art dealer, Lord Duveen, who sold to American million-aires masterpieces for enormous sums. One day, while walking in Central Park, Duveen stopped to admire a bonnie baby in a cot. He began to poke it, appreciatively. The alarmed nurse screamed and called a policeman, to whom Duveen had to explain that his behaviour was quite innocent, he was only admiring a masterpiece.

At the end of February I was astonished on being called up by ex-King Peter. He was in New York with his wife. I went round to see them, being delighted for a special reason There had been rumours current that they were separating, and now here they were, seemingly happy. Peter, nigh penniless, was looking for work. It was said that his father had left several millions in a Swiss bank under a code number but that after his assassination no one could find the number and the Swiss bank refused to pay the money to his son. He told me that he was now in New York because he had been offered a job as an automobile salesman. He took it, but it did not last. He was only given the job because his name was a bait to snobbish purchasers. "It wasn't enough to sell a car," he told me later. "They expected me and Alessandra to attend their dinner-parties, and say a few words." Harassed for the rest of his days, he died, aged forty-seven, lonely and impoverished in the United States. On his death a squabble broke out between factions of exiled Yugoslavs as to who should arrange his funeral. But now, here in New York, he seemed happy at the prospect of earning a living.

One evening, dining at Mrs. Vanderbilt's, I found the Duke and Duchess of Windsor among the guests. He was always an attractive conversationalist with an eager interest in everything. After the ladies had left the dining-room we somehow got on to the subject of Bonnie Prince Charlie. I found that the duke was under the impression that Henry, Cardinal Duke of York, was Prince Charlie's uncle, and not his younger brother, the last of the Stuarts! I ventured to correct him and quoted the inscription on Canova's cenotaph in St. Peter's, on which the Old Pretender and his two sons are depicted. "You seem to know a great deal about the Young Pretender," said the duke. I confessed the reason. I had written about him in my book *And so to Rome*. He said he would read it at once. A week later the duchess told me that he had sat up late, engrossed in the chapter on Bonnie Prince Charlie. Presently there came a letter from the duke.

I read the pages you recommended and despite the exhausted condition in which the completion of my Memoirs leaves me at the end of the day, I greatly enjoyed them. From the little I have read about him I have never been able to work up much enthusiasm for Bonnie Prince Charlie.

He seems to have had some good "public relations men" to build him up in Scotland in the years immediately before 1745. He certainly let them and all his brave, loyal Highlanders down about as badly as any self-styled leader could. Now my disillusionment is complete, and the fine old song "Bonnie Prince Charlie's gang awa, will he no come back again" can never again give me a lump in the throat.

II

On March 1st I sailed in the *Vulcania*, an Italian liner, for Gibraltar, accompanied by my friend, Mrs. Boehm. We boarded the ship in a snowstorm. On the second day out we were hit by a hurricane. The captain of the *Queen Mary*, heeding a warning, turned back to port. The *Vulcania* went on. The second night was one of alarm. The bridge was battered, the staterooms flooded, and all the furniture set out for the captain's cocktail party in the saloon was smashed. Many passengers spent the night roped together on the ship's staircase. I went along at three a.m. to see how my friend was faring. En route a great surge of water swept down the corridor and I had to cling to a rail, waist-high in water, until it passed. I found my friend had taken refuge in an upper bunk in her stateroom which had a foot of water. A seaman came in and moved her portmanteaux into the bath, the only dry place. For four days we were tossed in a tornado. There was no electric light. Three lifeboats were torn from their derricks and smashed. Nothing could have been launched in that terrific sea. The ship rolled thirty-eight degrees. At forty she would have capsized. The kitchens were all out of order and we were fed with soup in paper cups brought to us on the stairs. Oddly enough we were so near death that none of us was frightened. A famous American actress, on board, Katherine Cornell, said "You know, I somehow felt I was acting in a drama on a world stage!" Waves 160 feet high went over the ship.

The fifth day the tornado abated. The captain said it had been "molto pericoloso" and at one period he had feared we should founder. A hatch had been smashed, the hold filled with water. Twelve automobiles below were destroyed. The crew was magnificent, tireless, without a shade of panic. There was a touch of humour. In the doctor's office, my friend met a little Siamese passenger, also injured. It was his first Atlantic crossing. When Mrs. Boehm remarked on their terrible experience, he opened his eyes wide and said politely, "Oh, madam, I thought this was the usual sea journey."

Somehow throughout all this I corrected the proofs of my novel, *A Terrace in the Sun*, sitting on a roped chair in my stateroom. When the ship reached Lisbon many passengers deserted her. We went on to Gibraltar and entered the harbour but it was too rough for the tender to take us ashore. The sea had not done with us. I was astonished to find that we were moving all night. The ship had parted from her anchor and had had to cruise in the open sea! We landed on a calm, radiant Sunday morning. The most battered passengers were a Spanish ballet company pinned down in the steerage throughout the journey. Poor souls, they contrived to laugh and wave as they set foot on terra firma.

Within two hours of landing I stepped out on to the balcony of my room at the Rock Hotel. The Straits shone below me. In the noonday sun the shore of North Africa, with Ceuta, was visible. This was a sub-tropical paradise after the hell we had come through. Gibraltar was buoyantly British, the Spanish agitation for reclamation would hit it later. It had a Governor, nicely housed, a Colonial Secretary, and an Admiral Superintendent, commanding at Gibraltar, tall, silver-haired Lord Ashbourne. His home, The Mount, was superbly placed on a hill, a wide-windowed Regency house with fine views. It was filled with good English furniture and pictures, mostly of the eighteenth century. The Admiral gave a dinner, an American Naval Commander and his Consul among the guests. The naval atmosphere was set by the young orderlies in white service jackets who served at table. At the end of the dinner the port circulated. There was a Royal toast. Here was the very essence of traditional England on a rock above the Straits. The Admiral could not have been more English, very handsome in his mess uniform, a perfect host, a good conversationalist. I declined a car to take me home. I walked down from the Mount, through a scented, warm midnight, moonlit, with ships' lights scintillating in the harbour below.

There was a surprise in store for me. Lunching with the American Consul, I noticed, when signing his book, that the Bishop of Gibraltar had been there. I had a particular reason for wishing to meet him. So after lunch we called on him at the Deanery. I found a new friend in Cecil Horsley, the bishop. Young, rubicund, jolly, he was at once lovable. I told him that I had just finished a novel. It opened in Monte Carlo, and on New Year's Eve my hero had dined on board a friend's yacht, meeting there the Bishop of Gibraltar and his wife. Towards midnight he had motored home to his apartment, next door to the English church, where the bishop was conducting the Watch Night Service. I asked him if he had any objection to his inclusion. "Oh, none at all. What fun to figure in your novel! But there's one correction, please. There's no Mrs. Horsley. I'm a bachelor!"

As the bishop had no official residence in Gibraltar he moved into the Rock Hotel, with his secretary-chauffeur, Ian McDougal, a young South Rhodesian. For the next week we were almost inseparable. One day when we were lunching under the pergola, with a view across to Morocco, we began to exchange reminiscences. He told me that he had had a stern, taciturn old father, a retired admiral. He was the son of a second marriage and felt himself a neglected late chicken in the nest. Perhaps an awareness of the shortening years prompted the admiral to ask his son to reserve two consecutive Wednesdays for him. He gave no inkling of his purpose in making this request, a singular overture for a silent, undemonstrative man in his eighties. On the first Wednesday they went to Canterbury. His father had been at King's School there and had suffered under a sadistic master. They went into the cathedral where the old man led his son up to a pew by a pillar. "I want you to look at this pew, my son. This is the only place where I knew happiness in my boyhood. I would find a refuge here from the discipline and the beatings, and listen to the choir, whose music I loved." On the second Wednesday they went to the Royal Naval College at Greenwich. There, saluted by old servants who knew him, they dined in the great Painted Hall, with its ceiling by Thornhill, its naval portraits, flags, battle pictures and silver candelabra on the long tables. "Here, in my last years, I have again known happiness," he said. By those two pilgrimages his reticent old father had opened two windows of his heart to his son. When the admiral died, the Bishop, who knew how he had loved the music of a cathedral choir, succeeded in obtaining from nearby Chichester Cathedral the choir, which walked and sang beside his bier, covered with the Union Jack, and on which reposed the sword and cocked hat of an old sailor laid to rest.

The Bishop had an amusing story about going to see the Archbishop of Canterbury. Pressed for time, he went into a Lyons' Restaurant in London. He ordered a cup of coffee and a sandwich from the "Nippy". He waited for some time, and, receiving no service, called her, saying that he was in a great hurry as he had a train to catch. "Perhaps you have, little robin-redbreast, but you must wait your turn like the others," retorted the waitress.

Horsley had received an invitation to go to New York. He seemed very nervous about it. He envied me my experience there. I encouraged him to go, gave him some letters of introduction and cabled friends who would entertain him. Very hesitatingly he decided to go. Thereby Mrs. Boehm and I had a windfall. His car and secretary would have to return to England. He offered us the service of both, which we gratefully accepted. So while he toured the States we would be touring Spain, homewards, in his car.

A month passed very quickly in Gibraltar. Spring was there in full bloom. We made brief excursions, to Tangier, by a horrifying flight in an old plane that seemed unable to rise more than a hundred feet over the Straits. We went to Algeciras, to Cadiz, snow-white and fiercely hot, and to Tarifa, reeking with history.

We motored up coast to Torremolinos, south of Malaga, with an empty beach three miles long. While having tea in an hotel there, an agent tried to sell me an orange grove, twenty acres, a mile from the beach, at £10 an acre. He would build me a house on it for £400. With my pesetas I could have bought 100 acres and have built a house, but what did I want with an orange grove in distant Spain? When some twenty years later I was again in Torremolinos, the long beach was covered with broiling bodies and lined with hotels and apartment houses. Land cost £3,000 an acre. Never, never look back.

There was a farewell party at the Deanery. On the morrow the Bishop was leaving for New York, in a state of perturbation. We were leaving for Seville, in his car, driven by young McDougal. Our route in Andalusia was one long enchantment across a flat plain covered with mauve and yellow flowers. So I came back to the old Hotel Madrid. This time it was not the festival of Holy Week, but the Feria, a festival of horses in a flower-drenched city, heady with orange blossom, and ablaze with bougainvillaea that trailed over snow-white garden walls. By day and by night there was a lilt of guitars. No one went to bed till dawn. Surely there had been drawn into the narrow streets all the most beautiful women in Spain, Carmens galore, with flashing eyes and teeth and a rose provocatively stuck in their black tresses caught up in high combs.

This time the Duke of Alba was there, at his Palacio de las Duenas, hospitable, as always. His only child, Maria, the Duchess of Montoro, had two children. After lunch one day they were brought into the open gallery of the palace accompanied by their nannie, the elder son, four-year-old Carlos, and a baby, Alfonso, which Alba nursed in his arms while I photographed them. A little later an open carriage drew up into the courtyard with gaily caparisoned horses, in the

Alba Livery. The young duchess and friends were off to the bullfight. What a carriage-load of beauty they made! Alba and I followed later. I would have liked being spared another bullfight, but it would have been discourteous to have refused, for this was the great national pastime, and the Feria was a very special occasion. The sight in that vast arena was certainly magnificent, with its multitude of *aficionados*, tier on tier, its vivid colours, its flags flying, its great sanded arena in the afternoon sun. The march of the picadors and matadors opened the proceedings. Within twenty minutes the first slain bull was trailed by horses out of the arena.

But horses, not bulls, were the cherished animals of the Feria. Here were Spain's finest, ridden by young cavaliers in cutaway jackets, frilled shirts and black sombreros, each with a lovely girl perched side-saddle behind him, her magnificent flounced skirt spread over the horse's haunches. Round and round they went in a slow proud procession on the Fair ground. The chief avenue in the Feria was lined with the private boxes, the *casetas* of Seville society. Boxes is scarcely the word for these gay pavilions, furnished with carpets, tapestries, and a dining alcove where refreshments were served between parades. The Alba *caseta*, carpeted, bright with house flags, was almost a drawing-room with one side open to the avenue. On they came, the gallants and their señoritas holding slim waists, roses in their black tresses, scarlet-lipped, the allure of Spain in their dazzling smiles.

One morning a Spanish friend took me to see the training stables of Francisco Rodriguez at Triana. He told me that the horses in Velasquez's paintings were of Arab and Aragona stock, being bred specially for Charles V to carry heavy armour. We proceeded to Antequera in the afternoon to see the bulls bred for the arena. It was a social occasion with tea served in a pavilion overlooking the paddocks where the most costly bulls lived almost luxuriously, unwitting of their doom. Our evening closed with a flamenco performance, a short play by Lope de Vega, and then on to the Casino where my friend and I danced in an immense crowd with great gusto. When we drove home at 4 a.m. in the scented dawn there was the music of guitars eddying from the narrow alleyways. It would seem that Seville never went to bed during the Feria.

After only a few hours' sleep I could not refuse an excursion to

Huelva, where Christopher Columbus had set forth on his voyage of discovery of America. There is a little convent and church at Palos where he passed the last night before sailing. I stood on the wharf that had known the history-making departure, on the morning of Friday, August 3rd, 1492, after Mass, of the *Santa Maria*, 120 tons, flagship of Columbus, decked over, with a crew of 52; the *Pinto*, 50 tons; and the *Niña*, 40 tons, a caravel with a crew of 18. The total fleet, made in a local shipyard, cost £950. In the crew was one Englishman, Allard of Winchester, and one Irishman, Ires from Galway. At the tip of the estuary stands the gigantic statue of Columbus by Malvinia Hoffman. Its counterpart, across a once unknown ocean, is the Statue of Liberty, marking the new continent, the new age.

We left Seville in the early April dawn with the birds singing in the Jardin des Delices. At Ubeda, in the Davalos Palace turned into a *parador*, which overlooked the Plaza and the façade of the vast church of San Pedro, I slept in the largest bedroom I have ever seen. It was a long walk from the bed to the bathroom, converted from a small chapel. The cold in winter must have been terrifying.

On reaching Madrid I found the Duke of Argyll in my hotel, on his honeymoon. I got him to tell me about his plans for raising the lost Spanish galleon in Tobermory Bay, which was attracting so much attention. He had succeeded in getting the help of the Navy in this exciting enterprise. He was not positive whether the ship, driven north after the destruction of the Armada in the English Channel, was a Spanish or an Italian ship. At Inveraray Castle he has a cannon, retrieved from the wreck. It bears the cognisance of Francis I of France, and what is believed to be the monogram of Benvenuto Cellini. There is nothing impossible about this, for the cannon may have been left behind when Francis I, for whom Cellini worked, was driven out of Tuscany. One theory is that the wreck was a ship contributed to the Armada by the Grand Duke of Tuscany, named the *Florentia*, of 961 tons, commanded by a Spaniard, Periera. The duke discovered that Periera had been taken as a prisoner to Edinburgh, where he settled and where his descendants lived to this day.

In Madrid there was now a British Ambassador, Sir John Balfour, so fluent in their tongue that he astonished the Spaniards by reciting their medieval poetry. After lunching with him I discovered on the top of the grand piano a specially illustrated edition of James Elroy Flecker's *Poems*. I commented on having corresponded with Flecker. He told me that he had known him, and that a highly talented artist who had shared his, Balfour's, imprisonment with him in Germany, had been persuaded to draw the illustrations for the poems he recited to him. So there we were in a Madrid drawing-room talking about Flecker, dead these thirty-five years.

After five days in Madrid we motored on to Salamanca, stopping for lunch at Avila, a walled city crowning a hill. Our host was the lively Marques de Santos Domingo who had a house built into the walls. One could walk along the ramparts for two miles and look down on a house, now a convent, where St. Teresa had lived.

In Salamanca Wellington's former headquarters stood empty, except that a Spanish professor of English at the local university held classes there. We invited him to dinner and then in moonlight walked round the vast arcaded plaza. How the professor, educated at Oxford, enjoyed talking English! He wept when we said goodbye. "What a breath of wonderful English air, señor!" he exclaimed.

It was cold and misty when we arrived high up at Pamplona. On our second morning a *huelga*, a fierce strike, broke out. The Guardia Civil had been called in to suppress it and there was much shooting in the streets. We were locked in our hotel. This for me was intolerable, though well intended. I had come to Pamplona to see the Sarasate Museum on the top floor of the Town Hall. So despite warnings, I slipped out and went towards the arcaded plaza. There was a crack of rifle fire all around. Seeing a bookshop displaying my books in the window, I went in to greet the bookseller, The shop seemed empty. I called out and there arose from behind the counter three scared persons, the bookseller, his wife and daughter. They wanted to drag me down, it was too perilous. Yes, they said, it was terrible, the people were hungry and had struck against the high cost of living. I refused to hide, signed six of my books, and left them wide-eyed at the mad Englishman who went out in the noon-day gunfire.

Realising it was dangerous to walk under the arcades, where I might be accidentally shot, I stepped out into the middle of the Plaza. There could be no doubt I was a mad Englishman. I wore a blue double-breasted overcoat, a black "Lock" hat, carried a Brigg umbrella in one hand, and a red Baedeker Guide in the other, a camera slung on me. The cross-firing stopped at once. When I got into cover at the other end a young officer spoke to me, warning me. What did the señor want? I said I had come to Pamplona to see the Sarasate Museum. He conducted me by side streets until we reached The Town hall. The front was sandbagged, the place under siege. I ignored his protest, stepped across to the entrance, where another astonished officer asked what I wanted. I told him. I was hustled through a guarded door that opened for me. I started up a large four-tiered staircase, and as I mounted there was a reiterated refrain from below. "He wants to see the Sarasate Museum!" Arriving at the top floor, I hammered on the locked door. After some minutes a scared curator peered out. I stepped in. "But señor . . . " he began. I knew quite well the museum was closed, that a revolution was raging, but I had come a long way to see it. He unlocked another door, warning me not to go near a window, and disappeared. I was in the museum. I had it to myself for a whole hour, while rifle-fire sounded below. I examined the manuscripts, the photos, the violins, the walking sticks the sovereigns of Europe had given the great Sarasate. There was an ivory-handled one from Queen Victoria. Then I descended, emerged from the sandbagged portal, and made my way openly across the great Plaza, where again the shooting obligingly stopped. When I arrived home I found the hotel keeper, Mrs. Boehm, and other residents, almost paralysed with fear. They had watched from an upper window my perilous journey. Well, I had seen the Sarasate Museum.

Our car was escorted out to the town's walled gate the next morning. The fighting was still on. I had seen Pamplona, almost at war. And so to San Sebastian, to the calm of the Continental Palace Hotel. At Hendaye I saw my companion off for Florence, visited St. Jean-de-Luz and went on to Paris and London, arriving at Pilgrim Cottage at 11 p.m. on a starry night of mid-May.

III

At the end of June Lady Cecil Bingham gave a lunch at her house in Eaton Square. The twenty-six guests included Helen,

Queen-Mother of Rumania, Field-Marshal Lord Alexander and his wife, the American and Argentine ambassadors and their wives, the Duke of Wellington and Lady Kemsley. At lunch Lord Alexander, who was on leave from his Governor-Generalship of Canada, sat opposite me. He was a man with a great record as a soldier and of exceptional charm. We discussed the Monte Cassino battle as I had recently published my novel *Eight for Eternity* based upon it. He astonished me by saying that the bombing of the abbey, which had been much criticised, was due to an error of translation. A soldier of the American Signal Corps had intercepted a German conversation on the wireless. In the confusion of the meaning of two words "der Abt" with "die Abt" it was assumed that the Germans were in the monastery and using it as an observation post. Therefore its bombing was justified.

I was so utterly astonished by Lord Alexander's statement that when I got home I made a note of his *ipsissima verba* and wrote asking him to confirm the statement. He confirmed it, writing:

> The intercepted German message was "Der Abt ist noch im Kloster." Upon which those who did not know their German well enough, but interpreting Abt" as short for "Abteilung" (in common use in the German army) forgot, or didn't know, that if it was "Abteilung" it would be "die Abt", since "Abteilung" is feminine like all words ending in *ung*. Whereas "Der Abt" means "The Abbot is still in the Cloister", quite harmless and quite another thing under the circumstances.

So the monastery was destroyed owing to a ministerpretation of two German words!

General Mark Clark, whose Fifth Army led the assault on Cassino with General Freyberg's New Zealanders, had just published his memoirs. In them he deplored the bombing of the Abbey. I mentioned this to Lord Alexander, who showed no reluctance in discussing General Clark's strictures. "I accept full responsibliity for the bombing of the Abbey," he said, in reply to my question. "It was an absolute military necessity. As for General Clark's criticisms, we could never get from him a firm opinion about the proposition of the Abbey. He would not say he was in favour of the destruction of the Abbey. He would not say he was not in favour of it. He sat on the fence. I had the opinion of Freyberg and others, and after full consideration of the case I decided that it should be bombed as a military necessity." Although my questions must have struck rather a hostile note, he answered me with the utmost goodwill and frankness.

Ten years after our conversation, Lord Alexander wrote his *Memoirs*. He told the story of the translation error. He seemed to have thought it a small one and called it "a slightly comical incident". Comical incident, involving the destruction of a great historic monastery and many lives? The justification put forth in his book was "It was necessary more for the effect it would have on the morale of the attackers than for purely material reasons". With that argument you could justify the destruction of anything.

There was a different American version of the controversy. General Mark Clark, the American commander, wrote in his book *Calculated Risk*, "Freyberg insisted on the bombing as a military necessity. I was never able to discover on what he based his opinion." He wrote to General Alexander. "If the Germans are not in the monastery they certainly will be in the rubble after the bombing ends. If it were a matter for an American commander I would refuse to give authority but in view of the circumstances I am reluctant to cause an issue."

"General Clark," reported his Chief of Staff, Gruenther, to Lord Alexander, "does not think the building should be bombed. He is still of the opinion that no military necessity exists for the destruction of the monastery. He believes it will endanger the lives of many civilian refugees in the building, and that a bombing will not destroy its value as a fortification for the enemy. In fact, General Clark feels that bombing will probably enhance its value." Three hundred refugees and monks were buried under the ruins, and, as foreseen, the Germans immediately took up positions in the rubble.

The Americans were very critical of this campaign and after their appalling losses there had been a movement in Texas, whose sons had fallen so heavily, for the impeachment in Congress of General Clark, which had been resisted with difficulty. When the Librarian of the destroyed monastery, whom I met, visited the U.S.A. in order to raise funds for rebuilding the Abbey, the American Government repressed his tour, afraid of the bitter controversy that might follow his presentation of the facts.

Churchill wrote in his *History*, "The result was not good. The Germans now had every excuse for making whatever use they could of the rubble of the ruins, and this gave them better opportunities for defence than when the building was intact." The truth is that the Italian campaign was a blunder, even if political expediency made it necessary. In a burst of euphoric rhetoric Churchill had talked about "the soft underbelly of the Axis". In Italy it was an armadillo-spine. Churchill and Alexander should have known that the Abruzzi, and the Apennine mountains and the endless river crossings provided formidable defences. The battle of Monte Cassino was only one link in a chain of faulty strategy; Greece, Crete, etc. Montgomery, arriving at Vasto on the Adriatic, in November, 1943, assured the Eighth Army it would be in Rome, one hundred miles away, by Christmas. It arrived there in June, 1944, and many more months of costly fighting lay before the Allies, inching their way to the north.

In the drawing-room after lunch I asked the Duke of Wellington a question that had been in my mind for two years. When the Duke of Alba showed me pictures salvaged and conveyed from the Liria Palace to his new apartment after the bombing in Madrid, including a head of Pope Innocent X by Velasquez, we discussed the famous Velasquez portrait in the Doria Palace at Rome. "It is very fine," said the duke, "but I have been told it was not painted in the presence of the Pope. The portrait was painted from a head-sketch made direct by Velasquez for which the Pope gave him sittings, a method of work not unusual with portrait painters. I have a Velasquez head, as you see, but the Duke of Wellington possesses the original head-sketch, I think." I now asked the Duke of Wellington if his was the original version. "I'm doubtful. I should like to think it is, but that's not a battle I am prepared to fight!" He told me that it would be on view soon at Apsley House, which he had presented to the Nation.

At the private view for the opening of the house, in July, 1952, which I attended, it happened that the Duke of Wellington and the Duke of Alba were present in the gallery where the Velasquez portrait hung, and I heard them dicuss it. The question of authenticity has now been settled. I received from Mr. Walker, the Director of the Mellon National Gallery at Washington, the assurance that

Velasquez's original sketch was in their gallery! It was once owned by Sir Robert Walpole and then acquired by Catherine the Great. When the Bolsheviks wanted a dollar loan they approached Andrew Mellon, the United States Secretary of the Treasury, knowing he was a wealthy art collector, and offered to sell him works out of the Hermitage Gallery. They did not get their loan, but Mellon privately bought some paintings, including the Velasquez head-sketch, which he gave to the National Gallery at Washington. The Velasquez head owned by the Duke of Wellington is now believed to have been made by the artist for Philip IV. It was in the captured baggage of the fleeing Joseph Bonaparte, who had usurped the Spainsh throne, at the battle of Vittoria. Wellington offered to return it to King Ferdinand VII, who insisted on making him a present of it, with other works.

After lunch at Lady Bingham's, while taking coffee, the Queen-Mother of Rumania, asked "Can you tell me which is Cecil Roberts? I'm told he is here, I like his books so much." "You couldn't be more tactful, ma'am. I'm Cecil Roberts," I replied. I asked a question in turn. My housekeeper Giulietta had once run a teashop in Florence and often spoke warmly of the Queen, a customer. I said she was now with me. "Guilietta! Oh, what a wonderful character! Give her my love. And when you visit Florence come and see me at the Villa Sparta." Thus began a friendship that was to last down the years.

IV

I visited Aubrey Cartwright at Cambridge. He took me to Even-song in King's College Chapel. We sat in the choir stalls, under the high fan vaulting, with Tudor rose and portcullis decorations. During the reading of the lesson my eyes and mind wandered. I looked at the superb sixteenth-century stained glass windows with the arms of Henry VII encircled by the Garter and a thorn bush, recording the finding of Richard III's crown reposing in a thorn bush on fatal Bosworth Field, in 1485. I looked at the organ screen given by Henry VIII, carrying his arms and initials with those of Ann Boleyn, whose head was still on her shoulders while this screen was being carved.

Those pure treble voices of the choristers, ascending, flute-like, lifted my spirit above all mundane cares. I had been depressed by the state of affairs in England. Giulietta complained that the shopkeepers were unobliging, and they refused to deliver. The postal service was curtailed, and lamentable, and the laundry service was now fortnightly. We were still harassed by food rationing. I noticed a long queue outside the Kensington Town Hall. They were house-wives collecting food coupons. One weekend my American friend, Mrs. Boehm, came to Pilgrim Cottage. At Paddington Station she went into a confectioner's shop to buy a box of chocolates. Having selected one, she opened her purse to pay. "Two coupons, please," said the assistant. Astonished, she learned she could not buy chocolates without sweet coupons. She was again surprised when asked, on arrival at my cottage, if she had brought her meat and butter coupons. In Germany, Italy, and France, countries which had lost the war, you could buy all the meat, butter, and chocolate you desired.

Something had gone wrong in this England of ours. I foresaw growing disaster. We were throwing away our hard-won Empire. It had taken the Romans four hundred years to lose theirs, we had lost ours in under fifty, wallowing in a mush of United Nationism, with the Russian menace growing on the horizon, and the lesser nations ganging up on those who had built our civilisation. We comforted ourselves with the myth of the Commonwealth, whose links were rapidly dissolving. One day there would be an economic crisis like a thunderclap.

Travelling abroad so much, I observed all this more acutely on my return each year, with growing despair. I no longer pointed out what I saw. One could not penetrate the general complacency. They were not angry at me when I protested, they smiled as if tolerating an old fogey or an unbalanced alarmist. Did not dividends and bonuses increase, the old age pensions go up, the work hours decrease, the holidays grow? That it was all based on paper, paper, paper, few seemed to notice. Buy today, pay tomorrow. Loan interest went up from three to four to five, to six and seven per cent. One day it would go to ten. You might not own gold, visible only on your wife's fingers and ears. Two generations had never seen gold. Only those curious Swiss hoarded it—they knew that paper could be blown away.

In August I motored to Sutton Cheney, and to Church Langton, in Leicestershire. The latter church held the monument of Sir Richard Roberts who, at seventy-eight, had ridden in 1642 to Nottingham to join King Charles in the raising of the Standard at the beginning of the Civil War. He did not live to know he had backed the wrong horse, for he died two years later. The Cromwellians hacked the feet off the monument his son erected. The tomb was now very dilapidated and I went to talk to the Rector about having it repaired. I lunched with the Hazleriggs at Noseley Hall. Our families had been neighbours for some centuries. Sir Arthur had been an ardent Cromwellian, which must have created bitterness between him and Sir Richard. But he, too, backed the wrong horse for he died in the Tower of London after the Restoration, even though he had refused to sign the King's death-warrant. All this was forgotten, for in 1784 young Charles Roberts, a lieutenant of the 54th Regiment of Foot, on returning from the Siege of Gibraltar married Amabel Hazlerigg. Before lunch Lady Hazlerigg showed me the heir, in his perambulator in a sunny bow window. I breathed a prayer that the boy would not become another offering to Moloch.

The day after my return from this excursion John Betjeman came to lunch, from his home at Wantage. His eyes were shining when he walked in. He told me he had had an encounter with his Muse while motoring over the Chilterns. He had composed a poem! Standing there by the hearth, he recited it. And since one poem deserves another, I wrote one, about his hat which, on leaving, he forgot. I hesitated about posting the hat to him. It was an old brown felt one, shapeless, greasy, with the band missing and two holes in the crown. It seemed hardly worth the postage, but I sent it, knowing one has an affection for old things. My friend Norman Birkett learned my poem, "The Old Brown Hat", by heart and recited it in the Judges' Robing Room at the Law Courts to a fellow Lord of Appeal who liked poetry.

A week later I left for Bad Gastein and Venice. Giulietta was joining her sister, the English mistress at a girls' school in Florence. One September day in Venice I was called to the telephone. It was Giulietta in Alassio, where she was visiting a friend. She had been shown an apartment on the top floor of a palazzo, with a wonderful view. It was to let for five pounds a week, furnished. I told her to take it for six months from the begining of December.

In Venice I attended the première of Stravinsky's opera, *The Rake's Progress*. The Fenice Theatre was packed. People had paid £30 for a stall. Nothing can surpass the beauty of this theatre with its five tiers of gold boxes, its clusters of candelabra, its crimson stalls and painted ceiling. A frame to the beauty of the women's dresses were the eighteenth-century costumes of the flunkeys, and the carabiniers in their uniforms of dark blue with gilt grenades on the tails, red and blue pompons on their Napoleonic cockaded hats, white gloves and shoulder straps. Stravinsky had a great reception when he came in. Pallid, long-nosed, he picked up the baton. At seventy-one years of age this was his first serious, three-act opera. Everyone was determined that it should be a masterpiece.

The libretto was by Auden and Kallman. Tom Rakewell is taken in hand by an evil tutor, Nick Shadow. The action proceeded from a country house to a town house and a brothel. It was sung throughout in English, which was a little hard on the ear. "Your advice is needed in the Kitchen." Elizabeth Schwarzkopf was perfection in a difficult score. The curtain fell to delirious applause. Was it in tribute to the composer and not to the opera, which sagged at times ? It was a great musical event. The libretto was bizarre, the setting conventional, the score was curiously mixed. Opinions were varied and passionate. My friend Armand de La Rochefoucauld asked me what I thought of it. "Mozart and soda-water!" interjected someone. "No, gin and gimmick!" cried another. "No, a masterpiece!" "Favoloso!" "Wunderbar!" "Marvellous old boy, marvellous music, a marvellous night!" Judgement seemed impossible with us all in a state of euphoria. In the foyer and in the street the debate went on "Well, don't forget *Butterfly* was a flop the first night." "Flop! I call this a triumph!" I reserved my opinion. One was too near it on that heady night, and I am no avant-gardist. Three days later we read *The Times*'s balanced account. "It put the clock back to eighteenth-century opera of the Mozartian type, with occasional side glances at Gluck, Handel, Bellini, but the handling of recitative, aria, duet and ensemble were that of a consummate craftsman. Expressionless music used to be Stravinsky's aim. Here there were many passages of a lyrical, dramatic and witty nature."

I went on to Rome that week, staying at the Grand Hotel. Mrs Boehm, my American friend, now lived there, tiny, birdlike, known for her hats, never ill, never out of temper, never late, never tired, a phenomenon of hearing and sight, fluent in five langauges, ever exercising an insatiable curiosity. At the beginning of October, in glorious sunshine, I worked at an open window overlooking the Piazza Esedra with its fountain and the Baths of Diocletian, with the Alban Hills and Frascati on the horizon. When I arrived in Rome, Hodders informed me that *A Terrace In the Sun* had subscribed 30,000 copies, with a reprint of another 20,000 within a month, and that Foyle's Book Club had issued 250,000. But I did not allow myself any elation over this smile of Fortune. I had made a mistake in its title. It was a Nottingham novel, with much autobiography in it. I should have called it *A Nottingham Lad*, as more descriptive. A reviewer started the legend that I was a miner's son, like D. H. Lawrence. All that my novel had in common with his *Sons and Lovers* was the mining locale. My home circle had been one of great affection, whereas his revealed a pathological hatred of his father. And he skimped the Nottingham scene. But we had a deep devotion to our mothers, who witnessed the birth of our first novels, from the same publisher, and we had had the same early struggle.

As before, Sir Victor Mallet, our ambassador, and his wife, were very hospitable at the Villa Wolkonsky, to which the British Embassy had moved after the former one had been blasted by Palestine Jews. That autumn there was a memorable opera in the open Colosseum, under flares and a half-moon, with eight thousand people present. Roman Christians packed the arena, with no fear of lions.

The day before I left Rome I lunched with the Austrian ambassador, Prince Schwarzenberg, of the great Austrian family. The representative of a Socialist government, he called himself Dr. Schwarzenberg. He was very popular, a success he repeated in London when he proceeded there. My table companions included the Marchese Origo and his wife, Iris Origo, whose books delighted everyone. They lived in the famous Villa Medici at Florence. During the war the Germans occupied it. When they retreated the Nazi officers, in sheer spite, fired their revolvers at the ceilings, mirrors and bookshelves. The Marchese showed me a book with a bullet embedded in it.

I left the following evening for London. That morning I had noticed a red spot on my right foot. The irritation was only slight.

During the night in the *wagon-lits* I ran a fever and my foot became terribly swollen, so much so that I had to be carried on board the boat at Calais. Somehow I got to Pilgrim Cottage. After three days my local doctor, alarmed, took me to Reading Hospital to have my foot examined. They said it must be opened at once or I might lose it. I refused, I wanted a second opinion. The next day my Harley Street friend, Dr. Fergusson Hannay, came to see me. "Your wife and I are both novelists. If this foot was your wife's would you have it opened?" I asked. "No," he said, "but you must go into hospital at once." So I found myself in St. Mary's Hospital, Paddington. How very odd! Hannay had just treated Prime Minister Attlee for some foot trouble, and I was occupying the very bed he had vacated.

A tour of South Africa had been arranged by my publisher but this had to be cancelled. I was there a month. I nearly lost my foot. We never discovered what was the infection. In Rome I had walked on the Palatine, among the ruined palaces of the Ceasars. Perhaps I had kicked up the evil dust of Nero or Caligula and been infected. My hospital sojourn ended on a note of comedy. The evening before I left Hannay came to see me and said, very quietly, "I've some news for you. You'll see in the morning papers I've been knighted." A morning paper came, and there he was, Sir James Fergusson Hannay. Two nurses came in, very excited. "Dr. Hannay's been knighted!" they cried. "Yes, I know," I replied, "I always have my doctor knighted on leaving hospital." "Oh, how wonderful!" They left in a flutter. A few minutes later the Head Sister came in. "What a nice thing to have done for Dr. Hannay!" she exclaimed. I informed her it was a joke, I had had nothing to do with it. Doctors to Prime Ministers get rewards other than fees. Churchill's became a peer.

After three weeks I left for Alassio, arriving in the darkness. Giulietta showed me over our new apartment and then ushered me out through a French window on to the terrace. I stood speechless. We looked down on the Piazza garden, with its palms and flower beds, on the amphitheatre of mountains above the town, and on a moon-flecked sea in a crescent bay. "Well!" asked Giulietta, beaming. "What a find!" I replied, overwhelmed by the beauty of it all. We went in to supper.

V

"Breakfast is on the terrace," said Giulietta the next morning. I stepped out from the salon into a blaze of sunshine. An orange awning had been lowered to give shade. My breakfast table sparkled in the light. Something else sparkled. To my left was the sea, azure blue. In front there was the Piazza with a fountain, trees and ornamental gardens. It was like the drop scene in a theatre. It lay between the Corso Dante Alighieri and the Via Aurelia, Italy's ancient road which ran from Ventimiglia, at the western gate of Italy, to Rome, where it ended on a hill overlooking the Eternal City, by the gate of San Pancrazio, named for the fourteen-year old saint who defended the Christians before the Emperor Diocletian, and was executed. In London St. Pancras Church and St. Pancras Station memorialise his name.

I did not sit down at the table for some minutes. I was too excited by this scene before me. In the Piazza were palm, pine, magnolia, laurel, oleander and jacaranda trees. From a terra-cotta bowl on the terrace a rose tree spread its branches over the pergola. The terrace, walled in at each end, had a marble balustrade with four Ionic columns, two in the centre and one at each end, that supported a pergola. It faced south-south-west and was a sun-trap. A hundred feet above the Piazza, we were not overlooked. There was nothing before me but the great blue sky, the amphitheatre of mountains and the little town.

I sat down at last. Giulietta appeared through the french window, bearing the teapot. The whole apartment was very English. It had belonged to a bachelor, a member of the Ionides family, a London-Greek banking family. A row of his Eton prize-books were on a shelf. They had called him "The Emperor" because of the style in which he had lived here, but withal, I learned, he was a very modest and shy man. When he declined an invitation he said that he, unfortunately, would be out of Alassio that day. Being a truthful man he took a bus into San Remo and stayed there the whole day. The apartment had family portraits by G. F. Watts, which I found threatening. The senior Ionides had been a great patron of that Victorian mammoth. The walls also held a series of Burne-Jones engravings of woeful young women, barefooted, trooping up and down staircases, holding lilies. I consigned Watts and Burne-Jones to a cubby hole.

In due time I learned more about "the Emperor". When he died he left the apartment to his brother who lived in a villa in the town. A series of tenants had left the place in a very dilapidated condition. I set about remedying this. Next to using a pen, doing things with my hands has been my delight. So I bought a set of tools, brushes, and paint, and went to work in a cheerful frenzy. There were eleven double windows. It took me three weeks to paint them. The wooden, latticed shutters were a formidable problem. Sun-blistered through a dozen years or more, twenty-two in all and ten feet high, for two months I was busy with a blowlamp and a scraper. All this activity created wonderment. The ironmonger's shop where I appeared every few days was puzzled by the strange things bought by this "signore molto gentile." Finally, one of the partners stopped my housekeeper in the street and asked the real nature of my profession. Could it possibly be true that the signore was a famous English writer? If so, why did he buy chisels, screwdrivers, putty, glass, paints? "He enjoys himself that way," she explained.

I demolished the leaking plant boxes, I made new wooden traverses for the pergola, I cleaned the four Ionic stone columns and repainted the lattice work on each end-wall. I did this half-naked in the hot January sun. Lastly there was the matter of plants. A bougainvillaea and a jasmin were bought for each wall. Both dashed my hopes and became withered sticks. I came near to discarding them after four months and then they had a marvellous resurrection. The jasmin burst into golden flower and the bougainvillaea covered the end-wall with purple glory.

Among the amenities of Alassio I found an excellent English library. It had been founded in the years when a well-to-do English colony of about a thousand had dominated the scene. My old concierge, an ex-Genoese sailor, said sadly, "Ah, signore, you should have seen my English here! When they went out to dine the women were in evening gowns, the men in 'smoking'. You know, good style, good manners!" The community had now shrunk to about eighty. There were no more retired Indian civil servants, ex-Governors, judges, commissioners, an upper-class community, conscious of the prestige of a great Empire and a large navy ruling the seas. They had sung "Rule Britannia" without apology or diffidence. Too mellowed with long prosperity to be arrogant, they stood high in the affection of the local Italians. But they were a dying breed with no recruits, suffering from devaluations, a post-war rise in the prosperity of the Italian nation, and a growing scarcity of servants. The lovely villas had shrunk from two hundred to twenty. Gone were the days when Elgar rented a villa and wrote there his Overture "In the South". The gardeners were cut down from four to three, to two, to one, and then a day-jobber. From long custom the shopkeepers spoke English, experimentally. Over a dressmaker's shop was the sign "Fits upstairs", and, lurid with coloured lights below me, on a corner of the Piazza, was a "Snak Bar". But now there was a change of language. The Germans were sliding down from the Alps in their thousands. Their broiled bodies blotted out the beach. They bought so much gold that four new jewellers' shops opened and did a thriving business. "Wieviel?" and "Guten Tag" and "Dankeschön" were heard in the shops. A change in the class of English tourists puzzled the shopkeepers. The cafés put out signs, "Tea as Mom makes it".

I discovered some personal drawbacks. I found myself in time visiting too many sick beds and attending too many funerals of the the dying colony. I began to wonder who would be left to render me similar service. We were on the eve of the Age of Concrete, the fifteen-storey apartment houses, the crowded car parks, the coaches of "package tours", the collapsed pound that extinguished the reticent English of "private means". The sun was setting on a shrinking Empire.

Outside the British Club, stronghold of "the gentry" and bridge-addicts, soon to vanish, there was a stone lion. At the coronation of Queen Elizabeth in June 1953 I hung a string of red roses round its neck, and put out a Union Jack. We could still demonstrate. After all we British had been paramount here since 1875, when Sir Thomas Hanbury, a wealthy Scot from Dunfermline, had arrived with his wife and bought up villas and land. In her late widowed years Lady Hanbury kept a salon, ruled over the English colony like a queen, and quashed any gossip with a withering: "What you tell me may be true, but we never *say* these things in Alassio." The Hanbury line still persisted and when I arrived a widowed Mrs. Hanbury, very gentle and hospitable, lived at the big villa on the top of the hill. Its door was opened by an ancient butler in tails. We all regarded her as the Lady of the Manor.

The once-prosperous English colony had built a beautiful church. It now had a congregation of about a dozen and was only filled for funerals. It was kept going by "collections" from summer Germans who followed their Lutheran faith in this Anglican church. Our dear old honorary vicar, looking like Mr. Wordsworth, inaudible, was an exquisite water-colour painter. "When I came here thirty years ago I asked my parishioners if they liked sermons. They all cried "No!"—so I never preach any" he told me. The Secretary of the English Tennis Club (a Hanbury bequest), aged eighty, who wore red socks and played a good game, had a wife who was a descendant of Wellington. A very large ancestral nose on a very tiny body gave her much prestige.

The Italians were headed by the gentle, octogenarian Marchese Ferreri. He lived in a large palazzo with a garden bordering the Piazza. When I asked about his family's history he presented me with an enormous book, over six hundred pages, with four-fold genealogical tables. I spent a month digesting this tome, fascinated by a thousand facets of the family's life in Spain, Liguria and Piedmont through six hundred years. His daughter, Donna Anna, said, "My great-great-grandmother was the niece of Alfieri." She took me into the library and showed me the poet's manuscripts, a lock of his reddish hair, and a sword with which he had fought a duel in 1771 in London. He was having an affair with the wife of General Viscount Ligonier. Meeting Alfieri in the Spanish Ambassador's box at the opera, he called him out. They went to the Green Park and fought a duel. Ligonier could have killed the youth, being an experienced swordsman, but he satisfied his honour by pricking the young Italian in the arm. Half-an-hour later Alfieri was back in the Ambassador's box, his arm bound up, apologising for his absence. There was another exhibit in the library. "My great-grandfather went with Napoleon on his campaign in Russia, and lost his leg there. Here's his wooden leg, all that's left of the glory."

There was tall, handsome Count Galleani, English mother, who had founded the local bank. You could hardly exist without the Banca Galleani. It kept your account, cashed your cheques, registered you with the police, let your villa for you, arranged your wedding or funeral, in any Faith, made out your income-tax, arranged transport, sealed the property of the deceased until the English solicitor arrived, sold it or let it, found you a caretaker or a servant, always courteous, always reliable. Three sons would carry on the Galleani dynasty.

VI

In February the almond blossom was out. I worked each morning outdoors. The Piazza below me had become a blaze of colour. I had bought two small cypress trees for my terrace and they speared the azure sky dramatically. The café below set out its bright tables, hopefully.

In a halcyon spring I began to make excursions. I had two literary neighbours. One was Somerset Maugham, who lived at Cap Ferrat, two hours west of me, and the other was Max Beerbohm, who lived at Rapallo, two hours east. I had not seen Beerbohm for many years. In the year 1922, while editing the *Nottingham Journal* and standing for Parliament for East Nottingham, I was plunged suddenly into a by-election. Through overwork I had a breakdown and had to withdraw. In retrospect what seemed a serious check to my career was really beneficial. It seemed likely that I would have been elected. Norman Birkett, to whom I handed over my constituency, became the Member. The current of my life was changed by that breakdown, and instead of politics I devoted myself to authorship. For fifty years I have been a free man, able to live an independent life. In 1922 I had just written my first novel, *Scissors*. It had been accepted for publication by Heinemann Ltd. They were Max Beerbohm's publishers, so when, with a friend, I went to convalesce at Rapallo, I carried a letter of introduction. My friend also had a letter to Gordon Craig, who was Max's neighbour. To our hotel one bright May day came invitations from these two expatriates. My envelope was addressed "All' Illust'mo Cecil Roberts." What did that mean? "That means," said the obliging concierge, "To the Most Illustrious." Like all of Max's missives, it was written finely in pencil, the same kind of pencil-writing to be found in the inscriptions on his caricatures.

The Villino Chiaro where Max lived was on the Provincial Road at the coastal village of Zoagli, two miles out of Rapallo. It was a white, cube-shaped villa of six rooms with a very wide terrace built over the house. He had lived there since 1910. The view from the terrace was stupendous. It commanded the wide crescent bay with the castle-crowned promontory of Portofino on the horizon. On that first visit I was ushered up to the terrace, paved with black and white marble tiles, where Max received me, like an admiral pacing the quarter-deck. He put me at my ease at once. He was dressed in a flawless double-breasted shantung suit, a gardenia in his buttonhole, a straw hat rakishly set on his head. He was an elegant, middle-aged little man, with pink cheeks and round china-blue eyes. He led me into his small study, a room isolated on the terrace. It seemed like the charthouse of a ship sailing the Mediterranean. The walls of this retreat, painted blue, had a single shelf of books running round it. Presently Mrs. Beerbohm appeared and we went down to lunch, which was hilarious. He played skittles with a number of his contemporaries, and was reproved from time to time by his wife, quiet, reserved, who would say "Now, Max, dear, you are scandalous!" But he went merrily on.

Now, thirty years later, finding myself almost his neighbour at Alassio, I wrote asking if I might call, if he remembered me. The reply was immediate. "I remember so very well your visit to Rapallo. My dear wife and I took great delight in your company and in the brilliance of your talk. How very glad I would be to see you if you could come here and have lunch some day." So I went to the Villino for lunch. His wife had died and he was cared for by grey-haired Miss Elizabeth Jungmann. "Look after Max," his dying wife had said to her Viennese friend. She looked after him, affectionately, tenderly.

I found Max still debonair, beautifully dressed but slower, rounder, white-haired. "I remember what you told me when you were here thirty years ago, you looked out over the Mediterranean and you startled me by saying 'Exactly one hundred years ago on this very day in July, 1822, Shelley was drowned in that sea!' Dear me, ever since I've been expecting Shelley's body to be washed up on my doorstep!" "That couldn't happen. Shelley was cremated," I observed. "Yes, but you can't cremate a ghost," he replied. "It was his ghost you left here that day." He gave an endearing chuckle.

Living so near I became a frequent guest at the Villino Chiaro. The formula became that I would arrive soon after twelve. We would talk for an hour before lunch. Afterwards we retired for a siesta, he to his bedroom, I to a couch in the little salon-library. At four o'clock we met for tea. Before dinner I departed, having taken some colour slides of the villa, of the terrace, of his study. I was careful not to take him. He was plagued by visitors arriving with cameras. Miss Jungmann battled with them. The transatlantic celebrity-hunters were so persistent that the gate below had to be kept locked. You were given a code signal for the bell.

There were odd streaks in Max's character. For some reason he hated Kipling. His line was malicious whenever he drew him. He had an almost pathological dislike of King Edward VII. Once, when having a siesta in his study, I took down some books from the shelf and was startled to find he had been busy on the illustrations. The faces were maliciously perverted. I shuddered to think what Messrs. Freud and Jung would have deduced from them. All this seemed contradictory to the character of one so agreeable and polite.

Urbane and eclectic, some of the most enjoyable hours of my life were spent talking with him on that balustraded terrace. I discovered several astonishing things in those long talks as the afternoon wore on. I mentioned my repeated tours of the U.S.A. "I went there once, with my brother, on a theatrical tour. Once was enough! I have no desire to see it again," he said. He had never accompanied his American wife, the ex-actress Florence Kahn, on her visits to the homeland. He was not enthusiastic about the British colonies. "The only feeling they inspire in me is a desire not to visit them, nice people though they may be." He thought travel was a waste of time. I became aware that he lived in an ivory tower filled with Italian sunshine. He thought our civilisation had passed its peak. In London he had been dismayed by a "rabble of all shades." Even so, he looked on humanity with an amiable eye. But his disgust with the exploitation of sex came out in his *Getting Married*, and in *Misalliance*. His own adventures had been very mild and cautious. There had been a long indefinite courtship with an actress in his brother's company, which fizzled out. His engagement to Constance Collier, the actress, a strong character, came to a sudden end. She could not see enough vitality in a marriage with him. There came the tranquil years with his wife Florence, and now, after her death, Elizabeth Jungmann had come to housekeep for him. It was singular that he had married a Jewess, and now he was being cared for by a Jewess, but he was not a Jew. He was born in London. His father, of German Baltic origin, had been a successful business man there. His sister became an Anglican nun. He had no anti-semitic feelings, indeed he was on friendly terms with those he called his "cosmopolosemitics".

In appearance and manner Max was an English gentleman of the old school. He was a delightful conversationalist, with a spice of puckishness that made him endearing. But he had firm likes and dislikes. He had been sent a copy of T. S. Eliot's *Poems*. He picked up the book from the table. "What do you make of them?" he asked. I felt somewhat inhibited by their enormous réclame, but I risked being frank, "Probably I'm wrong, but I find little that I would call poetry," I said. "Some of the lines seem to me to be ludicrous. 'I shall wear the bottoms of my trousers rolled.' 'The yellow fog that rubs its back upon the window-panes.'" Max raised his hands. "Then I am not slipping!" he cried. "I find it rather forced. 'April is the cruellest month.' Why? Browning didn't think so! What is all the hullabaloo about? But we shall be consigned to outer darkness. We'll have our heads decapitated and carried on stakes by the *cognoscenti*."

Ezra Pound came into our talk. He had once been Max's neighbour in Rapallo, and mine in Venice. Again we agreed. "The good fellow's very puzzling to me," said Max. "I'm not alluding to him personally, though he's bizarre enough, a very original creature—but his verses, those *Pisan Cantos*—are quite incomprehensible to my poor wits." He thought D. H. Lawrence was too obsessed with sex. "Rather the ardour of the impotent, eh? The blood always at boiling point, and nothing boiled. Poor fellow!" He admired Henry James and envied me my friendship with Joseph Conrad, whom he had admiringly parodied in *A Christmas Garland*. We both knew and liked Arnold Bennett. We did not always agree. I could not share his enthusiasm for Lytton Strachey, who had visited him. Enjoyable, scholarly, yes, but I had reservations about his debunking of historical characters. Sometimes, it seemed to me, he had the zest of a gamin throwing a brick through a stained-glass window. And so we talked, until the sun began to sink and a cool wind came in from the sea.

In these latter years the Recluse of Rapallo had become a cult figure. His caricatures had made him an indispensable footnote to the Victorian and Edwardian scene. Indolent by nature, Max had done almost nothing for half of his life. He had just idled in Rapallo, with one interruption during the Second War, enjoying his premature immortality. There was never a lull in the disciples ringing his gate bell, bearing incense. His taste was fastidious. He had an eye for the absurdities of his fellow men, though he was full of contradictions himself. "The Establishment" had forgiven, or forgotten his vitriolic assault on King Edward, and the fun he had aways poked at Queen Victoria, to whom he gave a big belly, pudgy hands and puffy eyes.

I wondered who had pulled the strings for Max's knighthood. He had written a scathing essay about it. "In the future knighthood may be one of the lighter punishments of the law, 'Forty shillings or a knighthood,' sounds quite possible." He had made fun of his brother's knighthood in 1909. "Now the dear fellow's lost all hope of being taken seriously." There was a loud outcry when Max exhibited his caricatures of the Royal Family in 1923. Some of them had to be withdrawn. One caricature he had wisely withheld, a skit on the well-known engraving of the young Queen Victoria, awakened to receive from the Lord Chamberlain and the Archbishop of Canterbury the news of her accession. She gave them audience clad in her dressing-gown. Max's cartoon showed Edward VII in striped pyjamas coming downstairs to be greeted by Lord Salisbury and Archbishop Temple. The sting lay in the glimpse of the hem of a lady's nightgown vanishing from the landing above. Someone in the Royal entourage bought up the offending cartoons—possibly the Royal Family privately enjoyed them? Despite all this, in 1939 Max was offered and accepted a knighthood. One day I had the temerity to ask him about this inconsistency. He was in no way perturbed by my question. "My dear fellow, I had two good reasons, one false and one real. I felt I might contribute some respectability to it, and, as a discreet snob, give and derive pleasure."

We discussed racial prejudice. A Negro had been knighted. "I have often been quite lucky," he observed. "I was lucky to escape from Rapallo in 1939 or I would have been interned. With my name Beerbohm and my wife's Kahn, a Jewess, we would have gone to a concentration camp. I fear the fact that Beerbohms had married Prussian generals in the nineteenth-century would not have saved us. I am not at all anti-Semite, indeed I should be pleased to know that we Beerbohms have that very admirable and engaging blend."

One May morning I was called up from the Villino Chiaro. It was Elizabeth Jungmann. Next week, on my birthday, Max wanted me to come for lunch, to celebrate. "How do you know it's my birthday?" I asked. "Max found it in *Who's Who*, and he wants a copy of your *Pilgrim Cottage*." I had been very diffident about giving so exacting an artist any book of mine. I was leaving for Florence. This was almost a royal command. So I promised to be at the Villino on the 18th, on my way home.

In Florence I joined my friends Everard and Stella Gates. Two events stand out in my memory. In the Teatro Communale we heard Benedetto Michelangeli play Ravel and Liszt. He was said to be temperamental and sometimes did not turn up. On this afternoon he was in magnificent form, and drew seven encores, which did not produce a single smile on his pale, aesthetic face. I went to piano recitals with all the excitement with which some people go to race meetings. Here was another great artist, to be bracketed with Cortot, Arrau, Rubinstein and Rachmaninoff.

At the Grand Hotel in Florence I found my incredible friend, Darius Talyarkhan, who travelled with an electric vegetable-mincing machine and a vicuna bedspread. I always felt he was a reincarnation of Darius the Persian and not a Bombay Parsee. He took me to call on the old Countess Edith Rucellai, who was eighty-six. It became an event when I discovered that she was the daughter of Mrs. Bronson who owned "La Mura" at Asolo, where Browning had so often been her guest. The Countess had many mementoes of the poet. My hand trembled when I read a letter written to her mother from Venice by Browning's son, in 1889.

Palazzo Rezzonico. Dec. 12th 10.30 p.m.

Dearest Friend,

Our Beloved breathed his last as St. Mark's struck ten, without pain, unconsciously. I was able to make him happy a little before he became unconscious by a telegram from Smith Elder saying "Reviews in all the papers most favourable. Edition nearly exhausted." He just murmured "How gratifying!" Those were the last intelligible words.

Browning's last book was called *Asolando*, many of its poems having been written while staying with Mrs. Bronson at Asolo. It

Norman Birkett and the author

The British Ambassador, Sir Ashley Clarke, unveils the Max
Beerbohm memorial plaque

included the apposite *Epilogue*—"At midnight, in the silence of the sleep-time".

In the lounge of the Grand Hotel at Florence there was a comedy. Somerset Maugham was there, with Frederick Prokosch, the novelist, who had his cat in a basket, with which he travelled. Maugham, turned to me and said—"Freddie travels with his cat, Darius with his mincing machine, what do you travel with?" "A duck," I responded. "A duck!" he exclaimed, "Where is it?" At that moment my housekeeper, who had been visiting her sister, came in at the door. "There, just coming in," I replied, "That's my housekeeper. Her name 'Anatrella' means 'a little duck'." Behind her came Alan Searle, Maugham's assiduous young secretary-companion. "And you travel with your watch-dog," I added.

VII

On May 18th, 1952, I duly arrived at the Villino. That day I was sixty. In August Max would be eighty. He was in festive mood, in a white drill suit, very smart as always. It happened that my publisher had just issued a new edition of *Pilgrim Cottage*. It was specially printed, designed to be the first volume of a Henley Collected Edition. I gave him a copy. From him I received a small pocket edition of *Once More*, a collection of his delicate little essays. I mentioned that Maugham had given me a magazine in which he had written about Augustus Hare who, in the Eighties, had published his phenomenally successful *Walks in Rome*, a guide book that still led the field. Hare had had a great success visiting aristocratic houses where he was famed as a teller of ghost and mystery stories. Maugham had stayed with Hare when he was an elderly bachelor. He was surprised to find, in the family Bible from which Hare read each morning to guests and assembled staff, that parts of it had been heavily ruled out. On asking Hare the reason for this he had replied, "God is a gentleman, and being a gentleman he would have thought the fulsome praise of Him in very bad taste." When I mentioned Hare, Max darted off into the little study on the terrace and came out with a large photograph album dated 1865. "Here's treasure! It's Augustus Hare's photo album. I found it in a second-hand book shop in the Charing Cross Road. It has over a hundred photographs he took. He can never have met any Commoners. Princess, Peers, Dukes, Dowager Duchesses, everyone in his collection has a title." We went through it, giggling, until Elizabeth Jungmann called us in to lunch.

A few days after my return home there was a letter from him which set my mind at rest and gave me much pleasure. His fine pencilled letter ran—"I enormously enjoyed *Pilgrim Cottage*. How immensely alive from start to finish! What fun to be you!"

VIII

Very different was my other neighbour, Somerset Maugham, located at the western extremity, on the Cap Ferrat peninsula overlooking Villefranche harbour. Max, rubicund and suave, seemed to exude the milk of human kindness, though the claws were there. Willie, as we called Maugham, had acid in his blood. His face was grey and saturnine. He had a world-wide reputation for being cynical and somewhat treacherous in the manner in which he used, for fictional purposes, the people who had entertained him. I think this reputation was blown up by two things, envy of his success and his own sly pleasure in the bogy-man he had created. The legal down-turn of his mouth and the cool saurian eyes fitted the rôle. For myself, looking back on a friendship of nearly forty years, I never recall an unpleasant moment in his presence. I found him always agreeable and hospitable, nor can I, nor would I, record any stories of a lurid sex life.

He lived in his beautiful Villa like a grand seigneur. He cultivated a myth that he had been poor and known struggle. That boyhood in his uncle's Whitstable vicarage was given a twist, I believe, to make it in tune with the theme of human bondage that he turned to such profit in his work. His happiness lay in his determination not to be happy, to regard the human race as a mistake and to behave like a mischievous boy let loose in a plaster museum. He had to knock off the nose of his Venus and castrate his Apollo. It was a strange contrasting experience to visit Willie and then to visit Max; the former grim, highly industrious and prosperous, the latter urbane, idle, cheerful, and not at all prosperous but content with his humbler nest. Willie had an idea that Max was lucky and had "pulled it off" with a minimum of effort. As Malcolm Muggeridge put it: "He sometimes let fall a sigh in the direction of Rapallo along the coast where Max Beerbohm was growing ever more famous in literary and intellectual circles with every book he did not write."

Such were my two neighbours, both famous, one urbane, one grim, one in a splendid villa with a butler, six servants and four gardeners, still highly productive, world famous; and the other, with an eclectic fame, of modest means, living in a small one-servant villa. Both were verging on eighty. Max had been knighted. Willie had had no official recognition, but later would be made a Companion of Honour. No one acclaimed him as a genius, whereas there was Max, poor, unproductive for thirty years, with a constant stream of influential connoisseurs bearing incense; flourishing, as it were, on unearned increment.

My position as the friend of both was difficult. I liked them, admired them and had known both for many years, but since one never mentioned the other, I, too, never mentioned either to either. I never purveyed news between the Villa Mauresque and the Villino Chiaro. I considered myself fortunate to be on friendly terms with two such distinguished and hospitable neighbours.

IX

That summer, *in loco parentis*, almost, to young Aubrey Cartwright, we made a sort of Grand Tour to Florence, Rome and Naples. My twenty-two-year-old protégé was like a young thrush, he gobbled everything I fed him. On leaving Rome he gave me a book inscribed "To a generous and wonderful paedagogus from an ever-grateful pupil."

My coaching bore fruit later. In 1958 he published a *Guide to the Art Museums in the United States*, a first volume covering the East coast from Washington to Miami, illustrated. With his copy came a letter—"I have taken three years to do it and have had a unique and enjoyable experience. I shall never forget my debt to you for awakening my early love of painting, and encouraging me on our visit to Florence and Rome where you were the most perfect tutor any sensitive soul could have wished." So I had not wasted my time. I read his book with pleasure and pride.

CHAPTER SEVEN

The Fight for Freedom

I

The Palazzo Vairo was well planned, with two lifts, two marble staircases serving twenty apartments. Each apartment was reached by a small bridge from the lift. These bridges were gay with pots of geraniums, azaleas, cinerarias, lobelias, marguerites and cyclamen. I was amused by the names on my neighbours' doors. An English doctor lived on the first floor. His name was Cane, which is "dog" in Italian. On the second floor was Signor Topo (Mouse), on the third Signors Quadri (Pictures), and Lupi (Wolves). On the fourth dwelt Signor Vacca (Cow), and opposite me, was Signor Calandri (Meadowlarks). I called the café on the corner, below me, the Café Bohème. I liked to think that Mimi and Rodolfo went there as well as Maria and Mario. Sometimes from it arose a lilt of guitars, happily faint and romantic, so I was not disturbed. One sight delighted me. When all the beach-umbrellas, diversely coloured, opened up, it looked from above as if we had been invaded by a fairy Parachute Division. When they folded up at dusk they looked like sleeping tulips.

At the end of June I left for England, stopping over at Mrs. Cartwright's Casa Estella. So I went from one bright terrace to another, fronting the Mediterranean. One afternoon we went to cocktails at a neighbour's house. Among the guests was Greta Garbo, with her dark little man of affairs. Her eyes were hidden behind large blue glasses and I did not like her loose black stockings. She looked a little blowsy, with untidy hair. The company was so awed by her presence that conversation froze. My hostess began to be anxious, so I stepped in to break the ice. "Miss Garbo, is it fair for you to hide from us one of the most beautiful faces in the world?" I asked. She laughed, took off her glasses and said "Now, you see how you've exaggerated!" But no thaw set in. We all stood and looked at each other. Presently my hostess came to me. "Mr. Roberts, do tell Miss Garbo your story of Lady Mendl's gold unicorn." I demurred. "Phat eez a oonicorn?" asked Miss Garbo. I answered, "It is a fabulous animal of the Middle Ages, immortal, with a horse's body and a single long straight horn sticking out of its forehead." "You aaff seen one?" "No, Miss Garbo. It is an heraldic beast. But I saw a gold one that Lady Mendl owned." "I knew Lady Mendl, in Hollywood," said Miss Garbo, "She was remarkable woman who stand on her head. I want hear what she do with a oonicorn, tell me." So I began my story. In the silence I had the floor to myself and tried not to be self-conscious with her beautiful cool eyes on me.

"Lady Mendl, when living in Paris before the war, owned a golden unicorn. It was an exquisite work of art, about ten inches high, in solid gold. It was said to be the work of Benvenuto Cellini. At dinner parties she sometimes had it as a table centre-piece. A French poet burst into tears when he saw it. He said it was too beautiful to live with and no one should eat in its presence. When the war came Lady Mendl fled to America, leaving her enchanting Paris house in charge of a faithful old couple, Jean and Marie. For four years she heard nothing. When the war ended she returned to Paris. A bomb had damaged her house. After many enquiries she found her maid, now a widow. Jean had died. Marie had lived through the war in one little room, hungry and cold. Lady Mendl took her back to her hotel. After a while she began to enquire about her house and lost possessions. Marie told her that before it was bombed a German general had lived in it, and some soldiers. 'They stole everything, Madame.' 'Who got my gold unicorn?' asked Lady Mendl. 'Nobody, Madame. The day before the Germans arrived Jean buried it under the tree at the bottom of the garden. It is there.' The next day they went there, with a man and a spade. Marie told him where to dig. The unicorn was uncovered, unharmed, wrapped in a waterproof cloth. 'But Marie, you should have sold it, and have lived comfortably!' 'Oh, no, Madame. Jean said it is a sacred animal. It preserved your life.' Lady Mendl told me this story one day when

I went to see her at the St. Regis Hotel in New York. She opened a velvet-lined box. And there it was, a marvel of shining gold," I said, concluding.

"That is a most beautiful story. I tank you," said Greta Garbo, smiling. And then everybody began to talk, about Lady Mendl, the golden unicorn, the faithful Marie. And Garbo smiled, and talked and did not put on her glasses until her funny little companion took her away.

The owner of the Golden Unicorn had died in Versailles. She had made a fortune as an interior decorator and had amazed everyone by marrying, long after middle-age, Sir Charles Mendl of the British Embassy in Paris. When I saw her at the St. Regis in 1946, just back from Paris with the unicorn, she was over eighty. She was energetic, elegant, with a rasping voice, and a tense, parchment face. Every morning she practised Yoga exercises. A friend told me that at her seventieth birthday party, challenged, she stood on her head. She rose at six, did her exercises, and then went back to bed until noon, dictating to her secretary-companion.

II

It was exciting to be back in London, which I have always regarded as the most civilized of cities. It had not yet been degraded to a zoo with tourists thronging every nook and corner. In whatever other great city of the world could one take a three-mile walk on grass, amid trees, all the way from Trafalgar Square to Queen's Gate, where I had my London lodging? I have never been derisive about the Albert Memorial, classed with landladies, mothers-in-law and fish-and-chips as a standard music-hall joke; and I have an affection for that terracotta pork-pie, the Albert Hall. Take the roof off it and knock a few holes in it and you have a Colosseum, built for music instead of massacre. Hyde Park had not in 1952, been desecrated with an atrocious cavalry barracks nor with skyscraper hotels that mar the wide horizon. The Ecclesiastical Commissioners, worshipping Mammon, had not yet in their venality permitted a building to cut away from view half of the noble façade of St Paul's, at the top of Ludgate Hill. The headquarters of the Royal College of Art, a frightful towering bulk, had not yet settled next to the Albert Hall.

The irony of the name! A glass and black concrete monster—more suitable to house an elephant than art students.

But not all shocks were without diversion. I found in the Tate Gallery a clever portrait by Graham Sutherland of W. Somerset Maugham who, with Churchill, was another victim of that merciless artist. There was "Willie," commanding attention, perched on a stool, jaundiced, haggard, a sort of bamboo effigy, loosely draped. Then in a basement room my attention was arrested by a conventional painting of a dapper young man in grey top hat and morning coat poised against a screen in an elaborate Edwardian drawing-room. It was a fine period piece entitled. "The Jester". But surely that sleek young man was an early edition of Willie? The painting was by Sir Gerald Kelly, P.R.A. I wrote to him. Was I right in thinking that "The Jester" was a portrait of Somerset Maugham? If so, I felt it should be upstairs and the Graham Sutherland one downstairs. Sir Gerald replied:

> Yes. The picture that I painted of Willie in a grey hat was almost a quip; it was done just casually. He had just made a great success as a dramatist and had started to dress himself in a very dapper way and came in delightedly to show me his grey hat. It amused me to paint the Burmese cabinet and the Coromandel screen and Willie was introduced as a diversion in the foreground. It is so perfunctory in characterisation as to be quite valueless; it is just a gay little picture, whereas Mr. Graham Sutherland is, they tell me, a very important artist and his remarkable study of Willie is certainly revealing. To think that I have known Willie since 1902 and have only just recognized that, disguised as an old Chinese Madame, he kept a Brothel in Shanghai!

Pilgrim Cottage was lovelier than ever this summer and Henley Regatta had perfect weather. I was the Headmaster's guest at the Bradfield College Greek play. This year the boys performed *Antigone*, with their usual verve, in the sylvan setting of the Greek theatre. I had two American guests. One of them lost her heart to a small Christ's Hospital schoolboy, in his long, blue-belted gown and yellow stockings, who sat beside her. His manners were as beautiful as his face. "Oh, if only I could buy one!" she exclaimed.

Soon after that I went to Nottingham, with a triple bill; to visit my invalid brother, happy among his roses. All our lives, with over ten years between us, we had been strangers to each other, with nothing whatever in common, but this did not lessen the ties that bound us. I stayed with the Vice-Chancellor of Nottingham University, Bertrand Hallward. I remembered when the site of its buildings was daisied fields above the River Trent. That titan, Jesse Boot, founder of the great Boots the Chemists empire, paralysed after fifty, an open-handed Maecenas, had given the site, and money to build the university. I had been present at the laying of the foundation stone. The university had grown and grown, with a fine boulevard and boating lake below its long façade. I had ideas about a Greek theatre on the sloping hill, with a view towards the Trent and the Charnwood Forest. The Vice-Chancellor and I found a site. It has not been built, but I hope some day it will be.

My third chore during my visit was to go to Thrumpton Hall, on a bank of the Trent, to open a garden bazaar. I had been there in former days, when the local vicar was the Rev. Lord Byron, a kinsman of the poet. The brick mansion had an Italian loggia and a Grinling Gibbons staircase. I remembered the gentle old clergyman and his wife. He had peacocks walking on the lawn and he was the only man I ever knew who could call them to him and stroke their heads, inducing the spreading of their fantails. Usually they are strident and untouchable.

On my way back to Pilgrim Cottage I found myself in Banbury and near to Aynho Park, the ancient home of Richard Cartwright, a kinsman of young Aubrey. It happened to be Visitors' Day, so I called. In a wing of the house there was a museum with a fine display of Chinese and Persian ceramics. A youngish man was conducting visitors round. I asked him if Mr. Richard Cartwright was in. "I am Richard Cartwright," he said. When I mentioned my name his face lit up. "Of course I know you! You must meet my wife. We are closing soon, do stay and have tea with us."

When I was writing *And so to Rome* I discovered quite a lot about a Mr. W. C. Cartwright of Aynho, a Northamptonshire squire who stayed much in Rome. He had been a friend of Robert Browning and Lord Leighton when they sojourned there. One day, in 1850, Mr. Cartwright was walking across the Piazza di Spagna, just below the house where Keats had died, with John Gibson, the sculptor who worked in Canova's old studio. Gibson stopped in his walk and told Cartwright how, one morning on a balcony opposite, at No. 66 in the Piazza, he had seen Lord Byron, who had a lodging there. This Mr. Cartwright was the grandfather of my host. I found another tie. The lady he presented me to, his wife, was the daughter of Viscount Weir. In the First World War Lord Weir had been Secretary of State for Air, one of the creators of the Royal Air Force. He commissioned me to visit the new arm of the Forces and write articles for the Press on its various activities. I was then a young man of twenty-six. He expressed himself as very pleased with what I had written. I collected these articles and John Murray published them in a small book called *Training Our Airmen*. To this, Lord Weir had contributed a preface.

Before tea I was taken on a tour of this most beautiful house. It was full of treasures. There was an illuminated *Book of Hours* given by Charles 1st to a Cartwright bride before the Civil War brought unhappy divisions in the family. William Cartwright defended Aynho against the Cromwellians though his wife Ursula was the daughter of the great Parliamentary general, Lord Fairfax. There were fine Sir Peter Lely portraits of William Cartwright and his wife. Hogarth painted the grandmother of another squire, W. R. Cartwright. The beautiful curving white staircase was hung with other family portraits. From the central hall there opened a series of magnificent communicating rooms so perfectly designed that through one keyhole you could look through six in line. There was a French drawing-room, a Soane drawing-room, a library, a vestibule and dining-room, an orangery and a long terrace commanding the landscape. There was a superb miniature by Nicholas Hilliard of a Cartwright, and a fine Murillo Virgin. Rubens, Romney, Gainsborough and Lawrence were represented. There was eighteenth century French furniture, and, in a large leather box with the imperial 'N' a Meissen china service, a present from the Austrian Emperor to Napoleon. He abandoned it on the field of Waterloo and it was picked up by a General Cartwright. Treasure after treasure was in these rooms apart from the museum of ceramics Richard Cartwright had collected. It was a mansion that had passed from generation to generation through four hundred years. What an afternoon to remember, presided over by the handsome young squire and his gracious wife. Here was England at its best.

III

One July day I went to Knole for lunch and was surprised to find that the Sackvilles had three guests, so there were six of us lunching in the Poets' Parlour. Last year Anne had written: "I am defeated. With not one servant in a house of 365 rooms and 52 staircases, etcetera, and no chance to buy any decent food, life here is really a nightmare."

But now there was a butler, and a footman, waiting at table and, I assumed, a cook in the kitchen. I congratulated Anne on having solved the servant problem. "Dear Cecil, it's not what you think!" she said. "The butler is an old pensioner, having a summer holiday here, and he's brought his family with him. His wife cooks, their married son and daughter are footman and parlourmaid, so for two weeks we can have friends to lunch." It was Sutton Place all over again. But at Yattendon Court, when I went to lunch with the Iliffes, the faithful Hungarian butler was still in command of the staff there. Elsewhere there was grief. My friends Everard and Stella Gates had boldly bought a vast house at Ewhurst in Surrey, built like a Spanish castle by a man who wanted his Spanish mistress to feel at home. The last time I had spent the week-end there the house was staffed with a butler, a cook and two parlourmaids. Something about them puzzled me. They looked foreign but they were not Dutch, Swiss, Swedish, Norwegian or Danish importations, as so often, and they spoke English. "We are in clover!" said Stella. "They are wonderful! There's no trouble with them. They have British passports." "But they look foreign?" I said. "Yes, and no. They're British, they come from St. Helena! We've quite a colony of them here in the neighbour-hood, so they're quite happy, and not feeling lonely." Shades of Napoleon!

But this year when I arrived there was no agile butler, only a very feeble old man. I insisted on carrying my bag upstairs. And then I heard a lamentable but too common history. Paradise had suddenly dissolved. The St. Helena colony had departed after "an upset". "Ah, they were Saki servants," I observed to my hostess. "Saki servants?" she queried. "Yes, Saki, the essayist, wrote about them. He said of his cook: 'She was a good cook as cooks go, but as cooks go—she went.'" Alas, the beautiful Spanish castle, with its spacious gardens, proved unworkable. Young Christopher, the son of the house, newly married, baulked at inheriting it, so it was sold.

Arriving home, Giulietta had sad news. "Mrs. Barefield says she can't come in any more!" Mrs. Barefield lived up the lane. She had been a "faithful" for fifteen years. Honest, efficient, cheerful, I suspected she and Giulietta did not "get on". We had guests that week-end. It was the same story all around. The Birketts at Challens Green had two Swiss girls, but only for three months, who had come to learn the language. No wonder silver was disappearing from tables—too much cleaning. Visiting my old war-correspondent colleague, Sir Philip Gibbs, at Shamley Green, I made my own bed, and helped to wash up in the kitchen. All my life I had cleaned my own boots, sternly taught by my father, so that was no difficult task. Despite Philip's protest I cleaned his. "They've never been so bright," he observed, gratefully. I went over to Wantage to lunch with John Betjeman. There, too, a "help" came in. A friend there had inherited Lord Berners' house in Rome. He wished to sell it. Later, when in Rome, I went to look at it. The position was excellent, on the edge of the Roman Forum, in a quiet street. There was a growing desire in my mind to have a pied-à-terre in Rome. This was a slice of a house, four storeys, attractive, but there was one grave drawback, very steep stairs. The Mrs. Barefields of Rome would object.

I had had an experience of formidable Roman stairs. I had gone one day with Mrs. Cartwright to call on the Duchess of Sermoneta. She lived in a palazzo constructed on the ruins of the Theatre of Marcellus. This noble building, whose outer walls are one of the sights of Rome, had been built by Julius Caesar. Completed by Augustus, it was dedicated in 13 B.C.. to the memory of his young nephew, Marcellus, whom he had intended to be his successor, a youth cut off by early death, celebrated in Vergil's Aenead *Egregium forma juvenum et fulgentibus armis*. The Theatre had held 15,000 spectators and had three arcaded tiers. Fire partly destroyed it in the fourth century. Fallen masonry from the upper part had created a vast mound in the arena, which now formed a courtyard for the apartments built in the upper tiers. On the top floor the Duchess of Sermoneta lived in a palazzo with salons, library and private chapel, etc. There was a long gallery with an arched, painted ceiling, and windows that opened on to an enclosed garden with seven fountains, tangerine trees, and a pattern of box-edged flower beds. There was a view of the River Tiber below.

The duchess was a beautiful, energetic woman, with a passion for England derived from her English grandmother, Lady Burghesh. Lady Randolph Churchill was a close friend and often stayed in this palazzo. The duchess wrote a number of books and memoirs. She was a fascinating woman, very hospitable. To reach her palazzo there was a steep staircase of seventy-two steps. Princes, cardinals and ambassadors had mounted them through the centuries. Mrs. Cartwright, handicapped by a stroke, blanched on seeing the stairs but her visit had been arranged for. Two young footmen appeared with a portable chair and in this she was carried to the top of the flight. There would have been no room for two footmen with a chair to ascend the stairs in the Berners house.

IV

When in Seville I had met a very eager youth, Pardo de Santayana, who surprised me by his knowledge of our English literature. He had now been appointed the London correspondent of the Madrid *Pueblo* and he often became my guest at Pilgrim Cottage. One day I had given him a proof copy of *A Terrace in the Sun*. When he had read it he said, "You know, your Spanish publisher will not be able to issue the book as it stands. You open with a suicide in Monte Carlo. Editors in Spain are prohibited from publishing any story with a suicide in it—the hand of the Church is still strong." I replied that he must be wrong. In *Victoria Four-Thirty*, which had had a great success in Spain, there was the story of a German youth, Emil Gerhardt, a film star, persecuted by the Nazis, who had been driven to take his life. Santayana was quite positive the suicide story could not have been in the book. I showed him a tenth edition of the novel in its Spanish translation. He examined it and then astonished me by pointing out that two chapters telling the story of Gerhardt were missing in the Spanish version, a thing I had never noticed. I took the matter up with my Spanish publisher. I had a clause in my agreement that no alteration in the text should be made without my consent. He informed me that he had not deleted the chapters, he had never been aware of them! His wife had heard a Zurich German broadcast of my novel and recommended him to acquire the rights. The Spanish translation had been made from a Swiss-German edition from which the Swiss, nervous of their Nazi neighbours in 1938, had deleted the two chapters.

In that same year a Dutch translation was published. The publisher asked for permission to delete the Gerhardt chapters as Holland at the time was nervous of giving offence to their German neighbour. I gave permission. In 1951 there was another Dutch translation, made for an edition issued by the Dutch Book of the Month Club. I found that nothing had been cut out from my version.

V

In these last days at Pilgrim Cottage I had to make a serious decision. After the outbreak of the war I had sold my American investments and surrendered to the British Treasury $80,000 in accordance with its new regulations. I had also made it a free loan of £9,000 for the duration of the war. To continue in the U.S.A. at the request of the Government, as an honorary worker in the propaganda field, I had to have means to live. Throughout five years the Treasury refused me any of my own money. I borrowed from an American friend. In view of what happened I should have gone home and attended to my own affairs.

At the close of the war the Treasury refused me the dollars to pay off my debt, despite the endorsement of the Ministry of Information, for whom I had worked to their high satisfaction. Moreover, under the new currency regulations, I was not allowed to use abroad any of the money I now earned abroad. Everything from every source had to be remitted to the Bank of England, where it was blocked—and subsequently thrice devalued.

I saw no prospect of this economic tyranny ceasing. I decided, therefore, that I must emigrate, as had so many of my fellow authors. It was a decision long delayed, which caused me much sorrow for it entailed parting with my cottage, since I might not retain a residence in England. It meant surrendering a home that had given me the happiest years of my life and where I had written fifteen books that had brought me some degree of fame and fortune. I was now sixty and could not expect my industry and vogue to continue. There was old age to provide for. An author is wholly on his own; he receives no pension from his publisher. But it was my dollar debt that forced me to act. I could no longer, with any sense of honour, go on owing my generous American friend the $50,000 I had borrowed. He had never charged interest or pressed for repayment, "Don't worry, you did a magnificent job and I am happy to have contributed to it in a small way," he said.

I arrived at my decision after consultation with friends. Some of them opposed it. "What about your readers who come from all over the world, having read about your cottage in *Gone Rustic*, *Pilgrim Cottage*, and other books ?" they asked. I was aware of this but I had to deal with facts. The change was made easier by the English owner of the Alassio palazzo apartment being willing to sell it for sterling. I decided that when I returned to England next summer I would find a sympathetic purchaser of the cottage, someone who would be affable to those overseas visitors, and free myself from financial bondage.

Early in September, on a cold rainy day, I left for Cap d'Antibes, to stay once more, Mrs. Cartwright's guest, at Casa Estella.

VI

When, in the summer of 1922, I had first lunched with Max Beerbohm I went afterwards to call on Gordon Craig, who was entertaining my travelling companion, Duncan MacPherson. Craig lived just across the road with his Italian wife and young son, Edward. We were detained for supper. Our host was a massive, lion-like man with a tawny mane framing noble features. We ate in candle-gloom. It was almost one of his stage sets, with portentous shadows. He was famous in the world of the theatre as a revolutionary designer of scenery, but his productions had always been costly, and his extravagant demands wore out the patience of successive Maecenases. Handsome, the natural son of Godwin the architect, who had built Whistler's famous house in Tite Street, Chelsea, and Ellen Terry, he had all the Terry charm. He had had successes in Germany, Russia and Italy, but England had not given him the recognition he thought he should have had. His domestic life had always been complicated, his financial position hazardous, but he drove himself on in a gale of enthusiasm. Since that meeting at Rapallo I had never forgotten him. He was the kind of man who etched his personality on your mind.

I now learned, some thirty years later, that he was living in a French pension at Vence, in what are called "straitened circumstances". I suggested to Mrs. Cartwright that we should go and call on him. Would he remember me after thirty years? He was now eighty. In the interim he had never been wholly out of the news, a man who defied time and the conventions. It happened that we arrived at the pension in my hostess's chauffered Rolls-Royce car, and I wished our advent had not been so ostentatiously prosperous. I had prepared the way with a telegram and he must have been awaiting us, for the moment our car drew up he appeared. What an appearance! He was pure theatre on that hilltop, standing before a rather seedy pension. He was tall, with his magnificent head still crowned with tumbling waves of hair. Clad in a large camel-hair cloak with a burnous, he wore a wide-brimmed brown sombrero. As we got out of the car he dramatically threw a lap of his cloak over one shoulder and made a ceremonious bow with a full sweep of his hat. He took us on to the verandah where he had ordered tea. "Of course I remember you," he said, when I recalled our meeting. "You shook Max telling him that it was exactly one hundred years since Shelley had been washed up on the shore. You've been very busy since then, books and books and books. Well, I've never been idle, have I?"

Later, after tea, he said, "You must come up to my den—I'm writing my *Life*, I'm three-quarters through." I followed him up a flight of stairs to a very large bedsitting-room lined from floor to ceiling with books and files and papers. The table held them, the bed held them, the window ledges held them. Never have I seen such confusion. He sat himself majestically in a Gothic chair before his large writing-table. "You see, I work—I must get this book finished, and all this material"—he waved his hand at the crowded shelves—"has to be put in order." I looked round. A table by his narrow bed held a large reading lamp and three jars full of pencils. It appeared to me that all his wardrobe hung on hooks along one wall. If you moved you trod on docketed papers, magazines, books with markers. Yet how noble and impressive he looked, with his beautiful head, presiding over all this chaos, reflecting a long fervid life of incessant labour—and, alas, I feared, with little reward. A Civil List pension kept him from starvation. There was a crowning touch of irony in his life. His country had not recognised him and had given a knighthood to a man of the same name, aged thirty-eight, a film director.

He was now all alone in life, here on a hilltop, in a backwater, but apparently still irrepressible. When we left he accompanied us to the car. As we drove away, there he stood, with a last flourish of his cloak and a gallant sweep of his sombrero. We might have been departing from a Moorish palace rather than a meagre pension. "What a superb man!" said Mrs. Cartwright, "I hope we didn't embarrass him with the cost of those teas." The next day she sent him a case of champagne with an appropriate note. And all was well since it ended well. He completed and published his autobiography, *Index to the Story of my Days*, five years later, and, tardily, at eighty-four was made a Companion of Honour. He died at Vence, aged ninety-four.

VII

I was in Rome in October. One day sitting at Doney's café on the Via Veneto I had a shock. In the thirties at Pilgrim Cottage I had often entertained a young German artist, Kurt Winkler, who had fled from the Nazis in Berlin in 1934. He settled in London and somehow scraped a living with his drawings. When the war broke out, and just before I left for America, I had an agonised telephone call from him. They were going to intern him, could I do anything for him? Alas, I had only twenty-four hours before my departure, but I asked a friend to do what he could, in vain. Kurt Winkler was interned in the Isle of Man. Then later all the internees, invasion being threatened, were sent to Canada, some five hundred. Nearing the Labrador coast the ship was torpedoed and most of the passengers were drowned. I heard that Kurt was on the ship and had gone down with her. I mourned him. He had been a pleasant fellow, fiercely anti-Nazi. Now, sitting in the October sunshine outside the café I heard my name called and there was Kurt Winkler, a little heavier, in good health! He told me his story. He had been in the sea five hours when he was picked up by a trawler off the

Canadian coast. He was interned in Canada for the rest of the war. This ended, he had the choice of remaining in Canada or going to Australia. He chose Sydney, and there he built up a successful photographic business. He was on his way to Germany to collect his mother who had survived the destruction of Berlin.

One evening, Kennedy Cook, the director of the British Council in Rome, gave a dinner party for Sir Kenneth Clark, who was lecturing for the Council. John Betjeman's wife was there with Robert Heber Percy. He told me he had sold Lord Berners's house. We went to see it. I still wished it was mine. Berners's piano was there. He had vanished but the music he had composed on it was living.

The next day I lunched with our Ambassador, Sir Victor Mallet, at the Embassy. I learned from a guest that George Santayana, the philosopher, had died, aged eighty-eight, in the Blue Sisters' Hospital. They had looked after him wonderfully but all the time he was dying they had a priest nearby, in the hope that the old agnostic would embrace the Roman Catholic faith. He firmly refused all overtures. "I'll die believing what I've lived believing," he told a friend, "and disbelieving what I've always disbelieved!"

On my last evening in Rome Neville-Terry, the British Consul-General, invited me to dinner. Cecil Horsley, the Bishop of Gibraltar, was staying with them. I was delighted to see again this most jovial of clerics. There was a note of comedy. He was late coming into the drawing-room so Violet, the daughter of the house, went to his bed-room. She found him on his knees trying to retrieve from deep under the bed his buckled shoes. At dinner he told us about his American tour, a resounding success. "They drowned me in kindness." We had a merry evening.

Back at the Palazzo Vairo in November I packed and, at the end of the month, sailed in the *Saturnia* from Genoa for New York. Off Cape St. Vincent, beyond Trafalgar Bay, there was a flaming sunset. Browning came to mind:

> Nobly, nobly, Cape St. Vincent to the North-West died away;
> Sunset ran, one glorious blood-red, reeking into Cadiz Bay.

On calling at Halifax a welcoming telegram awaited me from Mrs. Cartwright, with whom I was staying in New York. My room in her large top apartment at 820 Fifth Avenue offered a magnificent panorama of Central Park, now familiar to me, this time not yet laden with snow but in the last rich tints of autumn. In the early evening the sun flushed the sky with crimson, silhouetting the great apartment houses across the Park.

It was my good fortune to have my friend Josephine Crane in the same building, two floors below. When I went to call on Lady Ribblesdale all the Christmas trees down Park Avenue were lit up, a fairylike scene ending in the towering pagoda tower of the Grand Central Railway. Ava Ribblesdale at eighty was still a woman of striking beauty. Svelte, long-necked, her head crowned with white curls, she moved like a swan. Small wonder she had created a sensation when a London hostess. She was exceptionally well-read. Soon after I arrived the two Sitwells came in; gothic, long-nosed Edith, dramatically dressed with a green-collared corsage that gave her an Elizabethan air, and Osbert, a replica of Max Beerbohm's cartoon, languid-eyed. I was distressed to see how laboriously he moved, impeded by the onset of Parkinson's disease. Poor fellow, within two years I would have to hold open the door of the Athenaeum to enable him to get through. He said he was still writing. With us, when the ink ceases to flow, the heart ceases to beat.

The following day Mrs. Murray Crane gave a lunch party for me. It happened to be Sir Shane Leslie's birthday. This time he was not wearing the saffron kilt of an Irish squire. A scholar, he always talked well and he was in good form. Padraic Colum read a little poem which he had written in tribute to him. The table had a complete set of porcelain Lippizaner horses as a centrepiece. Against one wall spread a fine five-fold Coromandel screen. The talk was good and lively. Josephine was a great collector. She owned an authentic water-colour portrait of Shelley and an Augustus John drawing of James Joyce. She had acquired a beautiful period piece, in a red-plush frame, a watercolour of Prince Jerome Bonaparte, the royal bigamist and ex-King of Westphalia, who had deserted his wife Betty Patterson. He had been painted posing in the study of his palace. Queen Victoria met him, during her visit to Paris, and disliked him.

In the New Year I signed a contract with my American publisher that would be productive of future income to enable me to pay off my debt to my American friend. At the end of January I had a pleasant surprise. The Duke of Windsor gave me a copy of his book *A King's Story*. It was an edition-de-luxe, bound in red morocco leather, with the royal arms embossed on the cover, and made more acceptable by what he had written in the flyleaf. "To Cecil Roberts, in appreciation. Edward." It contained facsimile pages of his beautiful bold handwriting which I envied, my own being execrable. I had contributed very little to his book, it being wholly his own work, but I appreciated the gesture. When I congratulated him on the book he said, "The conversion of a few of the old stuffed shirts of the hard upper crust, who disapproved in principle of my writing my memoirs, has been more than gratifying. The reviews, with one or two exceptions, were fair and generous."

In March I sailed for Genoa. When the ship passed the bay of Alassio it radioed that I was on board so everybody there was made aware of my return. I stepped into the riot of a Mediterranean spring. The Piazza below me blazed with flowers. The giant magnolia trees already had buds, soon to be white cups. Roses bloomed, the mimosa was a golden rain, yellow and red carnations grew on the terraced hills, the gorse bushes were afire in the mountain ravines.

There was a large packet of mail awaiting me. Suddenly, on opening a letter all the beauty went out of the day. Cecil Horsley, the Bishop of Gibraltar, had died in a London hospital after a short illness. It was difficult to believe that one so full of joyous life, so much beloved of everybody, had died aged fifty. Perhaps he had rushed around too much in his enthusiasm for work in his immense diocese stretching from Gibraltar to Asia Minor. High blood pressure had been the cause of death. What a merry eye and a warm hand he always had! I could still hear his laughter on the terrace of the Rock Hotel at Gibraltar in those first weeks of our friendship.

VIII

One morning looking down from my apartment I was surprised to see a number of covered wagons forming a complete circle in the Piazza. A circus had arrived. The wagons, dropping one side, were cages with animals, including a leopard, a tiger, a lion, cheetahs and monkeys. Soon a blare from a loudspeaker announced that the zoo had opened. I hated this business of caged animals despite the rapture evoked in children, but I found myself forced to make a visit. Then one evening there was something quite terrifying. A cable was stretched from the top of the palazzo down to the Piazza. Up this cable came a young man on a roaring motorcycle. As he reached the top the ascent was almost vertical. There seemed nothing for him but death on the pavement a hundred feet below. The powerful motorcycle had only grooved wheels. We held our breath. He arrived, turned the machine and then made his descent at a murderous speed, braking violently in the last ten yards. There was a collection in the Piazza. For this dare-devil act he did not net more than three hundred lire, the spectators meanly moving away. To risk your life four times a day for the price of a packet of cigarettes!

In that same week I was confined to bed. About three o'clock one afternoon, while I was dozing, there was an urgent ringing at the door. It was answered by Giulietta, aroused from her siesta. Then I heard Italian male voices mingled with her excited treble. This was too much for me so I rose, put on a dressing-gown and went into the hall. There I found three dark young men, all flashing eyes and and teeth, rain-drenched, attendants from the zoo. A monkey had escaped and had been seen sitting on the balustrade of my terrace. I was incredulous. How was it possible for a monkey to climb the façade of a five-storey building? "It's true, signore. We've seen him!" I led the way into the salon where the French window opened on to the terrace. I peered out, for it was raining heavily. There, on the edge of the marble parapet, sat the monkey. The men rushed out but he was too quick for them. With a great leap he was on the balcony of the adjoining apartment. There followed a hair-raising episode. My terrace was a hundred feet above the Piazza. One of the youths did not hesitate to mount the wet, slippery parapet and, like his quarry, take an acrobatic leap on to the next balcony. The monkey again leapt and scaled a rain-spout up to the flat roof. Defeated, we all went back into the salon.

The roof over me had an area large enough for two tennis courts. From it you had magnificent views of the town, sea and mountains. Since there are people who have a mania for hurling themselves from great heights, no one was allowed on the roof. The key was kept by Giovanni, the concierge. He was now brought into the chase. For the next twenty minutes there were the thudding sounds of four pairs of feet scampering overhead. The monkey was elusive. He leapt down to a balcony on the north side. It happened that a window was open. By this time he was a very wet and frightened monkey. Liberty was not all it had been cracked up to be in monkey village. He took refuge in a room, to the surprise of the maid. She approached the poor little fellow and in his terror he bit her. Wisely fastening the window and the door, she brought news of the prisoner. The chase was at an end. The men left with profuse apologies for the disturbance. Rough lads, they had the manners of Venetian ambassadors. We replied that it had been a great entertainment. Then I went back to bed.

There remained the mystery of how the monkey had got on to my terrace. Giovanni supplied the explanation. The monkey, escaping during the cleaning of the communal cage, had run across the avenue of palm trees separating us from the Piazza into the entrance hall. Here, disturbed by someone entering, he had leapt on the roof of the lift, to find himself transported to the fourth floor by an incoming tenant. As soon as the lift stopped he ran up the remaining flight of stairs and by agile climbing got on to the open roof. From there he had leapt down on to my terrace and been seen by the hunters below.

The zoo left as quickly and as quietly as it had come. The long wagons were skilfully manœuvred into the Via Aurelia, and headed in the direction of Albenga, the next town on the coast. The zoo story provided another which had filled the newspapers the previous year. One day during a performance with a lion and tiger the latter attacked the trainer. He was immediately rescued by the lion, who had an affection for him. But the tiger was a mean beast and had a long memory. Some weeks later, while the zoo was approaching Noli, a fishing village twenty miles from Alassio, the drivers heard a tremendous uproar in one of the wagons. They stopped and approached the cage with the lion and tiger, whence the noise came. When they lowered the shutters they discovered that the cage was swimming with blood and the lion was dead. He had been attacked by the tiger, which had taken its revenge. The tiger was so mauled it had to be shot.

Just before Lent King Carnival arrived. There was a band, its members dressed in sailors' blue trousers, striped jerseys and berets with red pompons. It was Neptune's band, with white violins, conch-shells, trombones, tridents and nets. There were highly decorated floats crammed with children in fancy costume, angels in white, with wings. There were large antediluvian animals, with great trunks, glaring eyes, long tails, made out of papier-mâché. Through-traffic to Rome was blocked for four hours. King Carnival ruled. At the end of the day all the monsters went up in a roaring bonfire. The Carnival was over.

IX

When I was in Rome the previous autumn I used to take an evening walk on the Pincio, in the Borghese Gardens. It presented a beautiful and dramatic scene with all Rome lying below in the valley, the lights coming on in the dusk. Across the Tiber the great dome of St. Peter's was silhouetted against a blood-red sky. I never walked there but what I thought of three young Englishmen who had known that evening scene some one hundred and thirty years earlier. They were young John Keats, his companion, Joseph Severn, and Lieutenant Elton, the son of a Sussex squire. As with Keats, consumption had driven Elton to Rome. He had seen service as an Ensign at Waterloo but his Army career had been broken by the onset of lung trouble. He was a dandy and rich enough to keep a couple of hunters, establishing himself with the Roman hunt as a spirited rider. With his ample fortune, looks and breeding, he was much sought after by English dowagers and mammas with daughters for disposal. The other two Englishmen, Keats and Severn, twenty-five and twenty-six respectively, unlike Elton were almost penniless. They lived in a small two-roomed apartment at the foot of the Spanish Steps, over which one room commanded a view. In that corner room within a few months Keats would die. His devoted companion, Severn, lived on in Rome until he died there, aged eighty-six, famous for his association with an immortal.

But on that far-off evening as they walked on the Pincio they were young and excited by the scene. It was the hour of the evening assembly. The princes, dukes and counts and their ladies rode in their carriages. They were attended by grooms in the liveries of famous houses, the Colonna, Borghese, Massimo, Ludovici, Ruspoli, Doria,

Chigi and Corsini. Young Elton, popular and known, was bowing constantly as the carriages circulated on the palm-bordered plateau. The women were beautiful, the men elegant, the horses superb. One of the ladies drew all eyes as she sat in a yellow landau, attended by her latest lover, Signor Pacini. She was the Princess Pauline Borghese, Napoleon's notorious sister who, at the age of thirty-seven, had not lost her vivid interest in any good-looking young man. And there were three of them, obviously English, one of whom had a handsome head and figure. Elton she knew and bowed to. The third young man, Keats, was too short for her taste. She required of any man that his legs should be long. Keats had seen her naked statue by Canova, exhibited for a small tip by the butler in the great Borghese palace and had been more disgusted than shocked by it. "Beautiful bad taste", he commented, but Severn was overwhelmed by the sheer genius of Canova's work. Shortly afterwards he visited the sculptor's studio, presenting a letter of introduction he carried as a Gold-Medallist student of the Royal Academy.

I began to be interested in the history of young Severn who, a second-rate artist, succeeded through a long life in scraping a living. By virtue of his care of the dying poet he became a legend. He defied the arrogant Countess of Westmorland, enamoured of him, by marrying her ward, the illegitimate daughter of a peer. A long, happy life produced seven children. Wordsworth, in Rome, attended the christening of one of them. A twin son, Arthur, and his wife, lived at Brantwood, Coniston, and nursed the insane Ruskin in his decline. If you went to Rome it was the "thing" to call on this remarkable young man, whom Gladstone made the British Consul at a youthful sixty-seven in 1860. Ruskin had described him. "There is nothing in any circle that ever I saw or heard of like what Mr. Joseph Severn then was in Rome . . . Lightly sagacious, lovingly humorous, daintily sentimental, he was in council with the cardinals of today, and at picnic in the Campagna with the brightest English belles tomorrow; and caught the hearts of all in the golden net of his goodwill."

That autumn in Rome I visited many of the places Severn had known, his lodgings, the palaces he had frequented, and, of course, Canova's studio. For the next six months I "lived" Joseph Severn. I planned a novel about him, to be called *The Remarkable Young Man*.

As soon as I had returned to the Palazzo Vairo I shut myself up and worked incessantly, caught up in the Roman pageant of his life, ending with his burial in the grave next to Keats's in the Protestant Cemetery. I began the novel in March. I finished it, 100,000 words, within nine weeks. Then I went to Rome, to check it.

Rome at all times was delightful. In May it was intoxicating with its beauty. I lunched and dined out, in bowers of flowers. The terraces at friends' apartments often commanded views over a city of mottled roofs, open loggias, domes of churches, obelisks, gleaming fountains, the brown Tiber by the great mole of the Castle St. Angelo, and always the dominating cupola of St. Peter's. One day at Prince Doria's, after lunch, we took coffee in the green salon. One's eye wandered over the paintings. On an easel stood Velasquez's masterpiece of Innocent X, a Pamphili. There was a beautiful Bronzino of the murdered cousin and heir of Andrea Doria, the great Genoese admiral, founder of the line. A huge tapestry covered one wall, a vivid fantasy of the life of Alexander the Great—he descended to the sea to fish and sat in a kind of bathysphere from which he calmly observed the fish around him. He ascended to Heaven, in a cage lifted by four griffons, God looking on; and there was also a battle scene of the assault of Ghent by Philip le Bel. How patient and gentle Prince Doria was, explaining what he must have explained a hundred times, and escorting his guests round the four-sided gallery as though it were for the first time.

One day I walked the whole length of the Appian Way which, with an aerodrome near the end of it, was rapidly disintegrating. Hundreds of Roman tombs lining it had been stolen and scattered, reappearing in churches, private palaces and museums. The automobile was rapidly destroying the ancient silence, broken also by zooming aeroplanes.

I returned to Alassio having checked the data for *The Remarkable Young Man.* I broke my journey at Rapallo to call on Max Beerbohm. I found him finishing lunch on the terrace with Elizabeth Jungmann. He was as alert and charming as ever. I had told him on a former visit that I had made a gate-leg table out of the shelves of an old walnut bookcase. I showed him a photograph of it. He was full of wonder. "What skill! I couldn't be trusted with a saw. There would be blood all over the place." He wanted to hear about the British

Council lecture I had given in Rome. "With no manuscript, with not a note—then you memorize it?" I denied this. "You know," said Max, "once when I went with my brother to New York with one of his plays, I was persuaded to try a small part. It had nine lines. When I walked on I forgot them. That was, thank God, the end of any theatrical career for me." They had finished lunch, so I had coffee with them. When I stood up to leave Max would not hear of it. "We'll have our siesta and then have tea!" So I stayed and took the evening train to Alassio.

Back at Palazzo Vairo I worked on my manuscript. One morning I was interrupted by visitors. I found in the hall Mrs. Duncan Sandys, Churchill's daughter, and her little girl, Celia. It was her birthday. They were spending a short holiday in Alassio, Mrs. Sandys recuperating from an illness. On this bright morning, mercifully, one had no foreknowledge of what was to be her sad destiny.

When my tenancy came to an end I was so enamoured with my apartment that I bought it. For I had made a decision. I was at an age when a man retires from his life's work, turned sixty. I had written thirty books, having published my first at twenty. It was time to compose myself, to travel as I wished, to write a little, to dream, to welcome friends, to bask on my terrace. Here, under a lovely sky, in a land inexhaustibly rich with treasures of art and architecture, peopled by the most genial race on earth, I had come to port after a voyage of rich experiences, still active in mind and body, and animated by an unquenchable curiosity. So I thought, optimistically.

In June I left for London, arriving in time to attend a dinner at the Garrick Club arranged by Hamish Hamilton in honour of H. M. Tomlinson, my old war-correspondent colleague, on his eightieth birthday. Poor man, stone deaf, he did not hear a word of the speeches we made in tribute to him, the author of *Gallion's Reach*, etc.

There followed the usual round of week-end visits, to Francis Jekyll at Munstead, the Gates at Hascombe, the Sackvilles at Knole, the Birketts at Chalfont St. Giles, Masefield at Burcote Brook, the Iliffes at Yattendon. And once again there was Henley Regatta and the Greek play at Bradfield College. I had guests all the time, and there was a stream of overseas "fans". But there was a shadow over the scene. I was emigrating and had to sell my cottage. What a revelation of human nature it produced! I weeded out most of the people the agent sent. Even so, the cranks got in. There was a monocled major who came in a Jaguar car. He called five times with his wife. She suffered from arthritis and would have to have a downstairs bathroom built on. Then his architect went up into the roof and reported it would collapse very soon. I laughed. I told him it had been there three hundred years and would be there another three; there wasn't a nail in the roof, it was all oak and oak pegs. The major appeared again with a mysterious man, who asked about the drainage. I told him there was none. By this time I was hot with shame for my beloved cottage. Then I discovered the man was from a building society! When I complained the agent confessed that the major lived in a cheap hotel. Pretending to buy houses was his pastime! He wrote me an abusive letter when I told him I had sold the cottage. He said I had tricked him and was no gentleman.

One day a Rolls-Royce with a liveried chauffeur arrived. A most lovely, tall lady, all pearls and powder, descended. She must have it, she thought the place divine. She had a house in Grosvenor Square, a villa at Cannes, and a staff of twelve. I pointed out she would bump her head all the time, and there was only one bathroom, and no room for a maid. She came twice. She found the cottage irresistible. She was charming, willowy, expensive with every breath she took. She had read *Pilgrim Cottage* and *Gone Rustic*. It would be so wonderful to live here. I suggested you couldn't live in a house just because you had read a book about it. This was a tiny cottage with no room for her five dogs, and no garage to hold a Rolls-Royce. She invited me to dinner. I found she was the wife of a steel magnate. I told her the cottage wanted a good Nannie, someone who would live in it and be kind to the fans who would come to look at it. I laughed her out of it and we became good friends.

Then one day a nice young couple appeared. They were local. I felt at once they would be kind to the old place, and agreeable to all visitors. So I sold it to them, and they were more than all I had hoped for. I often visited them in the following years, with much heartache, but it was good to see how they loved it and looked after it. It had been my habit to write the names of the books I had written there, on a door of the study. When they repainted they preserved the fifteen titles on its panel.

And so the last heartbreaking day of a farewell tea party came, given for the new owners. There was Giulietta, tearful, young John Smyth, still in the army, who had gardened here, and jovial Lord Parmoor, who was the brother of Stafford Cripps but all that his brother wasn't; and young Mr. and Mrs. Plater, the purchasers. We tried to be cheerful, aware that we were all acting a part, with tears only the other side of a thin partition. After twenty-four happy years the tendrils of love are not easily uprooted.

X

In mid-September, having corrected the proofs of *The Remarkable Young Man* I was back at Casa Estella, in all the blue radiance of Cap d'Antibes. After ten days I moved across the road to stay with Lady Norman at the Château de la Garoupe. I was the guest for a week of this highly capable woman who administered the La Garoupe estate, with its five houses to which she now added a sixth, built for her younger son. This was called the Tourelle and was in the shape of a starfish, with pointed wings, erected on a small promontory commanding the Bay of Nice. The position was magnificent with Nice at night like a collar of diamonds along the Promenade des Anglais.

Fay Norman and I were the first to sleep in the new house. With windows on three sides of my room I felt very much on view. It had everything except what I wanted most, a writing desk. Within a half hour of asking, two men bore in such a large one that a bureau had to be taken out. Five minutes later Fay came in with writing pad, ink, blotting paper, a box of clips and an indiarubber. What a woman! She could have governed an empire. Indeed, this Château de La Garoupe was an empire which she directed from a desk littered with papers. I remembered her handsome old father, Lord Aberconway, although I had seen him for only an hour some thirty years ago when calling at the Château with my friend Francis Jekyll, whose sister, Barbara, had married his son, killed in the First World War. By him she had two sons. Later she married Bernard Freyberg, V.C. After three days at the Tourelle we moved over to the Château.

One November morning from my terrace at Palazzo Vairo I saw Corsica on the horizon, very clear, its mountains capped with snow and glistening in the sun. The weather was so good that we had our meals outside. The sun sank behind the mountains across the bay at half-past four but there was a wonderful afterglow, and then the little town lighted up, the curving promenade sparkling through the crimson dusk. Above, on the mountainside, lay the small promontory of Santa Croce, with a ruined chapel and an ancient arched gateway, part of a fort that had defended Alassio from its near-by enemy, Albenga. Through that gateway ran a road known to the Romans coming up from the south to fight the wild Ligurian tribes. From a small platform one looked down on the great curve of the bay holding Alassio, shut in by mountains. That old crumbling gateway, which had known so much history, was like a portal to the paradise below. Returning homewards down the cobbled track it occurred to me that here was a title for a book, *Portal to Paradise*. It lodged in my mind. There was so much history and beauty in Alassio. I began a notebook but six months passed before I started writing.

Christmas had been spent in Rome. The Mallets had left the British Embassy. It was a loss for they had been most hospitable, but their successors, Sir Ashley and Lady Clarke proved equally so. The ambassador loved music. If he had not been a diplomat he might have been a conductor. His Italian was fluent. I heard him give an excellent lecture on Mozart, which he illustrated at the piano.

XI

In the spring of 1954 I made a Greek tour, sailing to Athens from Venice. In Mycenae I went through the Lion Gateway and climbed to the Acropolis where Agamemnon had been murdered in his palace by Clytemnestra on returning from the Trojan War. Sitting amid the ruins of the palace I found an Englishwoman, an elderly spinster. She was touring Greece on a donkey, now tied up to a wall. She sat on a stool painting. And there, in one of the most historic spots in Greece, I was thoroughly sat upon. When she got up from her tripod stool I saw she had heightened her seat with a couple of books. The top one was *So Immortal a Flower*, my novel of Crete. When I revealed myself, expecting her surprise, she said downrightly, "Well, I'm sure it does you good to be sat upon! And now you're here, you might autograph it." We exchanged addresses. A year later I went to an exhibition of her pictures in London. I bought one she had painted of the Lion Gateway. "Oh, I'm glad you've got it. I painted it on my eightieth birthday!" For four months she had ridden her donkey over the Greek mountains, sleeping in peasants' houses.

The highlight of my tour was not Crete with its palace of Knossos but Delphi, superbly lodged on its high mountain recess, still brooding over the mystery of the Oracle, and its sacred cult. This had long vanished but the weight of history was in the air and the ghosts of old anxieties pervaded the deep, wooded valley. Up the steep cobbles, past the Treasuries, we took the road to the vanished temple, and the gymnasium where the naked athletes had sought the victor's crown. Across the towering cliffs an eagle flew in the bright Parnassian sky. Surely Pan with his flute would be heard, could we but wait.

Back in Athens I bought a copy of *The Times* of April 2nd, to find what had been happening in England during our tour. My eye fell upon a paragraph which froze me with horror.

Mr. Richard Cartwright of Aynho Park, Banbury, Oxfordshire, and his only son Edward, aged 17, were killed on Wednesday night when their car was in collision with the back of a stationary timber lorry about three miles from Aynho Park. Mr. Cartwright, who was born in 1903 was the son of the late Rt. Hon. Sir Fairfax Cartwright, British Ambassador in Vienna, 1908–1913. He married in 1933 Elspeth Weir, daughter of the 1st Viscount Weir.

For the last 340 years the direct descendant of the family has been an only son. This accident wipes out the male line. The house at Aynho Park is one of the showplaces of Oxfordshire and has been in the Cartwright family since 1616 when it was purchased from a member of the Marmion family. After the Battle of Edge Hill Charles I spent some time there. Mr. Cartwright had a fine collection of Chinese and Persian ceramics and his monochromes were reputed to be the finest single collection in the world.

Later I learned that he had been to Eton College to fetch his son home for the Easter vacation. Planks protruding from the lorry had killed father and son instantly. I did not go out that morning to the Acropolis museum, as planned. We sailed in the afternoon from the Piraeus but all the way up the Adriatic my mind was full of the tragedy at Aynho.

How chill and damp was Venice to which the graceful new *Achilles* bore us! The most enchanting city on earth can be the most forbidding on a cold grey day, for April this year was delayed and winter still lingered. The rain fell in torrents. An icy wind from the Alps blew over the canals. But my mind was not in Venice. It had gone back to a bright July day, two years ago, in an ancient house full of treasures, where the young owner had upheld the Cartwright tradition.

XII

It was cold when I got back to Alassio. There was snow on the mountains around us. Calling on Max on the way home I found him in a muffler and overcoat, sitting over a wood fire. I thought he looked pinched. He had developed eye trouble and a London specialist had come out to examine him. For the first time he was not spruce and alert. I sadly realised he was old, eighty-two. Twenty years later, when I went to see my oculist, Marcelli Shaw in Harley Street, I learned that it was he who had visited Max. "Just before leaving, Max talked about his life in the Villino," said Shaw, "and he said something I shall never forget, regarding his neighbours— 'The English are the salt of the earth, the Italians are the sugar'."

On leaving the Villino Miss Jungmann endorsed my anxiety when she said "Do come again, soon." The emphasis was on the word "soon". I had made him laugh with a description of our classical tour. We had had a high proportion of learned bluestockings from the universities. They carried textbooks, dictionaries, maps, in cloth bags. They fell asleep in buses. One went to sleep on me, her head on my shoulder. I wondered if ever again I should support so much learning. She was a professor of Greek archaeology, and an authority on Ventris's Linear B discoveries. My stock went up when I asked her if she had seen, as I had, the earliest known Greek inscriptions carved on the seats of the stadium at Santorin in the Aegean, inscriptions from which our own alphabet had been derived. They were the ecstatic expressions of Lacedemonian boy-lovers who had watched the dancing of naked youths competing in the annual gymnopaedics. Yes, she had indeed, and asked, "Did you see the carved phallic symbols coupled with their declarations?"

That spring I began to write *Portal to Paradise*. Halfway through I received an invitation to join Lord Iliffe on his yacht *Radiant* for a cruise to the Dalmatian Coast. The yacht was in the harbour at Monte Carlo. Alas, I am a shocking sailor and a ship of 60,000 tons is not big enough for me. I had never crossed the Atlantic without being half the time in bed. So I reluctantly declined this offer but I went to Monte Carlo and lunched on board the yacht, a luxury ship with a crew of twenty-two.

By the middle of July, in a frenzy of work, I had finished *Portal to Paradise* and went to the Villa Mauresque to lunch with Somerset Maugham. I found him very sprightly at eighty, enjoying his persistent pessimism. He had been made, tardily, a Companion of Honour. His first impulse was to decline it. *The Remarkable Young Man* had just been published so I took him a copy. I told him he was under no compulsion to read it. "I shall read every word of it and be consoled by all your faults," he replied. When I told him I had just finished another book, about Alassio, in eight weeks, he said: "You should never tell anyone you've written a book in eight weeks. People are absurd. They'll think it's no good. If you say you have taken four years, they're impressed. Well, anyone who takes four years over a book just can't write, he gets coagulated. How many hours a day do you work?" "When the tide's flowing, twelve," I answered. "Good God, no wonder you've an ulcer! Four finishes me." I asked him if he was writing. "Y-yes. I'm a word-addict and can't -sh-shake it off," he replied. I noticed he drank two cocktails, and steadily ate through an excellent lunch. He expected you to leave at three o'clock, when he went to his siesta.

At the beginning of August I was in London. It grieved me that there was no Pilgrim Cottage to go to. The new owners invited me to lunch. I went and opened a wound. There were too many ghosts of lost happiness in the house and the garden.

At the end of the month I left with my friend Mrs. Boehm for Scotland, to attend the Edinburgh Festival. We were house-guests of a lady, Italian by birth, widowed, who lived in a huge, sham baronial mansion on the edge of a black loch near Peebles. The house was servantless, the long carriage-drive through the woods had been neglected and was full of potholes. The tennis court and gardens had all gone to seed during the war. In the hall there was a large organ that had not been played on for twenty years, and guns and sticks, all dusty. My kind hostess, an invalid, passed her time in front of a fire in the large oaklined library. Her elderly son shut himself in his study at the other end of the house. A companion-help, a cheery little woman, did the cooking and served the meals. There was a ghostly drawing-room with everything under white sheets, morgue-like. Upstairs along the corridors the wind lifted the carpets. The windows looked on a barren mountainside and a black loch. I tried to draw the heavy curtain in my bedroom. The whole thing came down on my head. Yet this mansion with sixteen bedrooms had once been full of guests, with butler, cook, and servants in the enormous kitchens downstairs, and gardeners and stablemen outside. Now, silence and decay. My hostess sat and dreamed of the Italy she had left as the bride of a Scotsman who had brought her to the sunless north. All day it rained. How it rained, incessantly, for ten days.

Each day the obliging son motored my hostess, my friend and myself into Edinburgh for the Festival. There were Rubinstein and Claudio Arrau playing, a performance of *A Midsummer Night's Dream* (the irony of that title!) with Robert Helpmann and Moira Shearer; there was the Edinburgh Philharmonic Orchestra with Karajan conducting Berlioz's *Symphonie Fantastique*. There was a ravishing performance of *Le Bourgeois Gentilhomme* by the Comédie Française Company, and an equally sublime *Count Orry* (Rossini), imported from Glyndebourne. Our thoughtful hostess omitted nothing. Her patient son drove us in and out of Edinburgh through sheets of rain. We were entertained by the Maxwell-Stuarts, descendants of the Earls of Traquair, living in the oldest inhabited house in Scotland. The forecourt of Traquair was an architectural gem, with stone piers and ironwork gates which had never been opened since the 11th Earl closed them when Bonnie Prince Charlie departed, after staying there on his way south. He vowed they would never be opened again until a Stuart king was on the throne. To this day you go in by what is optimistically called "The temporary entrance". Part of the house, standing on the banks of the Tweed, goes back to A.D. 1175. William Lyon of Scotland came there after

The condemned cottage, and the restoration

Driving to the Feria, the Duke of Montoro "in hand" with the quintet

The Duchess of Alba, in the mantilla, leaves for the bullfight

hunting and in the hall signed a charter allowing the Bishop of Glasgow to raise his "hamlet" to the status of a Royal Borough. On September 9th, 1513, the family saw the archers returning from the battle of Flodden Field. Wounded bowmen from Selkirk told them that King James was dead and "the flowers of the forest died around him".

Traquair has always been a Catholic house. In the King's Room, where Mary Queen of Scots slept, there is an entrance to a secret escape passage used by priests. In 1566 Queen Mary of Scots came with Darnley and the Three Marys, Mary Beaton, Mary Seaton and Mary Carmichael. They embroidered there the bedspread still in the house. Other exhibits are the Queen's crucifix, her rosary, her bed and the cradle in which she rocked her son, James VI of Scotland and the First of England. There is also a little picture she drew as a child, with her name on the back. The library was well-catalogued and bound, mostly classics. In 1745 the Earl of Traquair welcomed Prince Charles Stuart, coming in triumph from the battle of Preston Pans and the capture of Edinburgh. On his way to England, the Prince held a reception in full highland costume. The house preserves an Amen glass inscribed "God Bless the Prince of Wales".

We had tea with Colonel and Mrs. Maxwell-Stuart and Peter, their elder son, who was farming the estate. We ate in a candle-lit panelled dining-room with a log fire burning in the great fireplace. It was a dark, rainy day. The house seemed full of ghosts, lost causes, the debris of history. Colonel Maxwell-Stuart took me into his study and gave me one of the paperweights he made, a piece of oval glass with a photo of Traquair. Later it lay on my desk in Alassio and I felt that it revelled in a light and warmth it had never known. What a beautiful setting, but how dark and laden with time! "I'd love to live in London," said Mrs. Maxwell-Stuart. Well, the line will still go on. Some time after our visit young Peter married Flora, the twenty-two year old daughter of Sir Alexander Carr-Saunders, director of the London School of Economics.

There was a memorable lunch at Sir Walter Scott's home, Abbotsford. Sir Walter Maxwell-Scott, the great-great-grandson of the novelist, had died that spring, with no male heir, so the baronetcy was extinct. I had met him at Lady Ribblesdale's in New York earlier. His two lovely young daughters did the honours in the historic house.

They paid me an unrehearsed compliment. They showed me some of my own novels in this home of the great master of our craft.

In the train home from Edinburgh to London there was a comedy. This last spring I had been to Munich to give a lecture. On my way home I stayed in Merano. And there befell an adventure, an idyll, not "the Indian Summer of a Forsyte" but something very similar. I thought of various episodes in the key of romance, and suddenly they formed themselves into a book. One of my characters was taken from life. A few hundred yards from the Palazzo Vairo there was a villa in which lived a stone-deaf old man in his eighties. His younger wife had recently died, and this created a drama. Forty years earlier, in middle age, he had been a patient in the hospital of the Blue Sisters in Florence. He fell in love with one of the young nuns, and enticed her to leave secretly. They settled in Alassio. The marriage was perfectly happy. One morning on his wife's birthday, he being her senior by twenty years, he made her a present of the freehold of their villa so that when he died she would be assured of her home. But turned sixty, she died before him. Whether as an act of contrition, or from piety only, it was found that she had left the villa to the Blue Sisters, to use as a hostel. The old man was shaken at the thought of having to leave his home but he was consoled by the Mother Superior, who, after overlooking the property, told him they would give him a life tenancy. So he died, nearly ninety, in the villa he loved. This story was part of the book on which I was working that summer.

In the train three very fat Blue Sisters came into our carriage. One of them, observing me correcting a manuscript, said, shyly, "May I ask, are you an author?" I told her that I was, that I was working on the proofs of a novel. "Oh, may I ask what it is about?" she said, smiling. I smiled back. "Well, your question is rather singular. You are a Blue Sister, and part of my story is about a Blue Sister who ran away from her convent with an elderly patient. Later there was quite a drama. She bequeathed the villa her husband had given her to the Sisters of her Convent. The husband was still alive and it looked as if he would be turned out of his home but one day the Mother Superior came and told him he would have a life-tenancy. So all ends happily in my story."

The eyes of the fat Sister twinkled. "Was the Convent in Florence?

"Yes." "Was the villa in Alassio?" Startled, I said, "Yes." "Was the old gentleman named Warrack?" "Good Heavens, how should you know that?" I asked, quite shaken. "Well, I am the Mother Superior of the Blue Sisters in Florence. It was I who went to tell the old gentleman not to worry as we would not turn him out."

I asked if she had been with her companions to the Festival. No, they had a hospital in Edinburgh. She was on an inspection tour of their properties, from their headquarters in Florence. "You are not Italian?" I asked, hearing her good English. "Oh, no. I'm an Australian!" "Are you returning to Florence?" "Not immediately. I'm now going to our convent in Nottingham." Again I was startled. "I was born in Nottingham," I said, "and lived there during my first twenty years. I never knew there was a Blue Sister convent there!" The three fat Blue Sisters laughed. "Oh, yes. The founder of our Nursing Order, Mother Mary Potter, was born there!" Later in Rome I visited a friend in the large Blue Sisters hospital. In the hall stood a bust of Mary Potter.

XIII

In October, lunching with John Betjeman at the Garrick Club, I found him depressed. He was usually exuberant and treated life as a cheerful adventure. He worked very hard, writing for journals, and reviewing, but he felt he was not "getting there". It is a mood that comes upon all authors. We commiserated with each other, wondering why we had ever gone into this writing business. We would have had a safer, more steady life in a bank or a Government office, with regular hours, regular salary, a pension, and have been eminently respectable. Writers in England are never quite respectable, the shadow of Fleet Street vagabondage is over them. In France one became a *maître*, in Italy a *maestro*. You had reduced income-tax. There were societies that paid you homage if you had any success, and, if French, you could end up in a braided uniform with a feathered hat, an Academician.

By the time the oysters had come and gone, the burgundy had circulated and we had worked down a menu with which John was always expert, we became irrepressibly cheerful. The mahogany tables shone, the Zoffany portraits looked down on us benignly, and everyone in the room seemed prosperous and happy. A motherly waitress urged John to finish his steak pie. "She collects poetry. You must give her one of your books, signed," he said. So he wrote her name and address for me. By three o'clock we were certain that we were fortunate to be what we were, expressing ourselves, free of office hours.

The next day I left for Alassio and Rome. I called on Max when returning from Rome and found him better, though confined to the house. I went there on a delicate mission. Alan Pryce-Jones of the *Times Literary Supplement* asked if I could find out whether Max was in financial straits. He had a lot of fame these days but had nothing to sell and he had never made money, as the phrase goes. He told me he had never sold ten thousand copies of any book he wrote. "Why should I?—I'm too eclectic for the public." The famous caricatures? His editions were limited and, as he had written, "My gifts are small. I've used them very well and discreetly, never straining them, and the result is that I have made a charming little reputation." Alas, he had done practically no work for the last thirty-five years. He was now eighty-two. You can't live in an Italian villa, with ever-rising costs, on fame alone. No author gets pensioned like a bank clerk or a school teacher. Max never complained. He was always cheerful but things indicated there might be pressures. The lorry traffic on the Provincial Road under his villa had grown so enormous that he had to sleep elsewhere, in a little cottage he had bought on the hill behind. This was an extra expense.

I had a delicate task. I approached the subject obliquely, observing that I thought the Society of Authors, of whose Council I was a member, was doing good work with its fund for necessitous scribes. "Yes, there are such funds, I know," observed Max. "But would you believe it, Sylvia Lynd of the Book Society came out here to enquire if I was hard up! The cheek of the woman. They gave me a sum from the Queen's Bounty—I couldn't refuse it but I was deeply embarrassed." Warned, I changed the subject, my mission unfulfilled.

On the day before I left to spend the New Year at the Château de La Garoupe a letter arrived from Hollywood that caused me deep distress. My old friend James Hilton had died of cancer, aged fifty-four. He had frequently stayed at Pilgrim Cottage. With *Goodbye,*

Mr. Chips and *Lost Horizon* fame and fortune had come to him in a rush while young. I had been his guest in Hollywood in 1940, where he was the highest paid of all scenario writers. But I felt the place had destroyed him with its emotional strain. He had had two wives after the break-up of his first marriage. He was gentle and simple and somehow I felt he never fitted the Hollywood picture with its ebullient follies.

When I arrived at the Château de La Garoupe the Christmas guests had departed. There were only two of us in the large house. "You're an ideal guest," said Fay, "you don't arrive with a pile of laundry to have washed, like too many of them. It's not that I'm mean but I hate being imposed upon."

I was given a large bedroom with a view over the sea. The marble salon, covering the whole width of the château, would have made a fine concert hall. It was not used until tea-time when a resinous log fire was lit in the great gothic fireplace. At noon we lunched on the terrace, under a sun-awning. The land fell away in six terraces down to the sea and the little harbour. These were planted with orange trees heavy with golden fruit. There were agave, almond and cherry trees, mimosa and wisteria. The grounds covered one hundred acres, with olive groves and pine woods. Seven gardeners tended all this. Fay knew and loved every yard of the estate. When her father had made a mile-long sea-promenade around the rocky peninsula she told me that as a girl she had worked with the labourers. Even now, turned seventy, she frightened the family by going out in a canoe. On one occasion, capsized by a rough sea, she swam back to one of the coves. There was never the slightest sign of effort in all she did. I felt that she scared the estate employees with her efficiency. As a guest you had punctilious attention to every need.

A grand staircase led up to the first floor, serving a wide gallery that ran the whole length of the house, the bedrooms opening off on the south side. On the north side, when I went up to my room to dress for dinner, there was a breath-taking panorama. The rose of sunset touched the massed snow-covered Maritime Alps that backed the great Baie des Anges, where Nice lay along the shore in a fringe of diamond lights. It was an ever-changing kaleidoscope, until the last glow faded from the peaks. I stood motionless in this sunset hour, permeated with the enthralling beauty of the scene.

Sometimes there was a lunch party for twenty in the great dining-room, but in the evening we dined alone in a small room before an odorous wood fire, and we often talked until midnight. Fay had a no-nonsense mind. It frightened some people, it delighted me. Her father, Lord Aberconway, had been a man of large industrial interests, her late husband, Sir Henry Norman, was a scientist and a writer. You felt she had kept pace with both. She had an agnostic mind, with a strict moral code.

I worked in my room each morning. "I like guests who don't appear until noon!" she said, when I made an apology for my tardy appearance. Sometimes we made excursions. There was a delightful and amusing one to a villa on a hill, the Domaine de la Croix de Gardes. Our host was a M. Goldman, a not inappropriate name for the man whose fortune came from owning the "Burma Gem" business. The villa was crammed with works of art but what I appreciated most was a work of artfulness. He had had a special *gâteau* made, with coloured icing in the form of a large book. The title on it was *Pilgrim Cottage. By Cecil Roberts.* It was not likely he had ever read anything I had written, or heard of me until the day before, but I appreciated the compliment. One day we went to lunch at Casa Estella, where I had spent so many happy days. Beatrice's appearance confirmed what I had heard, my friend was failing. I took aside Anthime, the gentle butler. He was apprehensive. Our hostess, soignée as always, made a brave show, but she had had another stroke and her paralysis was increasing.

XIV

At the beginning of February I left for a short tour of Egypt, Cairo, Luxor, Aswan, the Nile, the Valley of Kings, the Colossus of Memnon. The high moment of the tour was the tomb of Tutankhamen. It was like a descent into Eternity, the final low room where the young king had slept through centuries until Howard Carter had walked into the death chamber.

In Cairo I went without lunch for three days to visit the museum with the Tutankhamen relics. It was the only hour that you could see them, the crowd of tourists absent. On the second day there was only a little slant-eyed Japanese who for three-quarters of an hour took photographs with his Leica. Should I tell him? "Excuse me, but do you know that you've got the cap on your lens?" He bowed so low that he nearly bumped his brow. "It is of an imponderable kindness, sir!" he said with marvellous sangfroid, and started all over again. From the balcony of my room at the Semiramis Hotel I could watch the gold of sunset fade over the Pyramids in the plain beyond the Nile. (Invisible in 1970, with skyscrapers built along the opposite bank.) On my return to Venice, I ran into a thick, cold fog. But on my terrace that evening at Alassio there was a full moon over a silver sea, and a warm air from the south.

A week later I had callers, en route to Cannes from Rome. When my housekeeper showed them into the hall. I was a little puzzled. Who were Mr. and Mrs. Robert Kennedy, of Washington, as their card proclaimed? Mr. Kennedy enlightened me, apologising for their call. In January, 1940, I had lectured to the Foreign Affairs Study group in Palm Beach, Florida, in the drawing-room of one of the members, facing the Atlantic. His mother, Mrs. Rose Kennedy, wife of the American Ambassador to England, lived next door and had taken him to the lecture. He was then a boy of fifteen.

On this occasion they stayed for a pleasant hour. On that sunny February morning of 1955 we could not know that in 1968, a Presidential candidate, he would be assassinated, like his brother earlier, President John Kennedy.

Soon after this visit, returning one day to the palazzo for lunch, I was hailed by a man in a passing car. He was accompanied by two ladies. They were motoring through. Seeing that I was English, he asked if I could direct them to a good restaurant. I told him that he would be well accommodated at "The Ligure", facing the pier. He thanked me and drove on. As soon as the car had passed I began to wonder where and when I had seen him before. In a few minutes I thought I had recollected. It was so extraordinary that I turned and went to the restaurant. I found them sitting at a table and went up to him. "Will you excuse me, but may I ask you if your name happens to be Cain?" I said. He looked surprised. "Yes, my name is Ronald Nall-Cain, Lord Brocket. This is Lady Brocket and my daughter Elizabeth," he replied, introducing me. I asked further questions. "Was your father Charles Cain, who, in 1916, lived in a suite in the Adelphi Hotel at Liverpool?" "Yes." "Were you then a small boy at Eton ?" "Yes," he said, very surprised. "Did you know my father ?" "Yes, I did," I replied. "In 1916 I was Literary Editor of the *Liverpool Post*. One evening your father had a dinner party at which I was a guest. After dinner in his sitting-room he asked me if I would play the piano. I sat down and began an *Étude* of Chopin's but soon stopped. There was a silver photograph frame on the piano, containing the photo of a boy of about twelve. The frame rattled so much I asked my host if I might have it removed. He came to the piano and said 'Certainly—that's my boy at Eton,' showing me the photo. I never saw your father again, moving to London. Today I have recognised you—the boy on the piano."

They were, of course, astonished that I should now identify him, a grown man, after nearly forty years. I invited them to the palazzo for coffee. Before they left they extracted a promise that when in England I would visit them at their home, Brocket Hall, in Hertfordshire. "Wasn't that once the home of Caroline Lamb, enamoured of Byron?" I enquired. "Yes, and later Lord Melbourne, and Lord Palmerston lived and died there." I said I would visit them with great pleasure. They went on their journey. Eight years would pass before I could keep my promise.

I was leading a halcyon life. For six months my inveterate enemy had not laid me low. I was writing easily, in all the excitement of an opening spring. The flower beds in the Piazza below me were in full bloom. I lunched al fresco on my terrace, and had a series of guests from England and America. The view from the terrace was entrancing. I looked over the palms, trees and flowers of the Piazza, the red-tiled town, the wide amphitheatre of the mountains and the roofs of buildings on the left side of the Piazza. I had a view of the blue sea with, at certain times, Corsica visible on the horizon. Sometimes the moon shone above the bay, laying a silver path over the water, and I could see the fishing boats by Cape Mele, in a floating crescent of lights.

Immediately below me, on a corner of the Piazza there was a small hotel. I often watched its life with amusement. One morning, when I went on to the terrace for breakfast, the whole town in early sunshine, I noticed some scaffolding being erected in front of the hotel. I thought it was for repairs but on the fourth day the scaffolding became ominous. It had reached the hotel roof and was continuing.

I had a shock when I learned that another storey was to be added to the building. This meant that my sea-view would be cut off. I was told not to be alarmed. There was a local by-law that prohibited any building in the Piazza being higher than four storeys. Within a month it became clear that the hotel was adding a fifth. I invoked the law without result. I learned that builders often added another storey, paid the fine, and kept it! Not only was I likely to have my sea-view cut off but there was the menace of having the hotel washing put out to dry on the new roof. At some cost I got an injunction against this. Even so, my paradise had a flaw, and despite the fact that three-quarters of my panorama was intact, the obstruction entailed a permanent loss of view. It was like a mole on a beautiful face.

I was in Vienna in mid-June. I did not stay this time in the old König von Ungarn hotel, just behind the cathedral. I had formerly parked my car under an outside altar where Mozart's funeral service had been held at 3 p.m. on December 5th, 1791. He had died at 1 a.m. that morning, penniless. It cost money to have a service inside the Domkirche. Then, in a snowstorm, with not a mourner to follow, he was hurried to an unidentifiable pauper's grave in the churchyard of St. Marx. Mozart's home, now a memorial museum, was next door to the König von Ungarn which, in better days, had been the haunt of officials at the Court.

This time I went to a pension recommended by a friend. It was good and cheap enough, with board and lodging at twenty-five shillings a day, but my rest was disturbed by the early morning gargling of a man next door. When I made a protest the landlady looked on me with horror. The man in the next room was the great Dietrich Fischer-Dieskau who was singing at the Opera House. He was tuning-up. It sounded a fearful business and I had my room changed.

I had arrived in Vienna for the P.E.N. Conference and found friends there, Charles Morgan, Alec Waugh, Louis Golding and Leila Williamson. There was a reception at the lovely Schönbrunn Palace. Shades of the unhappy Duke of Reichstadt, whose deathbed is a relic! I reflected that had the son of Napoleon lived he might have caused a lot of trouble, as is the way with claimants to lost thrones.

My young protégé, Günther Bauer, was now making progress as

an actor, getting good rôles. He took me to see him act in a Zuckmayer comedy at the Deutsches Theatre, young, handsome, enthusiastic and excited with life. His father, the Salzburg lawyer, was placated by his studying for a degree at the university. It was clear that the theatre would win. Excitedly he showed me the room he had furnished, his very own, in an old courtyard bright with flowers. He was writing a play. I bought him a typewriter as a housewarming gift.

John Gielgud was in Vienna with Peggy Ashcroft. They were playing in *King Lear*. I took Günther behind afterwards and introduced him. Gielgud was his invariable gracious self.

One morning as I was dressing, Günther rushed in. He was excited because he had seen in a bookshop on the corner of the Kärntnerstrasse a copy of *Portal to Paradise*, in English. A book written in Italy, published in England, on sale in Austria! This seemed to him to be visible fame. I bought him a copy and took him to lunch. He had finished his play. One day, perhaps, it would be produced. (It was.) We ate in the Stadtpark, off the Ring. An orchestra played in a bower of flowers, the sun shone and we sat under coloured umbrellas. We were surrounded by happy families, and I was struck once more by the beauty of these Austrian girls, with their blue eyes, wavy light-brown hair, and a piquancy of dress and manner that made them appear as if they were all starring in a musical comedy. It might have been *Das Alte Wien*, had they had officer-escorts in gay uniforms. I looked at Günther's eager face. To be young, to be ambitious, was a wonderful thing. I had once been like that. He brought back a lost springtime. He had great news for me. He was engaged! Later, at a café in the Graben, we met. Dolores was a tall, beautiful girl, who had taken her degree at the university and was working on a newspaper as a journalist.

On a Sunday morning I went with an Austrian friend, Rudi Sommer, to a performance of the Lippizaner horses in the Spanish Riding School. Afterwards Colonel Podhajsky, the commandant, showed us round and we drank a glass of wine at a table in a stall, with his horse looking on. Then Rudi, the soul of gaiety, invited me to have tea with his mother, a piece of Meissen china, beautiful, Viennese to her finger tips.

That July, all the old operettas were trotted out, *Zigeuner Baron*,

Fledermaus, Lustige Witwe. The most memorable of all was a performance in the open courtyard of the Schönbrunn Palace of *Der Vogelhändler,* on a starry, warm evening. I went to eleven performances of ballet, opera and operetta. Straus and Strauss got into one's blood.

I motored out to Mayerling, always fascinated with the Crown Prince Rudolph-Vetsera affair. I saw where the tragedy had taken place, but not the actual shooting lodge, for the Emperor Franz-Josef had had the place demolished, and a small chapel built on the site. In a hillside cemetery was the grave of the ill-fated, foolish little Marie Vetsera. To think that Sir Shane Leslie's father had once danced with her in London!

My Vienna sojourn was made very agreeable by my friend, Lieutenant-Colonel William Ballance, who was *en poste* with the Allied Commission for Austria. I went with him one morning to the Hofburg Platz. The city was still occupied by French, English, American and Russian troops. We witnessed the changeover of the Russian and French forces. What surprised me was the smallness of the Russian soldiers, and their untidy uniforms and clumsy boots. For some reason I had expected sternly disciplined giants. Naturally they were not popular with the Viennese, and all fraternisation was forbidden. An ugly Russian statue dominated Stalinplatz, a square that had been named for the dictator. After the ceremony we went to a cocktail party in the Allied Headquarters. Officers from the four armies were there. They were punctiliously polite to each other. Perhaps they all wished to be elsewhere, for here they were, sitting on the chests of the Austrians ten years after the close of hostilities. By error I rushed one day into the Imperial Hotel and found I had run into the Iron Curtain, guarded by bayonets. It was the Russian Headquarters!

One evening my friend took me to visit an American, Miss Mores. She was lodging in a wing of a house on the bank of the Danube. There was a large writing-desk in the sitting-room. It had an engraved brass plate recording that at that desk Franz Lehar had written *The Merry Widow, The Count of Luxembourg, The Gipsy Baron* and *The Land of Smiles.* I was in the house he had shared with his brother, General Lehar. There was a private chapel cut through two floors. A steep vaulted stairway led down to a garden on the bank of the river. It was lined on both sides with the playbills of the First Nights of Lehar's operas in all parts of the world. After seven weeks of Viennese gaiety I drove back via Tarvisio and the lovely Friulian Alps to Alassio. Here a pleasant letter awaited me. *Portal to Paradise* had been reprinted twice.

On an August day I was called up by Lord Iliffe. He was not at Monte Carlo but at Roquebrune. "I've bought a villa here. Come over to lunch tomorrow. I want you to see it". Whatever Tod Illiffe did was usually worthwhile. The onset of old age in no way diminished his enterprise. As he was building a winter home for himself in Nassau, Bahamas, what did he want with a villa in Roquebrune? I motored over the next day and had my breath taken away when I arrived at the Villa Egerton, hung on the cliffside, with terraced gardens going down to the beach. It had a magnificent view across the bay to Monte Carlo. When in Nassau last winter Tod, as we all called him, had received a cable from his son, Langton, who had just seen this villa at Roquebrune for sale, including the furniture. It was an executor's sale. The price was £17,000. Should he buy it? Yes, replied Tod. So here it was. What did I think of it? I said I would not have been surprised had he paid £100,000 for it. It was a jewel. He showed me over the villa. It was very well furnished. "The furniture alone is worth what you've paid for the place," I said. "Oh, no!" he replied, "£17,000 for the furniture?" "Have you had it valued?" I asked. "No."

The villa had a big glassed-in salon, like the prow of a ship sailing down the Mediterranean. There was something Medicean about Tod. He had a country mansion, Yattendon Court, with its covered tennis court, and swimming pool, and terraces looking over the Berkshire hills. He had a house on the beach at Nassau. He had a yacht; and now a villa at Roquebrune. With all this he was the quietest and simplest of men. I stayed to lunch and dinner and motored back to Alassio in a golden dusk, a large harvest moon rising out of the sea. Rounding Cape Mele there was a view below of Alassio, a half-circle of silver lights along its promenade. Such beauty; I stopped the car on the downward road to contemplate my good fortune in living in this paradise.

Ten days later Tod rang again. "I want you to come over to lunch, I've something to tell you." So I went. His eyes twinkled when I had descended the steep stairs down into the hall. "Were you ever in the antique furniture business?" he asked. "Never!" I replied, surprised by his question. He pulled a folded paper out of his pocket. "You estimated the value of the furniture at what I had paid for the whole house, £17,000. I've had a valuer in. Here's the figure. £17,600." I looked at the inventory. "Those executors must have been crazy!" I commented. "Executors of a rich man's estate often are crazy," said Tod. "They just want to get the thing off their hands. The victim isn't there to protest!" We joined his wife, Charlotte, in the observation salon. Langton and his pretty wife arrived. We went in to lunch. "Would you set me up in an antique business?" I asked. "I would set you up in any business, my boy," Tod replied.

XV

At the beginning of September I left for London and stayed in Queen's Gate. One morning the housekeeper announced that there was a clergyman downstairs who wished to see me. I found a very frail old gentleman in a clerical collar. He apologised for calling but he had just read *The Remarkable Young Man*. He told me how much he had enjoyed it and found it a wonderful portrait of Joseph Severn and his life in Rome after he had nursed John Keats on his death-bed there. I thanked him. "Are you particularly interested in Joseph Severn?" I asked. "Yes," he replied, gently, "I am the Reverend Henry Severn, his grandson." Somewhat shaken by this revelation, I invited the old gentleman up to my apartment for a drink. I lived two flights up and on arriving there I saw that he was frail and out of breath. I made him sit down and got him a glass of sherry, with-holding my questions. "A compliment coming from you is indeed a compliment," I said, after a pause. "It is most kind of you to call. May I ask, did you ever know your grandfather?" He smiled at my question. "I am eighty years old, I have just retired from my 'living', and am visiting a niece near here. I could not resist coming to call on you. My grandfather, Joseph Severn, about whom I don't think I can tell you anything you do not already know, died in 1879. I was an infant then, in England. He lived in Rome and died there. Alas, I never saw him."

We talked for three-quarters of an hour. He asked me how I contrived to know so much about his grandfather, more than he had ever learned elsewhere. I told him that I had spent many months visiting almost every place in Rome where Severn had lived after Keats died. I made some hundred pages of notes before I began to write my novel. "I felt that perhaps too much of my labour had gone for nothing. But today you have made me feel that it was all worth it," I said.

I escorted the old gentleman downstairs and got him a taxi. I never saw him again. He lived another ten years, dying at ninety. Longevity seemed to be in the Severn family. His grandfather had lived to be eighty-six, active until almost the end. He had lived frugally, with a faithful Italian maid, in Rome, on a pension of £80 from the British Government as a retired Consul, and a Civil List pension of £60.

I had one more fan. On publication I had given a copy of my book to Max Beerbohm. He wrote—"Your historical novel has given me great pleasure and instruction. Severn's name had never been anything but a name to me but now I know all about him and greatly like him, and have, moreover, been having an exciting and delightful time in Rome of 100 years ago—all thanks to you and your recreative powers."

XVI

The drawback of foreign residence is that when you go home for a visit you rush madly around visiting old friends. I went to the Norman Birketts at Challens Green, Bucks, a house on the edge of a golf course; the library had a curved panorama window commanding a view of the Amersham valley; to Francis Jekyll, battling with his famous garden at Munstead, exhorted by the menacing shadow of Gertrude Jekyll. He knew everything about plants, but nothing about finance, and I spent my time there amid accounts and bank statements. He could not understand why the bank wrote figures in red ink. "Debit" and "Credit" were mysteries to him. He was the same delightful, infuriating Timmy who in Venice years ago had given a party for a sham Titian he had bought with what was "a large dividend on some Japanese Bonds", to discover later that it was not a dividend but the repayment of capital. I wondered why it was that one's incompetent friends were often the most lovable.

I went to stay with Brigadier Williamson, a tall, rumbling, warm-hearted man who lived in a wind-blown white house on the edge of the estuary at West Wittering. His wife, Leila, who was "Eve Orme", retreated upstairs to write a new novel, after she had peeled potatoes and got the pressure-cooker going. They were both crazed by their daughter, fragile, lovely Mary, who worked in a flower shop in Bond Street, in which the most beautiful flower seemed to be herself. Despairing beaux trailed her. When she went to New York for a time, working for Constance Spry, she was followed by more suitors. There was a quiet young man, devoted and persistent, Lord Nicholas Gordon-Lennox. One Sunday morning Mary and I walked along a sea-wall, haunted with sailing boats. I warned her that the loveliest roses wilt in time and are not forever for plucking. She laughed her golden laughter, heedless.

That summer I did a lot of talking, speaking at the Women's Press Club, with Lady Georgina Coleridge in the chair, an appro-priate name for a literary occasion, and at The Lunch Club, with Lord David Cecil in the chair, and yet again at Harrods for one of their Book Teas organised by their librarian, Cadness Page. Lady "Polly" Monckton, to whom I was furniture-repairer-in-chief, gave one of her Cadogan Gardens lunches. Among the guests were Sir Neville Pearson, President of St. Dunstan's for the Blind, dainty Dorothy Dickson, and my hostess's son, Gilbert Monckton, the youngest Major-General in the British Army. How did Polly cook a lunch for twelve, with only an odd woman coming in, and show not the slightest sign of effort ?.

I visited my old colleague, Sir Philip Gibbs at Shamley Green. A widower, a little man with gimlet eyes and a deep voice. He was the soul of sincerity and nobility of mind, undismayed by recent events, a Sir Galahad among scribes. Verging on eighty he was still busy at his typewriter. "My boy, if I don't write a novel this year I can't pay last year's income-tax!" His eyesight failing, he had typed part of a book a line too high on his typewriter and had to have the manu-script transposed to lower keys, like a musician.

I gave some lunches in my club restaurant, overlooking the trees and lawns of Carlton House Gardens, before the view and the sylvan scene were destroyed by a concrete pigeoncote of offices with a sense-less pool buried at its base, an architectural gimmick. It was on the site of a house Gladstone had lived in. Polly Monckton, Rafaelle, Duchess of Leinster, Stella Gates, no more migrant St. Helena servants in her life, and John Betjeman, hurried and diverting as always, formed my lunch quintet.

In mid-November I went to my native Nottingham to raise ghosts. Now in "The Distinguished Old Boy" category, I was asked to distribute prizes at my old Grammar School. Over two thousand were present in the Albert Hall, from whose platform I had made my first speech as a parliamentary candidate thirty-three years earlier. I had a shock when a small boy, receiving a prize, said "My father sends you his compliments, sir." "Oh, do I know your father?" "Yes, sir. You gave him his prize, in 1927." Dear me, so I was that old! Would I live to be giving them to the grandchildren?

On that evening I took a neat revenge. I had never won a school prize. The only thing in which I had excelled was the General Intelligence paper, in which I scored four consecutive firsts. For this no prize was given. It riled me to see numskulls walk off with piles of prizes just because they had sponge-brains that could suck up information and squeeze it out on examination papers. I announced that, with the consent of the Governors, I was founding a new prize. I had given them £2,000 for annual travel prizes for the two leaders in an Intelligence Paper. I was well rewarded by the most astonishing letters from them. It was amazing what they accomplished in Europe with some fifty pounds each.

At the beginning of December I left for Cap d'Antibes. For once a thick London fog gave me pleasure. They had become so rare, with something nostalgic about them. I stepped out into brilliant sunshine from the Blue Train the next morning. I stayed four sad days in Casa Estella. My hostess, failing, lay on a chaise-longue before the window overlooking the sea. There was all that wealth could give her, which was nothing. Sometimes she was conscious, sometimes not. After four days with much heartache I went on to Alassio where I spent Christmas. It was incredibly warm. On Christmas Eve, with a full moon over the bay, we dined in candlelight on the terrace. The streets below me were bright with Christmas lanterns. A giant fir tree in the Piazza was festooned with sparkling little globes. I went to the parish church. Everyone seemed to be present for the midnight Mass. A decorated manger was illuminated, the altar sparkled with candles. The priests were in their embroidered vestments, the acolytes were robed in white and red. At the *Gloria in Excelsis* an old shepherd from the hills appeared in the open west door. He slowly walked down the nave, up to the altar. He carried in his arms a newborn lamb. The eyes of the little creature shone in its woolly white head. While the shepherd knelt the priest blessed the lamb. Then, without word or gesture, the shepherd turned and walked down the nave through the great door, out into the night. He would carry the lamb up into the hills, returning it to the flock which shared the blessing it had received. In the church they sang a special carol, originally set to shepherds' pipes.

I went home through the illuminated streets. Going out on to my terrace I looked down upon Alassio. The clear sky was spangled with stars. A light breeze came from the calm bay. The bells rang their Christmas tidings from the campanile. I recalled how I had heard other bells, out of the past, the bells of Westminster Abbey, by radio, in my old Chiltern cottage, where the fire burned cheerily and the candles in the silver candelabra cast a soft light on the Christmas fare spread beneath the old beams, while outside the poplars swayed in my garden, netting a misty moon. The heartache for old lost things of beauty seized me momentarily. And so to bed.

CHAPTER EIGHT

Vienna, Geneva, Nassau

I

On the last day of December, 1955, I was Lady Norman's guest again for New Year's Eve. This time I was not in the Château but in the small villa, the Clos, down on the inner harbour. New Year's day has been perfect with crystal air, a hot sun, a cloudless blue sky and the Maritime Alps glistening with their mantle of snow. Roses and mimosas were in bloom, the oranges hung golden on the trees. From the upper gardens there was a magnificent view, over the roof of the Clos low-lying by the Garoupe bay, of the pinewooded promontory of Antibes crowned by a lighthouse. During the war the Germans had built a block-house adjoining The Clos, mined the whole of the little bay, and laid a chain barrier, fastened to concrete pylons. Nevertheless, a British submarine would enter this harbour and from it, under cover of night, a man would swim ashore bringing money and radios wrapped in oilskins for the members of the French Resistance. On one occasion, making the return journey, he could not find the submarine so the commander took the enormous risk of turning on his light to aid the man in the water. None of the German sentries saw the light and the submarine got away. And now, on New Year's Day, 1956, I sat writing in a window of the Clos, overlooking the scene of this exploit.

The next morning I motored with Fay around the estate. At the Château there were 2,000 pieces of linen which she checked. She told me that on the terrace one day, many years ago, a tenant, Mme Pulitzer, had given an evening party and Pavlova had danced before four kings. A man with blocks of ice had stood by to check any overheating of the electricity cables. Fay had built two houses for her sons, the Folie and the Tourelle. The latter was on a site on which had stood a Napoleonic battery. It was marked with a tablet. In the evening we dined at The Clocher with Antony and his pretty wife Anne. It had a large salon with long windows.

One day we went to lunch with Barry Diercks and Eric Sawyer, architects well known and esteemed along the coast for thirty years. They lived in a house at Point de L'Equillon, vertiginously perched on a red cliff over the sea, with a view of the Golfe de Napoule. Among the lunch guests were Princess Maria Pia of Italy and her husband Prince Alexander of Yugoslavia. She was the daughter of ex-King Umberto II. She had a head of black curls and bore a striking resemblance to one of those Byzantine mosaics seen in St. Vitalis at Ravenna. She might have been a reincarnation of a Byzantine Empress. Talking with her, I found she was an ardent admirer of the novels of D. H. Lawrence. She was intensely interested when I was able to give her an account of his Nottinghamshire background and of early events in his life there. Her husband was tall and handsome. They had two small sons, twins.

While motoring home Fay pointed out the Villa Garibondy which Diercks and Sawyer were altering for a new owner, Mr. Douglas, brother of the American ex-Ambassador to the Court of St. James. When the war broke out it was occupied by a Miss Paget, an elderly spinster, related to the famous hero of Waterloo known as "One-Leg Anglesey", he having lost a leg and buried it there. The French warned Miss Paget of the approach of the Germans. She refused to move out. When they arrived and found themselves confronted by a determined old lady they thought the best thing was to give her the opportunity to escape. She declined to escape and said she had every intention of staying in her villa, "on my own terms". Startled, they asked what they were. "That you allow me to fly the British flag from the roof." They gave her permission and she stayed on in the villa flying the Union Jack until the Liberation.

II

In March I motored from Alassio to Rome. En route I arrived at the Villino Chiaro about eleven o'clock one morning. I had not warned Max of a call so I did not ring his bell, but stealthily went up to the door and hung on it a tin of the Earl Grey Mixture which I knew he liked. I got a reproachful note from Elizabeth saying I should have rung the bell, Max was very disappointed. How I wish now that I had! When I returned at the end of the month I learned that Max was in hospital. Elizabeth Jungmann had gone into Rapallo that morning. I was aware of confusion and anxiety. I left a card and went on to Alassio. The next day I was called on the telephone by Elizabeth. Max was very ill in hospital and could not receive visitors. She had news for me. Yesterday she had been privately married to him. I said I was happy to hear this. Alas, I was about to leave for Spain to see my publisher.

I went to Barcelona with my friend Ballance. My publisher had good news. All my twelve translated books were selling well. After a few days we went on to Palma, Majorca. It was the time of the Easter festivities and we witnessed the bearing of palms in the cathedral. My main purpose in visiting Majorca was to see the Carthusian monastery at Valdemosa, where Chopin had spent the winter of 1838–9, with George Sand, her son, daughter and maid. I had been a Chopin lover since a boy of fourteen when I had been entranced by a recital given by Vladimir de Pachmann. From that moment I was a Chopin addict. I learned to play his music. I journeyed to all the Chopin shrines I could find. I had visited the Château de Nohant where he had spent the summers, composing, dominated by Madame Sand until the unhappy break with her. In 1929, in Poland, I had been to his birthplace at Zelazowa Wola, and to the church of St. Croix in Warsaw, where his ashes are enshrined in a pillar.

When he came to England in 1848 he was already a dying man. He played in Manchester and Glasgow, and in Edinburgh, where he collapsed, complaining bitterly of the cold. In London he played at a Guildhall concert for Polish charities, and in the drawing-rooms of Lady Blessington at Gore House, and of the Duchess of Sutherland at Stafford House. He gave two morning concerts, for which the tickets were a guinea each, at Lady Falmouth's in St. James's Square and at Mrs. Sartoris's at 99 Eaton Place. He had to be carried upstairs but played with much vivacity. He died the next year, aged thirty-nine, in Paris. He was given a great funeral at the Church of the Madeleine, crowded with the élite of Paris, when Mozart's

Requiem Mass was sung and the *Marche Funèbre*, played. Theophile Gautier wrote an account of it for the Press.

Soon after arrival at Valdemosa in November, 1838, the Sand ménage was compelled to leave the house in which they first lodged. The owner said Chopin was consumptive and ordered them out. They had to pay for their rooms to be disinfected. The monastery to which they went was beautifully situated, commanding a verdant valley, but the low white building was grim, and one realised how much the ailing Chopin must have suffered from the cold and the ceaseless rain. The Customs held up his piano for three months. Nevertheless, he composed two Preludes, the *Ballade in F Major*, the *Polonaise in C minor* and a *Scherzo*. They reflect the melancholy that engulfed him but enriched the world of music.

The monastery is now a Chopin shrine. Three large tourist buses arrived while I was there in 1956. The terrace-garden, on to which Chopin's room opened, was now full of spring flowers and almond trees in pink blossom.

We stayed at a good hotel in Palma, at the ludicrous price of thirty shillings all in per day. Evidently Spain was the place to live. I could have bought myself a beautiful ten-roomed villa on the sea coast, two miles out of the town, for £8,000. Spain had not been "discovered" and was not yet swarming with charter-plane package tourists. But I had my own place at Alassio, and many friends there, so I did not buy.

In May, after my return to Alassio, I learned that Max Beerbohm had died in hospital in Rapallo, aged eighty-three. Just before he lapsed into unconsciousness his last words were *Grazie per tutto*— "Thank you for everything", a final gesture of his natural courtesy. The deathbed marriage had had an economic purpose. He had wished to leave the Villino to Elizabeth Jungmann. There would have been an exorbitant estate tax had it been left to one with no relationship. Since Max had no near relations, which Italian law takes care of, the inheritance for the widow was clear and the tax nominal.

Max was cremated and his ashes were sent to England. At a memorial service in St. Paul's Cathedral they were interred in the crypt, keeping company with Nelson and Wellington in the national pantheon. In a sale at Sotheby's Max's library fetched £26,654 for 383 items. American institutions were the chief buyers. Many of the books carried his barbed perversions of their illustrations and some wittily astringent mock prefaces. In a copy of Queen Victoria's *More Leaves from a Journal of Our Life in the Highlands,* he had written, imitating the Queen's handwriting: "For Mr. Max Beerbohm. The never-to-be sufficiently-studied writer whom Albert looks down on affectionately, I am sure. From his Sovereign, Victoria, R.I. Balmoral, 1898."

III

At the end of May I motored to Vienna. En route I called at Kitzbühel. It had been the scene of *Spears Against Us,* which had brought some publicity to it. During that period the Prince of Wales, soon to be Edward VIII, went there to ski. He took lessons from Count Lamberg, a champion skier, who was the original of the young count in the Schloss I had written about. His mother, faced with disastrous losses, in 1918, had turned her Schloss into a pension. I found it temporarily closed. It had become a flourishing pension and the count was building on a wing. I learned that he was living in a gardener's house up the lane. I called. He was excited when he discovered who I was. He introduced his wife. They had two young sons. Above the fireplace there was a triptych painting. The left panel held the count, the right the countess, in the middle panel were the two boys. "Was that painted by Baron Kurt Pantz?" I asked. "Good heavens, how do you know that?" cried the count, astonished. "He drew my portrait in New York in 1942. I recognise the style," I replied.

Arriving in Vienna I returned to the old Hotel König von Ungarn near the Stephanskirche, where I had stayed when I first visited the city. It had not then recovered from the war and the Russian occupation. My friends thought I had gone "slumming", but I loved it dearly. The bedroom doors still carried the names of the court officials at the Imperial Hofburg, and next to me was the bedroom Franz Schubert had once occupied. I could look out of my window into the sitting-room of Mozart's house next door, in which he had written *The Marriage of Figaro.* It was now a museum. On his birthday I threw from my window, into his, a tributary bunch of flowers.

It was very hot in Vienna. I lunched with Rudi Sommer in the Hofgarten. Vienna seemed buried in roses, and was full of music. I went to *Rosenkavalier, The Marriage of Figaro,* and the ballet *Giselle* at the New State Opera House. I lunched with Günther Bauer who was acting at the Berg Theatre. I ran into Yehudi Menuhin, playing in the Redoutensaal. Two nights later there was an excellent performance of Cimarosa's *The Marriage Broker,* which offset the grimness of *Turandot,* which I had seen the previous evening. Dr. Felix Schwarzenberg gave me lunch in a garden-restaurant in the park of Prince Eugene's Belvedere Palace. Behind us was a grim reminder of the war, the bombed site of Baron Eugene de Rothschild's house. I evoked from the ruins the ghost of Kitty Rothschild who had set all the young men of Vienna afire with her beauty.

At the Opera House one night Berg's *Der Sturm* proved too much for me. I walked out halfway. I am a great walker-out when I dislike a thing. Concerning this kind of music I agreed with Pablo Casals:

> Modern music is a language no one understands. The word "music" is misused. The most I will concede is that modern music is an art made with sound but it is definitely not music. Why invent a new language which nobody understands, when the masters all spoke the same language? The public does not like to listen to this stuff, neither do I.

Unfortunately, it is too often inflicted upon us. I have seen a beautiful ballet, *Romeo and Juliet,* ruined by Prokofiev's cacophonous score. I am, of course, ignorant, and out of the fashion!

Before leaving Vienna I went to look at the new tenements built by the Socialist Government. They were well-planned, well-built. In the reign of Franz-Josef there was an aristocracy indifferent to the appalling poverty of the working-class. It had taken two crushing wars to reverse their positions.

On the morning that I left Vienna Rudi Sommer called with some flowers as a farewell gift, in the Austrian manner. He begged me to return next year. He had once stayed at Pilgrim Cottage. Just over thirty, he possessed all the Viennese élan. A year later I was shocked to hear that he had committed suicide, for no known reason. A love affair? I thought of his devoted mother.

I motored across Austria and returned to England via Bad Ischl and Baden-Baden. The beauty of the latter place induced me to stay a week. The grounds of my hotel went down to the canalised river that ran in a series of little waterfalls through the leafy Lichtenthaler Allee. There was a nineteenth-century Kursaal, a birdcage-like bandstand where an orchestra in frogged uniforms played rumty-tumty music, with a heavy proportion of Strauss and Lehar. From Baden-Baden I went to Heidelberg and finally to Le Touquet. The British Channel crossing had always been a nightmare to me, a shocking sailor, but that horror was now wiped out. I flew with my car in about half an hour to Lydd airport and thence to London.

In 1956 the P.E.N. held a reception for the delegates to its International Congress in the great upstairs drawing-room at Lancaster House, the former home of the Duke and Duchess of Sutherland. "I have come from my house to your palace," said Queen Victoria to the duchess, making a call. I looked down the long drawing-room wondering just where the piano had stood when, in 1848, Chopin had given a recital there.

I restricted my engagements. I had begun work on a new novel, *Love is Like That*. Halfway through the novel I ran out of invention. I went to spend my customary annual week-end with the Norman Birketts at Challens Green, Chalfont St. Giles. Norman and "Billy" were a devoted pair, full of kindness, some of which they lavished on me. We had been friends for thirty-three years. Norman was now a Lord Justice of Appeal. "When you two get together, it's like watching a steeplechase," said Billy, who would stop us towards midnight with bedtime Ovaltine. I told Norman that I had dried up. In his long career at the Bar he must have had many singular experiences. Which had been the most harrowing? "Can you give me something that will supply me with an episode for my novel?" I asked. "Let me think it over," he replied. Towards noon the next day, as we walked in the garden overlooking the golf course, he said, "I think my saddest experience was a murder case. As you know, I've had to deal with quite a lot of murders, often as defending counsel. There was one case of a mother charged with murdering her mongoloid child, to which she was deeply devoted. A mercy-killing, she was condemned but reprieved. I defended her." Norman gave me details of the case. I had got my new episode. When I had written it I sent him the manuscript to check. He replied, "You've got it all correct, there is hardly a detail to alter. It's aroused all the emotion I felt at the time." I thus found the material for the tragic story of Mrs. Callender in *Love Is Like That*.

The following week-end I stayed with a friend who owned Seyton Manor, an Elizabethan house near Chequers, the great mansion presented to our Prime Ministers for a country retreat. The custodian there, a former secretary to Winston Churchill, Mrs. Kathleen Hill, was our friend. She had a beautiful sitting-room overlooking the grounds. One day when I lunched with her she took me up into the Long Gallery, whose stained glass windows carried the heraldic arms of all the Prime Ministers who had stayed there. She brought out of the safe the historic ring which had belonged to Queen Elizabeth. When you pressed a catch the lid opened revealing inside a miniature of Ann Boleyn, her tragic mother. This was the ring that on Queen Elizabeth's death had been sent to Scotland to James VI in token of his succession to the English throne.

One Sunday morning there was an urgent telephone call from Chequers. The house was full. It was during the early days of the Suez Canal crisis, and Churchill had come to lunch with Anthony Eden, the Prime Minister. Kathleen was short of one peach. Winston liked peaches. Could we send one over at once? So we motored up to Chequers with a peach. It was an amusing episode. Policemen in guard boxes were on duty at the main gate and down the long drive. Evidently they had been informed and the peach-bearer's car proceeded to the house without a hitch, the crisis solved.

There was a small library at Chequers, with beautiful portraits on the panelled walls, as elsewhere. This room was used as an office by the Prime Minister. A white telephone lay on the desk. "Pick it up," said Kathleen, one day. I did so. A voice spoke, "Number 10 Downing Street.' It was a private direct line. What momentous conversations had passed over it!

One morning in August, just as I was about to leave to stay with the Everard Gates, at Hurtwood, Ewhurst, I received a cable that threw a deep shadow over me. Beatrice Cartwright had died after her long illness, at Casa Estella, Cap d'Antibes. I had been over to see her frequently, so that her death was not unexpected. What wonderful hospitality she had dispensed at Palm Beach, in New

York and at Cap d'Antibes. She had had four husbands, three children and a large fortune, her zest for life undiminished, extravagant, elegant, kind-hearted. So another door had closed forever in my life.

IV

I left England in October, motoring to Geneva to stay with Dr. Antoine Cloetta at his Château de Vernier, high on a cliff above the River Rhone. From the terrace you could see, over the ridge of the distant woods, the silver spear of the great *jet d'eau* on the Lake at Geneva. Below the château the river made a loop in the plain between us and the *massif* of the Grand Salève. There was a house party, and one evening after dinner I read to them the first episode from *Love Is Like That*. I was now three-quarters through the novel. After a few days I continued on my journey via Modane, Grenoble, Avignon and through Cap d'Antibes to Alassio. It grieved me to pass Casa Estella.

I had let my palazzo for the winter and stayed with my friend Mrs. Alida Bock at her Villino Romano. It was one of the many fast disappearing villas in Alassio. Lovely houses and old gardens were being ruthlessly demolished to make way for concrete skyscraper apartments, one blocking the view of the other. In three years I had seen twenty villas with splendid gardens reduced to rubble. Alida Bock loved her villa, with its palm trees and rose hedges, but she knew it was doomed. The skyscrapers were shutting her in. Dutch by birth, she had had a varied career, and was a great lover of England. When the Germans occupied Belgium in the First World War, a young trained nurse, she had crossed the Channel, and nursed wounded Belgian soldiers in a Bournemouth hospital. She was pretty and vivacious. A Scotsman, of an old family, fell in love with her, and, a young bride, knowing very little English, she found herself in the midst of the Scottish landed gentry. She was rather overwhelmed when she first met her husband's cousin, the Duchess of Atholl. "But I don't know how to call you. Do I say Duchess?" "No," replied the duchess, "you just call me Kitty!" They lived in their property near the Firth of Forth. One day a lady was announced. The young bride went into the drawing-room straight from the kitchen where she was cooking, "I've come to call on you," announced the stranger, beautifully dressed. "Oh, yes, what about?" asked Alida, surprised. The elderly lady smiled. "My dear, it is usual to call on newcomers to the district—it's a social custom which is known as 'calling'," she explained.

The stone mansion proved too large and too cold. They sold the place and emigrated to the South of France, and later settled in Alassio. Her husband died, and she remarried, this time a retired Dutch tea-planter. They had been interned during the Second World War in Boccaccio's home town, Tuscan Certaldo, along with some British internees, all of them in a state of near penury. The war over, the Bocks went back to their Alassio villa. I had just come to know this hospitable couple when the husband died. She kept open house and was loved by everybody, a good linguist, with all the virtues of Dutch housekeeping. There was a stream of Dutch and Scottish relations, the more the merrier. She often took charge of Palazzo Vairo during my absence.

I finished *Love Is Like That* at the Villino Romano, in a small garden-study bowered in wistaria, roses and plumbago, a perfect retreat. From the outside world came news of the Suez Canal imbroglio, mismanaged by Eden who was forced by Eisenhower to withdraw from his adventure. Eden, crushed, resigned the premiership. Years of unrest in the Mediterranean would follow this débâcle, unrest that would breed future wars between Egypt and Israel.

I had heard some time earlier of Günther Bauer's forthcoming marriage to his Dolores. A letter arrived with an account of the wedding and some photographs. I was sorry to have missed it, a very Austrian affair at Gmunden in the Salzkammergut. The happy couple walked across a bridge to the church of Schloss Orth on the lake, with little bridesmaids holding posies.

v

At the end of December I was again at Lady Norman's Château de la Garoupe. Not a mile away was Casa Estella, closed and silent. One day lunching at Eric Dunstan's domain at Morgins-Sartout, I found there ex-King Peter of Yugoslavia and his wife Alessandra. They were living in a two-roomed apartment near Nice, she doing the cooking. The American experiment had failed. It is bad enough to be impoverished, but to be impoverished with a royal status round one's neck is a double misfortune.

On the last day of 1956 Lady Norman and I lunched again at M. Goldman's Domaine, where something incredible happened. He had some house guests, among them three ladies and a gentleman who were Hungarians. They had recently succeeded in getting out of communist Hungary. They had arrived in Cannes with almost no clothes. M. Goldman took them into Nice and fitted them out. The man of the party had spent four years in gaol in Budapest.

My Hungarian friend, Baron Jancsi Wolfner had often entertained me in that city. He had escaped at the end of the war and visited me at Pilgrim Cottage. His money in an English bank was still sequestrated. Penniless, he decided to go back to Budapest, thinking things would get better. He was thrown into gaol by the Communists and his property was confiscated. We heard no more of him. I now asked this guest if by any chance he had known Wolfner and could give me any news. He stared at me in amazement. "We shared the same cell for over two years. When we were released together he refused to leave the prison. Poor fellow, his nerves are quite shattered, and he fears the world outside." I felt something must be done. I enlisted the help of my friend George Maddocks, who had often been his guest, and spoke Magyar. We began wire-pulling. In four months, in May, 1957, we got Wolfner out of gaol, over the frontier, and safe in the London he loved.

VI

For some time I had made excursions to the country behind Alassio. There were romantic-looking villages in these Ligurian mountains. On my way by car to England I often went via the San Bernardo Pass that led down into the Piedmont plain and distant Turin. Amid olive groves and cypresses, little villages clustered on the precipitous cliffs. It seemed that they might slide down the mountain at any time. They were all ancient. The olive groves had originally been cultivated by retired Roman soldiers who had settled there. They had built, on dizzy heights, little fortresses against marauding Saracens who came up the Mediterranean. Picturesque they were, but close inspection of these villages. with their delightful baroque churches and slender bell towers, proved fatal. They were mostly dilapidated hovels from which the inhabitants had vanished, leaving only a few crones, decrepit old men and poor priests. The young men had all departed, to take their chance in the fabulous United States, or in Germany and France where they earned good wages. The young women had gone down to work in the factories or hotels on the coast, where they had congenial company, and boys to dance with in cafés at night. Grandmother and grandfather were left derelict. The houses were dark and cold, with no sanitation. We used to visit the old parents of Alida Bock's maid in their mountain village. With only a bare table, rough chairs and a bed they showed us rare courtesy. A chair was wiped and a bottle of wine was brought by the toothless old pair. I gave the old man a Savile Row suit that fitted him like a glove. He made a parade in it every Sunday morning to the church and piazza. He had aristocratic features. No hidalgo ever looked prouder. His daughter, our maid, had the bearing and features of a Roman duchess. Soon there will be no olive groves, cultivated through a thousand years. A storm comes, the soil moves, the dry-stone retaining walls burst, and the terraced groves slide down the mountainside, with no one to rebuild the walls. In summer the villages look idyllic, at a distance; in winter they are shut off, through bitter days and long cold nights.

The route to the San Bernardo pass ran up the mountain valley from Alassio's ancient neighbour, Albenga, which had once been a busy Roman port, and later an important medieval town of many towers. The communal palace was built in A.D. 1300. There was a cathedral with a fifth century octagonal baptistry. The walled town had narrow streets, with ancient Gothic-windowed palaces, still occupied by old families. It had known Queen Isabella of Aragon and Francis I of France, on his way to the disastrous battle of Pavia. Napoleon had made it a headquarters during his march into Italy in 1796. But this ancient town was associated with another great conqueror. In 205 B.C. Mago, the brother of Hannibal, landed troops there, going to the relief of his brother. The town had been thronged with dark Numidian soldiers, twelve thousand strong, and earth-shaking elephants. Hannibal had come out of Spain, crossed the Alps and, hard pressed, had waited in northern Italy for reinforcements. Mago marched up over the San Bernardo Pass. In battle he was defeated, gravely wounded and carried back to his galley in Albenga. It dodged the Roman fleet but Mago died on the voyage to Carthage. I never drove up the narrow Neva valley, down which a torrential stream poured, without thinking of those Carthaginians and dark Numidians who had taken the road to the Pass.

There were old villages up the valley, with high-perched castles on gaunt summits. After little Cisano-sul-Neva came the walled, arcaded town of Zuccarello, built over its river, and then, higher up, Castelvecchia, with a gaunt, half-ruined castle on the summit. It was for sale. Tempted, I looked at it. The panorama was immense but you cannot live on a view. The end of the road up to the castle was only a mule track. A miserable peasant family lived in the half-ruin.

It was in this valley of the Neva that I often saw, built on a ledge across the river, a fourteenth-century castle with a battlemented tower. It was backed by a forest-covered mountain. One day motoring by with my friend Alida I remarked on its romantic character. "I wonder if anyone lives in it," I said. "Let's go and look," she replied. So we crossed the stream by a little bridge, mounted up through a straggling village, and came to a drive leading to a castle. The great gate was open. We drew up in a grassy forecourt. The castle was thronged with workmen covered in plaster. We walked in. A foreman there looked at the trespassers. We asked him whose place it was and its name. It was the Castello di Conscente. It was being renovated and modernised by the owner, who had just inherited it. What was the name of the owner? The Marchese Rolandi Ricci del Carretto. The white-dusted foreman was very affable and halted his work to show us over the castle. Before leaving we apologised for our intrusion. "My friend is a writer and interested in local history. We live in Alassio," said Alida. He asked our names. "Are you the author of *Portal to Paradise*?" he asked; I confessed I was. "I hope when the castle is finished you will come and see it," he said. "But we do not know the Marchese. Is he hospitable?" I asked. "I hope so. I am the Marchese, Rolandi Ricci," was the reply.

Thus started our friendship. The renovated castle was a showplace,

restored with exquisite taste down to the last detail. It was in one of
the vitrines there that I found Fabergé gold cigarette cases that had
belonged to my eccentric, ill-fated friend, Maurice Sandoz. There
was a fine old portrait of a Grand Master of the Knights of Malta,
Fabriano del Carretto, my host's kinsman. The Marchese had two
flags that he sometimes flew from the battlemented tower. You saw
them as your car crossed the bridge in the valley and mounted to
the castle. One was the flag of the Sovereign Order of the Knights
of Malta, a white star on a red ground, the other was the British
Union Jack flown in compliment to the Englishman coming to
lunch.

Luigi Rolandi Ricci, Marchese del Carretto e Lusignano, to give
him his resounding title, was a man of delightful gestures.

In the grounds of the castle there was an old fifteenth-century
house. He thought it would be nice to have my friend Alida and
me living near him, so he restored the place, and converted the
attic, which had been a pigeon loft, into a library for me. The flat
roof of the house had a fine view of the castle, and the surrounding
mountains. I put in some books but, alas, had too little time to spend
there. He wrote out, playfully, a transfer of the house to us, and
since I was an honorary citizen of Alassio he created Alida a "baroness
of Castello di Conscente". The coloured parchment was decorated
with the del Carretto and Lusignano seals.*

VII

One day soon after returning to Rome I lunched with the Swiss
Dr. Paul Niehans and his English wife at the Tre Scalini, a pleasant
little restaurant in the beautiful Piazza Navona, with its three
fountains. Its elliptical form conserves the shape of the original
circus of the Emperor Domitian. Neihans was one of the most
talked of physicians in the world, having invented cellular therapy
for the prolongation of life. He was at the moment attending Pope
Pius XII, with whom he was on confidential terms. Niehans was 6 feet
3 inches, seventy-five years of age, fresh complexioned, extremely

---

* Lusignano is a village, once a fief of Genoa. When the Republic held
James Lusignan, King of Cyprus, a hostage, one of his family settled there,
and the village took his name.

agile. He had Hohenzollern blood in him. His Swiss father was a surgeon who had married the daughter of an Italian countess who was the morganatic wife of the Crown Prince Frederick who later, in 1858, married Queen Victoria's daughter. In this manner Niehans was the grandson of the Emperor and the nephew of Kaiser Wilhelm II. His relationship was acknowledged by the Hohenzollern family. Niehans bore a remarkable resemblance to the Crown Prince Wilhelm, his cousin, and like him was tall and fair. His uncle, Kaiser Wilhelm, wished him to become a Staff officer in the Prussian Army but Niehans insisted on taking up medicine. In the First World War he served in the Dolomites and was wounded several times. He had specialised in endocrinology, studying under the Nobel prizewinner, Carrel.

When in Rome the Niehans stayed at the Grand Hotel and thus I had come to know them. I liked them, but he was a German *au fond* and one day we had a collision. He had referred to "that monster, Winston Churchill who massacred the Germans with his merciless bombing". I sharply reminded him that the Germans had caused two world wars, were guilty of frightful atrocities in the extermination camps, and that they had started the bombing of open cities, and only got what they deserved. Otherwise our relations were affable. A gifted diagnostician, which helped him in his cellular therapy, he was a good advertisement of his own cure. He moved without effort and was devoted to his invalid wife. A surgeon, he had pondered on the theory of everlasting youth, and in 1931 by an accidental treatment had stumbled on his cellular theory. He had experimented on himself to a point of danger. His "cure" was based on the injection of the pulverised glands of ewes, calves or young pigs. The glands had to be freshly used and when he came to treat the ailing Pope a special slaughterhouse was set up for him in Vatican City. He had cured the Pope after the first consultation. He was often received by Pius XII and in 1955 his fame was endorsed by his being elected to the seat in the Pontificial Academy formerly held by Sir Alexander Fleming, of penicillin fame.

There was a rush by the famous and wealthy wanting to be rejuvenated, and despite the fact that the medical profession on the whole regarded him as a charlatan, he never lacked patients. His fees ran from £500 to £3,000. Naturally, many of the patients were

The author receives the keys of the castle, the Marchese in uniform, with attendants

Günther Bauer's wedding at Schloss Orth, Gmunden

Eight and eighty. Nicholas, son of Michael Gilliam, and the
author

The Château de la Garoupe, Cap d'Antibes

loath to confess to having had treatment. These included the Pope, King Ibn Saud, President Heuss, Thomas Mann, William Furt-wängler, Christian Dior, Georges Braque, Bernard Baruch, the Aga Khan, Sacha Guitry, Somerset Maugham and Noël Coward. At first Coward denied he had been treated, afterwards he confessed to having been "rejuvenated" by Niehans. Somerset Maugham was very nervous about having the injections. "I don't like the sound of it but will go to see Niehans anyhow," he said. He took his secretary, Alan Searle, to the clinic with him. "You have it first," he said. Searle bravely obeyed. After Maugham had had it he exclaimed: "I have never felt better in my life!" and began to write again. But some years later a repeat treatment failed because he ignored Niehans' demand that the patient should lay off all smoking and drinking. Maugham persisted in both. But it carried him on to a vigorous eighty. There was no truth that Churchill took the cure, but years earlier he had been treated with cellular therapy by a French doctor. When Stravinsky secretly came, Niehans refused to treat him. His blood pressure was too high. So the two men spent a couple of hours discussing music.

Niehans became known as the man who was keeping the seventy-seven-year-old Pius XII alive. He attended him three times. In 1954 the Pope was dangerously ill with hiccups. Niehans, called in urgently, saved him. Later he successfully treated him for a dia-phragmatic hernia, which caused him great pain. He again cured him. Maugham believed Niehans had stopped his increasingly desiccated "Chinese" appearance, which Graham Sutherland had mercilessly revealed in his portrait. Maugham had spent hours deploring his features in the mirror. Such was the extraordinary man with whom I lunched that day at the Tre Scalini. My own opinion is that he was an extremely sincere man and he really achieved cures. He was sprightly until the last time I saw him, when he was eighty-five years old.

In London that summer I saw my liberated friend, Jancsi Wolfner. "Do you notice anything wrong with my mind?" he asked, pathet-ically. I assured him he was his own bright self. "You know, it was one long battle to keep my sanity—in fact I went mad for a time." He was deeply touched that the Reform Club, to which I had got him elected in 1936, had only suspended his membership, with no back dues, although an enemy subject. On his death he left legacies to its servants. A still greater surprise was that his London bank, where he had deposited before the outbreak of war a large sum of money, now released, had allowed him four per cent interest, without tax, on Funding Loan bought for him. "You English are a very wonderful, magnanimous people," he said quietly.

I made my usual round of visits, to the Birketts at Challens Green, the Williamsons at West Wittering, the Iliffes at Yattendon and the Sackvilles at Knole. Lord David Cecil lunched with me at the Athenaeum. He was struggling with the biography of Max Beerbohm. He found it difficult to keep it lively. "The trouble is dear old Max did almost nothing for the last forty years of his life,' he said. I dined with Alan Pryce-Jones at his Albany flat. He suggested that the Villino Chiaro should be bought for a memorial museum. I did not think this feasible. Beerbohm's fame was restricted to the English-speaking world. Upkeep and gradual decline in interest would create problems, more complicated on foreign soil. I suggested a plaque on the roadside wall of the villa.

Before leaving for Alassio and Vienna, I went to Shamley Green to see Sir Philip Gibbs, still writing. I found him as buoyant and optimistic as usual. "There's nothing wrong with our younger generation!" he affirmed when I indulged in a little pessimism. Small, frail, handsome, he waved me off down the drive. He was much loved in Shamley Green. I wished that I might have as good an old age.

Norman Birkett was the Master of the Curriers Company. He asked me to respond for "The Guests" at the annual banquet. The age-old ceremony was followed in the great hall: the silver loving-cup went round. I had taken as my companion Rafaelle, Duchess of Leinster. She always looked beautiful, and, having a title, fulfilled the social formula for such occasions. Norman's speech, as usual, was a gem of composition and delivery. He had a persuasive, golden voice. The flower-laden tables, the silver-plate, the candelabra, the ladies in beautiful gowns, the excellent speeches, here was England at its traditional best.

In mid-July I was back in Italy and made myself "incommunicado" at the Palazzo Vairo, working on the proofs of *Love Is Like That*. It was eighty-four degrees in the shade. I lived in a state of nudity with the awnings down, and at noon walked fifty yards to the beach where I bathed. One evening a glorious great yellow moon came up out of the sea over the bay of Genoa. The nights were warm and starry. The strong scent of tuberoses came across the Piazza from the Marchese Ferreri's garden, pervading my terrace and awakening nostalgia, for I remembered how, at dear Estella, in Palm Beach, it had been so strong at midnight in my bedroom that I had had to get up and shut my window.

My proof-correcting finished, at the end of the month, I left by car for Vienna, stopping en route at silvery Sirmione on Lake Garda to see the astonishing Naomi Jacobs, proudly Yorkshire, trousered, monocled, crop-headed, robust, downright, one of the town's characters with her heart of gold. My Hotel Catullus recalled the famous lament of the Latin poet, once a citizen, *Ave, Atque, Vale*. I spent a night at the Lamberg Schloss at Kitzbühel, and had a royal welcome. I was delighted to encounter Leonide Massine, an old friend of the Diaghilev Russian Ballet days. He had with him a bright-eyed boy, his son. Somehow I had never envisioned the light-footed choreographer of *The Three-Cornered Hat* as domesticated.

Salzburg was crammed with Festival addicts, and I found here my indefatigable friend Mrs. Boehm, who had been to five operas and seven concerts. She at once took me to a performance of *Figaro*. But the chattering, music-crazy crowd irritated me. ("But my dear, her breath control isn't . . . wasn't Inge Borkh divine last night . . . The prices are really an outrage . . . Did you see the ex-queen of the Belgians wearing a . . . Poor Koussevitsky was quite exhausted when he came in to supper afterwards . . .") I went on to Zell-am-See, with its lake and background of snowy alps, and to Bad Ischl. The famous teashop had a plaque above a table. "Here, Edward Prince of Wales took tea on September 10, 1935." Visiting Franz Lehar's villa, I looked with amazement on a hideous oak sideboard that George Edwardes of Daly's Theatre had presented to the composer. In Vienna I stayed at the Ambassador Hotel, faithless to the old König von Ungarn. One day I lunched at Schloss Enzesfeld with Baron Eugene de Rothschild and his wife. The Russians occupying it had gone off with the furniture. Eugene had refurnished it. Here, King Edward VIII had come immediately after his abdication, in the hope of eluding the Press. It was his second visit. In 1935 he had visited the Schloss, back from a Mediterranean cruise, with Mrs. Simpson. He had had a bad cold then. It served as a clue. Just before the abdication there was a telephone call from London to the Schloss. It was Lord Brownlow. "Can I come and stay with you and bring my brother, you remember, who had a bad cold?" They knew who had the bad cold, and were not suprised when the Duke of Windsor stepped out of the train. He stayed there, telephoning Mrs. Simpson on the Riviera every day, most of the time until her *decree nisi* became absolute. But the Press got there all the same, two hundred of them. "We had to pull one photographer out of a tree on our golf links!" said the Baron. The trouble with the Duke as a guest was that he never wanted to go to bed until 3. a.m. The Rothschild, worn out, had to get a dispensation.

This month Vienna, too, had a musical festival. The supper tables at Sacher's were crammed, beds were at a premium, as also opera tickets. There was a gala performance in the new opera house, Strauss's *Elektra*, with Inge Borkh in great form, and Mitropoulos conducting. Since there was no Royal Box any more the visiting King and Queen of Greece occupied a loge. The house applauded when the conductor appeared betwen them. It was a Greek occasion. The new opera house was a triumph. I looked and marvelled. Could this be an Austria twice beaten to her knees, impoverished, occupied, and now, phoenix-like, risen triumphantly from her ashes? Should one lose a war to start afresh? In 1972 I was going to wonder still more when a firm schilling looked down on a badly sagging pound.

VIII

Every year I went to Harley Street to be vetted by my friend Sir James Fergusson Hannay. He was usually cheerful and optimistic when he had gone over me but on this visit he severely admonished me. I was running down the batteries. "Must you work like a demon and live like a goat?" he asked. "A goat?" "Yes, you run all over the mountains," he replied.

I went to Rome for Christmas, back to my old room at the Grand Hotel. Warned that my health had become precarious, I decided to take a year's rest and do no writing. With twenty-two novels and ten miscellaneous books written by my sixty-fifth year, perhaps I was entitled to retire. It proved again a vain intention.

I found many friends in Rome. At my hotel Princess Aspasia of Greece had arrived with her grandson, Alexander, aged twelve. A few days later his parents, ex-King Peter and his wife, Alessandra, joined them. We made excursions together. Italian children do not celebrate Christmas, their great festival is in the New Year. The Piazza Navona is lined with booths stocked with toys that the witch Befana bestows on good children. At night, lit up with flares, it was a carnival scene. Before his departure for his Swiss school I gave Alexander a leather portfolio, having become "an uncle".

Rafaelle Leinster had also arrived, the guest of Sir Marcus and Lady Cheke. He was our Minister to the Vatican. They lived in a large baroque villa up by Monte Mario. There was a magnificent view over Rome and the River Tiber in the plain below. The villa had been the summer residence of an old Roman family and had painted ceilings and frescoed walls. I greatly admired Sir Marcus. He was intelligent and elegant. He wrote a very good biography of *Cardinal de Bernis*, who had settled in Rome in the eighteenth century as King Louis' ambassador. Little Bernis was a protégé of Madame de Pompadour, frivolous but kind, a *littérateur* and *bon vivant*.

On Christmas Day I lunched with the Chekes. Afterwards Rafaelle and I motored down into the city and, like a pair of green tourists, did not resist having ourselves photographed in front of the Trevi Fountain where we threw in our coins. Like feeding the pigeons in St. Mark's piazza at Venice, it is a tourist gambit. Happily, we could not know that within eighteen months Sir Marcus, a vital and gifted man, would be dead, aged fifty-four.

I did not go out on New Year's Eve. I knew it was dangerous to be walking in the streets around that hour for the Romans have an old custom of throwing out of the windows any objects they no longer want, furniture, crockery, etc. I had a friend who had been knocked senseless by a chamber-pot, having ignored advice to walk in the middle of the road.

Two evenings later, on January 2, 1958, there was a sensation at the Opera House. At a Gala performance, with the President in his box, the great Maria Callas sang in the title role of *Norma*. After a time it was obvious that she was not in good voice. The audience grew restive, there were calls from the gallery and someone shouted—"Is this what we've paid a million lire for?" There was general consternation but the act proceeded to its end. Taking the curtain the diva glared up at the gallery. A long interval followed before the second act. When the audience had assembled the curtain did not rise. After a very long wait a loudspeaker bluntly announced that Madame Callas was indisposed and the performance would not continue. There was amazement and disbelief. Most of the audience thought that it was a diva's tantrum following the catcalls. It was considered a gross affront to the President and the distinguished house. The audience slowly filed out into the foyer where it had a long wait, cars and chauffeurs being absent. An angry crowd assembled before the diva's near-by hotel. The Press clamoured for an interview. Madame Callas remained invisible, but a notorious American gossip-writer, Elsa Maxwell, posing as her dear friend's champion, told the Romans that they had no manners and were a disgrace. This, reported in the Press, caused further uproar. The American ambassador privately intimated to Miss Maxwell that she should leave Italy.

Lady Beerbohm arrived, a guest at the British Embassy. She lunched with me and we talked of Max. I found her very depressed. Should she not leave the Villino Chiaro, with too many ghosts haunting it, I asked. She shook her head. "I have no other life but there," she replied, sadly. When we parted I was perturbed by her condition. She had been part of a legend and felt bound by it.

My morning mail had a pleasant surprise. Elusive Mary Williamson had married young Lord Nicholas Gordon-Lennox. The persistent pursuer had been rewarded, and Mary had been netted. Nicholas, in the diplomatic service, en poste in Washington, was motoring to Heath Row for his plane. Mary was in the car with him. Somewhere on the Bath Road he proposed to her again and this time she said "Yes". They stopped the car and went to the nearest call-box. From it they informed their parents, the Duke and Duchess of Richmond and Brigadier and Mrs. Williamson, that they were engaged. He would come back soon from Washington to marry Mary—and live happily ever after. I regretted missing the wedding, but I had been ill again and a winter flight was impossible.

I got up in time to fulfil an engagement at the English College in the Via Monserrato where I had been invited to lecture to some seventy novices at this ancient Catholic College. It was founded in 1575 by Gregory XIII. It adjoined the ancient church of St. Thomas à Becket, whose arm was conserved as a relic. The college has a long hall with portraits of English Catholic martyrs under Henry VIII and Queen Elizabeth. John Milton had been a guest here in 1638 and the cloister contains the beautiful tomb of Christopher Bainbridge, Archbishop of York, created a cardinal, who died in Rome in 1514 under a suspicion of having been poisoned.

I dined with the students in the refectory. The rector warned me that the Latin grace, written by St. Benedict, would be very long. I told him I knew it and quoted the first words, to his great surprise. But I was not as learned as he thought. Investigating the life of St. Benedict, and the history of the Monte Cassino monastery for my novel *Eight for Eternity*, I had come across this long Latin grace. I expressed my enjoyment of the excellent dinner, observing that they must have a good chef. No, the dinner was cooked by French nuns! I lectured on my various tours of the United States, and mentioned the strange places I had visited, including two towns called Humbug Mines and Ticklenaked. I was puzzled by the uproar of laughter that greeted this statement. Only later did I learn that the rector, who took the chair, was Monsignor Tickle. At the close of my talk there was a vote of thanks proposed by a youth in a black soutane. He said it gave him particular pleasure, his home was near Pilgrim Cottage, and, a shy boy, he had often seen me, the "local lion", going to the village post office. What an enjoyable evening!

My pleasure was shattered the next morning by the news of the death of Prince Filippo Doria Pamphili. I was sad at the thought that never again should I see this great Roman gentleman, so gentle in manner, so brave under trial.

In the summer I left Alassio to stay at Château Vernier, near Geneva. One evening in an ancient bakery on the estate my host gave a Swiss "period" dinner. We sat at long wooden tables, lit by candlelight, and ate off wooden platters a traditional *fondue Bourguignonne*, dipping our raw meat in boiling butter and oil. At midnight when we went back to the house, the fountains were playing in the long pool. A full moon added silver to silver. The scent of verbena and roses mingled in the warm night air. The Rhone below the woods was a gleaming scythe.

With my friend Ballance, a fellow guest, I motored home via Holland. We wanted to see the paintings at The Hague, and the Rijks and Van Gogh galleries in Amsterdam. Often, dining until the early hours, we walked back to our lodging under the leafy trees bordering the canals, hearing the dawn birdsong in the fresh air. And so to England where I began a round of visits.

My first duty there was to straighten out a fellow scribe's financial affairs, and since I knew he could never manage them I made him buy an annuity to secure his old age.

Every summer I went to visit John Masefield at Burcote Brook. He lived in a vast, ramshackle old house at the end of a long, potholed, overgrown drive with lawns that had not been mown for years. Gentle, white-haired, patriarchal, he had been my friend for forty years. I was alarmed at the austerity of his mode of life, like another Poet Laureate's, "plain living and high thinking". I asked Judith, his devoted daughter, how he kept warm in winter, for there was no sign of heating. "Oh, father never feels the cold," she said. His study was a large, uncarpeted, bay windowed room facing the stripling Thames, open to the winds. In winter he worked with his feet in a box of straw! His muse still visited him. When I left he gave me his latest book of poems. With old-world courtesy he followed me out to my car and stood there until I disappeared down the drive.

A friend of mine had a beautiful property, near Westerham, Kent. He was a neighbour of Winston Churchill at Chartwell, whose gate on the road was always open, with miscellaneous cars in the gravel forecourt. Frequently passing, I often resisted the temptation to call, but one day I turned in, without appointment, taking a chance. The Times Bookshop had held an exhibition of Churchill manuscripts and books. It had requested the loan of the manuscript of my Churchill poem *A Man Arose*. I had attended the opening ceremony. When the poem was published, in a new English edition with a preface by Wendell Willkie, who had introduced me at the National Broadcasting Company's broadcast in New York in 1941, I sent Churchill a copy. He thanked me saying "It will have an honoured place in my library." The N.B.C. presented him with a

double disc of the broadcast. He was also delighted with the Kodachromes I had given him, taken in the stadium of Miami University,
holding 20,000 people, when he had received an honorary degree, in
February, 1946. A fortnight later he made his historic 'Iron Curtain'
speech at Fulton, Missouri.

Cordially received, I was shocked by the change in his appearance
in twelve years. At Miami he had seemed a vigorous man. He was now
bowed and deaf, the voice shaky but the eyes vital. He was eighty-four.
We talked of various things. I congratulated him on his *History of the
English Speaking Peoples*. Before leaving I said there was something I
had always wanted, an autographed photo. He sent for a portfolio,
drew one out and shakily wrote on it "Dear Cecil Roberts, yours
sincerely, Winston Churchill". The photo he gave me was one that
greatly pleased me. He was not glowering, as in Karsh's famous
study. He had been taken in a benign mood, relaxed, cigar in hand.

I never saw him again after this visit. He had seven more years to
live. In 1965, in the billiard room of the gunroom in the Castello di
Conscente, I saw his funeral in a relayed television service. My host,
Rolandi Ricci invited his staff in, postponing lunch. We watched that
deeply moving pageant progressing through the London streets,
to St. Paul's and up the Thames to Waterloo station. I was the only
Englishman present and my Italian companions were as moved as I
was.

IX

As before, I spent a week-end with Norman and Billy Birkett.
He had just been created Lord Birkett of Ulverston, an honour which
he had expected after the Nuremberg Trials. Though he had retired
as a Lord Justice of Appeal he was still in much demand as a public
figure, esteemed by everybody. Recently he had presided very
successfully as the chairman of a Ministry of Labour inquiry into
a printing trades dispute. He showed me with pride a de-luxe edition
of *The Oxford Dictionary of Quotations* with signatures of all parties
in the dispute, a token of their esteem.

Soon after my arrival Norman took me into his little study and
produced a large red morocco leather attaché case. The inside lid
contained the parchment of the Warrant of his appointment to a

Barony. Oddly enough, though in the Queen's summoning words, it was not signed by her but by "Coldstream". The bottom of the case held the Great Seal, about six inches large, not in red wax as formerly but in a greenish plastic. On one side there was the Queen enthroned, with orb and sceptre, on the reverse a plaque of her on her horse, in the uniform of a Guard's colonel. For the crest of his arms Norman had chosen three full-bottomed wigs, "Do you know, the College of Heralds has extracted three hundred pounds from me for this!" he exclaimed. "Never mind, Norman. It has cost some peers a hundred thousand," I said. "You wicked fellow," he retorted, laughing and closing the case.

He talked of the House of Lords. He thought some of the members looked quite moribund. "They have to use earphones and you can't tell, when addressing them, if they are asleep all the time. He named three who he thought were in a state of senile decay. But there were some very bright independent minds. The best plum in the House was the Lord Chancellorship, with a salary of £17,000. He had fine quarters in the House of Lords, overlooking the river. "Of course men like Birkenhead on the Woolsack sacrificed £50,000 a year at the Bar," said Norman. "Birkenhead by tradition couldn't return to it. He was a ruined man on losing office." The House was the world's best club, with a fine library, reception rooms, a very good bar, a restaurant with subsidised meals, a fee for attendance, and a hush-hush of deference as you walked over the red-pile carpets along the Gothic corridors. Even the cloakroom was impressive, like the writing paper.

We had just heard of the death of Brendan Bracken, long Winston Churchill's "wonder boy" whom we had both known. "A dynamic, wild, full-blooded fellow who pushed himself up from Irish obscurity to the top. He had a fortune, a peerage, a lovely house in North Street," remarked Norman, "But he was very secretive about his origin, and he got involved in a libel action, which I tried. I summed up against him severely. It cost him £5,000 damages but he remained warm and friendly. He was a great book collector. Dead now, of cancer, at sixty-two. Well, what is it all about?"

That evening I mentioned that a friend of mine was much perturbed because he had been unable to renew the lease of his flat in Queen Anne's Mansions, the tall block that overlooked St. James's Park. It was going to be demolished. "I never see it without thinking of poor Henry McCardie," said Norman. "Mr. Justice McCardie, who committed suicide?" I asked. "Yes, he lived there. I got mixed-up in that unhappy business." I asked how and he told me the story.

"He was a nice fellow and a good judge but he couldn't resist making jokes about married life when conjugal cases came up before him. Everyone knew him as "The bachelor judge". One day he asked if I would come and see him, so I went round to Queen Anne's Mansions. I found him in a very distressed state of mind. What he told me seemed unbelievable. He had been playing the stock market, with ruinous effect. He was on the verge of bankruptcy, which would, of course, end his career. Could I lend him £2,000? I was rather stunned by this. There was a very serious obstacle. I was a practising K.C. It was not improbable that one day I might find myself conducting a case before him. What would be said if it leaked out that I had lent a sum of money to one of His Majesty's judges before whom I was pleading? There could be very damaging insinuations. He was in such distress that I made a proposal. If he would agree to my informing a mutual colleague about the loan then I should feel safe in making it. The next day I went along to Queen Anne's Mansions with Stuart Bevan, K.C., also a friend of McCardie's, and in his presence agreed to the loan. I was very puzzled by all this. How could a man who had earned £20,000 a year at the Bar and now had a judge's salary of £5,000 a year, with a £3,500 pension one day, be in such straits? Also, the sum was relatively insignificant. Soon after our visit there was a frightful sequel. He was found dead in his flat, with a shotgun beside him. Later, a lady called at my chambers. My clerk refused to admit her at first as she had no appointment through a solicitor, but she forced her way in. She told me that she was in financial trouble. For some years she had been McCardie's mistress, residing in the country. She asked if I could help her. Of course I refused. Later it transpired that McCardie had been having relations with a society woman also, and she was pregnant. McCardie was a charming fellow, and everyone liked him, but the fact is he was a womaniser, and probably there were other ugly things raising their heads. I suspect he was being blackmailed. Two notorious blackmailers made confessions during a trial that they had obtained money from him."

I was given, subsequently, a macabre footnote to the suicide story. In Rome I had a friend, Chance Quarrell, a retired solicitor. He was a man of some wealth and of much culture and, despite his name, shy and gentle. He had a very fine library of which I had the use. I also profited by his wide knowledge. He was a Winchester and Oxford scholar and I got him to check my proof sheets. One day when I went to dine with him I mentioned that I was sorry to learn that they were demolishing Queen Anne's Mansions, where I had always thought I would like to live. Quarrell said, "I had a strange experience when I went to dine with some friends who had a flat there. During the course of the meal there was a white sauce served with the mutton, but, to my hostess's surprise, it wasn't white but pink. Later she asked the cook, whom she found very agitated, the reason. She said: "I put the sauceboat on the sideboard just before sending it in and couldn't think why it was pink. Afterwards, I noticed there was what looked like a splash of red ink on the side-board. Look, ma'am, it's still dripping from the ceiling!" It wasn't ink. It was blood. It had come through from the flat above where Mr. Justice McCardie lay in a pool of it."

On Monday, after leaving Challens Green, I went over to Chequers to lunch with Kathleen Hill. The Foreign Secretary had just departed after a conference on the crisis in Cyprus. Calm had settled down on the great mansion. We lunched in her sitting-room with its mullioned windows overlooking the north terrace. Afterwards in the Long Gallery Kathleen showed me the octagonal table that Napoleon had used at St. Helena. On it was the small red leather briefcase, embossed with "N", which Napoleon had used all his life. One of the windows had four new Garter arms, in colours, of Chamberlain, Churchill, Attlee and Eden. In the corridor there was a watercolour painting of the Long Gallery, with a letter of Queen Mary's to Stanley Baldwin, P.M., from Buckingham Palace, saying that she had found this painting by Augustus Hare in an antique shop and recognised it was Chequers, so she sent it to him for the house.

Two days later I made a B.B.C. broadcast, *Young, but not angry.*

I had seen a play, *Look Back in Anger*, by a brilliant young play-wright. Before the end I left the theatre, nauseated by it. I had had enough of a very angry young man who seemed to have a very squalid character. He was abusive of the world in general and of his wife and relations in particular. I felt that she should have resorted to a remedy very popular in the pantomimes of my youth. She should have gone into the kitchen, picked up a rolling-pin and given him a crack over the head. A friend to whom I made this observation remarked that there was probably no rolling-pin in the house—this being the age of ready-made pastry. Nor did I like the audience that guffawed and applauded. They appeared to have come out of the King's Road, Chelsea, the kind of bearded "hippies" who live in mouldy bedsitting-rooms, with large cars, a girl in the bed and nothing in the bank. Why should the modern young man be angry? He is very much more fortunate than his father, with shorter working hours, longer holidays, bigger wages, pensions, and a Welfare State to cushion him? Never before has he been able to be so irresponsible. The Talks Director wrote to me—"I hope you can now feel that all the work you put into it was worth it. I should like to add to those of your friends my warmest congratulations on the final result." I had ended my talk by saying I thought the play was a libel on many of the younger generation who comported themselves with cheerfulness, courage and good manners.

One August day Lady Monckton took me down to see her old home, Ightham Mote near Sevenoaks. It was a moated manor dating back, with its twenty-five-feet wide moat, to 1340, with Tudor additions. The great hall had its original oak timbers and fourteenth-century corbels. There was a Tudor chapel with a seventeenth-century clock in the gable. The manor was four-sided with a drawbridge giving access to an inner courtyard. It was a thing of sheer beauty, with black and white timbers and mullion windows. It had had famous guests, Sargent, Ellen Terry, Irving, Burne-Jones, Henry James, William Morris and Meredith. It was considered to be one of the most perfect Tudor manor houses in England.

For some time it stood empty, needing expensive repairs, and then an American, Mr. Charles Robinson, saw a print of it in a shop in the Strand. He went immediately on a bicycle to look at it and bought from Lady Monckton's family, in 1953. He went to work restoring it, with great patience and skill. A bachelor of seventy, he lived at Cape Elizabeth, in Maine, and came over each year to supervise the work. He always travelled tourist-class and slept in the village inn at forty pence a night. He kept three permanent gardeners for the grounds, and a relay of restorers. He worked on it for ten years.

The house was half empty when Polly Monckton took me there, rather ghostly and eerie with the sense of dead generations, but of great historic beauty. "Will he come to live here?" I asked. "I don't think so, I think it is just a hobby, to restore something to its old perfection," she replied. By 1963 he had finished his work, filled the house with period furniture, and then handed it over to the National Trust. What a delightful way for a millionaire to spend his money, and what a gesture to the England he loved! It might be expected that a manor as old as Ightham Mote would have a ghost. Edmund Gosse, the critic, once stayed there. Afterwards he showed Osbert Sitwell a photo he had taken by chance of a spectre, a monk, walking with a rope round his neck!

In August I was a guest again at Yattendon Court. My host, Tod Iliffe, farmed in a large way on his land. He had an up-to-date estate office down in the village, where Robert Bridges, a former Poet Laureate, had once lived. Yattendon Court, with its long terraces, stood on a high ridge. It overlooked a deep valley and the rising Berkshire hills beyond. It was the time of the harvest, and the opposite fields, climbing up to the horizon, were a deep golden brown. On Saturday afternoon Tod said he was going to watch the haymaking and asked if I would like to go with him. He drove me off in a vintage Wolseley open car. It roared and rattled but it went. He said it never broke down and liked rough country. How true that was! For the next two hours I had the most exciting ride of my life. We went madly steeplechasing over mown fields. We jumped ruts, we rose and fell, sometimes careering through gates, sometimes through hedges and briars. I understood why the Rolls-Royce had not been taken out! What astonished me was the driver's tenacity. Tod let nothing deter him. We sailed up to and round threshing machines and wagons whose operators waved joyously at our reckless progress. He said a few encouraging words and was off to another field. When

we returned home from this steeplechase, the Wolseley having behaved like a tank, I was exhausted and shaken. Tod, aged eighty-
one, was as boyishly fresh as when we had set out.

That morning after breakfast I had watched him playing in a
doubles on the indoor tennis court. He was President of the Lawn
Tennis Association, as well as Chairman of the trustees of the
Shakespeare Memorial Theatre. A month later he invited me to be
his guest at the Shakespeare Memorial Theatre Dinner but I was
in Alassio. Tennis, haymaking, presiding at the London Chamber
of Commerce, a Governor of Pangbourne Nautical College, entertaining for the Greek Play at Bradfield College, a director of the
Daily Telegraph, chairman of two insurance companies, the owner
of a group of newspapers and magazines, calm, smiling, he was
equally capable in any role. He had bought the villa on the French
Riviera without seeing it, he had built himself a winter home at
Nassau in the Bahamas. Age did not weary nor the years condemn.
In the morning and in the evening he remembered everything, to
paraphrase Binyon's noble verse.

X

In September I returned by car to Alassio, this time going via
the St. Gothard Pass to Lugano. I had first visited this Swiss resort
almost forty years before. It was then a sleepy little lakeside town,
Italian in atmosphere, with its half-moon promenade of cropped ilex
trees bordering the blue lake, and a few scattered villas on the
mountain slopes. I was horrified by what I now found, the streets
full of automobiles, new glaring hotels along the lakeside, the town
transformed with skyscraper apartment houses. In a few years it
would have a crop of small banks busily engaged in aiding Italians
to smuggle their money out of Italy, just over the border.

Alassio, too, was crowded. I remember the days when no one would
dream of being on the Italian Riviera in summer, but now there
were no seasons. Hordes of Germans poured down over the Alps
until the end of October. The beaches from St. Raphael to Genoa
were lined with naked bodies broiling in the sun. The prices of deck
chairs, sun umbrellas and car parking soared. New jewellers' shops
had opened to cater for Germans buying gold ornaments. The

English, with a fifty pound travel allowance, could only look in the windows.

I opened the Palazzo for six weeks and then sailed for New York. On arrival I was the guest of Dorothy Quick, the poet, who had an apartment only a few yards along Fifth Avenue from where Mrs. Cartwright had lived, so that the view over Central Park and down the Avenue from my bedroom was almost identical. Dorothy and I had had a "writing friendship" for twenty years.

I found that Aubrey Cartwright had established himself in a Lexington Avenue flat. He asked me to lunch and had a surprise for me. In walked Mary and Nicholas Gordon-Lennox, from Washington, so young, so happy. He had come to see his father the Duke open the British Week exhibition in New York. Meanwhile my Australian friend, Guido Wertheim, down in Palm Beach, Florida, had agin demonstrated his genius for finding cheap lodgings. The widow of a ruined millionaire had let him the porter's lodge on her large estate. She had divided the main house into eight apartments, but Guido had his own little house, with a garden of palms and giant eucalyptus trees, and a private beach. His landlady lent him a piano, as he was musical. There was a sittingroom with a long, open balcony, two bedrooms, bathroom and kitchen, furnished. The rent was $150 a month. Would I share it ? We should do our own cooking and housekeeping. It would not be Estella of happy memories but it would be an ideal jumping-off place for Coconut Grove, and Nassau, in the Bahamas, for which I had invitations. I sent him a cheque for the rent. When I posted the letter New York was wrapped in a snow blizzard, five degrees below zero.

On New Year's Eve Josephine Crane, a few yards from Dorothy, gave a dinner for twelve, and had a string quartet to entertain forty guests afterwards. Champagne flowed at midnight. I thought how, six years ago, in the apartment three floors higher, we had drunk champagne on New Year's Eve, 1953, at Beatrice Cartwright's party, New York white under snow as now on this eve of 1959. I toasted my hostess. In her eighties she had lost none of her zest for life. Forty-eight hours later I stepped out into brilliant Florida sunshine, with eighty degrees in the shade, blue sky, blue ocean. "Well, what do you think of it ?" asked Guido when we reached the house. "Paradise!" I replied. All this without having crossed a single frontier between blizzard and heat wave.

In the third week I flew to Nassau, to visit Sir Guy and Lady Henderson, old friends. He was Chief Justice of the Bahamas. They had a house overlooking the golf course and on the other side was the one Tod Iliffe had built for himself. I walked across the links to lunch one day. I found him busy on the loggia with a tray of typed sheets. He was writing his *Life*. He gave me a chapter to read. "Rather an unpleasant story," he said, laconically. It was about a grim battle between the newspaper magnates, the Berrys and Rothermere, involving himself. The battle became too ruinous, and they cried quits. It was quite hair-raising. The *Life* was not published. It was for the family.

Charlotte Iliffe appeared. "It's time to bathe," she said. The house was on the beach. The sand was so hot you could hardly walk over it. I stayed on to dinner. Ann and Guy joined us with the Sutherlands, the Bede Cliffords and the Norman Armours. The next day, in church, I saw all the island community. Guy read the lesson, the Canon preached, the Governor and his wife were in the official pew, where the Windsors had worshipped. It looked all very peaceful and "Establishment" but there had been a frightful murder on the island. A local tycoon, Sir Harry Oakes, had been foully murdered in his house in 1943. There was a sensational trial, with no result. The murderer was never found. The Oakes house was still locked up. One shivered motoring past it.

Two days later I was taken to lunch with the Governor, Sir Raymond Arthur, at The Residence, which the Duchess of Windsor, immured there with the Duke, had termed "St. Helena", though their reign had been popular. Sir Raymond, hearty and kind, said, "You know I am very delighted to meet you." I looked surprised. "I'm one of your fans. I've read *So Immortal a Flower* twice. I want to go to Crete again with your book in hand." He began to ask me about my other novels. I always become nervous on these occasions. You are asked about characters in a book your reader has just read, but it is often ten, fifteen or twenty years since you wrote it, and you look rather stupid, unable to remember who they are and what they did.

When I got back from the Governor's lunch a cable awaited me that took the sun out of the sky. Lady Beerbohm had died. Later I learned the details. She was overdue as a guest at the British Embassy. The Clarkes started enquiries. The police called and broke in. She had been dead in her bath for ten days. I recalled the lament "I am so lonely" on that photograph of Max she had sent me. She had been part of those happy Villino days.

The cost of my return fare to Nassau was thirty-six dollars. It was, I think, the best value I ever received. The flight from Palm Beach to Nassau, over the Cays, was one long enchantment. One looked down into a luminous rainbow-coloured sea that washed against the small, low-lying islands. It was a world of blue and gold on a radiant morning. My ever thoughtful hosts, Guy and Ann, saw me off on an evening return flight. A crimson sunset faded over the blue ocean, then in the growing darkness the long flat littoral of Florida, from Miami north to Palm Beach, glittered with coloured lights. We veered over palm groves and jungle and backwaters, in the warm February night, with little towns and villages like jewels set on velvet.

A week later I left for Leafy Way at Coconut Grove, south of Miami. It was almost like going home. My hostess, Mrs McWilliams, had bought the house where I had written much of *Gone Sunwards*. "My house is almost part of your literary property and I want you always to feel welcome here," she said. Gestures like this are the rewards of an author's life. So here I was again, in a house full of canaries singing in a patio where, in 1936, at breakfast, I had listened to the funeral service for King George V at Windsor. The Negro gardener had bowed his head and said. "We are all mourning for our good king." Our? "Oh, yes," said my hostess, "he's a Jamaican, and isn't he proud of the fact." The only menace in the garden were the coconuts, huge things that fell with a plonk. There was a swimming pool, whose water matched the blue plumbago trailing over the pergola. Oranges and grapefruit grew on the same tree, and for breakfast you could pluck an avocado pear. One day I was taken off to Marineland to see the performing dolphins. I was enraptured by one who changed bonnets in the water, and by another who played "America the Beautiful" with its snout on an organ. It bowed to the applause and took an encore. My hostess, eighty, had a large studio, and painted watercolours. After an idyllic week I was back in Palm Beach en route to New York.

Before I sailed for Genoa early in March Mrs. Crane gave a lunch party for me at which the guests included Mrs. Roosevelt, Count Orlovsky, Lewis Einstein and Professor and Mrs. Walter Starkie. I was delighted to see Starkie again, now retired from the British Council in Madrid. He was in American on a lecture tour. He gave me news of Spain. The young Duke of Montoro, married to the late Duke of Alba's daughter, had now taken his wife's title, and become the Duke of Alba. The title later would pass him and go to their son. They had three bonnie boys. The destroyed Liria Palace in Madrid had been wholly rebuilt in the same style and all the saved treasures had been returned to it. Starkie told me that he had been responsible for bringing Leslie Howard, the film star of "Gone With the Wind", etc., to Madrid to lecture during the war. He had organised a large party of flamenco dancers, gypsies, for his entertainment. When he asked one of them why she was not dancing, she replied "I cannot dance for a dead man" and refused to take the floor. Four days later Howard was shot down, with his party, in the plane flying back to England.

Lewis Einstein, a retired American diplomat at the lunch, a born raconteur, who resembled Henry James, had had a distinguished career, having served in Turkey, China, Bulgaria, Czechoslovakia, France and England. He had been a close friend of President Franklin Roosevelt and for many years was a leading figure in the State Department in Washington. He had published very interesting memoirs, and spoke eight languages. He told us a story of a man in Georgetown who was held up by a hoodlum. When the man proceeded to feel his pockets he told the thief he was a priest. The thief abjectly apologised. The priest, thinking to make a convert, talked with him and offered him a cigarette. "Oh, no," he replied, "I never smoke during Lent."

On leaving Mrs. Crane's during a snow blizzard I ran into Salvador Dali who stopped me. He fished in his overcoat and brought out a green pamphlet which he gave me. It was a prospectus of a new magazine *Rhinoceros* which he and his life-long friend Skira, the art publisher, were founding. According to Dali the magazine would be "of supreme importance to all people interested in the Cosmogenic Unity of our Century, the future Ecumenical Congress of Pope John XXIII, the new moral and scientific values of Soviet Russia". All this was imparted to me in a snow blizzard, ten below zero, on a corner of Fifth Avenue. I fled, clutching the green pamphlet. Dali had become a snowman.

XI

In the spring the Queen Mother and Princess Margaret came to Rome on a five-day visit for the purpose of unveiling in the Villa Borghese a statue of Lord Byron. It was a fine copy of the excellent one of the seated poet, by Thorwaldsen, which had had such ignominious adventures, being declined by Westminster Abbey, lying boxed under the arches of Charing Cross Station, and finally housed in the library of Trinity College, Cambridge. When the Queen unveiled the statue, provided by public subscription, I could imagine the poet smirking at the antics of Fate. Exiled from England and Westminster Abbey for his scandalous conduct, with charges of incest, adultery, homosexuality, scarcely smothered by a tragic end, he must have found the presence of England's Queen Mother in an act of homage distinctly satisfying. The plinth on which he stood carried quotations from his magnificent tribute to Rome. "Oh Rome! my country! city of the soul!" The fact is Byron visited Rome for only a few weeks in April and May, 1817, when he was writing the fourth canto of *Childe Harold*. During that time he sat to Thorwaldsen for his bust. Byron put on a scowl. The sculptor complained about his posing. "Will you not sit still—and you need not assume that look!" he cried. When Byron saw the finished work he said "It doesn't resemble me at all—I look much more unhappy!" We must be thankful to the Dane who would not be humbugged by the poet.

When the shroud fell from the statue, amid applause, though beautifully carved there was a shiver of disappointment. It seemed too small. Had we not subscribed enough? It offended Byron's *amour propre*. Walking by the statue next day, I thought he spoke to me. "Just look at that fellow down the Avenue, and look at me—a dwarf!" I knew to whom he was referring. The fellow down the Avenue was Goethe, four times his size, magnificently throned on a great base. I tried to console him. "After all, the Queen Mother and Princess Margaret did come here to honour you, with one ton of luggage, three maids, one hairdresser, two footmen and two detectives," I said.

XII

Before leaving Rome I went to call on a young couple who were at the British School of Art, being interested in their careers. The manner of it was this. One day in my Queen's Gate lodging I had gone down to the basement to get out my baggage for departure to Italy. In a dim, narrow corridor, as I went to the cupboards, I was astonished to be confronted by a completely naked young man who was carrying a lamb over his shoulders. When I got back my breath I discovered that the naked Adonis was made of bronze plaster, life-sized. As I stood examining the work a door opened behind me and a slip of a girl came out. I asked her if she knew how this statue came to be blocking the corridor. She laughed. "It's mine!" she said. "Yours?" I cried, incredulous. "Yes, I'm studying sculpture. I've won the *Prix de Rome* with it." "The Prix de Rome!" I echoed, "You?" I looked at her. "I think you are the most fortunate girl on earth. There are three highly desirable things, to my mind: to live in Rome and be a cardinal, an ambassador, or a pupil at the British School. You will have the most wonderful time of your life." "But I'm not going," she said quietly. "You see, I'm just married. I can't leave my husband, can I?" At that moment the door of the front area opened and a young man walked in. One look told me that he was the model of the statue. She introduced him. They had the basement apartment and invited me in for a drink. He was a qualified architect, just starting in London. After some talk I said, "You must go to Rome. Perhaps I can arrange something to make it possible." "For both of us?" she asked. "For both of you. It happens that I know two rather influential persons in Rome, one is the British Ambassador, the other is the Director of the British School. I feel Fate has sent me to you. I am going to see what I can do."

I wrote to Sir Ashley Clarke, and to the Director, Ward Perkins. I had a line on both. One day at the British School, Perkins, a renowned archaeologist who had excavated at Leptis Magna, showed me the work of two of his pupils. "They've gone as far as they can with us. They should really go on to our School at Athens," he said. "Why can't they go?" I asked. "It needs money." I asked how much it needed for them to complete their training. He told me. "I'll give you a cheque," I said. They went to Athens. I now wrote to Sir Ashley and to Ward Perkins, telling them about the girl who had won the *Prix de Rome* but could not take up the scholarship because she would not leave her husband who was an architect. Could they not somehow find employment for him, to enable her to get to Rome? In a few weeks it was arranged. They were to live at the school, and work would be found for him in connection with British Government properties there. So now I visited them at the school. They were happy and working hard. After a time they left for Cornell University in the States, where she obtained a post in its Art Department, and he in its School of Architecture. In due time they came home to Oxford, where they found positions in the university.

While in Rome I took the opportunity to discuss with Sir Ashley the memorial to Max Beerbohm. It would have to be done before the Villino Chiaro was sold to a stranger. He promised me all help, which also came from our successive Consul-Generals at Genoa, David Balfour and John May. It was to prove a long business. After dining with Sir Ashley he took me to a concert in a new Rolls-Royce car they had sent that spring to the Embassy. He was dismayed by the size of it. "It can't get into some of these old Roman streets," he complained. There was an elaborate panel inside. "Look!" He pulled down the lid revealing a large cut-glass cocktail outfit. "Can you imagine Elizabeth and Philip driving down the Via Veneto shaking a cocktail?" he asked, derisively.

Leaving Rome I joined Richard Church, the poet, and his wife at Pisa, and here again I was on Byron's tracks. I took Richard to see the sixteenth-century Palazzo Lanfranchi by the River Arno, where Byron had lived, with his menagerie invading the house, to the alarm of Leigh Hunt and family, who came and outlived their welcome. Byron was in Pisa at the time, writing *Don Juan*, when Shelley was living in a palazzo on the other side of the river. Neither of them with their ménages were considered respectable by the local aristocracy, but fame, Byron's rank, and wealth, curbed their censure.

In June on my way back to England I went via Lake Maggiore
to stay with my friend Neil McEachern at the Villa Taranto near
Pallanza, one of the finest gardens in Italy. I had known him in the
twenties in Venice. He was a rich shipowner, cultivated, who
leased the Palazzo Labia, and started to restore it. He discovered
under the whitewash magnificent Tiepolo frescoes, "Cleopatra
and Antony's wedding". Alas, it was a fatal discovery for the state
came in and declared the palazzo a national monument. He was not
willing to spend money on a place he could not buy. It was leased
later to the Mexican millionaire, Charles Bestegui, who made Venetian
history by giving a fabulous costume ball in the palazzo he had
filled with treasures.

In 1930 Neil McEachern was in a train travelling from Venice
to London. He saw an advertisement in *The Times* offering for sale
a villa on Lake Maggiore. He left his *wagon-lits* and inspected the
villa, a dilapidated house with garden. He found he could buy more
land and make the garden he had always desired. He bought a
hundred acres, demolished the house and built a château and horti-
cultural laboratories. A fine botanist, he created one of the great
gardens of the world. He called the villa after a kinsman, Maréchal
Macdonald, whom Napoleon made Duke of Taranto. He brought
a water supply through seven miles of pipes and employed over a
hundred men for two years tunnelling and terracing above the lake.
He dug a fosse, thirty feet deep, and made five large rock gardens,
ten fountains and two miles of stone walks. He brought plants and
trees from Tibet, the Himalayas, Japan and Siam, etc. He created
a valley of rhododendrons, one of heather, and an "autograph"
park consisting of trees planted by royalties and famous persons who
were his guests. He lived in his Swiss-like château fronting a great
lawn. At the bottom of this there was a deep cutting by which visitors
passed from one side of the gardens to the other. Near it he had
a hidden fountain. Sitting on his veranda, hearing the tourists, it
amused him to touch a button whereupon a great jet of water rose
in the air to their astonishment and needless alarm. For "tulip
week" at the end of each April he had ninety thousand tulips in bloom
and another eighty thousand were flown in from Holland to distribute to visitors.

Neil was a world-famous horticulturist and possessed a magnificent library of garden lore. He was a rather shy, quiet widower and loved to entertain. He often had twenty house guests. I was given a bedroom, lined with Russian leather, from whose veranda I had a panorama of mountains, including Monte Rosa crowned with snow, and Monte Mottarone. He employed six guides in uniform to conduct tourists over the estate, which had 100,000 visitors a year. When he died, some three years after my last visit, he left his garden to the Italian Government, with funds for its upkeep. The villa itself was bequeathed, as a summer retreat, to the President of the Republic, the gardens being kept open to visitors. He was buried in a private chapel built in the grounds. We affectionately called him "The Marshal of Flowers". I introduced my friend Rolandi Ricci to Neil and he visited him at the Villa Taranto. He had found an old engraving of Maréchal Macdonald. "I want to give it to him and it would be nice if you would write some verses on it." So I wrote:

> Better, dear Neil, I think, to be
> A Marshal of Flowers in Italy
> Than emulate a sire who stood
> Engulfed on fields of foreign blood.
> He used the sword, but you the trowel—
> Better to plant than disembowel.

CHAPTER NINE

Honorary Citizen

I

On arriving in London I found a letter awaiting me with the information that the City Council of Alassio, by a unanimous vote, would confer on me its honorary citizenship. My first visit was to Oxford for the Encaenia, as the guest of my friend Dr. A. L. Rowse, at All Souls College. I watched the procession passing by its wall to the Sheldonian for the conferment of degrees, headed by Lord Halifax, the Chancellor of the University, looking very feeble, in his robes, with an undergraduate train-bearer in knee breeches. Margot Fonteyn and Sir Robert Menzies, the Australian ex-Premier, received degrees. My friend had a beautiful suite of rooms in the second court at All Souls, whose windows looked on to the long façade of the Codrington Library. In this magnificent, high-ceilinged hall the College gave a luncheon to one hundred and fifty guests. Above the shelves the marble busts of dead worthies looked down on us. My host presided at his own table of twenty. His suite in All Souls College had a large, light sitting-room, the width of the wing, with a great lawn in front and a small garden behind. Here, a prodigious worker, he wrote the books that made him the foremost Elizabethan scholar of the day. There was a long, booklined corridor connecting my bedroom with his sitting-room. Late that night, after retiring, I wandered into the corridor in the deep silence. A full moon hung over Oxford. I looked across a moonlit lawn and saw silhouetted roofs and towers, with the great dome of the Radcliffe Camera, almost like St. Peter's, rising into the bright sky. The beauty of it all in that still summer night!

Leslie, volatile, omniscient, was a compulsive talker. His positiveness enraged many but woe to them if they challenged him. He flourished a battle-axe of learning over their heads, exulting in the fray. I envied not his brilliant mind but his large writing-desk. All my life I have been frustrated in this respect. My Pilgrim Cottage had not room for one, the places I rented always had miserable drop-lid bureaux. The seignorial space of Leslie's room accommodated not only the large writing-desk but a round library table, mountainous with books, and a great Chippendale bookcase lining a wall. In such circumstances, with all the amenities of a rich college, of course you could write masterpieces. Lawrence of Arabia had written part of *Revolt in the Desert* while residing, as an Honorary Fellow, in this luxurious nest, so chaste, quiet, richly endowed, with its portraits of Lord Chancellors and Bishops, shining silver plate, soft-voiced servants, and a renowned cellar.

II

One evening in July Lady (Polly) Monckton gave a dinner at her flat in Cadogan Gardens. Her guests were always chosen with a view to variety of interest. The occasion of this dinner was for us to go on later to an evening reception at the Royal Academy. One of the guests was Lord Methuen. When I was writing *And So To Bath*, in 1939, I had called at his home, Corsham Court in Wiltshire, to see its fine art gallery. In it there was a marble figure of a Sleeping Cupid, reputed to be by Michelangelo. Lord Methuen was very modest about it but thought it was genuine. The Cupid's history was singular. Michelangelo, aged twenty, working in the Medici gardens, carved a sleeping Cupid which was so like a Greek marble that a dealer took it to Rome and sold it to Cardinal Riario as an antique. The fraud was discovered and the dealer had to take it back. The Cardinal, impressed, invited young Michelangelo to Rome. The agent then sold the Cupid to the Pope's son, Cesare Borgia, who gave it to the Duke of Urbino. Some years later he treacherously sacked the Duke's castle. Among the loot was the Cupid. Isabella d'Este, of Mantua, coveted it for her collection and although the Duke of Urbino was her brother-in-law she did not hesitate to ask Cesare Borgia to give the Cupid to her. It was in the Mantua collection until 1630 when the collection came on the market. An agent of Charles I bought it and shipped it from Venice in 1632. Thus the sleeping Cupid went into the Royal Collection and was there until its dispersal after the execution of the king.

I had had a very pleasant correspondence with Lord Methuen about his copy. He wrote:

> So far very little has been done by way of establishing this copy as the missing Cupid of Michele Angiolo (Michelangelo in the French form looks to me all wrong) but there is an account in the 1896 Dublin University Magazine. In this the writer traces the known history of this statuette, which you have summarized in your letter. The article quotes a letter from my grandfather, Sept. 16, 1876, where he said that it had been covered up for many years and had been bought by Sir Paul Methuen about 1725–1730. My father used to tell me that my grandfather had found it in a wooden box kept in the cellar of his London house. It had apparently been overlooked when Sir Paul Methuen's effects were sent down from London after his death in 1759. Personally, I am convinced that this is the missing Cupide Dormiente; but the pundits are naturally very chary as to what they commit themselves to.

This correspondence with Lord Methuen had taken place twenty-three years earlier. I had been unable to accept a cordial invitation to be his guest at Corsham Court. Now I had the pleasure of meeting him. He was a man in the seventies, distinguished in appearance and achievement, a Royal Academician, an excellent artist, and a Trustee of the National Gallery.

After dinner we left for the Royal Academy. Lord Methuen wore a faded black ulster, with a hood, and a floppy felt hat that made him look like a conspirator. He offered us transport in his car at the door. It was a battered station-wagon. He drove with some abandon. Nearing Hyde Park Corner we nearly had a collision with a taxi. His lordship put his head out. "Why don't you look where you're going, you silly bastard!" he shouted. The taximan shouted back "Who's let you out in that hencoop, you bloody old fool!" We ran side by side into Piccadilly, with the altercation waxing. "It's hooligans like you that do murders on the road," shouted his lordship. "It's bastards like you that are a bloody menace!" came the retort. The debate went on, getting fiercer and fiercer. A lady in the taxi lowered the window. "Really, sir, can't you behave?" she said, glaring. "You'll end in hospital, madam," replied his lordship. The taxi tried to get ahead, but Lord Methuen clung to it, neck and neck. The language between the two drivers got more and more lurid. Where had his lordship picked up his vocabulary? Polly and I looked at each other in wonder. There was nothing we could do. Both men were driving and swearing like demons. Lord Methuen's car bore a label on the windscreen that entitled him to park in the Academy's courtyard. As we turned into it he said "I'll get rid of that fellow here!" But he didn't. The taxi had a right to deliver its alarmed occupant at the door. We parked our car and walked to the steps. The taximan, leaving, had a farewell shot as he went by. "I'll bet you're a bloody rotten artist, like your cloak and your car!" he cried, and drove off triumphantly. I learned later where Lord Methuen had obtained his vocabulary. He had served in the First World War in the Scots Guards.

This summer I made the usual round of visits to my friends. They were certainly diverting with their various interests. There was Alec Lacy, a retired naval commander, married to an admiral's daughter. A delightful fellow, his real passion was painting so I was not surprised when he announced that he was holding an exhibition of his works at a London gallery. I thought them quite awful; he was a disciple of Braque, Klee and Miró. To my amusement he sold some of his paintings. "I am in advance of Picasso," he observed, humorously. There was no limit to his interests. He had been in the U.S.A in 1942–1944, his task being to superintend the mounting of guns on merchant ships. He was one of the fathers of the Greek Navy when our Admiralty sponsored its creation. He spoke fluent Greek and French. In the first two years of the war he had been British Liaison officer to Admiral Muselier, commander of the Free French navy. He had vivid stories of Muselier and de Gaulle embattled over naval affairs before the great split. He wrote an excellent book about his experience with the Greek Navy, which he never succeeded in getting published. He also wrote a learned book, *Greek Pottery in the Bronze Age* which had a *succès d'estime*. He bought a neglected eighteenth-century manor house in Kent, and proceeded with his own hands to reconstruct it. It was here I made happy visits.

I went to West Wittering to the Williamsons. Leila cooked in the kitchen, and, the oven going, retired upstairs to write her new novel. The Brigadier surprised me one day by producing a manuscript.

After service as an artillery officer in the First World War, he had volunteered for service with the Don Cossacks, in an abortive attempt to bolster the White Russians fighting the Bolsheviks. It was one of Winston Churchill's enterprises which almost proved successful. Admiral Kolchak advanced in Siberia, General Wrangel in the Crimea. General Denikin, in June 1919, came near to victory, crossing the Don and the Volga, reaching within two hundred miles of Moscow and taking Kiev and Tsaritsyn (Stalingrad). But we gave the White Russians too little support. This, and the corruption that ran through all Russian enterprises, frustrated a victory that might have brought about the defeat of the Bolsheviks. Williamson had no illusions about the Russians. "I offered myself in a spirit of adventure and of preservation of the traditional ethics of the caste to which I belonged (Eton and Woolwich). I had no more time for mutinous soldiers and sailors who ill-treated and massacred their officers than I had for political adventurers from the criminal classes who murdered their Tsar and his helpless family." His story was in the form of a diary. I found it absorbing and felt it should be published. But in 1959 no publisher was interested in what had happened in White Russia in 1920. So here was my host, Brigadier Williamson, D.S.O., M.C., Belgian Croix de Guerre, working hard in his wind-blown, sea-edge garden, and, being a man of public spirit, serving on the parish council. There was to be a happy ending to the story of his diary. A friend edited it and it was published as *Farewell to the Don* in 1970. It was a success and had a second printing. So he emerged as an author, aged eighty-three, the year before his death.

I did not visit Knole this summer. Charles was away. There had been a tragedy. Anne Sackville, mounting a chair in the baggage-room to get portmanteaux for the winter migration to Monte Carlo, had fallen, baggage on top of her, and died as the result of her injuries. So Charles, nearly ninety, was all alone in that vast servant-less house. His was a second marriage and it had been wholly successful.

Yattendon that summer, as always, was a delight. We did no harvesting this time. Tod Iliffe had gout. "All because I failed to keep my rule of drinking a gallon of water a day," he explained. So we went no more a-haymaking by the aid of a Wolseley car.

I visited the Birketts at Challens Green. It was almost like going home, in perfect July weather, the Amersham Valley lushly green below us. I had begun to write again, working on a novel, so I kept to my room until noon with the ever kind Billy bringing me a nourishing cup of beef-tea. Norman had just made a television appearance in a "Face to Face" series of frank interviews with John Freeman. We watched a re-play. "Lord Birkett, you are known to the world, I suppose, as one of the three or four greatest criminal lawyers of the century," blandly began Freeman. Later, he became almost merciless in his personal questions. He asked Norman if he had had time when young and away on circuit to attend to the upbringing of his children. "Not very much, but everything went easily. We had a good nurse and household staff," he replied. "Oh you brute!" interjected Billy. "There I was, left all alone, housekeeping and slaving for the children!" "I'm sorry, darling—how remiss of me. You were quite wonderful!" replied Norman, "I should have said you relieved me of all anxiety." Freeman asked, later, "Lord Birkett, I believe you were once a Wesleyan local preacher, in your youth. Do you still believe what you did then? Are you still a Christian?" Norman hesitated and then said. "No—I suppose I might describe myself now as a sort of Christian-Agnostic." Norman shook his head at the screen. "I'm afraid that's going to get me into trouble," he commented.

On another occasion Norman had given some radio talks on famous advocates he had known. One of these was the late Sir Edward Marshall Hall, K.C. He had told me that he had shared chambers with Marshall Hall when starting his career but eventually the famous advocate became so jealous of his junior's success that he had had to leave and move into his own. Hall's erratic behaviour had also worried him. After we had listened to the replay, I said, "You were very tactful and forgiving, Norman." He spread his hands. "How could I be otherwise? The fellow has sisters living who adore him."

He had a well-stocked library. The stairs and passages were lined with books. He was widely read and had a deep love of literature, especially poetry. Billy used to laugh at us, we were always jumping up to find a quotation from some book. On birthdays they gave each other a fine edition of a book, by which the library was enriched.

How we talked, sometimes when walking in the garden, with its pergola, rosebeds and a deep dell with a pond over which presided a fine copy of the bronze mermaid of Hans Andersen's fable that flanks Copenhagen's harbour. In those talks I became aware that, deep down, there was a sense of discontent despite his sunny, extrovert nature. On this Saturday afternoon he said to me, as we walked the lawn before tea, "You know, I've made a great mistake in my life. I should have been an author not a lawyer. When I went to Cambridge my father hoped I would become a Wesleyan minister. But at Cambridge I knew I had no 'call' as they put it. I certainly had 'the gift of the gab'. If you don't go into the Church there are only politics or the Bar where you can capitalise on it. So I went to the Bar, but I've never liked it, with its miserable odour of the Law Courts."

He had a grievance over the delayed peerage. He should have had it after the Nuremberg trials in 1946. His colleague there had been made a peer. He complained that Lord Chief Justice Goddard had deferred his elevation as a Lord Justice of Appeal. "With the result I did not arrive at my pension until last year, aged seventy-five. And what have I to show for it all? Can you recall the name of any Lord Chancellor or Lord Chief Justice of fifty years ago? Look at you, my dear fellow, with a long list of books to your name, something to show, and you've given pleasure to millions."

I stopped in our walk. "Norman, how can you talk such nonsense!" I exclaimed. "You've had a wonderfully successful career, a K.C., a Knight, a Privy Councillor, a Lord Justice of Appeal and now a Peer. You've earned thirty to fifty thousand pounds a year as an advocate. You're one of the best-known, most liked figures in the Kingdom. You've made a fortune, you've got a fine pension. You've a wonderful wife, a handsome son, a happily married daughter, and this lovely home. How do you know you would have had any success as an author, or been able to make a living at it?" "But you've done very well, haven't you?" asked Norman, "You're very comfortable, aren't you?" "If I am, my dear Norman, it's not from writing books," I replied. "I've never earned one fifth of what you've earned each year. And I've no pension awaiting my old age. My grim boyhood taught me a lesson. I'm independent because I've always lived on less than two-thirds of my income, whatever it was. The Society of Authors recently had a poll. Only ten per cent of its members make £1,000 a year, the average only £500. True, I've been a 'best-seller" for over thirty years but under our iniquitous free-lending-library system my books have been loaned out a million times and all I get is a shilling or two royalty on the single copy bought by the library. You can't perform a drama, play a record or a piece of music, or use a photo, without paying a fee. But when an author asks for a penny on each copy lent, the libraries rise up in wrath and block all attempts to pass a Bill giving him a lending-right fee. Just where would you be if you'd relied on a pen instead of a wig? For one Somerset Maugham there's a thousand derelicts. Don't think I'm complaining. I've always wanted to be an author, I've been an author, and I've enjoyed every year of my life, as you have done. You mustn't talk rubbish, my dear Norman. You've had a wonderful innings!"

He blinked at me through his glasses and smiled. "Dear me! You've read me quite a lesson," he said, putting his arm over my shoulder. "You are quite right. I should not talk such nonsense. I've been quite a success, as you say, and I've enjoyed my life. I often think that my deepest pleasure was in addressing a jury in a murder case, but that was ephemeral, and good writing has a chance of being remembered."

At that moment Billy bore down on us, carrying a camera. "What are you two talking about? You look as serious as judges. Now please sit down on that bench, I want to take your photograph." We sat on the bench, meekly. She was a skilled photographer and developed and enlarged her own photos. She took us several times, and then we went into the loggia for tea.

I had decided to publish a selection of my poems written between 1910 and 1960. I had brought with me a set of proofs for Norman to read. Another set I had left with John Betjeman. On returning to London I went to see him. He was living in a tiny flat over a butcher's shop in the City area. His windows looked on the grave-yard of St. Bartholomew's, one of the oldest in London. I found him in bed in a state of happy disorder, books, letters, papers, proofs, covering the bed and the floor. He had finished my proofs. It was a service we did for each other. Our friendship had covered over thirty years. It was past noon. John got up, dressed and took me off to lunch at a local chop-house frequented, he told me, by wool

Dr. A. L. Rowse and the author at All Souls College

Judith Masefield, the author, and John Masefield

Somerset Maugham painted by Sir Gerald Kelly, P.R.A.
(*left*) and Graham Sutherland

Lunch at the Crouching Lion, Honolulu, the author with
R. Dudley and Mrs. Boehm

dealers and butchers from near-by Smithfield Market. The chop-house was Dickensian, with a special table reserved for John who evidently was *persona grata* in this odd milieu. They knew he was a poet, a strange business they could not understand but were awed by it. He was enfolded in an affectionate bonhomie and today, far from being sunk in gloom and apprehension, he was exuberantly happy.

In August I left to spend the week-end with Leslie Rowse at his home, Trenarren, at St. Austell, Cornwall. He had a stately Georgian house, stone built, at the summit of a deep combe, umbrageous with chestnut trees, that fell swiftly towards the sea. Leslie lived in almost squirearchal state in this former home of the gentry, which gave him a certain wry pleasure of achievement, for he came of a claymining family that had laboured in the local pits. He was now a famous son of Cornwall, after a brilliant Oxford academic career which he owed entirely to his own prodigious industry. He has told his story, movingly, in *A Cornish Childhood*. His house had a large Louis-Seize drawing-room with Aubusson carpet, etc., which he seldom used for he shut himself up in a book-lined study, a hermit, pursuing Elizabethan trails in a domain he has made his own.

We often walked on the rocky seacoast headlands. He took me one day to Mevagissey, a little Cornish fishing port with an almost land-locked harbour, and hideous Victorian houses on the horizon. It had a crowded summer season and burst with tourist prosperity. For some elusive reason we both had a fit of the giggles and we built up between us a fantastic life there and nearly fell into the harbour. Its very name moved me to hysterics. It was a relief to take our aching faces off to lovely Fowey where he showed me the swallow's house of Quiller-Couch, "Q", the novelist, one-time Professor of Literature in the University of Cambridge, best remembered now as the compiler of the first Oxford Book of English Verse. "Q" had shown Leslie much kindness at the beginning of his career. With a huge public in the U.S.A., where the Shakespeare industry flourishes, he was now high in the top-earning category of the Society of Authors' poll. Prosperity had neither dimmed his industry nor his combatant sense of humour.

What would our American audiences have thought of us, seeing two elderly authors, swaying giddily with mirth in Mevagissey?

I don't know why we had that effect on each other. One day I fell flat on my face outside All Souls College, tripped up in a storm of laughter that some remark of his had provoked. "You know this sort of thing is fatal to our reputations," he warned. "The public is impressed by the solemn owl, and Oxford is its nest." Our friendship had begun many years ago when I had written to him pointing out some grammatical errors in one of his books. I feared he might be angry. Not at all. We visited each other. One day a letter came from him addressed "Cecil Roberts, K.C.M.G." I asked what he meant by that. "Kindly Correct My Grammar," he replied.

Early in September I flew with my car from Lydd airport to Le Touquet en route to stay with my cousin Walter Robert in Paris, where he had lived for some fifty years. His wife was French. His history was a singular one. A good linguist, as a youth he had gone out to work in the office of a marble quarry firm near Athens. During a riot at the quarry he got a bullet in his lung. After a short spell in hospital, the bullet still there, he was sent home. In the train he met a Frenchman who, alarmed that he should be travelling in such a dangerous state, persuaded him to go into hospital as soon as the train reached Paris. It was found that the bullet was too near the heart to be extracted. The kindly Frenchman took him into his home and nursed him. On recovery he offered the youth a position in the Western Union Telegraph Company, of which he was the Paris manager. So Walter never went back to England, married a French girl, and eventually succeeded his benefactor as manager. He was now almost a Frenchman, but resolutely kept his British nationality. The bullet was still in his lung. He read my manuscripts for me, an acute critic.

One morning in Paris I had an odd adventure. I had never seen the Conciergerie with its grim prison where Marie Antoinette and other victims of the Revolution had passed their last hours. Emerging from the Metro, I asked a gendarme to direct me to the entrance. I was received by a porter in a somewhat elaborate uniform who, taking my hat at the cloak-room, asked me to wait until others had arrived. Presently there entered a party of about forty men and women. We were led up a grand, carpeted staircase, then along what seemed to be a columned ballroom, to a room overlooking the Seine. It struck me as a very odd way into a prison. I then noticed in glass cases all round the room what appeared to be illuminated addresses, with the names of famous people on them. I read on one that, on October 7th, 1896, there was a reception in honour of the Emperor and Empress of Russia. A vase had been given by Czar Alexander III to the City of Paris. On Saturday May 2nd, 1903, Edward VII and President Loubet were received by M. Deville, President of the Municipal Council, and M. Selves, Préfet de la Cité and members of the Council. As I examined these documents, more and more puzzled, a double door was flung open and a gold-laced flunkey announced "Monsieur le Préfet!" A dapper gentleman in a tail coat, wearing a gold chain stood there. Behind him was a large buffet. He shook the hands of the visitors who filed before him. Unable to escape the line, mine was shaken in turn. On a table there was a large book which the visitors signed. This was too much for me. I slipped out of the room, almost ran through the ballroom, down the crimson carpeted stairs to the cloakroom where, to the attendant's surprise, I retrieved my hat. "Is this the Conciergerie?" I asked. "No, m'sieur. This is the Hotel de Ville!" "And the ladies and gentlemen who have just gone upstairs?" "They are the mayors and mayoresses of France, m'sieur. They are here attending a conference, and the Préfet is holding a reception for them." I hurried out. I was on the wrong side of the Seine! When I told my cousin I had been received by the Préfet of Paris he looked surprised, and when I explained he collapsed in mirth.

In Paris I met my old friend Armand de la Rochefoucauld. I enquired about his uncle and aunt, the Duke and Duchess de Bisaccia. In 1927 Armand had taken me to visit them at their beautiful Château d'Esclimont, built by François I, *parrain* of a La Rochefoucauld. Yes, they were alive and often enquired about me. "Why don't you go and see them, they would be delighted," said Armand. So on leaving Paris I went to see them. What memories! In 1927, going there, we had crashed into the gates of the Château de Rambouillet. Armand's racing car had been utterly wrecked but somehow we emerged alive. We were taken on to his uncle's château, where I had been semi-delirious. With what kindness they had treated me!

Thirty-two years is a long time but I found little had changed. The château and its grounds were as lovely as before but my host and hostess had, of course, aged. They produced the visitors' book in which I had signed my name. Why had I stayed away so long? Their two pretty daughters were now married but at lunch that day, seated with a dozen shooting-party guests, I learned that an old wound had been healed. When I had left after my first visit, the Duchess, in tears, had said to Armand, "If you see my poor Stanislas, give him my love." I enquired what this was about and learned that the son and heir had been forbidden the house because he had married, defying them, an actress, a liaison the duke would not condone. Now at table I found myself sitting next to a lady who proved to be Count Stanislas's wife. The actress, after all? I felt my way cautiously and learned that the first marriage had been annulled, and now he was married to this lady of whom the family approved. Alas, for human destiny. Stanislas did not succeed to the dukedom and the château. He died prematurely, and the duke, in his eighties, was without an heir.

III

I was in Alassio for Christmas, 1959, having previously been in Genoa to consult our Consul-General about the memorial tablet for Max Beerbohm. I did not live at the Palazzo Vairo as I was without a servant. and stayed with my friend Alida Bock at the Villino Romano where I had every comfort. Three days after Christmas I motored along the beautiful Middle Corniche road to Cap d'Antibes, once more the guest of Lady Norman at the Château de La Garoupe. I found "Fay", as ever, efficiently managing her various houses. I was given my usual room in the château with its veranda overlooking the gardens and the terraces falling to the sea. A mauve wistaria covered the loggia below. In the evening, when I went up to dress, walking along the wide corridor to my room, I saw again the magnificent panorama of the snow-capped Alps, and the bay of Nice glittering with lights. On New Year's Eve a crescent moon hung high over the fabled shore.

Fay's family was present, her son Willoughby at the Folie, her second son and his wife, Antony and Anne, at the Tourelle. There were sixteen for lunch one day and it was so hot on the terrace when we took coffee that the awning had to be lowered. That evening we went to Cannes to see the Marqués de Cuevas's Ballet Company

228

in *Gaieté Parisienne*. I was shocked to see George de Cuevas in a wheel chair, very thin and pale. In New York during the war he had shown me much hospitality. His parties were always memorable for their gaiety and his inventive spirit. He had a temporary wooden floor put down in his salon on which La Argentinita gave her Spanish dances. Sometimes Segovia played the guitar. Warm-hearted, George was an exuberant little man who had a habit of kissing everybody. Once, in the hall of the Grand Hotel in Rome, he resoundingly saluted me on both cheeks, to my embarrassment. Now when I went up to his box to greet him, between the acts, I saw that he was a dying man.

IV

After my return to Alassio I was surprised to find at the door my old friend Seddon Cripps (Lord Parmoor). He had arrived with a bag of golf clubs. He was as full of fun and life as ever, despite his seventy-seven years. We had then no golf links at Alassio, though my friend Rolandi Ricci would soon back an enterprise to create a magnificent course at Garlenda, ten miles away. After a couple of days Seddon went to San Remo, on whose heights he found a course.

I went to Florence in March to collect some data. I was contemplating a Renaissance novel. I lunched again with ex-Queen Helen of Rumania at the Villa Sparta, halfway up the hill to Fiesole, all Florence spread below. I found there her widowed sister, the Duchess of Aosta, from her villa across the road. Then I went on to Rome, taking up my usual quarters at the Grand Hotel. I had made a momentous decision. I had decided to sell my apartment at the Palazzo Vairo. My friends were aghast but they did not know the reasons that led me to this step. I had found myself isolated in a dying English colony. From a thousand we were down to fifty and most of these were in their seventies and eighties. I seemed always to be visiting the sick, writing on pads for the deaf, or reading to the blind. There were endless memorial services. I had just attended one for our oldest colleague, a grand old man of ninety-four. On Christmas Day, my host, Sir Louis Rieu, eighty-two, had not been able to come to the table. Severe Exchange restrictions and British currency devaluations also played havoc. Villas were being torn up, giving place to gigantic concrete apartment blocks. There were other reasons. My visiting friends were beginning to desert me. They were very happy to come once, but naturally they wished to spend their annual holidays in new places. In the winter months I found myself looking down over a deserted, silent town. To lack of company I found other drawbacks.

In Rome the winters were lively with concerts, operas, plays and exhibitions. More important was the availability of libraries necessary to my researches. Alassio had an excellent English library attached to the church, but it was well-equipped only in books marking the high tide, the nineties onwards, when there was a well-off, flourishing British colony. It could not offer the amenities of the Rome libraries. I had many friends in Rome, from the Embassy down. There was a stream of visitors from all over the world. So with reluctance I instructed an agent to sell my apartment. In despair I revoked the order, and then repeated it. I sold the place with everything in it. I had pensioned Giulietta, my house-keeper, too ill to work. I sought to be free from the servant trouble that had ensued. Servants were getting scarcer and scarcer, with growing competition from the hotels.

Even so, closing down Palazzo Vairo tore at my heart-strings. I had received much kindness from everybody. It passed into a remembered dream of happiness. After the dismantling I left for England, staying, via Geneva, at Antoine Cloetta's Château Vernier, with its blue swimming pool presided over by a bronze dolphin. We lunched one day at my host's chalet on Lake Geneva, reached by his terrifying speed boat. One evening there were four exceedingly vivacious and pretty English, Canadian and American girls to dine on the long terrace above the Rhone.

I flew the Channel with my car and in July was again Leslie Rowse's guest at All Souls College, Oxford had all its old enchantment, and how we talked and laughed, with open windows overlooking the green seclusion of the second Quad. A week later I suffered the loss of Tod Iliffe. Crossing the Atlantic, after the winter in Nassau, he had been thrown down in his cabin during a storm, causing a slight concussion. This developed, necessitating a brain operation. He survived this but one day, while dictating to his secretary in the clinic, his heart stopped. He was eighty-three.

Warned of mortality, I made a Will, then went on my usual visits to the Williamsons, John Masefield, more sweetly venerable than ever, the Birketts, the Lacys, and to Richard Church with whom I had much in common. We had both walked out of the Civil Service, taking a risk with our pens. He had come through after the success of his autobiography *Over the Bridge*. He lived in a converted Kent oast house, with a large garden. He had an amusing story for me. By the high wall of his garden ran a lane. One afternoon, while dozing, he overheard the conversation of two passing "locals". "Who lives there?" "A man called Church." "What does 'e do?" " 'E writes books." A silence except for the sound of feet, then a voice: " 'E seems to make a bloody good thing of it!"

My *Selected Poems* had appeared. It had a still birth, and only two reviews. I complained to Richard, an excellent poet. "My last book had three reviews," he said, gently. "We haven't cultivated the coteries, and offered incense. We commit a grave offence. Our poems have rhyme, rhythm and reason, and lack obscenity and obscurity. All this abstract theory, which bedevils letters, painting, sculpture and music today, is an 'iron curtain' excluding folks like us. What can we do except to leave the last decision to that grim old critic, Father Time?"

I sent a copy of my poems to Somerset Maugham. He had once complained to me, as also had Joseph Conrad, that he was utterly incapable of writing a line of verse. He wrote: "Thanks for your *Selected Poems*. I have read them with particular pleasure. They are a relief and a comfort to me after the volumes of very, very modern poetry that are sent to me by authors who have won my Award. After reading them three or four times I find myself completely bewildered. The explanation they have offered me is that modern poetry is written, not to be read, but to be heard. That may be all very well if you have a television set in your house, but if you haven't, as is the case with me, you are left where you are."

v

On my return journey to Italy I stayed in Paris with my cousin and lunched with André Maurois at his apartment which overlooked the Bois de Boulogne. He lived in considerable state, with a butler and a magnificent library. He also had a large château in the south of France. It was not all from books. His father had owned a prosperous silk factory. We had met on platforms in the United States. He was a fluent English speaker and a true *homme-de-lettres*. At Eze I joined the Churches, having a Riviera holiday. I took them to lunch at the Château de La Garoupe, informing Fay that my friend was a well-known writer. "Oh, what do you write ?" she asked him. "Novels," replied Richard, meekly. "Oh, what a pity! I never read them," said Fay. We two novelists exchanged looks. It was one of her frank moments. The lunch was a success, nevertheless.

I arrived back in Alassio for the ceremony conferring on me its Honorary Citizenship. Sir Ashley Clarke came from Rome for the occasion. He followed the Mayor with a charming speech in fluent Italian. This ambassadorial visit delighted everybody, particularly the British colony. I received a beautiful illiuminated address, in coloured Gothic lettering, with views of Alassio, which graciously ran: "In recognition of his fame as a writer and of the great worth of his *Portal to Paradise*, written to celebrate the beauty and history of the city which has the honour of giving him hospitality for the greater part of each year."

I took this opportunity to ask Sir Ashley to unveil the plaque on Max Beerbohm's villa at near-by Rapallo. Two days later, on November 4th, 1960, we journeyed there for the ceremony. I was glad to see the end of my labour. It was surprising the number of persons who had advice to offer, who thought they should be consulted. Some of them had not been near Max for years. There was a controversy over the name. Some wanted "Sir Maximilian Beerbohm" on the plaque, a Christian name he had never used and which would have puzzled many. Then there was an objection to quoting Bernard Shaw's famous tribute "The incomparable Max". We were assured Max never liked the description and had said deliberately, "I am not incomparable." He said this, but it was done jokingly in a letter. The tablet should be in bronze, not in marble, said some. It should not be a tablet at all but a bust in an alcove in the wall, said others. The inscription should be in Italian. An Oxford don complained he was not on the committee. There was no committee. No one did anything until I took action and enlisted the support of our Ambassador. Two successive Consul-Generals, David Balfour and John May, at Genoa, had been of the greatest help. And now here was the plaque, carved in white Carrara marble, lettered in lead, well-placed above the road fronting the villa. It said:

Here lived 1910–1956
Sir Max Beerbohm
1872–1956
English writer and caricaturist
'The incomparable Max.'

There was a brief inscription in Italian below. For the unveiling ceremony on that bright November day we were a party of about forty. As there was heavy traffic on the road the authorities sent *carabinieri* to halt it. Sir Ashley made a brief speech and then pulled a cord, releasing the Union Jack from the plaque. There was no relation of Max's present but his friend, Rupert Hart-Davis, an avid collector, his lawyer, his publisher and an art gallery director had come from London. The Mayors of Genoa and Rapallo and some officials were present. The Consul-General gave a lunch at the Hotel Savoia in Rapallo.

Everything had gone without a hitch. I presented the architect's sketch for the plaque to Max's Merton College, Oxford, which was making a memorial collection. After the ceremony I went up alone on to the wide terrace where we had talked through sunny afternoons. Poor Elizabeth was in my thoughts, too, as I surveyed the silent, empty scene. *Sunt lacrimae rerum.*

When Somerset Maugham heard of my Alassio honour, he said: "It's time somebody gave me something!" They did. Ten months later he was given the Freedom of Nice. It was consigned to him, not in a casket, but, symbolically, in a dry gourd!

At Christmas there was the unfailing invitation to the Château de la Garoupe. I had to stay in bed under attack by the old enemy the first two days. I read through Compton Mackenzie's *Greece in my Life*, and came upon a description of Princess Aspasia my Venetian friend. She and her sister, daughters of Colonel Manos, had been two famous beauties in Athens. Aspasia had swept the ill-fated King Alexander off his feet.

Fay and I often talked confidentially. We discussed our beliefs, being much in accord. She did not want a second life. "Once is enough, and I could not have it as good a second time," she said, "and what in heaven would one do with everlasting life? The idea's frightening!" I felt the same.

On Christmas Day there was a lunch for fourteen, to which I could not do justice. It was a marvellous day of sunshine, eighty degrees in the shade. I was delighted to see a dwarf hummingbird hovering over a tuberose. As I watched the sun go down on the last day of 1960, I reflected what a wonderful life I had had, enjoying my work, delivered from early hardship and obscurity by my pen. I had been able to fulfil the three great desires of my life, writing, reading and travelling.

Two mornings later when I came downstairs in time to go and lunch at the Tourelle with Anne and Antony, Fay asked, very quietly, "Were you disturbed in the night?" I had not been, in fact I had slept for eight hours. "Early this morning," said Fay, "I was called. One of our staff who, with his wife, housekeeps at The Clocher committed suicide. I had to call the police, have the body taken to the mortuary, move my alarmed tenants to another house, and have the placed cleaned up. It is all over now. I am glad you were not disturbed."

Fay told me the tragedy behind the story. Some years earlier the police trapped a lorry in the mile-long drive in the grounds. It was loaded with contraband tobacco which had been landed from a boat in the cove below. The question arose how the lorry came to be in the grounds, when the gate was locked at night. It transpired that one of the staff had been in collusion with smugglers and had unlocked the gate. He was sentenced to a term of imprisonment. "We took him back when he came out. We have always been a happy family here. But the disgrace proved too much for the poor man's mind and this morning he shot himself." I listened and looked with amazement at Fay, so efficient, so calm and under control through it all.

I stayed on into the New Year. The other guests departed and we dined quietly in the small sitting-room before a log fire. Our talk ranged far and wide, often until past midnight. Fay was very frank and downright about everything. The subject of marriage came up, something I had not embarked on. I said I thought sex was largely a youth-storm, designed to perpetuate the race, hence it had been made one of the highest of human pleasures in its gratification but that most sexual relations seem condemned to disintegrate. For the fortunate few marriage was the greatest possible happiness. The bogy in most people's lives was loneliness. In old age it became acute. "I've been warned about that," I said, "You know what they say— the bachelor lives like a lion and dies like a dog. But some dogs have a happy end. Three of mine had!"

"Well," said Fay, "I've been singularly fortunate. My husband had been married before. He had one son whom I helped to bring up. Henry was a scientist, journalist and an M.P. I was able to help him with his work. Nigel, his son, had a brilliant career and founded the Paratrooper Regiment in the Second World War. He was killed flying in 1943. He had a strong character. At Winchester, resenting the pressure to be confirmed brought upon him by his housemaster, he requested an interview with the headmaster, telling him he simply could not accept the Christian theology. He did not believe in the virgin birth. It was not original. Earlier religions had claimed it. He asked to be protected from those who were endeavouring, however sincere and well-meaning, to drive him to a declaration of belief in things he found incredible. Somewhat surprisingly the headmaster saw the reasonableness of the request and gave instructions for him to be left alone. Nigel married a beautiful girl and had three sons. As for my own marriage, I've had a wonderfully happy and interesting life. My husband loved me dearly. He recalled your coming to our country house, Ramster, and the vivid conversation you both had. He thought you very precocious. 'I hope he doesn't die young,' he said, you seemed so delicate—transparent, in a way. I loved Henry and there was never a moment in our lives when we were not in the deepest accord and devoted to each other. When he died, I died and my life was really finished." She may have thought this, but no one else did. She was dynamic to the end of her life, aged eighty.

What wonderful evenings they were in that pine-log-burning room. It was somewhat like a game of tennis, with a quick opponent giving you a good return of the ball of conversation.

CHAPTER TEN

Shadows in Sicily

I

In the New Year of 1961 on my way to Alassio I called at the Villa Egerton and lunched with Charlotte and Langton, now Lord Iliffe, and his beautiful wife. But the ghost of Tod was there all the time. There was no one to tease me. Two days later I dined with Rolandi Ricci at his castle on the mountain-side above the silver stream rushing over the rocks. He was witty, even regarding food. On the menu was "Les demoiselles en chemise. Sauce Fragonard." How much better than Picasso's frightful trio, *Les Demoiselles d'Avignon*, which I found so visually indigestible.

On arrival at Alassio a book awaited me. It was from John Betjeman, a copy of his new long poem *Summoned By Bells*. The year previous he had written to me from a house near Killarney about the phenomenal sale of his *Collected Poems* (1958), with all the publicity it evoked. He was now apprehensive. I had recommended him to go into a sort of Wordsworthian "retreat" and to get on with a blank verse poem, à la "Prelude". He wrote: "I would have written before had I not spent two weeks of Irish peace, walking and driving and loitering and in the mornings going on with my blank verse autobiography, which few will read and fewer praise, but which is what I want to do. I hope you will not be disappointed with it. I am going to stop when I am twenty-three, as after that I got into the old literary groove we all know. It covers early childhood, Cornwall, Dragon School (as far as I've got), London in the twenties, Marlborough, Oxford, ending with being a private schoolmaster after being sent down. So the Wordsworthian seclusion you prescribed is being indulged in so far as it is financially possible."

He had sent me the proofs of his poem and as soon as I had read them I felt that he need have no apprehension about its reception. There is often a bad reaction when an author follows up a great success. After my *Victoria Four-Thirty* I had had the same apprehension. I read his proofs at one sitting, with moments of excitement. It was down to earth and yet reached to the skies.

> The eucalyptus shivered in the drive,
> The stars were out above the garage roof,
> Night-scented stock and white tobacco plant
> Gave way to petrol scent and came again.

Here the automobile moves into poetry without incongruity of time or language. I felt that he had done it again. Then, emotionally relieved, I set to work going over the proofs with a cold, dissecting eye. And now here was the published book, warmly inscribed, fit to come out of the Albemarle Street of Murray and Byron.

II

In February I left with a friend to make a tour of Sicily. I little knew that 1961 was to be a year overshadowed by the wings of the Angel of Death. In those first days at Syracuse the world seemed a very lovely place. I sat in the hot sun in the auditorium of the theatre, the largest known in the Greek world, with its seventy tiers of seats cut out of the rock on the hillside, and its magnificent view of the harbour and the blue Ionian Sea. I had brought with me a copy of *Persae* by Aeschylus, the tremendous historical drama written by the poet around the story of Salamis. Aeschylus himself had produced the play here, in 472 B.C. I tried to imagine myself one of the twenty thousand spectators of that far off day. Afterwards I went to the quarries of the Latomia which had witnessed the last tragic scene of what Thucydides called "the most important event in Greek history", the defeat of the Athenian expedition in which Demosthenes was captured with six thousand men who were shut up in the quarries to starve for nine months. The survivors were sold as slaves, with the exception of a few who were set at liberty because they could recite verses from Euripides. How vividly

Mary Renault has evoked the scene in her classic story, *The Last of the Wine*.

A little below Taormina I found an hotel that had a balcony from which I looked on snow-crowned Etna. At night there was a wicked rift in its side from which red flames shot up, the sky above quivering with a ruddy glow. It was a terrifyingly beautiful scene. The next morning I saw the Carnival in Taormina, with an astonishing ballet of pretty painted youths, wearing the chlamys, flower-crowned, nigh naked, dancing down the main street. It was supposed to be in the Virgin's honour, but the spectacle was wholly pagan and looked like a scene out of a Greek comedy, with a chorus of Ganymedes. The halo of the Madonna had somehow slipped and got attached to Aphrodite.

At Rolandi Ricci's I had met Viscount Bridport, Duke of Brontë. The Viscount was his guest along with Lady Bridport, and a small son with the beauty of an opening rose. He invited me to visit him at his Sicilian home. He lived near Randazzo, at the foot of Etna, in the Castello di Maniace. I called him up from my hotel and he invited me to lunch, sending a car to take me there, about forty miles. The village lay on the outer northern circumference of Etna, whose snowy mass dominated the landscape. The last five miles were like a ride through hell, with vicious-looking fields of black lava from former eruptions. The castle lay in a valley at the end of a steeply descending road. The River Saraceni ran through the plain, deceptively over three thousand feet high. The castle itself, low and built of massive stone, was originally a Benedictine monastery founded in A.D. 1174. Here in A.D. 1040 the Greek general, Maniaces, with a Norwegian and Norman army, defeated the Saracens. Margaret, the mother of William II, founded the monastery. It was a rectangular two-storey block with courtyard and a ruined abbey at one side. The title of Duke of Brontë, with the castle and 60,000 acres, had been granted to Lord Nelson by Ferdinand IV, King of the Two Sicilies. Nelson had rescued the King, Queen Carolina, the Court, and the British ambassador, with Lady Hamilton, from the City of Naples, threatened by Republican France. On their return to Naples, Nelson, having committed the judicial murder of Prince Caraccioli and hanged dozens of Neapolitans, going back on his promise of a safe-conduct, was rewarded by the poltroon king with the Brontë title and estate. Nelson never saw his property. Later the title and estate passed to the second Lord Bridport, who had married Nelson's niece.

Arriving at the Castello I was welcomed by Lord Bridport. He was a tall, bald, taciturn man, an ex-naval officer with a distinguished record, descended from a famous naval family. I was taken through a wide gateway into a large courtyard with the abbey on the right and the house on the left, in which one ascended to an upper floor with a long gallery, salon and study. In the centre of the courtyard there was a prominent runic cross. It was a memorial to William Sharp, who wrote under the name of "Fiona Macleod", a friend of Sir Alexander Nelson Hood, the previous Duke of Brontë. Sharp often stayed at Maniace and died there in 1905. He had some fame in his day as leader of a Celtic Revival group, now quite forgotten.

Lord Bridport farmed his land. One half of the estate had been confiscated by the Government for a cooperative farming scheme, but after long litigation in the courts he had been given £52,000 compensation. Oddly enough, I was staying with Rolandi Ricci when I read in *The Times* of this decision of the Italian Appeal Court. Bridport was in the next room playing bridge. I went in and gave him the good news. He showed not one quiver of excitement, put down his card, and said, "Well, what else could they do? They had stolen it!"

Lady Bridport did not like Maniace and stayed in Rome. Their little son, Alexander, was now at Eton. Bridport told me that he had much difficulty with the peasants. He wanted to restore the abbey, which had a fine Norman arch, but they resented his spending any money except on festas and fireworks. "Their ignorance and superstition are appalling," said my host. "You will have noticed that there was no one working in the fields. This morning about noon there was an eclipse of the sun. They all left their work to go back to their homes. If the end of the world came, as they feared, they wanted to die with their families."

I left Maniace in the early evening, and wondered much at a man who was prepared to bury himself in this lonely valley. But he was an enthusiastic farmer and plainly loved his estate. It was singular by what devious genealogical quirks the Bridports found themselves Dukes of Brontë. Lord Nelson died without heirs. An earldom was created for his brother, the title passing to the heir-male of his sister. The Dukedom of Brontë was similarly transferable. Lady Mary Nelson, Duchess of Brontë, was the heiress of the first earl. She married the second Lord Bridport. The Brontë title passed to their son. My host inherited the title from his great-uncle, Alexander Nelson Hood. Viscount Bridport, Duke of Brontë, died in 1969. His son Alexander carries both titles and is farming the Brontë estate.

It was sad that I was never to see the Duke of Brontë again. There was an air of melancholy about him, and, it might be, a touch of shyness. Obviously he was devoted to his isolated castle. I asked him, on leaving, how fertile his land was. He smiled slightly, saying, "Moderate. At one time it was well-manured with Saracen blood."

There is a little D. H. Lawrence footnote to my visit. The previous day I had walked down to Giardini on the coast, Taormina's bathing beach. At Fontana Vecchia there was the house in which Lawrence had lived and written in 1920. I was just in time, it was about to be pulled down to give place to an apartment block. On May 20th, 1920, he wrote to Lady Cynthia Asquith, "Meanwhile life at Fontana Vecchia is very easy, indolent and devil-may-care. Did you ever hear of a Duca di Bronte, Mr. Nelson Hood—descendant of Lord Nelson (Horatio), whom the Neapolitans made Duca di Bronte because he hanged a few of them? Well, Bronte is just under Etna and this Mr. Nelson Hood has a place there—his ducal estate. We went to see him—a rather wonderful place. But perhaps you know him. If I was Duca di Bronte I'd be Tyrant of Sicily. High time there was another Hiero. But of course money maketh man, even if he were a monkey to start with."

Leaving Taormina, I continued my tour of Sicily, arriving in Palermo towards the end of February. I had not been in that city since 1925 when for a month I had been seriously ill with ptomaine poisoning. I thought I would go to the new Jolly Hotel and not to the old Hotel des Palmes, with its unpleasant memories. The first news I received there was of the death of the Marques de Cuevas in his villa in Cannes. It did not surprise me for when I had seen him last year, going with Lady Norman to a performance of his ballet company, it was obvious that he was seriously ill. He had been carried into his box at the theatre where I went to greet him.

The source of his wealth was his marriage to Mary Strong, the granddaughter of John D. Rockefeller, the oil tycoon, "the richest man in the world." There was a story that de Cuevas was an adventurous gigolo who had caught the young heiress. It was utterly untrue. His title was not bogus. He was born in Santiago, Chile, in 1885, a descendant of a famous *conquistador*. He studied in Paris and took a job as publicity agent for a tailor's shop that had been opened by Prince Youssoupov, the killer of Rasputin, and by his wife, Princess Irin, niece of the ill-fated Czar Nicholas II. It was said that Rockefeller had strongly disapproved of de Cuevas, and was not happy at having such a flippant, dapper little foreigner as his granddaughter's husband. Her mother had already displeased him by marrying a Baptist minister. One day at his Palm Beach dinner-table de Cuevas kept turning away the dishes. Rockefeller, irritated, said, "I suppose our food isn't good enough for you?" "It isn't. It's atrocious! You've no idea how to choose a menu," replied de Cuevas. The astonished multi-millionaire said: "Then you take over and let's see what you can do!" De Cuevas took over and the result was such a success with Rockefeller's guests that the millionaire, a chronic dyspeptic who lived on bread and milk, handed over the ordering of his dinners to de Cuevas. From that day the tycoon respected him. George, as everyone called him though his name was Juan, was histrionic, highly strung, eccentric but always *simpatico*. He loved the limelight, whereas his wife and two children were shy and retiring. You never knew whom you would meet in his New York house, really two made into one. I once encountered on the staircase a Roman Catholic bishop, a Negro pugilist, and my friend, Donna Lucienne de Cardenas, and her husband, then Spanish Ambassador at Washington.

In 1939 de Cuevas decided to found a ballet company with the aid of Nijinsky's sister, Bronislava, and Balanchine. The company soon had great success, appearing in the capitals of Europe. He told me that he founded it in the hope of losing money and thereby writing down his income-tax. He was alarmed when it began to make money. In 1947 he took over the direction of the Monte Carlo Ballet, and he organised "festas" at Venice in 1951 and Biarritz in 1953 that by their extravagance drew world-wide criticism. He always surprised you. He once received me in his bedroom, lying on an iron bed decorated with black iron rosettes and hung with crucifixes. A Carmelite monk stood by his side. He had given him money for a mission in Africa. For his Biarritz festa he spent two hundred million francs to create sixteen buffets for three hundred guests. In Paris, when the word went round that he was dying, he appeared on the stage at the end of a performance of *The Sleeping Beauty* and said: "The ballet is not dying, neither am I. We shall go on until the very end." In 1958 he quarrelled with Serge Lifar and they fought a duel. It was a spectacular farce, pure theatre. All the Press was at the 'secret' duelling ground. George pricked Serge's arm. Honour was satisfied. The duellists embraced.

I once told him of the sad case of a Polish refugee, a violinist, whose right arm had been fractured badly in an accident. He and his wife were almost destitute, and only an operation could save his bow arm. "Get him the best surgeon, put him in a good clinic. Send me the bills," he said. I did so. He not only paid the bills, but went to see him in the clinic and turned his room into a bower of flowers. The arm was saved. A year later he arranged a benefit concert for the violinist. De Cuevas's death saddened me, and I felt the poorer.

III

There was something wrong in Palermo. A week later I had another shock. My friend Sir Thomas Beecham had died, a character as rich as de Cuevas's, equally free with money, histrionic, gifted. It is generally conceded that he was one of the four best living conductors, and there were connoisseurs who regarded him as the equal of Toscanini and Furtwängler. His personality with orchestras and audiences was magnetic. He had no money sense, ran through one fortune, went bankrupt, and tried to spend another fortune, tied up fortunately in a trust fund. I had known him, not intimately, for some twenty years, but in New York, in 1940, I was turned into something of a buffer-state in the breakup of his lifelong affair with Lady (Emerald) Cunard. He took up with a pianist, Betty Humby, a clergyman's wife, got a questionable divorce from his discarded wife, Lady Beecham, and married her. I used to meet him, until the final break, in Emerald's suite at the Ritz Hotel in New York.

As the rumours grew of his affair with Betty Humby, Emerald reached a stage of hysteria. She had a habit of ringing me at two or three in the morning, saying we must stop Tommy behaving so outrageously. In vain I pointed out that one man cannot interfere in the amatory affairs of another. Finally, broken-hearted, Emerald left for England in 1941. She never recovered from the blow.

In 1944 I had a bad haemorrhage from a duodenal ulcer, brought on by overwork. I had made over two hundred war propaganda speeches. I was found in my room in a pool of blood and rushed to New York Hospital. When the time came for me to be discharged Beecham and his wife would not hear of me returning to my bed-sitting-room. They fetched me in their car and nursed me in their apartment. So I had reason to remember this remarkable man with affection. Now in my Palermo hotel I received a cutting from the *Daily Telegraph* announcing his death. Martin Cooper in an obituary notice wrote:

> His intelligence moved like lightning and his life was lived in a kind of incandescence that made ordinary lives seem tepid. He was one of the most gifted executant musicians that England has ever produced, the most brilliant orchestral conductor of his period; a man of infinite wit, variety, courage and vitality. These gifts, and with them a princely fortune, he dedicated to music, and the art has perhaps never known another single benefactor on quite the same scale, spiritual and material.

I had not recovered from this second shock when I had a third. I had met, while he was an undergraduate at Oxford, an extra-ordinary youth, Richard Rumbold. He had written a sensational novel. It was the story of alleged homosexual practices at his Catholic school and of a youth who had committed suicide, unable to stand up to the public school system. Rumbold was ostracised at Oxford, refused Holy Communion by the Roman Catholic Church, and excommunicated. He visited the Vatican for an audience with the Pope but his appeal to have the ban removed failed. Meeting him in the rooms of an Oxford don, I felt sorry for this overwrought youth and invited him to Pilgrim Cottage for Easter. He almost wrecked my house-party with his outrageous statements, which I refused to take seriously. Then suddenly he became a charmer. In the war he had a good record in night-bombing expeditions. After the war he came to see me. He had spent most of his life wandering about the world. He again created a sensation with a book about his father, who, he alleged, had driven his mother to suicide. Later his sister committed suicide. He was consumptive and neurotic. He toured with a constant companion, the 59-year-old Mrs Hilda Young, a friend of the family. Handsome, vivacious, with an adequate private fortune, he sought fame as an author, and spiritual peace. Both evaded him.

I did not know when I arrived in Palermo that Richard Rumbold was there. Had I gone to the Hotel des Palmes, as formerly, I should have met him. One morning, while dictating to Mrs. Young, who acted as his amanuensis, he walked into an adjoining room and did not return. His body was found in the courtyard fifty-feet below. Perhaps if I had met him and talked with him, for he found me understanding, he said, this would not have happened. I had last seen him in 1949 when he came to Pilgrim Cottage with Lady Margaret Stewart, with whom he was about to set off on a motor safari across the Sahara. He had been in a Zen monastery, he told me. He seemed happy and in good health then. His friend Archibald Colquhoun arranged the sending of Rumbold's body to England. He left behind a remarkable diary covering the last thirty years of his life, *A Message in Code*, which his cousin, William Plomer, edited.*

I travelled on to Sorrento. There, ill fate pursued me. I went down with an attack of the old enemy. Three weeks later I struggled back to Rome, and was sent by my doctor to the Salvator Mundi Hospital, on a hill overlooking the city. Alas, I was no stranger there. As soon as I was out again I attended a dinner given by John Leslie in his sixteenth-century palazzo, and read to his guests from my recently published book of poems. Then I went on to Alassio, to my friend Alida Bock's Villino Romano, my home since I had sold Palazzo Vairo. I had nursed her through an operation for double cataract and now she looked after me. But, alas, the Villino would soon be no more. It was set in a beautiful garden with palm trees and cypresses, and was embowered in roses. In the grounds there was a charming little lodge, buried in blue plumbago, in which I wrote. The Villino had been built in the grounds of a larger

* See *Sunshine and Shadow*, Ch. 4, II.

villa whose owner had had quite a history. She was the retired Marquise de Montelembert, the daughter of the Duc de Praslin-Choiseul. He was charged with the murder of his wife while having an affair with his children's governess. The trial created a great sensation in Paris. He was acquitted. This episode was the basis of a successful novel and film, *All This and Heaven Too*.

When I arrived at the Villino I had disturbing news. All over Alassio the old villas and their gardens were being ruthlessly destroyed to provide sites for huge apartment houses. Anyone who resisted this pressure found himself hemmed in by cliffs of concrete. The squeeze had now begun on the Villino Romano. Two neighbours had been forced to sell. My friend was offered a good sum to surrender the property. Otherwise she would have sun and light cut off by concrete behemoths. She was a woman of seventy and the villa had been her home for forty years. She had no choice. So at the end of the year she would have to move into another abode.

I had been very happy there, with the garden, the casetta, and excellent servants. My friend relieved me of all domestic cares. I had written there my novel *Love Is Like That*, some of its Alassian sunshine got into its pages. Now on arrival, with only a few more months of this sub-tropical setting, I began my South American novel, *Wide Is The Horizon*.

In May, while working on this, I received a letter from our ambassador, in Rome, Sir Ashley Clarke. I had declined an invitation to be present at a reception for the visit of Queen Elizabeth and the Duke of Edinburgh. "You must come," he wrote. "You will need a white tie." It was almost an official command. Alas, my full dress clothes were in London. I therefore asked an Alassio friend, Count Rogeri, a retired diplomat, if he could oblige me with the loan of tails, shirt, waistcoat, tie and collar. I had my own evening trousers, and black shoes. "But my dear fellow, I am short! You are tall. My clothes can't possibly fit you," he said. I suggested that they would, since, though he was not as tall, his chest was almost the same. So he lent me his suit. He also offered me an Order, a blue sash and a star. I demurred. "Don't worry, they'll never know it's not yours. It's a Latvian knighthood which they gave me when I was Minister there. Now Latvia doesn't exist, Russia's swallowed it up," said Rogeri. I declined the Order but borrowed the coat and waistcoat. Before leaving Alassio for Rome I had a dress rehearsal. His clothes had been made in Savile Row, London. Nothing could have been better.

I was unable to get a room at the Grand Hotel in Rome, so I went to a smaller one. On the night of the reception I dined first and ordered a taxi. I went up to dress. I tied a perfect white bow, and all was well until—horror!—I had forgotten to pack the white waistcoat. In despair I sat on the bed, frustrated. With only a few minutes to spare, where could I get a white waistcoat? Desperate, I pulled the lapels of the coat across my stomach—there was a wide gap. I sent for some safety pins but these would not hold and the gap still showed. Then, determined not to be defeated, I took out of a shoe a black shoelace, made a loop at each end, fastened one loop on the right button of the jacket, one on the left, pulling it together. Alas, there was still a narrow white gap between the jacket. I had a pair of white kid gloves. By holding these in my left hand over the gap all was well, if I kept my hand there.

I arrived at the crowded Embassy and in due course made my bow to Queen Elizabeth, my hand over my stomach. All the evening I kept my hand there. I was the last to leave the Embassy and Sir Ashley was standing at the door. When I told him how I had come to Court on a shoestring and showed him, he burst into laughter. As I left I asked him a question. On a previous visit of the "Royals", then Princess Elizabeth and Prince Philip, Mallet, our ambassador, had been given a pair of gold cuff-links, with the royal arms. "What did you get, cuff-links?" I asked Ashley. His face expanded into a bright smile. "No, better, a G.C.V.O.," he replied.

IV

One June day Rolandi Ricci took me to see the family palazzo in Albenga. His family had been established there for over four hundred years. The palazzo had twenty-two rooms. He had lived there, before going to the castle, with his mother, who had recently died. The palazzo had a fine library. Some of the books, autographed, were by Ferdinand Bac whom Luigi had known in Paris. He was the illegitimate son of Prince Jerome Bonaparte. The library also had complete first editions of Molière and Voltaire.

The Rolandi Ricci family had owned another palazzo in Albenga where Napoleon had had his headquarters during his campaign in Italy. He had walked through five consecutive salons whose open doors provided a long promenade, talking and giving orders to his staff. He often kept them awake all night. He took over the command of the army in Italy from Massena, in Albenga. He made my host's great-great-uncle a Bishop in Paris, and had another on his staff. The sword given to the latter by Napoleon I had seen in the castle at Conscente.

At the end of June I left Alassio by car for London. It was the end of the Villino Romano days, and Alida Bock and I were near tears. Count Rogeri gave a farewell party for me. The Alassio saga was ended. I would be living in Rome, but some of my heart would always be in the delightful town which had shown me such kindness, making me an honorary citizen.

v

I flew my car from Le Touquet to Lydd, a convenient landing place since I made a point after passing Rye to call at Staplecross in Sussex, where there was a little cottage called Wideview. There lived the mother of my beloved Lucien, who with his sister used to row me about Venice. I had made him my heir, sent him to school in England, to lose him in all his beauty and gaiety at twenty-two in the North African campaign. Beryl Reid, his mother, was an astonishing character. With her artist husband she had lived enthusiastically, though meagrely, many years in Venice, and now, widowed, she had settled to live alone in a tiny cottage whose view justified its name. Motoring out to Lydd, and coming in from it, this was for me a place of call. In her seventies she was still of vigorous mind. Horrified by the processions of old horses that passed her door en route to a Belgian slaughter-house, from time to time she purchased an ailing donkey. In the paddock behind the cottage she fattened him and let him end his days in ease. All animals and birds knew her kind hand and eye. Beryl was seventy-five when she surprised us by publishing a book of poems. In it was one evoked when I arrived, wearing a green shantung suit I had bought in Palm Beach.

Although you came a day too soon
This advent I did not deplore,
Though unprepared in every way
I'm glad you did not pass my door.
In shimmering iridescent green
You hailed me from my gate, en route;
To be believed it must be seen
That glorious Palm Beach silken suit,
Such splendour held me there in trance
Till I became aware 'twas he,
It really was "C.R." from France,
And took you in to give you tea.

I would call there for another nine years until she died, aged eighty-four, her beautiful face framed in a halo of white hair.

Leaving Wideview, my next house of call en route to London was Richard Church's converted oast house at Curtisden Green, with its garden overlooking the Weald of Kent. My poet-friend, frail, soft-voiced, was a prodigious worker, poems, novels, essays, book reviews, one wondered how so frail a body supported so much labour. He talked to one in a whisper, his eyes twinkling behind glasses. He had once quite seriously claimed to practise levitation and told how, crossing London Bridge from the Custom House, a civil servant homeward bound with other officer workers, he would "take off" over their heads. He was quite serious about this and even put it into print. A little fey perhaps, but a truthful man. Pressed on this matter, he always turned it aside with a twinkling refusal either to confirm or deny the experience. A strain of illegitimacy in his forebears related him to the Duke of Bedford. At any moment when talking to him in that delightful garden amid his apple and pear trees I thought that he might rise up like thistledown and float away over the hills.

That summer in England I made a round of visits, but there were gaps now, no Knole, no Yattendon. Happily, John Masefield at Burcote Brook was alert and beautiful to look at aged eighty-three and still interested in everything. There was, of course, the annual, visit to Norman and Billy Birkett at Challens Green. He was always astonished by what he called my "orbital progression", and on my departure for a world cruise he had written:

You will soon be off on your great adventure and your already marvellously-stored mind will be beyond all telling. Three weeks is enough for me at any one time. After that I pine for England and Challens Green. I love all the changing seasons, the winter with the snow making all the trees so beautiful and of course those wonderful days of February when the sun begins to shed a little warmth and the daffodils are getting ready; and the summer days by the swimming pool; and London with all its fascinations at all times. But I envy you your power to travel the world round and to enjoy it as if you were still one-and-twenty.

When I arrived I found Norman somewhat agitated by what he considered too savage a sentence inflicted by Lord Chief Justice Parker on George Blake, a young Secret Intelligence clerk who had been found guilty under the Official Secrets Act. Although the Prime Minister had admitted that Blake's disclosures had not done irreparable damage, he was sentenced to forty-two years' imprisonment. This, thought Norman, was "administrative and political" rather than judicial. He wrote to Blake's counsel offering his support in any action to deal with what he considered a travesty of justice. He was very indignant when charged by the Lord Chancellor with subjecting the judiciary to outside influences. "Is it not a dangerous thing to suggest that judges are immune from outside criticism? Is it not the right of every citizen to criticise a sentence imposed by a judge? If a citizen thinks that a sentence of imprisonment of forty years is an intolerable thing he should be entitled to say so," wrote Norman, indignantly. He was busy with the papers concerning the case when I arrived. Billy was worried. "You know Norman is supposed to have retired, and to take things easy," she said. But Norman could never take things easy, and earlier he had been busy sponsoring the Obscene Publications Act in the House of Lords. He had never been happy since he had defended Miss Radclyffe Hall in the prosecution over *The Well of Loneliness*, in which he could not find one obscene sentence. He privately expressed the opinion that there would never be a satisfactory law in England against obscenity. "Roman Catholics regard a book about birth control as obscene. And how do you prove that reading a book tends to deprave and corrupt?" he asked. Retired? He would never really be retired. He was in great demand as a public speaker. In vain Billy remonstrated. "I'm rather naughty about it," he said to me one day, "but I suppose it's vanity really—the old *prima-donna* who can't leave the stage!"

Eleven years ago he had had a severe operation for a duodenal ulcer, from which we were fellow sufferers. I was against any operation. He was not wholly cured and his heart was affected. He was now president of "The Pilgrims" and last year had gone to New York to speak at a banquet of the U.S. Pilgrims. "Cecil, do talk to Norman," pleaded Billy, "The pace is too much." I did talk, in vain. On Monday morning I left. In my room I had finished my novel *Wide is the Horizon*, with Billy bringing me nourishment while I wrote. What a happy home!

At the beginning of August I went to stay with Leslie Rowse at Trenarren, at St. Austell in Cornwall. We always had an amusing correspondence. In a letter he had once addressed me as Cyril and I had protested, provoking this reply.

> *All Souls College* (actually from
> the Royal Station Hotel, Newcastle-on-Tyne)
>
> My dear Cecil,
>   Marooned in this comfortable hotel, with the snow piled up all round me (like Emily Brontë's grave) and with a remunerative Ladies' Luncheon Club awaiting me across the road, I take this opportunity to explain my confusion with Cyril. Now don't mistake me, my boy, it is the greatest possible compliment to you both that my subconscious has you and Cyril Falls clamped together; he is one of my oldest and finest friends at All Souls, a man of extreme national distinction and charm, a soldier, Military Correspondent of *The Times*, a very attractive personality. So there you are. That is how I betray myself and evidently my subconscious feeling for you both. For bear me out, I always call you Cecil verbally in your presence, in talk with you.
>   I long to see you, and am beside myself with envy of your "Snobs Progress" through France. (Remember Cosmo Lang's own description of his annual pilgrimage to Scotland via Welbeck, Chatsworth, Alnwick?) Why can't I accompany you— because we should disgrace ourselves by falling over with laughing. Marthe Bibesco is always trying to lure me to her cousins, the Rohans, at Josselin. But I know what a fatal yoke that would be to that *princesse fatale*. I much prefer the simple delights of Cornwall and the quay-end and the sights of

Mevagissey, and you there to enjoy them with me. It is always a revealing bond when people have the same sense of humour and laugh at the same things. Never have I giggled so much as on your visit. Agree?

I shall expect you in May and possibly in June if you can manage too, when I may have a little literary party. Now comes the pill. Not unless you take up your pen and begin the second half of your Autobiography. It's all there in your head, waiting to come out. What's the objection, or obstacle?

I expect, if I am to be your friend, and you have to be my Cecil-Cyril, to have a good influence on you, in addition to the fun. So take up your Autobiography or I won't come to see you.

Affectionate wishes,
Yours
Leslie.

So to Trenarren I went. He sent me to bed at ten o'clock because he wanted to retire and get on with his book, which exactly suited me. Each day we walked and talked and went again to Mevagissey, and giggled there as before. Is the air there full of laughing gas? The effect on us was immediate. Then after five lovely days of work and fun, back to London I went to find awaiting me a letter from my American friend, Mrs. Boehm. She wished to make me a present for my seventieth birthday. She was joining the *Kungsholm* at Naples next February for a three-months' cruise around the world. It was a luxury cruise with the whole ship at the disposal of the 385 passengers. It started from New York, calling at Naples where we could join it. I hesitated about accepting, fearful of being cooped up for three months with a cargo of American millionaires, boisterous, noisy, cocktail-soaked. But my friend insisted. I needed a rest. The ship would return in time for my seventieth birthday festivities next May, when my new novel would be published. There was to be a Foyle Lunch in my honour and I had planned a party for two hundred friends. I rang up to check with my doctor, Sir James Fergusson Hannay, in Harley Street. He had been my medical guardian for over thirty years, since he had first come to practise in London, in a little Knightsbridge room, wearing a monocle, and driving a second-hand Rolls-Royce. The reply to my call stunned me. Hannay had died four days ago after a long illness.

I went to lunch at the Garrick with John Betjeman. "You look pale," he said. I told him why. "Somehow you don't expect doctors to die, and he was a dear fellow."

In September I saw Armand de la Rochefoucauld, in a torrid Paris, and motored on to Saulière, to visit the grave of young Louis Tissier, my former devoted secretary; then on to Aix-en-Provence and, via Moustier and the glorious Gorge de Verdon, to Italy. With no book on the stocks I was going to enjoy six months of freedom. In Rome I dined with the ambassador, and with a friend with whom, in Nottingham fifty years ago, I had played tennis, Dorothy Boot, now The Hon. Mrs. Bruce, daughter of Jesse Boot (Lord Trent), the sister-in-law of Captain Scott's widow Kathleen, the mother of Peter Scott. I had found by accident that Dorothy had settled in Rome on the ancient Appian Way. The manner of it was extraordinary. Motoring one day along that road she had seen a villa. Liking the appearance of it she called and asked the proprietor if he would like to sell it. He would. So she found herself the neighbour of Gina Lollobrigida, on a road where Romans had been buried two thousand years ago.

One day I dined with Orietta Doria, now married to a young English ex-naval officer, Frank Pogson, who set to work reorganising that vast palace and its art gallery and museum. A few days later another friend lunched with me, the Marchese Stella Vitelleschi, whose life-story was beyond the bounds of fiction. In my gallery of remarkable friends she had a special place. Nearing eighty, she possessed formidable energy. She owned a small flat in Monte Carlo but she commuted between Paris and Rome, using this as a half-way house. She augmented her income by working for the Bibliothèque Nationale of Paris, which employed her copying the correspondence in the Vatican archives of Cardinal Mazarin to his two nieces in Rome. She copied all this in a firm bold hand, without glasses. She had a singular knowledge of those two vast libraries. When I wished to discover the Latin manuscript of the *History of England*, written in A.D. 1513 by Polidore Vergil, who had been a priest at Church Langton, my ancestral village in Leicestershire, she found it for me in the Vatican.* When I wanted the newspaper account of Chopin's funeral service in Paris, written by

* See *The Growing Boy*, Ch. 8, v.

Theophile Gautier, she unearthed it for me in the Bibliothèque
Nationale.

The strangest thing about Stella was that she had died when she
was four months old. Her father was the Marchese Vitelleschi, of an
old Roman family, her mother was Scottish. The Vitelleschis had
taken a villa at Nice. The father, receiving news of the death of his
infant daughter, hurried there for the funeral. While carrying the
small coffin down the stairs he bumped it against the banister,
whereupon he heard a small cry coming out of it. They opened the
coffin and found the child alive. Stella wrote a book about this,
published in London, under the title *Out Of My Coffin*. When she
was a vivacious young woman visiting relations in England, George
Alexander, the actor-producer, was so struck by her ability in some
amateur theatricals that he asked if she would like to go on the stage.
He gave her a small part in his production of *Turandot*. The leads
were Godfrey Tearle and Mrs. Stella Patrick Campbell. During a
rehearsal a telegram arrived for Stella and a stage hand shouted
out "Miss Stella Rho!" Rho was the name under which she
acted. Mrs. Patrick Campbell stopped the rehearsal. "Who's Stella
Rho?" she demanded, and on Stella coming forward, she said:
"You'd better change your name. There's going to be only one
Stella in this theatre!"

Later she appeared in *Romance* in the part of Vanucci, the "dresser"
to Cavallina, the prima-donna, played by Doris Keane, opposite
Owen Nares. It failed in London at the Duke of York's, moved to
the Lyric Theatre and ran there for two years. Stella toured with
the company for fifteen years in England and the U.S.A. I surprised
her by saying I had met Edward Sheldon, who, when a young
man, had written *Romance* which brought him a fortune. In 1941
I gave at Radio City, New York, a N.B.C. broadcast of my Churchill
poem *A Man Arose*, with Wendell Willkie introducing me. Afterwards Austin Strong, the playwright of *Seventh Heaven*, asked if
I would let him take me to call on Sheldon, who had heard my
broadcast and would much like to meet me. Since early manhood
he had been totally blind and paralysed. We went to his apartment
off Fifth Avenue. I was shown into a shuttered bedroom where
Sheldon lay, all in white. He asked if I would kneel and let him
trace my features. I knelt. Then he asked if I would be kind enough

to read the poem to him. I did so. He thanked me and on my departure held my hand in his for some time. I left deeply moved.

When Stella came to lunch with me one December day I found her a little distressed. Her brother-in-law had sold the family palazzo where she had lived most of her life and now she had to find a lodging in Rome. However, all was well, a cousin with another old palazzo had given her accommodation. "I'm not really sorry to be evicted," she said, "I had four flights of stairs and there was no heating. The great rooms were iceboxes in winter, and the electric lighting failed. So I don't wonder my old brother-in-law moved out to a modern apartment. And I don't have so far to go to the Vatican library." She went there every morning at nine and copied all day. She copied and translated from a spidery Italian script in which the Cardinal had written to his nieces. In moving her things Stella had come across letters to her mother, an excellent pianist, from Liszt, Gladstone, Mazzini, Mme Chaminade, Jenny Lind, etc. She was the only woman who had been allowed to play the organ at the Crystal Palace.

CHAPTER ELEVEN

The Grand Cruise

I

I began the New Year of 1962 having to enter the Salvatore Mundi Hospital with which I was all too familiar. Its beautiful situation above Rome did not compensate for being confined there. On returning home I found in the lobby of the Grand Hotel Dr. Paul Niehans. He had just flown from Tripoli where he had given a five-days' rejuvenation treatment to the King of Libya, aged sixty-two. I asked if he thought I should have it and he laughed. He was eighty years of age, clear-eyed, pink-cheeked and sprightly, looking like his cousin the late Crown Prince Wilhelm. He had just come in from the street, where it was twenty-six degrees in a phenomenal cold snap, without wearing a hat or an overcoat. He was certainly a good advertisement for his treatment, if he had had it.

The next week I lectured at the British Council but my voice was feeble. I had been wondering if I should be fit enough to embark on the Grand Cruise, the prospect of which now excited me, but on the last day of January I left with my friend Mrs. Boehm by car for Naples. I still could not believe that I was going round the world calling at eighteen ports, covering 26,457 miles, as the copious brochure announced. I wondered about those odd seven miles. It was a fine calculation that seemed to ignore tides, typhoons, fogs and eccentric pilots. I had a last sight of Rome. The beautiful fountain of the Piazza Esedra in front of my hotel, lit up at night, was one of the joys of living there. And now to other fountains in distant lands. "Are you all right?" asked my companion, solicitously. "I'm perfectly all right. If I'm giddy it's with excitement," I replied. "Nearly fifty-five years ago I saw at Belvoir Castle a portrait presented by the tenantry to the twenty-one year old Marquis of

Granby, the Duke of Rutland's heir, and the brother of Lady Diana Manners (Lady Diana Cooper). I was told he was making "The Grand Tour". It was the first time I had heard of such a thing, and I've dreamed of it ever since. I'm not twenty-one and I'm not the Marquis of Granby, but I'm making the Grand Tour—more correctly the Grand Cruise. It's a fairy-tale come true fifty-five years later!"

We lunched en route at Formia, near the villa where Cicero was murdered. We drew into Naples past the Bay of Baia where Nero failed to drown his mother. On our journey southwards the promise of spring was about us. There was golden genista in bloom and a glory of peach blossom, pink against an azure sky. When we reached the bay of Naples, there lay the *Kungsholm*. As we drew alongside the dock, how white, how regal she looked, with three gold crowns on her twin funnels! She was 600 feet long, 21,400 tons. The whole ship was ours, with one hundred and fifty stewards and stewardesses to administer to the needs of three hundred and eighty-five passengers. How they cosseted us. They were mostly young Swedes, with a small international quota. Our two table stewards were Austrian and Italian. One steward came in the dining-room carrying a salver with the grace of a ballet dancer entering from the wings in *Swan Lake*. I was not surprised when I learned he was a member of the Royal Swedish Ballet who had taken this means of seeing the world in the company of a friend, a fellow steward. The stewardesses, also blonde, in a happy minority, never lacked escorts. The ship's seamstress always had an Adonis at the doorway of her workroom. Twice, calling, I interrupted a charming idyll.

On the voyage down to Alexandria I was able to examine my fellow passengers. I had thought I was the only Englishman on board until I discovered that the ship's photographer and the tour lecturer were English. The ship had come from New York with its American passengers. They had exhausted themselves with three days in Rome and Naples, and were now resting before the onslaught on Egypt. They were well-groomed, all of sixty years of age up, mostly retired tycoons, with wives determined to defy time by the help of a "boutique" on board. Though everything cried money, some of the suites cost £20,000 for the three-month tour, they were never ostentatious or arrogant. Marvellously, they were never drunk. No one ever had to be assisted on board or missed the boat. What verve they had! In the mornings, when at sea, they joined a dancing class, and boys and girls of seventy up learned the latest steps from the professional teacher. In all those three months there was only one drawback. Birthdays produced in the dining-room that frightful American wail, "Happy Birthday to You!" with the ship's band playing each tune. One evening there were five birthdays to be wailed over.

No one was allowed to be ignorant or unaware of what he was going to see. Our cabins were flooded with literature and before landing we were lectured to in the cinema theatre by a young Englishman of whose diction and knowledge I was proud. Private cars and planes awaited us on landing, hotel managers genuflected at our approach. There was no trouble about currency exchange in a score of different countries. A banker came on board to change our dollars into the local currency, and came back before we left, to give us dollars for any currency left over. The librarian was a retired Roman Catholic naval chaplain, the Rev. Frederick Meehling. He had a flood of anecdotes that never ceased. The world was his parish, he exuded goodwill. Three years later he was created a Monsignor. He became devoted to me, a firm agnostic. My hotel was puzzled later by letters that arrived addressed to *H.S.H.* Cecil Roberts. "Are you a Serene Highness?" asked the concierge. "No," I explained, "*H.S.H.* stands for 'Holy Stinking Heretic'." No matter where the boat called the padre knew a priest or a nun, and got the inside story; the Church Universal indeed.

Arriving at Alexandria he took me in hand, determined to alter my poor opinion of the town, which I had visited before. It was the place where the great Alexander's corpse had been buried and lost, and where Cleopatra had failed to "vamp" Augustus Caesar, who executed her son and put Ptolemy XIV, the last of them, on the throne. The padre took me to the church of St. Catherine, the martyr of the wheel. Behind the altar there was a plain stone. On it was written, simply *Vittorio Emanuele III*. That was all. King Alfonso had died in the Grand Hotel and lay in Rome awaiting transfer to the Escorial. Now this deposed monarch, dead here in exile in 1947, awaited transfer to the Pantheon. Mussolini had made the midget king an emperor, and through him he had lost his throne. I was buttonholed by a little, seedy monk. "Would you like to confess?" he asked. "Confess what?" I replied. He smiled. I slipped him a dollar bill. He looked famished, the guardian of a dead king.

We entered the Canal which Nasser had seized. The statue of de Lesseps at the entrance had been tumbled from its plinth, but the canal was open. The Israelis had not yet pounced nor the Allies bungled the business. The Red Sea is not red or blue, but muddy. It is only red when the sun strikes the red algae that floats in the water and the reflection incarnadines it. But I did witness a phenomenon. One evening walking on deck I was amazed to see that the brown desert on each side of the canal had turned emerald green. Before I could call my friend it had gone, eerie, miraculous, brief. Then the light left the land and it was immediately dark. This phenomenon is called "The Green Flash." At Port Said some of our passengers who had left the ship at Alexandria came on board. They had been up the Nile to Karnak, to the Valley of the Kings and to Aswan. Some passengers were always hopping off on extra excursions.

Ninety halcyon days saw us in Alexandria, Aden, Bombay, Colombo, Rangoon, Penang, Singapore, Bangkok, Hong Kong, Kobe, Yokohama, Honolulu, Los Angeles, Acapulco, the Panama Canal and finally New York. In Bombay we took an afternoon plane for Delhi. At the airport, eager for news from home, I bought a copy of the *Daily Telegraph*, three days old. I opened it in the plane and suddenly grew rigid in my seat. There, as Bombay faded away below us, the icy finger of Death touched me. ". . . the late Lord Birkett did not desire any funeral service . . ." ran a paragraph. The *late* Lord Birkett! It seemed impossible that one word should convey to me so much loss, closing a friendship of forty years. There were no details. I was to learn later, in a letter from his devoted Billy, that he had died after a final triumphant speech in the House of Lords, by which he had saved Lake Ullswater from vandalism. I felt at that moment, airborne, that the returning earth and the wonders of Delhi, Jaipur and Agra would offer me only muted pleasure.

India bewildered and depressed me with its swarming millions, its poverty, dirt, superstition and racial animosities. The dhoti-clad, skinny-legged Indians, like black crows settling on offal, the long tyranny of the princes, the temple addicts, the *gurus*, all the human misery, created a horrifying kaleidoscope. To govern this land generations of Englishmen had eaten out their lives and their young wives had filled the English cemeteries—for what? The British Raj was now a creaking skeleton, boned by the slippery Gandhi, the bland Halifax, and the royal Mountbatten armed with a sword by a Socialist Government to cut the Gordian knot and get rid of the ghastly thing at any cost.

At the Taj Mahal, the pearl of pearls, an Indian Oxford-educated guide lamented Curzon, the last truly great Viceroy—whose zest and money had saved this masterpiece from collapse. A masterpiece certainly. Of all I saw in India that was the most memorable. Under its great dome, in the octagonal chamber, lay the tombs of Mumtaz-i-Mahal and of Shah Jahan. Never was a beloved wife so marvellously interred. From the centre of the dome hung a slender lamp. It was the gift of Curzon, leaving India after a collision with Kitchener. "May it hang there as my last tribute of respect to the glories of Agra which float like a vision of eternal beauty in my memory," he wrote.

My Indian holiday was marred by Norman Birkett's death and by an attack of influenza that confined me to my cabin for four days at Bombay, so that I missed some excursions. One morning, the steward announced that a gentleman had called to see me. I could not get the name, so asked for him to be shown to my cabin. To my utter surprise in walked Armand de la Rochefoucauld. He was staying in Bombay with the Maharanee of Cooch-Behar. He had just read in the paper of my arrival on board the *Kungsholm*, and had come to take me to lunch with his hostess. It was impossible for me to move, so I lost the opportunity of learning how a maharajah or maharanee live when they are at home. Armand came the next day with flowers and fruit, hopeful, but I could not move. Two days later, still with a temperature, I boarded our plane, resolved not to miss the Delhi—Agra—Jaipur excursion.

When we got back to the *Kungsholm* after our five-day tour of India and had sailed out of the harbour I went into the lounge. I found there three agreeable old ladies, sisters, one eighty. I sat down and had tea with them. I had surmised they had stayed on board for a restful time, but someone at the table had flown to Katmandu. "What struck you most about it?" I asked. "I should say the colour everywhere, the temples, the shrines, the roofs, the clothes the natives wear. One hates to think that place is going to be opened up and westernised. Thank God, we were just in time. In ten years everyone will be swooping down on it!" (In ten years it was infested with hippies.) One of the Chekov Sisters, as I called the trio, said, "We've been lucky, too. It was well worth getting up at five in the morning." I asked just what was worth getting up for at five in the morning. "The sunrise over Everest," she replied, putting down a tea cup. "We'd always longed to see it, and there it was!" "You don't mean to tell me you've been to Mount Everest?" I asked. The three sisters looked at each other happily. "Yes, not Everest itself, of course, that's 29,002 feet high. That two extra feet seemed odd to me. I asked Mr. Tensing if he'd measured it. How he laughed!"

"Mr. Tensing? Do you mean Sherpa Tensing, the first man on Everest with Hillary? Where did you meet him?" I asked. "At Darjeeling. We flew there first and then went to Tiger Hill and he took us in a jeep to his chalet for the night. We saw Everest the next morning, one hundred and forty miles away. The sunrise was emerald, green and pink, and then it looked as if the snow had caught fire. I do hope our Kodachromes will come out all right."

I thought I had done well to have seen Delhi, Jaipur and Agra in those few days. There were others, more adventurous, who had seen Samarkand and Bokhara. One couple at that table had been in Tashkent. "We went to see an opera there, a very good French company in Delibes' *Lakmé*." I felt I should never again think of myself as a traveller.

II

We sailed at midnight for Colombo. The Bombay Police Band, one hundred strong, played us out lustily, rendering *Anchors Aweigh* and *Auld Lang Syne*. We now had a run of eight hundred miles over a silken sea. The ridiculous thing about this part of the trip was that we had only sixteen hours in Ceylon. Early in the morning, after a trip round the town, our cars headed for Kandy, the former capital of the island, seventy-five miles away. The Kandyan Kings had lived and ruled there. The town stood on a lake-side. A road took us up a deep valley where a torrent fell in successive cascades.

It was an excursion into an exotic fairyland. First came rice paddy fields and the tea plantations. We seemed to be buried in a paradise of purple bougainvillaea, jacaranda, frangipani and giant-leaved banana trees. After two hours we came to this wonder city of the hills, 1,674 feet high.

All the Kandy restaurants were crowded with tourists. Outside ours there were slim dark men in sarongs carrying sun umbrellas and shaven monks in their bright saffron robes, with begging bowls. A dark, young mother with jewelled ears and nose, and jet-black hair, surely not seventeen, held a naked baby at her breast. She watched with big moon eyes the lords of creation stuffing themselves. I gave her a sandwich over our veranda. She was so solemn I wondered if she thought it was poisoned. She opened it, tasted it and then fed the baby. A native policeman shooed her off with half a dozen touts. After lunch we were given a performance on the lawn of the Kandy dancers, and then hurried to the famous Temple of the Tooth, fronted by a moat filled with tortoises and guarded by elephants. Here, to enter, you put off your shoes, but only at the Festival of Perchera could the Tooth of Buddha be exhibited during what has been acclaimed by many as the most magnificent religious festival in the world. Sixty sacred elephants form part of the holy pageant which takes place on the night of a full moon.

We were rushed back to Colombo and our ship, to sail at sunset for Thailand and Bangkok. There was a dramatic episode. In the years before the Second World War I had a German friend, Dr. Auer, who was Second Secretary at the German Embassy in London, and then in Paris. He had great difficulty in hiding his detestation of the Nazis. We were apprehensive of what might happen to him if we were plunged into a war. He was recalled to Berlin and no more was heard of him. We feared he had been "liquidated". Now, from a piece of paper, as the *Kungsholm* passed the jetty lights sailing in to the darkening Indian Ocean, I learned that my friend was alive. The note read: "Greetings from Teddy Auer, German Ambassador in Ceylon." He had seen in a Colombo evening paper an interview with me, but too late to make contact. For two years he had been a prisoner in the notorious Berlin-Plötzensee gaol, where Hitler had many of his opponents executed. Eleven thousand had been hanged, often after hideous torture. Auer awaited death daily for two years, then in May, 1945, he was liberated by the Russians, who arrested him and imprisoned him for seven years. In 1952 he recovered his liberty, resumed his career, and was sent, in March, 1956, as the West German ambassador to Ceylon. It was maddening to know we had missed each other by a few hours.

For sheer beauty the Palace complex at Bangkok in Thailand is supreme among creations of the Asiatic world. On entering the Royal Palace grounds it was as if one had walked into the jasper-gated paradise promised in the hymn-books. The glory, the colour, the fantasy of it all! From throne-room to temples, the eye was delighted and dazzled. Everywhere one looked on the sparkle of gold leaf and mosaics, on grotesque statues, lions, hippogriffs, dragons, shining gold-roofed audience halls, gem-encrusted altars, belled canopies, gilt pagodas, turquoise monuments, painted eaves, dragon-headed—all this without one lapse into vulgarity. How had so much delicacy and wealth survived through the centuries? And, awful thought, how long might it continue to survive in the turmoil of the East? The name changes, Siam becomes Thailand, but the royal palace of *Anna and the King of Siam* survives, a miracle of fragility in a dissolving world.

The trip from Bangkok to Hong Kong was fifteen hundred miles. We were three whole days at sea. The *Kungsholm* had a cinema theatre that held one hundred and fifty people. Asked to give a lecture, I agreed. This suited me admirably. On boarding the ship at Naples I had been much embarrassed to find in its gift shop some twenty of my books displayed. Unknown to me, someone had arranged this, but I was dismayed. How awful it would be to travel for three months seeing my books unsold!

If I had announced that I was going to give a reading of my poems it would have frightened the audience away. So I called it "Some Persons, some Places". In a packed theatre I gave a reading for an hour and a half. The next morning the dance instructor came up to me and after some complimentary words, said: "But of course you're a professional, like myself." "Professional?" I queried. "Oh, yes, it's no use saying you're not. I saw by the way you handled that audience you're a professional!" I smiled and thanked him. It had never occurred to me. Perhaps I was a professional. I had been appearing before audiences for over forty years on two continents.

Later I had to repeat it for those who had been unable to get in. The agreeable result was that every one of those embarrassing books of mine disappeared, sold out. The second reading took place on a day that was doubled on the calendar. We were en route to Honolulu, and in the Pacific we crossed the International Date Line, with two 27ths of March.

"See Naples and then die," they say, but you should not die before seeing Hong Kong. The port is ravishingly spectacular. We entered the wide harbour, with the capital Victoria spread over the mountain island of Hong Kong. A mile across from it, served with a ferry-shuttle service, lay Kowloon, taking its name from nine low hills called The Nine Dragons. There we docked, with Hong Kong, and all its shipping, spread before us. I was called for the next morning by a friend, Kenneth Kirby, an ex-naval officer who had retired there and had a villa up in the hills.

On arriving in Hong Kong a letter from Billy Birkett awaited me. I read it on the *Kungsholm* deck, looking across the harbour, but I was far away in England. Norman Birkett's end had been a fitting close of a great career. He had gone out with his words still ringing in the House of Lords. On the afternoon of February 8th he had made a great speech opposing a Government-backed Bill whereby the Manchester Corporation sought to turn the Lake of Ullswater into a reservoir and thereby destroy its beauty, and drown its villages. He killed the Bill in a polished speech. His beguiling voice and pure enunciation cast a spell over the House as he had cast it over juries in court. Billy wrote:

> Two days before Norman died he had one of his happiest and most brilliant days in the House of Lords. I went to hear him and he was in great form. The House was packed as I've never seen it before. I did not stay to the end as I wanted to get back and have his bed and the house warmed and some light supper for him, and to be ready to pick him up in the car at the station when he got back. He came home as happy as a schoolboy on holiday by the 11 p.m. train, with his beloved Lake District saved. Next morning I insisted on breakfast in bed and he enjoyed his letters and telegrams and newspaper reports.

But a slight pain persisted in his side. The local doctor called in a specialist who had him taken at once to London in an ambulance. As they put him into it he said to Billy: "What amazes me is the calm with which I'm taking this." She accompanied him. An operation was decided upon immediately.

> I was with him when he fell asleep before he went off to the theatre but thank God he never woke. The surgeons found he could not be saved. He slipped away with the minimum of pain and anxiety. So I'm glad for him and hope you will be, too. But, alas, that doesn't fill the terrible vacuum after 42 years of wonderful companionship and love. Please don't worry about me, I've all my life been rather a "solitary" and I've been used to being on my own for long spells while Norman was away on Assizes, etc., and know I can manage though the gap will be hideous—I will still expect the 'phone to ring and Norman's voice saying: "Darling, I'll be catching the 11 o'clock, will you meet me."

I read the letter in a quiet corner of the deck, twice, because the first time I could hardly see it for tears. So I had lost, as many others, a most gifted and wonderful friend. On the very day of his death I had written to him, unknowingly, asking him to be my Chairman at the Foyle Lunch. Of all my friends through forty years he had been one of the most cherished. And I should have had on this highwater mark of my life the kindest, most understanding man in the Kingdom as Chairman.

The morning after I had received Billy's letter I heard over the radio, while shaving in my cabin, that Philip Gibbs had died. I sat down on my bed quite overwhelmed by this second blow. We had been war correspondents in France in the First World War, we had nourished a warm friendship ever since. He was my Sir Galahad, handsome of feature, noble of mind, frail but indomitably courageous and an unquenchable optimist. Aged eighty-four, he had had a long, vivid and useful life, beloved by all who knew him. To lose him and Norman Birkett within a month was a great impoverishment of my life. What next had Fate in hand for me, I wondered.

In Hong Kong I had a little business to transact. I was marking my seventieth birthday next May with a party in London for two hundred of my friends, on which day I was publishing my twenty-third novel, *Wide Is The Horizon*. I wished to send out some fifty inscribed copies before I sailed, but the books were not ready and would have been too bulky to mail out to me. This was overcome by my London publishers sending blank leaves for me to sign which would then be bound with the books. They had an agent in Hong Kong. It was to his office, situated on the sixth floor of a building overlooking the harbour, that I went one day. As I signed the sheets I thought how extraordinary were the strands of Fate which should bring a youth, who once dreamed in a Midlands town of fame as a writer, to be autographing, for a seventieth birthday, his latest book, high up in an office in Hong Kong.

My next mission was in Kowloon. I had gone to a tailor there who was making six costumes for my friend within thirty hours. I fell to temptation and ordered three suits and two overcoats, cashmere and vicuna. I ordered something else, madness now in the blood. I saw a roll of flaming silk on a shelf. I asked what it was. "It's a bolt of mandarin silk, very rare." The tailor spread it on his counter. It seemed to set the shop on fire. I asked if in the remaining twenty-four hours he could make me a dressing-gown of it, quilted and lined with lilac silk. He said he could.

On the last evening before sailing the ship's gangway was thronged by errand boys delivering costumes and suits. In my parcel was the mandarin dressing-gown. Dozens of costumes, suits, gowns, shirts, had been made to measure within forty-eight hours, at nearly half the prices of Europe and America. My conscience troubled me. Was it sweated labour? I raised the question with the tailor. "It all depends what you call 'sweated'. If you are desperate to get out of China, and arrive here starving, you are glad to get any work at any price. These Chinese work all the hours of the day and night, but they live and eat on a scale they have never known before. Give them a holiday and they are wretched. They don't understand leisure. I employ two hundred smiling faces and busy hands. If you tourists didn't come here and empty your pockets these people would starve. And the community is able to house them in new apartment blocks where they have running water and closets, luxuries they have never known. The Crown Colony has done a miraculous job for three million people. Every immigrant believes he will work his way from a shanty, with ten in a room, to an apartment. They sweat, but it's a happy and ambitious sweat. They don't sit dreaming of a motor car and a holiday in Paris. They work and they save."

III

Alas, I was disappointed in Japan. I found its villages squalid with their unpainted wooden houses and paper windows, but I was there before cherry-blossom-time, which probably transforms the scene. My friend Edward and Grizel Warner, *en poste* in Tokyo, gave me lunch at the Embassy, and took me to a Kabuki theatre. In the boxes, if you wish, you can lie down on a mattress. The play is interminable. The text, like that of the Koran, is almost sacred and known by heart by the audience.

Tokyo itself seemed to me a shoddy Chicago. The last shattering disillusionment was to find that the cherry blossom fluttering down the famous Ginza boulevard, was artificial—plastic. The Imperial Palace Hotel had lift girls in kimonos, otherwise one might have been in any capital. There were touches of humour. After we had been touring in a motorbus we halted at an hotel and the smiling guide announced: "There will be a twenty minutes halt for a Must Go." The whole busload "musted". Half an hour later we were at Nikko to see the three famous monkeys, of "See no evil, Speak no evil, Hear no evil". They were carved in wood on the façade of a cabin with a curving roof. The building itself was called "The Sacred Stable" for it was built to house the ghostly horses ridden by the temple deities. There were eight panels depicting the monkey philosophy. It was the second panel with its trio of monkeys that had caught the world's fancy and spread the fame of Nikko abroad.

Japan gave me one unforgettable moment. We were flying in the evening to Tokyo from Osaka. We went over land and water, mountains on our left, and glimpses of the Pacific Ocean on our right. Darkness had fallen over the plain below and the lights of the city began to twinkle. Then, like a miracle, framed in the left window of our plane, there rose from the land-darkness into the light of the higher sky an immense cone, its upper slopes and flat top covered with dazzling snow, flushed with the pink after-glow of sunset. It was Mount Fuji, awe-inspiring in its majesty. Its noble shape, familiar the world over, the epitome of all that the word "Japan" meant, made it instantly recognisable. We seemed to be flying level with its summit, at some 12,397 feet. As we slowly watched it pass away behind us, and turned towards Tokyo, illuminated below, I could well believe why many account it the most beautiful mountain in the world.

IV

We were now on our longest stretch, Honolulu-bound. We found the island all we imagined it could be, a paradise, but one of the most sophisticated places on earth. It was Palm Beach, Nassau, Monte Carlo, Jamaica, Newport and Hollywood rolled into one. Immense luxurious skyscraper hotels lined the half-moon beach which ran from massive Diamond Head to the U.S. Naval station at Pearl Harbor. My companion and I were destined to have a surprising welcome on docking, but not from the smiling Hawaiian maidens who shook grass skirts over their sturdy legs and waved brown hands above flower-crowned black tresses. When we were about to go ashore a steward said that someone was asking for us at the bottom of the gangway. As soon as we descended a young man rushed forward and looped enormous *leis* over our heads and embraced us. The manner of this welcome was thus. In 1955 I went on an excursion to Neusiedlersee with an Austrian friend from Vienna. We stopped to pick up a young man in lederhosen with whom I began to talk German. He burst out laughing and said that, despite his Tyrolean attire, he was an American, de Wayne Fulton. He had graduated in music at Berkeley University and had now taken his Master's degree in the harp at the University of Vienna. That evening we went back to his rooms, where he enchanted us with his playing. He was later appointed Professor of the Harp in the Conservatoire of Music at Istanbul, and asked me to visit him. He had a beautiful apartment overlooking the Golden Horn, and a Hungarian cook. Perversely, I did not go. Then he toured with the Berlin Symphony Orchestra. We missed each other in Berlin, Munich, Rome, Florence, Paris and London. And now here he was, exuberantly roping us with frangipani *leis*.

The next day we toured the island, seeing place after place of incredible beauty. But my lunch by the blue Pacific shore, in an enchanting pavilion-restaurant at the foot of a mountain that gave its name to the Inn, "The Crouching Lion", was ruined by finding on the menu "Snow-white fillet of Dolphin, dropped in egg and pan-fried to a golden brown". I felt I would like to pan-fry the cook who perpetrated such an atrocity on docile and friendly dolphins. Then over more mountains we went through luscious valleys and pineapple plantations, ending in a glimpse of Pearl Harbor with the American flag flying over a sunken battleship as a memorial of a great disaster, the Japanese bombing—"the blackest day in American history", as one chronicler put it.

That evening de Wayne Fulton collected us and took us up to a hilly spur, twelve hundred feet above Honolulu, where he had a delightful chalet with Japanese sliding screens and a long veranda. The view was stupendous. It took in the whole sweep of the bay from Diamond Head along the curving Waikiki beach, across the town with its avenues and palm trees, to the end of the sickle where lay Pearl Harbor. As we talked the light faded, an immense crimson sun went down over the ocean and thousands of lights twinkled in the town below. We dined, and then there was music, a harp and an oboe, under the starry sky, with a soft, scented breeze. What a happy reunion after seven years of frustrated meetings! We sailed at midnight. As we rounded Diamond Head, according to tradition, we dropped our *leis* overboard and saw them float away. In Rome, to assure return, you dropped coins in the Fontana di Trevi. Here in Honolulu you dropped *leis* in the sea.

A day at Los Angeles, then an hour at the uninhabited Pacific island of Guadalupe on a bright morning to see the lumbering elephant-seals, sixteen feet long, with trunk-like snouts, on their breeding ground. They never moved for us, unmolested on this inaccessible island, their last home. Then on to exotic Acapulco, the winter playground of millionaires, and then the thrilling transit of the Panama Canal. And so to New York and the close of the cruise. I was sad to bid farewell to my companions. What a delightful company they had been! Together we had known three halcyon months with not a rough day or an unpleasant incident.

In Honolulu I had received a cable with news of yet another friend lost. It was planned for me to be again the guest in New York of Dorothy Quick, the poetess. An invalid now, she was almost

a prisoner in her beautiful Fifth Avenue apartment overlooking
Central Park. She had published ten books of poetry. Her rare mind
and nature were revealed in her verses. She had sent me her last
book of poems called *The Bold Heart*. What a title from one who
for long years lay on a bed of pain and never complained! It contained
To a Canary.

> Who fill the air with fluttering song
> Despite your cage, the whole day long,
> Know that I have no right to be
> Unhappy, songless, who am free.

When a little girl she had been a particular friend of Mark Twain.
They had met on board ship in 1907 just after the author had received
an honorary degree from Oxford University. He was seventy-two,
she was eleven. Between the two began a great friendship which was
to endure until his death some years later. He was so impressed
with her ability that he formed an "Authors League for Two" and
began to direct her talent. In 1959 I had been her guest for two
months, and on leaving she gave me a letter to open when I had
sailed from New York.

> Dear Cecil,
> When I was a little girl and visited Mark Twain for the
> first time in Tuxedo, he sent me home to my mother with
> a letter of recommendation. So I am giving you one in the
> Mark Twain tradition.
> "Cecil Roberts is the most perfect house-guest in the world.
> He eats everything, is always there when you want him, never
> there when you don't, which is seldom, for he is the most
> charming and entertaining guest, and, to quote Mark Twain,
> "he takes the sunshine with him wherever he goes." Bring it
> back soon, Cecil dear. With my love and a welcome for you
> always at 880 Fifth Avenue.

Alas, I was not able to take her any sunshine when the *Kungsholm*
docked at New York. I was too late. Two days later I sailed for the
ship's home port in Sweden, calling at Copenhagen where I left
it and stayed a week.

CHAPTER TWELVE

The Birthday Party

I

I arrived in London on a May morning, to complete the plans for the party in celebration of my seventieth birthday and the publication of my novel. Last autumn, when I had considered where I should hold this party, my friend Lady Illingworth said, "Why not hold it at my house?" I accepted the offer at once. She lived in what was the last private house in Grosvenor Square, soon to be demolished. In 1725 the *Daily Journal* recorded: "There is now building a square called Grosvenor Square which for its largeness and beauty will exceed any yet made in and about London." Sir Richard Grosvenor, the ground landlord, erected some fifty houses round a large ornamental garden, in the centre of which stood an equestrian statue of King George I, in Roman costume. It is ironical that little more than two hundred years later the Square should be practically taken over by the Americans, whom George III had failed to suppress, with a moated monstrosity for their Embassy and a fine statue of England's friend in the hour of need, President Franklin Roosevelt.

Lady Illingworth's house had seen much history. From 1804 until 1908 it was the residence of the Earls of Harrowby. The first earl was Secretary of State for Foreign Affairs. It was customary then for the members of the Cabinet to dine at each other's houses. On the evening of June 21st, 1815, the Cabinet, presided over by Lord Liverpool, Prime Minister, dined there. It was three days after the Battle of Waterloo, but the Cabinet did not yet know the result. There were rumours that Napoleon had been victorious. While the Cabinet was dining there was a commotion in the Square and a chaise-and-four clattered up, out of which jumped an officer in a red tunic. He was Major Percy, an A.D.C. to the Duke of Wellington. He had dashed over, the journey taking three days from Belgium, with the news that Napoleon had been defeated near a small village called Waterloo.

On February 23rd, 1820, there was another exciting episode at the house. On that day a group known as the Cato Street conspirators had planned to assassinate the Prime Minister and the whole Cabinet as they dined there. It was the intention of the conspirators to carry the severed heads on poles to the Mansion House and declare a People's Provisional Government. But someone betrayed them. The Duke of Wellington was for holding the dinner, with guards posted to trap the assassins, but the rest of the Cabinet, not fancying being murdered over their soup, outvoted him. The plotters were arrested in their hideout in Cato Street and went to the gallows. The French chef was so infuriated when the dinner was cancelled that he threw all the carefully prepared dishes in the fire. The kitchen, the scene of this episode, was still in use by Lady Illingworth.

A fine staircase with a bronze balustrade led up to the drawing-room. The downstairs morning-room opened on to a long garden-court with alcoves and classical statues. Such was the setting for my party on May 17th, on the eve of my seventieth birthday. The house was thronged with two hundred guests, some from America, France, Italy, Austria and Poland. The drawback was that when Lady Illingworth and I had finished receiving them there was little time for personal conversation. But it went off excellently, in a unique setting. Within three years this house, the last in the Square, was demolished and an hotel was erected on its site.

That evening when the last guest had departed I left the house, having refused all invitations to dine. I wanted to be alone. I walked across Hyde Park, under its splendid trees, to my hotel near Queen's Gate. I reviewed my seventy years, what had been accomplished, wherein I had failed. I thought of the fatherless boy almost burnt up with ambition, in the hateful bondage of a municipal office. I had seen then, as my first objective, that I must achieve independence. By the time I was forty I had accomplished this. I could do what I liked, live where I liked, with no man to command me. I had travelled over two continents and was not wholly unknown on them. A degree of fame, not too much to harass me, had brought me wonderful friends and the entry to circles which neither wealth nor rank could have commanded. I had written twenty-three novels and ten miscellaneous books, in addition to which I had made ten American lecture tours. The war work in U.S.A. had broken my health but the need to guard it may have assisted longevity. How many years would I have in hand, with less work, and more leisure? Perhaps a vain hope. Already I had in hand a final crowning work, an autobiography that might reflect the times and the scenes filling my varied life. I had lived in many places, known remarkable persons, had lovely homes in which to entertain my friends: it may be I had something worthy to record. It would probably take ten years.

Such were the assets, but there were losses. I was very much alone. I had missed marriage. In Hong Kong I learned that the beautiful Myra who might have shared my journey had just died. It was difficult to think that someone once so vivacious in youth, so entrancing in spirit, had vanished. Perhaps it would not have worked; our flames too ardent and windblown.

Others passed in review before me as I trod the soft turf; young Lucien, the boy I had made my heir and been so hopeful for, killed in Algeria in the flower of his youth; and Louis, my devoted secretary, for whose life we had fought for four years in vain. Too many old friends were departing. The road grew lonelier. I was aware I must make a new address book, the black lines in it were too many.

How beautiful was this May evening, with the chestnut trees in flower! Physically I was in good form. I could write and read without glasses, and work without fatigue, and with no failing of memory. My life had straddled two wars, six reigns, seen great nations collapse. More and more I became aware of the ruthlessness of change, the callous indifference of Time, the basic futility of all human things. *Vanitas. Vanitas.* Yet there were riches in the harvesting, my zest for life had not diminished.

Thus thinking, I came to Queen's Gate, where, amid the trees and the traffic, a forgotten Field-Marshal sat on his bronze horse. I reached home in the last glow of twilight. The next morning I went to my desk and began to write *The Grand Cruise*, the story of my voyage round the world. To rest is to rust.

II

Two days after the party I lectured at a Harrod's "Tea with an

Author" series. Three weeks later Christina Foyle, an old friend, for whom I had spoken and taken the chair through some thirty years, gave for me one of her Literary Luncheons at the Dorchester Hotel in Park Lane. The Duke of Bedford took the chair in a ballroom packed with 350 persons. He provided a note of comedy. It had been agreed that no messages or telegrams should be read, holding up the proceedings; but one telegram slipped through and confronted the Duke. He opened it and said: "I have here a telegram for our guest—'Dear Cecil, I hope you have a very successful lunch. I am sorry I cannot be present. With best wishes and my love, Jayne Mansfield.'" There was a look of utter astonishment on the faces of all present. The film star, Jayne Mansfield, was one of the most lurid products of Hollywood, an American sex symbol, with the blondness of her hair and the magnitude of her bosom. What was Cecil Roberts doing, cavorting in such company? I picked up the telegram and pointed to the name on it. The Duke put on his spectacles and looked again. "Oh, I am very sorry! The telegram is not from Jayne Mansfield but from John Masefield, the Poet Laureate," he said, provoking great merriment.

Despite this, the luncheon was a great success. I recovered before I got up to reply. Knowing what a superb showman the Duke had proved himself to be at Woburn, there were some who thought the telegram error was one of his gimmicks. When later there was a Foyle lunch to celebrate Noël Coward's seventieth birthday I wrote telling him to keep an eye on the chairman! In his case he fared well, a knighthood, but too long delayed, too near his death.

I was whisked away from the Dorchester, after much handshaking and autographing, to be interviewed at the B.B.C.'s television studio, an impromptu affair that suited me, for I detest set speeches. I was amused by the pretty girl who approached me with a powder puff and dabbed the top of my bald head to prevent it reflecting too much on the screen. *Ou sont les boucles d'antan?*

III

My first visit that summer was to Challens Green. I feared the ordeal but found Billy Birkett her usual serene self. I heard from her the full account of Norman's end. The house was now much

273

too large for her, being alone. On the Sunday morning I went with her and her son, Michael, and his wife, to look at a smaller place. It was a brick and flint cottage that stood on a high ridge of land above a deep valley. It did not look promising to me, and it was remote. Worse, it was at the end of an unmade road, but it was the name that put me off. Grubbin's Lane. And where would the domestic help come from, and the gardener? "I do most of my own housework and cooking," said Billy, "so that's not a problem."

She had plans. She would build on an extension, with a large ground-floor bedroom for her mother. Challens Green was put up for sale and she bought the flint cottage. I could hardly bear to think that I should never again sit in that booklined lounge, with the great bow window looking over the Amersham valley. And everywhere the cheerful figure of Norman, jumping up from his chair to verify a quotation, or working in the little study, typing his letters very perfectly with two fingers, in contrast with the chaos of my own performance. But I tried to be cheerful, and so Monday came and I left Billy, brave and smiling. "Until next year," she said, kissing me goodbye on the platform.

I made a number of visits that summer. Alec Lacy, at The Croft, Farningham, was no longer painting futurist canvases. I found him in a state of excitement. He had bought for £5 a large mahogany door from a house being demolished in Mayfair. It was a superb eighteenth-century piece of work, beautifully moulded, the grain magnificent, the carpentry of superlative craftsmanship. He was fitting it into his drawing-room doorway. I valued it at £300, which was his estimate. "I wonder how often the Duchess of Marlborough had her hand on that door knob?" queried Alec. "And the Prime Minister Disraeli, when he visited her in the Seventies," I added. I closed the door quietly. "Ah, thank God, you're not a door banger!" he said. I told him that my father had taught me to "feel in" a door.

I went to stay with Leslie Rowse at All Souls College. He gave a lunch party for sixteen in the great college dining-hall, with portraits of all the worthies looking down on us. I was in luck with my neighbours at table. Beaming Agatha Christie was there. I asked an American on my left, named Boise Penrose, if he was the author of a book on the ancient trade routes, which I had bought and enjoyed ten years ago. He was. His mouth opened in astonishment, his face flushed with pleasure. There was a little lady on my right. Her place-card said "Miss Joan Wake". I asked if she was the authoress of that fine piece of genealogical research, *The Brudenells of Deene*. She was. Her hand trembled with excitement. "To think that you have read it!" she exclaimed. Later my host wrote: "You are a prize guest and a great charmer. You always pull something out of the bag!"

I worked hard that summer on my new book, *The Grand Cruise*, and finished it. At Frankfurt, en route to Alassio, I visited a friend, Professor Arthur Bouvier. He was Dean of English Literature, from the University of Baltimore, which had a branch in Frankfurt for the American military colony. I gave two lectures to his students. He lived in a room walled to the ceiling with books. He had cultivated an ivy plant in a window pot. It had grown so vigorously that it went all round the room and began to obscure the shelves. He could not bear to cut it down . . . "a green thought in a green shade". I went on to Alassio.

The beautiful Villino Romano was a heap of rubble. Alida Bock had found a little apartment just behind the Palazzo Vairo. After some nights there we moved on to the Castle of Conscente where Luigi Rolandi Ricci had restored for us the fifteenth-century Casa Vecchia at his gate. My library on the upper floor now had a bathroom. The view was superb, the silence absolute. It was there that young Michael Gilliam of the B.B.C. came to interview me. He stayed the night. "But you're in paradise!" he exclaimed, when I told him I was going to live in Rome. Luigi put on a little show, a mock reception for me on my return, pretending I had completed a successful Governorship. The ceremony was reported in *The Radio Times* by Gilliam.

At four o'clock in a tiny village in Italy the Rolls came from the castle to fetch the English *maestro*. On arrival the Union Jack burst from the tower, the National Anthem was played, and a page presented the castle keys on a velvet cushion. Thereupon the Marchese approached, resplendent in gilt and blue and read a solemn address of welcome. And after a magnificent dinner in the castle this self-styled "intellectual vagabond" painted a picture in prose for me of his life there beside the Mediterranean.

The National Anthem came from a gramophone hidden in the chapel in the courtyard. For the occasion Luigi wore a braided court uniform and lent me a silk top hat once worn by his uncle attending King Umberto.

IV

Now homeless, that winter I took up my abode in the Grand Hotel at Rome. There was nothing here for tears. I had no domestic worries and downstairs a continuous pageant of life. My window was a casement opening on two thousand years of history. Immediately below me was the Piazza Esedra, on the ancient site of the Baths of Diocletian. It had what I considered the loveliest fountain in Rome, though comparatively modern, with a bronze triton holding a dolphin that shot a sixty-foot jet of water into the air, and three concentric pools that were rimmed with lights at night. Across the Piazza my view extended over a small park of cypresses and palms to the distant Alban Hills. The sun rose behind them, a scarlet scimitar cutting the horizon and then a ball of fire. On the slope of the hills lay Frascati with its vineyards. Immediately to my left rose the great mass of the ruins of the Baths. Part of these was now the National Museum. Michelangelo had converted the vast hall, where the bathers had promenaded in the fourth century, into a church whose roof was supported by gigantic marble columns. He had also created for the Carthusian monks a large arcaded cloister, now holding an overflow of the museum's statuary. I could walk there in winter in the sun, in the shade in summer, away from the crowds and the roar of traffic.

The Baths in the Emperor Diocletian's time could accommodate three thousand bathers. They had been built in A.D. 305 by an army of workmen, including forty thousand Christian slaves. At one corner was an octagonal steam room, or nymphaeum, still intact, with a rotunda roof. It had been converted into a planetarium, alternating as a cinema. My hotel room faced south-east. I required of any room I lived in that I should be able to enjoy the three daily wonders of the world, sunrise, sunset and the moon high in the heavens. These I had.

The hotel had long been the haunt of emperors, princes, presidents and prime ministers. When they made official visits to the Quirinale and the Vatican they often stayed here. Axel Munthe had laid one of the scenes of his fantastic allegory, *San Michele*, on a floor of this hotel. King Alfonso in exile, the American financier Pierpont Morgan had died here. There were official receptions and parties in the great chandeliered salons. Not only were there Government-sponsored gatherings of diplomats, beribboned and bemedalled, but it was a favourite setting for wedding receptions. A thousand guests would assemble in a salon converted into a bower of flowers. I had seen there the kings of Greece, Sweden, Denmark, Afghanistan, the Emperor Haile Selassie, the Sultan of Morocco, the President of the German Republic, and King Ibn Saud, with a harem of six wives and thirty children, in transit. Barbara Hutton, "the poor little rich girl", had vacated the royal suite for President Tito, and received from him a bouquet of red roses, a gesture from Communism to Capitalism. The Count of Paris, the Count of Barcelona and his son Prince Juan, heir to the Spanish throne, the unsmiling Gromyko, with guards, had all stayed in this hotel. There were some film and pop stars, and ballet dancers, but most of these preferred the flashier hotels.

Sometimes a pageant passed the entrance, a Guard of Honour with thirty cream horses and thirty brown horses, mounted soldiers in shining horse-tail helmets, and a mounted band, returning to barracks after escorting a visiting potentate. At one corner of the hotel stood the fountain of *Aqua Felice* with four stone Egyptian lions that spouted water under a cascade. When I walked in the cypress-shaded garden of the nearby museum I passed a collection of ancient tombstones. I always looked wonderingly at the mean one of "Helena. Obstetrix." How many little Romans had this midwife brought into the world, possibly soldiers who had died fighting on Hadrian's Wall or against Queen Boadicea?

My hotel had assets often missing in this age of concrete box-architecture, utilitarian and hideous. It had a noble staircase and wide carpeted corridors, a fine promenade when the weather was bad. Alas, some of its splendour was vanishing. A grand staircase leading only to the floor of the royal suites had been taken out. "Royals" are getting scarce, and impecunious. And no more shall I see a page-boy in white gloves carrying a candelabrum, escorting a robed cardinal to the grand salon. Cardinals don't count as they did. A great asset for me was that I was only ten minutes' walk from the British Council Library, where I found many reference books I needed for my work, as well as magazines, papers and a fine lending library. It occupied an old Roman palace in which the lecture hall was the former gilt-mirrored ballroom.

On my arrival in October the first Ecumenical Council had gathered, three thousand bishops all told. Thirty of them lodged in my hotel. When the bus from the Vatican sittings discharged them each day it was like a river of blood, such waves of gay cassocks. There were many stories about them. One American bishop arrived late to find his room taken. They put him in a double one. He unpacked and went out to dinner. When he returned the maid had laid his pyjamas on one bed and his lace cotta on the other. The bishop next door to me smoked a cigar after breakfast. Meeting him in the corridor I said I had always been curious about the odour of sanctity. I did not know it was an Havana X.

Everybody loved Pope John XXIII, even the heretics. He was genial, roly-poly, with a twinkle and consummate tact. I had known him when he was the Patriarch of Venice. A predecessor there, going to the Conclave in Rome, had been elected Pope, and never returned. "Take a single ticket for me, in case . . ." it is reported the Patriarch said to his secretary. He was not popular with the Conservatives, the "Black" Roman aristocracy. At Christmas he went to the Aracoeli Prison and blessed the convicts. Sniffed one— "A peasant's son—a communist!"

When the Conclave had elected him Pope in 1958, aged seventy-seven, it was thought he would be only a "caretaker" pope. He proved to be one of the most energetic popes ever seen. He called the Vatican Council to effect reforms he thought long overdue. The last Council, held in the Vatican in 1870 under Pius IX, was almost catastrophic. During a tremendous thunderstorm it pronounced the unpalatable doctrine of Papal Infallibility. It had to hastily suspend its sittings when Italian troops swept into Rome, ending the territorial dominion of the Papacy, and creating a united Italy with Rome as its capital.

Now, meeting again after ninety-two years, the Council's theme was Christian Unity, under the direction of a strong Pope, impatient of the old taboos, of long diplomatic experience, and firmly tactful. Old and ill he insisted on walking into St. Peter's and up its long nave behind three thousand bishops, archbishops, patriarchs and eighty-one cardinals. Wearing white mitres they occupied tiers flanking both sides of the nave. It was a stupendous sight. The Council began its long discussions. It nearly split on the subject of Divine Revelation, as between scriptural tradition and scientific historical studies challenging some of it. The Pope intervened and saved the Council by appointing a commission.

He was very ill in the last weeks and could not attend the thirty-four sessions with their 587 speeches and 523 written arguments, but his influence was felt. He insisted on freedom of discussion. He gallantly appeared at its last sitting before it reassembled next year. He gave it his blessing, with a characteristic touch—he hoped next time that there would be more deeds and fewer words. They would not see him again, the most popular and heart-winning Pope since the Reformation; all this achieved within a period of five years.

I had a Tribune ticket in St. Peter's for the anniversary of the coronation of the Pope. The Tribunes were filled with the Corps Diplomatique, and special guests, in uniforms, evening dress and decorations. I was only a few yards from the Pope seated under the great baldacchino. It was a stupendous spectacle. He had been carried down the nave borne aloft in the Sedia Gestatoria, Pharaoh-like, between plumed fans. All the cardinals came up to him to make obeisance. Some of them, very old, had to be helped up the steps. After the two hours' service ended I stood at an exit door where his car awaited him. He came out, waving to the applauding crowd, under a blazing noonday sun. His young attendant, Monsignor Capavilla, put the flat, broadbrimmed scarlet hat on the Pope's head, tilting it to shade his eyes, but he lifted it and waved it as the car bore him away to the papal apartments. He looked like a happy schoolboy on holiday but many of us knew that, aged eighty-three, he was dying. Within seven months he was dead of cancer, an heroic soul.

v

Rome was full of surprises. You entered a door of a narrow, slummy street, climbed a staircase and found an apartment whose terrace, gay with roses, geraniums and azaleas in terra-cotta jars, overlooked the hills of Rome and the winding Tiber. There were endless receptions and musical soirées in palaces with fine tapestries and frescoes under coffered ceilings. Rome was choked with diplomats, with ambassadors to the Quirinale (the Republic) and to the Vatican (the Pope). They all entertained ceaselessly and lavishly. The local aristocracies competed, with historic names like Colonna, Doria, Borghese, Orsini, Massimo, written into the history of Rome. The Pecci-Blunts had a palazzo with a private theatre, fronting the great steps sweeping up to Michelangelo's Piazza Campidoglio, with its bronze equestrian statue of Marcus Aurelius. One evening John Gielgud gave a Shakespeare recital in their little theatre. Afterwards there was a reception with a buffet, in a series of rooms with splendid paintings, and fires in great fireplaces. "I see now why you live in Rome. It's one long pageant," said Gielgud when I took him back to his hotel.

Living in Rome one was not spared from being converted into a guide by friends. Having written *And So to Rome* I was considered to be well-qualified. There were times when I groaned, having to describe things I had described a dozen times, and to appear interested and cheerful. But I was delighted when in mid-February, 1963, the Brockets arrived. I had not seen them since that time at Alassio when I had identified Lord Brocket with the Eton schoolboy in the photo on the grand piano, and I had not yet responded to their repeated invitations to visit them at Brocket Hall. Ronnie and Angela proved delightful company. For a week I took them around, ending with the Palazzo Doria, where Orietta Doria and Frank, were, as always, hospitable. When they left I again promised to visit them.

VI

One April morning when I was going out of the hotel the concierge asked me if I could help him to decipher a telegram someone had requested him to despatch. He had difficulty in reading the signature. I looked at the form. It was to Lord Baldwin, and signed "Evelyn Waugh", a name difficult for a foreigner. I knew that Waugh had a reputation for being aggressive but I happened to have an affection for his family. When I published at nineteen my first book of poems it was highly praised by his father, Arthur Waugh, a well-known critic and publisher. A few years later I received a fan letter about a poem of mine in *The Poetry Review* from a schoolboy at Sherborne. It was signed Alec Waugh. It happened that our fledgling novels were published at the same time by the same publisher. This resulted in a warm friendship that had endured for over forty years. Arising from this Waugh association I felt friendly towards Evelyn. I therefore dropped him a note saying I was in the hotel and that if I could be of any help to him with my connections in Rome I would gladly be at his service. My letter was sent to his room that morning. When I came in after lunch the concierge gave me my letter back saying the gentleman had said it was not for him. The letter had been opened and read by Evelyn Waugh.

I dined out the next evening and came in late. Just as the lift was ascending Waugh got into it. I recognised him by photos I had seen. He was an unprepossessing-looking fellow, puffy-eyed, apoplectic, pot-bellied and short in stature. He looked flushed and unhealthy. I said nothing. My room was on the floor to which he also ascended, and when I stepped out he followed. There was a long corridor, and another at the right-angle, leading to my room. Somewhat to my embarrassment we were walking side by side. We looked at each other and presently I could not resist saying: "I am sorry you found it necessary to be so discourteous, saying my letter was not for you." He looked at me angrily and cried: "I know all about you! I thought you were in gaol in Brazil with Jumbo Howard for sodomy!" I stopped in my walk. When I had recovered my breath I said: "I've never been in gaol, nor in Brazil, nor known anybody called Jumbo Howard. You must be mad!" We walked on. To my dismay he turned the corner with me. "I suppose you've sold a lot of your bloody books! What are you going to do with all your money? I've a wife and daughters to marry off!" he shouted, his face flaming. Arriving at my door, I replied, "I shall probably leave it to the Society of Authors to found a home for derelict writers like yourself." I put my key in the door. He turned, holding his key, and I saw that his room was opposite mine.

I am a friendly person, of an even temper. It takes a lot to stir me. In my room I began to recover from the impact of his words.

I was so angry that when I got into bed I could not sleep. At dawn, waking again, I made up my mind to go to his room and give him a sound thrashing. It was the only way in which to deal with such people. He had come to Rome to write about the Pope. Well, I would give him something else to write about. At eight o'clock, dressed, I went to his room. A card hung on it. "Non Disturbare". His shoes were outside the door. I tried the handle. It was locked. I went back to my room, and breakfasted. When I went to his room again the notice had disappeared and also the shoes. I knocked, and, getting no answer, tried the handle. The door was locked. At that moment the floor waiter came along. "The gentleman's just gone out, sir," he said.

I worked all that morning in an upset state of mind. I lunched out and returning before dinner found Waugh standing opposite the revolving door. He looked at me, smiled and said: "Good evening, Cecil!" I walked right past him.

When I narrated this incident some weeks later to A. L. Rowse, he said: "My dear fellow, you should not be surprised. He's a writer of some genius, but we all know that he's a paranoiac." After his death his appalling diary was published and confirmed this. The whole thing saddened me. I had an affection for the Waughs.

CHAPTER THIRTEEN

Irish Excursion

I

In the spring I motored home to England, via Florence, Alassio, and Geneva. I had houses of call at each of these places. I lunched with Queen Helen of Rumania, at the Villa Sparta on the hillside of Fiesole-San Domenico, overlooking Florence. Here at last, after a stormy passage, she was anchored in a haven of peace. Married to the irresponsible and unfaithful Crown Prince Carol, her father, King Constantine, exiled, her favourite brother, King Alexander, dead from a monkey bite, she had seen her country overrun by Germans and Russians, her husband vaunting his liaison with Madame Lupescu all over Europe, her son Michael, the boy-King, with all the Royal family, driven into exile in 1947. She had survived all this with quiet dignity. By nature a shy, reserved woman, I looked upon her with admiration. Happily she now had her sister, the widowed Duchess of Aosta, living in a villa across the road. We all met at lunch, to which Harold Acton came, a neighbour, from his beautiful Villa Pietra.

I went on to Alassio, passing the Villino Chiaro at Rapallo, with its sad-sweet memories of Max and Elizabeth. At Conscente I found Luigi Rolandi Ricci. I had only a brief time to look at my library in the Casa Vecchia. I stayed four nights and then went to Geneva, breaking my journey at Dr. Antoine Cloetta's château above the Rhone. I was in London at the beginning of June and went to stay with the Brockets, keeping my promise at last.

Brocket Hall, near Hatfield, surpassed my expectations. We entered the grounds through a pair of fine lodge gates, driving a mile in parkland with rhododendron bushes and fine trees. Then came the first view of the house, nobly placed on rising ground above a stream over which we passed by a balustraded bridge. The house was a fine example in rosy brick and stone, pilastered, of the early Georgian period. The entrance hall, of noble proportions, into which we immediately stepped, had a wide staircase under a dome, branching at the first storey. There was a morning-room on the left and on the right a large dining-room. A drawing-room led to the great saloon with a high vaulted roof. Its walls were hung with full-length oil paintings. There were portraits of Charles I by Van Dyck, another by Mytens; Charles II, James I, Queen Henrietta, Anne of Denmark, etc. The high, painted ceiling was the work of Zucchi, the husband of Angela Kauffmann, by whom there were several works. A fine Adam marble fireplace graced the long wall. The great saloon, really a gallery, was lit by ten twenty-foot windows. There were thirty bedrooms. My own was almost regal, with a bow window commanding a wide view of the lake, the bridge and the park. On the horizon stood a pair of tall, ironwork ornamental gates. These bordered the Great North Road. I was reminded of the *Gloriette* crowning the gardens of the Schönbrunn Palace in Vienna similarly silhouetted against the sky. Every room and every corridor was crammed with pictures. Ronnie could not resist the sale rooms. Lady Hamilton as "Euphresyne", by Romney, hung in the dining-room. In the drawing-room there were portraits by Lavery of Lady Brocket and her two small sons, and of her daughter, who had been with her parents that day in Alassio, now the Marchioness of Headfort. I looked at the two little boys. There was deep tragedy here. The elder was dead. A fall from a hay wagon had brought on cancer. He had left a widow and two small sons.

At the foot of the staircase stood a fine marble statue, French, delicate, amorous, of *Paul and Virginia*. The passage to my room was lined with hunting prints, a complete set of *London Cries*, and a delightful Paul Sanby watercolour of Brocket. A six-foot *Madonna* by Murillo (1617–82) had come out of the collection of the Infante Don Gabriel, son of Carlos III. At the top of the staircase I disdiscovered a small Romney, a delicious study of a sleeping infant, entitled "Horatia, daughter of Lord Nelson". In a back sitting-room I had a surprise. There was a striking canvas of an Italian shepherd boy, in a rich landscape. My attention was held by the quality of the painting. I was astonished to find that the artist was English, Richard Buckner, R.A. I possessed portraits of my grandfather and great-uncle by the same artist. When I remarked on this, "That was one of the favourite pictures of Queen Helen of Rumania when she stayed here," said Ronnie. I was amused by a plaque in the entrance hall. The house had been lent during the Second World War to the City of London Maternity Hospital, to ensure safe births during the blitz: 8,256 mothers were accommodated and 8,338 infants were born. There must have been twins around!

My bedroom in the left bay was over the library. It was glorious June weather and I never ceased to delight in the vista of the shining lake below, swan-haunted, and the three arches of the baroque bridge mirrored in the water so that they made perfect circles. There was a right-of-way across the bridge. Louts had destroyed six pillars of the balustrade.

I noticed in every room the tables were loaded with new books. It was my host's habit whenever he travelled to send one to Angela with a greeting inside it. Wandering through the rooms at Brocket I evoked the figures of the past. In historic houses I often speculated upon what the walls could tell us had they the power of speech. Brocket had witnessed a life of high fashion in the eighteenth and nineteenth centuries. The vigorous, rich Lamb family had inhabited it. Penistone Lamb had bought himself an Irish peerage, and as Baron Melbourne sat in the House of Lords where he opened his mouth once in forty years and said nothing of consequence. He had married the beautiful daughter of a Yorkshire squire, Elizabeth Milbanke, a woman of brains and beauty, and easy morals. It was said that the father of her second son, William, was Lord Egremont; the fourth son, George, was fathered by George, the Prince of Wales, whose interest was shown by adding "god" to "father"; and the daughter, Emily, destined to be the wife one day of Lord Palmerston. She seems not to have known who her father was. This easy-going family mingled with the Devonshire House set, a singular ménage-à-trois, with its brood of legitimate and illegitimate children.

One day the Devonshire children came to Brocket bringing with them a cousin, an elfin creature of fourteen, Caroline Ponsonby. She was a mixture of curly-headed tomboy and precocious infant. The handsome, twenty-year-old William Lamb, looked at her and was captivated. Six years later he married her, his overtures favoured by the fact that his elder brother having died he would be one day the second Lord Melbourne. He was destined to know ecstasy and utter misery. On their wedding day she was hysterical. Enraged by the bungling bishop she tore her wedding gown and was carried screaming from the London drawing-room where the ceremony was held. Her young husband took her to Brocket where they spent the honeymoon in lyrical happiness. They went about in London, entertaining at their town house and at Brocket. A son was born, alas, mentally deficient. She had two miscarriages. There were frightful scenes at Brocket and by the fourth year their marriage came to wreckage. Lord Byron appeared in London, the lord-poet-hero of *Childe Harold's Pilgrimage*. Every door opened to the dark-headed, surly, handsome Adonis. Caroline flung herself at him. For a short while his vanity was flattered, and then she became a pest. She pursued him, and forced herself into his rooms, with every suggestion of seduction. William watched, powerless. One night at a ball, repulsed, by Byron, she went into the supper room, smashed a glass and cut her arms and hands. She was borne off bleeding and shrieking. Society shut its doors to her. She went to Brussels, thrust herself on the Duke of Wellington and paraded the streets, half-naked. The Lamb family beseeched William to get a separation, to which he proved reluctant. He had married an elf and now found himself living with a tigress. One evening she smashed £500's worth of china in a tantrum. She turned Brocket into a lunatic asylum. She arranged a lavish dinner for eighty. Only ten came. She published a novel exposing herself, Byron and the Lamb family. It created a sensation. William, a scholar with political ambitions, entered the House of Commons and then withdrew from it. A separation became inevitable, and reluctantly he had the Deed drawn up. Distressed, he went down to Brocket to have a peaceful night before signing it. While undressing he heard a noise at his door, and found Caroline had followed him and was proposing to sleep on the mat. The next morning when the lawyers arrived with the Deed for signing they were astonished to find Caroline sitting on William's lap and feeding him, in gusts of laughter. The Deed was not signed. He entered Parliament again and George IV prophesied that one day he would be Prime Minister.

After twenty years of this frantic marriage he again considered a separation in Ireland. While he was there news came that Caroline was dying at Brocket, in a contrite mood. They corresponded tenderly. He was still in love with her. "Send for William," she whispered one day. He came and was with her when she died. The whole story of this shipwrecked marriage has been skilfully told by Lord David Cecil in his biography, *The Young Melbourne*.

William Lamb was forty-nine when Caroline died. Another great adventure was before him. He was the Prime Minister when the girl, Victoria, ascended the throne. The old Minister of sixty and the young Queen of eighteen were in rapturous accord. Almost father, lover, counsellor, he gave her three years of devoted service. "His manner towards the young Queen mingled with perfect facility the watchfulness and respect of a statesman and a courtier with the tender solicitude of a parent," wrote Lytton Strachey. But when Albert appeared on the scene his tutelage ended, his day was done. His government fell, he resigned office. There was a sad leave-taking of his sovereign. He retreated to Brocket, feeling that his life was finished. A year later he had a stroke but he lingered on at Brocket, his days spent reading by the fireside. He was alone, terribly alone, off the great stage he had occupied. There was no son and heir, no children. His sister Emily, now Lady Palmerston, came over from her near-by home to see him. He was still handsome but the flame was out, and he had no inner faith. His hedonistic philosophy had collapsed. The Archbishop of Canterbury suggested prayer. "Yes, but who is one to pray to and what is one to pray for?" he asked, petulantly. He mused on the past.

"It was natural that he should end at Brocket," writes Lord David Cecil in his *Lord M.*, "The chintz-curtained bedrooms, the gilded elegant salon, the leather-scented quiet of the library, the park with its grassy vistas and the swans sweeping down on thunderous wing to settle in the river reeds, all these were heavy with memories for him stretching back as far as he could remember at all." In this twilight he lingered for six years. Then one November day in 1848 Lady Palmerston coming into his room found him sleeping peacefully, his handsome face unravaged despite all he had suffered. The following morning he gave a long sigh and died. Palmerston sent the Queen the sad news. He was sixty-nine, the last of the great Whig politicians, twice Prime Minister, and almost completely forgotten. He joined Caroline in the churchyard at Hatfield.

II

Ronnie took me round the grounds and some of the estate. The gardens were now much reduced, instead of the ten gardeners of Lord Melbourne's time there was now one. At the back of the house there was a large formal garden, with two long lawns, red brick walls, and ornamental urns. There was an architectural gimmick, pure Regency, with a portico and an octagonal room under a dome, known as the Sillabub House. Here the elegant company had come to drink sillabub, a dish of cream curdled with wine.

We walked up the hill to the gates on the North Road. Here on July 12th, 1824, Caroline, out driving, with her husband accompanying her on horseback, saw coming along the road an ornate funeral procession, with black plumed horses, and a large flower-laden funeral coach. William went ahead to enquire whose funeral it was. He learned it was that of the late Lord Byron, whose body was being conveyed on the last stage of the journey from Missolonghi in Greece to the Byron vault at Huchnall Torkard, Notts., near the Byron ancestral seat, Newstead Abbey. Westminster Abbey had refused him burial. William did not report his discovery until they were home again, fearing the effect on his wife. She took to her bed for two weeks in a state of collapse. I observed this place on the road where the funeral had passed, with particular interest. The long procession had lumbered up the Great North Road to Nottingham at five miles an hour.

One Sunday morning Ronnie took me into the village of Ayot St. Lawrence and showed me the old rectory which he was re-decorating, and then gave me a drink at *The Brocket Arms*. He told me of another visitor to the inn. When George Bernard Shaw came to live in the village, one morning to the company in the inn he said, "I've taken a house here to keep my mistress in." For a year Mrs. Shaw wondered why no one called on them. After Shaw's death a mob of sightseers stormed "Shaw's Corner" and made life in the village a nightmare.

The Villa Taranto, Lake Maggiore

The Château de l'Echelle, La Roche-sur-Foron, Haute Savoie

Aubrey Cartwright (1930–72) at Eton

Sir Max Beerbohm at Villino Chiaro

I asked Ronnie if he knew which bedroom the Lambs had occupied. "I think so. I believe it is ours," and he showed me the large bay-windowed room with its view of valley and stream. It looked so calm, beautiful and sunny, but what agonies and ecstasies it had known! I looked at the mat on the threshold where the harassed husband had found his wife on the eve of the separation. He was William Lamb then. He succeeded to the title and became Lord Melbourne six months after Caroline died. He had lived on in the house with his half-witted son. Then the son died, eight years after his mother.

It was in the long, cosy library, with its book-laden tables, the rich leather bindings of books lining the walls, the writing desk in the window, where, in turn, two Prime Ministers had worked, that I came nearest to the presence of William Lamb. His last years had been spent here amid the books he loved, in a deep chair by the fireplace, the scholar-statesman, the hedonist to whom a young Queen had brought an Indian Summer of love. Ronnie opened the window. "Look," he said, "I am told that from those flower beds he cut flowers every morning and sent a rider across country with a bouquet for the Queen at Windsor, until Albert appeared."

III

Emily, the sister, who had attended Melbourne in his last hours at Brocket, had married the handsome Earl Cowper, a dull, good man. Then, widowed, she had married Lord Palmerston, the Foreign Secretary who had collaborated with Melbourne in his Ministry. He was something of a Lothario when young; now still a bachelor of fifty-five, he proposed to Emily, aged fifty-two. It was at the time when Queen Victoria had succumbed to Albert. "They are both of them above fifty, and I think they were quite right so to act since Palmerston, since the death of his sisters, is quite alone in the world . . . Still, I feel it will make you smile," wrote Victoria to Albert.

The whole world smiled on learning that this Lothario who dictated Europe's destiny should have succumbed. He took his adored Emily to his lordly seat, Broadlands. This belated union proved a perfect marriage. Even thirty years earlier, when a young

Secretary of War, he had danced with her at Almack's and loved her. They were often at Brocket. When Melbourne died he had left it to his sister and the Palmerstons lived in it through the years when "Old Pam" made Europe's history with his bold moves, and England stood at the zenith of her prestige. After twenty-five years, now eighty, he was still in love with Emily. Brocket was often filled with young couples, and taking Emily's arm in his, he would say to them "Here we are two pairs of lovers!" But in 1865, once more Prime Minister, he was failing. Hearing of his illness, Queen Victoria, who had never liked him, so different from dear Melbourne, sent kindly enquiries. His tart humour had not deserted him. He replied:

> Viscount Palmerston begs to thank Your Majesty for your kind and considerate message sent him by Lord Granville, whose head and time being full of the cattle disease and matrimonial arrangements and preparations, the message was not delivered quite as soon as it might have been.

During his illness he was a restless, naughty patient. He would not take his medicine. He walked out on to the drive without a hat and twice climbed the railing. "I wanted to see if I could still do it," he said when Emily remonstrated. Confined to bed, he told stories, quoted Virgil, dealt with matters in the red despatch boxes, ordering that civil servants should be given a half-day's holiday each week. His doctors, feeling the end was near, gently touched on religion, enquiring whether he believed in salvation as promised through Jesus Christ. "Oh, surely!" he said, and to a further enquiry about life immortal, "Oh, certainly!" A tactful agnostic to the end, he supported the Church of England as a national stabiliser.

The morning before he died he had a hearty breakfast of mutton chops and half a glass of port, and told his wife he "should not have lived so long without discovering what a good breakfast it is". On the last day of his life, as the evening sun gilded the trees at Brocket and crimsoned the lake, he was told the Queen had made enquiries about him. "It is very kind of Her Majesty. Tell her I am much better." Later, half-conscious, he was heard to say, his mind on foreign affairs, "That's Article 98—now get on to the next." He died at dawn the following morning, October 18th, 1865. two days short of his eighty-first birthday.

The Queen proposed that he should be buried in Westminster Abbey, an offer Lady Palmerston accepted on the condition that when her time came she could lie there beside him. The celebrated author of *The Life of Christ*, Dean Stanley, preached the sermon in the Abbey, extolling the dead statesman's merits. He was probably unaware that many years ago Palmerston had tried to seduce his cousin's wife, Lady Stanley of Alderley.

So, in the strange workings of destiny, two Prime Ministers had died at Brocket, brothers-in-law, tended in their last hours by the same devoted Emily, sister and wife.

I left Brocket Hall on Monday morning. The weather had been glorious throughout my visit. The whole place was a sylvan enchantment but the threat over it all was the servant problem. There was a temporary butler, a cook, and a woman who "came in". Repetitiously, butler and cook were leaving. The house, they complained, was too far from shops and a cinema. Once it had had thirty servants.

IV

Returning from Brocket Hall I gave a lunch to celebrate the fortieth anniversary of the publication of my first novel, *Scissors*, still alive in its twenty-first impression. What memories of one's anxieties and hopes in the launching of that firstling of a family that now comprised twenty novels, most of them "in a state of good health." *Scissors* had been launched at a lunch given in the Reform Club in 1923 by Harry Brodie, to whom I dedicated it. Of those then present I was the only survivor. At this anniversary lunch my guests were the son of the director of Heinemann's when the book appeared, Brodie's son, Patrick, Richard Church, Cadness Page, Dr. A. L. Rowse, John Betjeman, Beverley Nichols, Lovat Dickson and Dr. E. V. Rieu. There were to be no speeches, but Dr. Rieu of the Penguin Classics, made one in terms I will not repeat. Perhaps now I should retire. I had fathered a large family, I was seventy-one.

The next day I went to Nottingham to see my remarkable only brother, the survivor of seven operations. He looked like an animated skeleton when he met me at the station. He was eighty-two, and his car was ancient also, one I had given him thirty years ago. When I suggested buying him a new one he said: "On no! I know this old girl and love her. She'll 'go out' with me." He was widowed now, having worn out his devoted wife with nursing. What a singular relationship ours was! I had never known him. He was eleven years my senior. He rarely read a book and thought my means of livelihood most singular, and my mode of living quite crazy. Polishing his car and cultivating his roses in the garden of the little house I had bought him absorbed his days. In contrast with me who had circled the globe, he had been abroad only once, on the disastrous occasion when, having given him a holiday in Venice, he had coloured the canal with his blood. Withal, he was a completely happy man, knowing none of my anxieties and exultations. He once remarked that I had been lucky. I retorted that he should add a "p" to the word.

I knew another happy man, very different. I took Lady Monckton on my annual visit to John Masefield, the Poet Laureate, at Burcote Brook. Polly could not believe he was living in that half-ruined house, the part left after a fire, in a wilderness of a garden. White-haired, blue-eyed, I found him more feeble this year, aged eighty-five. He shaded his eyes with his hand, looking like the sailor on watch he had once been. He still retained his beautiful voice, his courtly manners. I told him that in a walk near St. Pancras Station I had just seen the alterations they were making in Woburn Place, where Yeats had lived at the beginning of his career. They were extending the Ambassador Hotel. I had been assured that Yeats's rooms would be carefully preserved and the memorial plaque, "William Butler Yeats, Irish poet and dramatist, lived in this house from 1895 to 1919", would be replaced. "When I was a young man I visited Yeats often—he was a glorious creature," said Masefield, "and a delightful talker. He used to preside over Monday evening gatherings, attended by the leading poets and artists, sixty years ago. Dear me! How very interesting what you've told me."

The report aroused his curiosity, for two months later he went to Woburn Place. The manager of the hotel asked him to describe the room where Yeats and his friends had gathered, in order that they could restore it as near as possible to when he visited Yeats there. "Jan" as we called him, was in very good spirits. He asked me what I was writing and discreetly remarked that he was quite unable to appreciate the work of the modern poets. "I suppose the poets of the future? Well, it seems to me they dislike all laws of metre, rhyme and technique, but no doubt it pleases them," he said, gently.

Two hours of talk passed like twenty minutes. He gave Lady Monckton a reprint of his book on Shakespeare, autographed very firmly. "You'll come again, won't you?" he said, escorting us to the door. Of course I would come again. I had been doing so for some forty-five years.

Lady Birkett had moved to her new house near Speen. She had built on a wing, with a fifty-foot library-lounge whose wide windows overlooked lawn and valley. One side was filled with books she and Norman had collected. But the ground floor room, specially built for her mother, aged ninety-two, had not been occupied, for she died before it was ready. Billy cooked all the meals that week-end with no apparent effort. No, she was not lonely. "I always have so much to do and think about," she said, answering my query. When I left she gave me a gramophone record of Norman's speeches, his mellifluous voice marvellously preserved.

I lunched one day at the House of Lords with Ronnie Brocket. There was a green envelope on my plate. I opened it wondering what it was. Inside there was an air ticket for Dublin. "You shocked us by saying you had never been to Ireland. So you are coming to the Horse Show, to stay at Carton, and later to make a tour of Ireland," he said. Within a week I was invited to the wedding of Aubrey Cartwright to a beautiful girl in Stockholm. It was not likely that either event would occur again, but Dublin had priority; two whole weeks with a wonderful host.

V

At the beginning of August I flew to Dublin and was met at the airport by Ronnie. We motored through Dublin and after some fifteen miles reached Maynooth, in County Kildare, with an entrance lodge to the Carton domain. The seat of the Dukes of Leinster had been bought by my host, a snap bargain, twelve years earlier, with 1,600 acres, for £63,000. He sold the timber in the park for £35,000 The Leinster family had vanished. The Premier Duke of Ireland was a spendthrift, with no sense of money, a happy-go-lucky, good-looking Romeo. He had sold his life interest to a speculator, Carton was no longer his. In time he would acquire four wives. The first one was a Gaiety Theatre actress, who ended by putting her head in a gas-oven after providing the duke with an heir. His second duchess was an American, my friend the beautiful Rafaelle. They had met in a popular café on Fifth Avenue, New York. Both married, they quickly got divorces and remarried. The duke, dogged by creditors, had no means of livelihood and had been sent by his speculative backer to make a rich marriage in America! His new wife had little money. The marriage ended in disaster. As premier Irish duchess, Rafaelle went to Court. The duke, a bankrupt, was banned. She divorced him in 1946.

Ronnie re-furnished Carton, retaining some of the pictures, and Angela redecorated it. They heated the vast house electrically. In the large park Ronnie placed a herd of his prize-winning cattle. In the grounds there was what was termed "The Royal Canal", connected with the River Liffey. It was so called because Queen Victoria, the Prince Consort and the young Prince of Wales had been rowed on it in 1849 to Shell Cottage, a whimsy created by the third duchess with 30,000 shells.

We turned in at one of the four lodge gates. There were eight miles of twelve-foot stone walls round the park. After a mile-long drive down an avenue of trees and crossing an ornamental bridge, we came in view of the house. It had been built in 1739 by the nineteenth Earl of Kildare on the site of a former one. The house had then cost £21,000. It could not be built to-day for less than a million. His heir became the Duke of Leinster in 1766.

The size of the house and its beauty left me speechless. The rooms on the south front, opened up, provided almost a Hampton Court vista. There was a long saloon with an Italian stucco ceiling, by Paolo and Filippo Franchini of Italy, the theme "The Courtship of the Gods", and a green drawing-room, 1815, with a fine Carrara chimney-piece with lapis lazuli panels. At the end of the saloon Lord Edward Fitzgerald, fifth son of the first duke, a fine musician, had built a Telford organ with gold pipes, which occupied two niches and the arch of the door-way leading to a state dining-room, fifty-two feet long and twenty-four feet high. Angela prevailed on me to play the organ. It was originally operated by water but now it had an electric motor. The tone was sweet and balanced. I could not help thinking of the musical Lord Edward who had installed it, and much wondered who had touched its keys down the years.

The great dining-room, beyond a circular small dining-room, with a plasterwork ceiling and two marble chimneyplaces, had portraits by Sir William Beechey of members of the Leinster family. In the hall were Allan Ramsey portraits of the first duke and his duchess, a Hamilton portrait of the ill-fated Lord Edward and of the beautiful Duchess Emily, daughter of the Duke of Richmond. Fitzgerald died of wounds resisting arrest during an insurrection. He was regarded as a great Irish patriot.

Life at Carton had been on the grand scale we shall never see again. A visitor wrote in 1788: "Everything goes on in great state here. The duchess appears in sack and hoop and diamonds in the afternoon, French horns playing at every meal, and such quantities of plate that one would imagine oneself in a royal palace, and there are servants without end." There were forty-seven servants, accommodated in thirty bedrooms. When I asked Angela how she managed about servants she told me there was an old Leinster retainer, Christopher the butler, and his wife the cook, with a family of ten children. They were all willing "fixtures", in various roles!

From the entrance hall a stately winding staircase led to the first floor. On its wall hung a tapestry recently bought by Ronnie at a Sotheby sale. It was sixteen feet by twelve. He had guessed whether it would fit. It was French, eighteenth century, called "The Little Gardeners". It so fascinated me that it interrupted my movement up and down the stairs. On the wall hung a twelve foot painting of Hermione, the beautiful young duchess of Leinster, the mother of the present duke, who had died widowed aged thirty-five, of consumption in Mentone. Opposite hung a portrait of Wentworth, the seventeenth Earl of Kildare, who died in 1664. There were forty bedrooms. Twelve of these had been given bathrooms and were beautifully furnished by Angela. They had Adam fireplaces and high windows overlooking the park. There seemed to be acres of close-carpeting and everything glowed with white paint. There were 340 windows to be kept clean, and those on the ground floor were twenty-feet high. What incomes these Irish aristocrats must have had! I found in a housebook that the first duke had an income of £20,000 a year, with no taxes—at today's value, £200,000!

When Ronnie bought the house, part of the conditions was that fixtures should be left intact. Unhappily, the contents of a fine library, with hundreds of books, calf-bound, with ducal arms, were gone, and also sixty red leather fire-buckets, with the ducal arms, which had hung on brackets throughout the house. A picture over a fireplace in the saloon was thought to be a fixture but proved detachable from its frame. Ronnie bought it from the duke, who didn't want it, for £6. During an insurance inventory it proved to be a Claude Lorraine landscape!

VI

One morning I explored the two floors above me, all empty. I counted twenty-two rooms on the second floor, twenty on the third. These, with eighteen rooms in the two wings, made a total of sixty, and I may have missed some. So there was plenty of room for those forty servants. Outside had slept twenty-two gardeners, and others in the four lodge gates. The two wings of the house had colonnaded porticoes. On the ground floor there were two interesting period exhibits. One was the bedroom of Queen Victoria, who stayed at Carton. In a corner there was a cabinet with a perforated ceiling. It was a shower-bath. On a cord being pulled, a servant above poured hot water down through the sieve. The other exhibit, next to the entrance hall, was the Footmen's Waiting Room. Round its cornice hung thirty-eight bells, listed. The chief were for the Duchess's Sitting-room, Spring, Summer, Autumn and Winter bedrooms and dressing-rooms; the Duke's Spring, Summer, Autumn and Winter bedrooms and dressing-rooms; the Earl of Kildare's Spring, Summer, Autumn and Winter bedrooms and dressing-rooms. Sixteen bells for the family, and others for the guests. When Ronnie put in electric light and bells, he removed three miles of wires.

There was a long high corridor which led to the stable courtyard and its fifty stalls. On the walls Ronnie had hung over two hundred coloured rosettes from agricultural shows where his cattle had won prizes. "Shall I call this the 'Cattle Prizes Gallery'?" he asked. "Oh no," I replied, "Call it 'The Rossetti Gallery', it's quite a P.R.B. palette." And so it was named.

The view from the windows of Carton on the south side was magnificent. The front lawns were broken by low, clipped privet hedges, scalloped. There were two large parterres with rose trees and down the centre a gravel path that led to a fountain with a large bronze Mercury, after Giovanni di Bologna. Beyond there was a meadow, planted with small trees, a mile deep that ended in a vista of the blue Wicklow Mountains. At one side of the garden there was a little railed-in forgotten cemetery where members of the family had been buried. The flat tombstones were illegible under moss. I chipped some away on one of them, to discover the name of a forgotten duchess. It was all too sad, so I stopped.

There was one other guest at Carton, the Hon. Grania O'Brien, the daughter of Lord Inchiquin. She was delightful company, and was in our touring party. We were to meet again at her home, Dromoland Castle, Co. Clare. From Carton we made excursions. Ronnie had taken a box for the Dublin Horse Show. It was behind that of President de Valera's. We went in on three exciting days. There were sixty thousand spectators. The weather was glorious. The great event was the jumping for the Aga Khan Cup. The British team was poor, the Italian fair, the Swiss good, the German good. In delirious excitement the Irish team won for the first time since 1949, so the Cup stayed in Dublin. The kilted Irish band played, and the old President went out to present the cup. Poor man, he was almost blind and had to be piloted. In the evening we saw the Russian Ballet. Ronnie wanted to have the whole company to Carton for lunch but it wasn't feasible.

One day we visited his daughter, Elizabeth, married to the Marquess of Headfort. They lived in an Adams house with eighty bedrooms, adjacent to Kells, the home of the *Book of Kells* (eighth century). There was a vast park and a lake. They were young, with two small children, inhabiting a wing of the house. A preparatory school of a hundred boys occupied another wing and also the top storey, and used the great dining-room as an assembly hall. We saw nothing of them in this caravanserai. The young Marquess had his own aerodrome and flew his own plane.

After a week at Carton we began our tour of Ireland. In the afternoon we came to Cashel with its giant rock in the Vale of Tipperary. The Dean's Palace there had been bought by Ronnie, to save it. He had converted it into a de-luxe hotel. Built for the Anglican archbishop in 1730, of red brick with stone quoins, part of it had latterly been used as a deanery. From my bedroom window I looked on the famous Rock, "the Acropolis of Ireland", where St. Patrick had baptized King Aengus in A.D. 450. The Munster kings had been crowned there on the coronation stone. Grania's ancestor was one of them, in A.D. 977.

The view of the great ruined abbey, castle, and towers on the Rock, silhoutted against the sky at evening, was unforgettable. In moonlight it was eerie, the black skeleton of Ireland's grim history.

When we entered the courtyard of the Palace I saw an enormous crate standing there and asked what it contained. At Christie's Ronnie had bought a large chalk-and-watercolour cartoon, "Galway", by Augustus John. Boldly drawn with fine characters and colouring, it showed in a foreground of rocks and sea a woman at a table selling apples and drink, and a group of about forty peasant men and women listlessly standing around. When it arrived at Cashel it was so large that it could not be got into the house. I made an inspection and a suggestion. With the help of men from the fire brigade with ladders, it was hoisted in through a large end window of the long first-floor corridor. It was hung exactly opposite my bedroom so that on one side I looked out on the Rock, with a thousand years of history, and on the other side on this work of Augustus John. Ronnie was so pleased with my solution of the hanging problem that he insisted on buying me a Donegal plaid rug in the hotel-shop. It is a treasured memento of him and our happy excursion for he died suddenly within four years.

On Sunday morning we attended divine service in the cathedral. The Dean of Cashel preached. He was flying to Toronto next day to attend an Anglican Congress. He sounded apprehensive as he told us this. The cathedral was vast and empty. All told, ten of us. "If you had not been here we should have been six," said the Dean.

When he came to dine I asked him how many Protestants to Roman Catholics there were in Ireland. "About 150,000 to 2,700,000" he replied, sadly.

The next day we left for Kerry, and passed through world-famous Tipperary, immortalised by the soldiers of the First World War, then along beautiful Lake Killarney and on to Lake Caragh, where Ronnie had a small fishing lodge. From its windows we looked on the low mountains between the lake and Dingle Bay, a landscape of exquisite pastel shades. Two days later we arrived at Shannon from whose airport I was to fly home. That noon we came to Dromoland Castle, the ancestral home of the Inchiquins, with towers and seventy-seven rooms. We lunched with Grania and her mother. Too large to keep up, they had sold it, thirty servants having dwindled to two. An American spent a £100,000 converting it into a de-luxe hotel, hoping to catch the New York-Shannon air passengers. The Inchiquins were building a smaller home in the grounds.

At three o'clock that afternoon I was taken to Shannon airport. We were almost tearful at parting. I had seen Ireland in a manner given to very few. As the plane rose over it, I felt a little of my heart had been left behind.

VIII

It was not long before we met again. Two weeks later, at the beginning of September, I flew to Venice and there Ronnie and Angela joined me. Venice always meant a gathering of friends and soon "Perry" Boehm, Alida Bock and Lady Monckton arrived. But there were sad gaps and many ghosts, and always there was my Lucien, a phantom boy rowing his boat on the canals. There I had once walked with Myra in the ecstasy of youthful love. It requires fortitude to march into one's seventies; familiar faces vanish, doors close forever, the years spin like a child's toy. I was glad, therefore, to make two new friends in Venice. One was Madame Romola Nijinsky, the widow of the dancer whom she had supported and nursed through the long years of his insanity. The other was Baron Paul Bohus, whose joy in living had not been lost by imprisonment in an Hungarian communist gaol.

The pleasure of Venice was dashed by a story that King Peter had gone to Paris, seeking a separation from his wife, Alessandra. Distraught, she had attempted to commit suicide in her mother's home, the Garden of Eden on the Giudecca. She had been rushed into hospital in a perilous condition and her husband had hurried to her side. Peter had accused her of extravagance, she had accused him of impoverishing them by helping exiled Yugoslavs. They were nearly destitute. Tito had confiscated the properties of the royal family. His father, assassinated in Marseilles in 1934 by a Croat revolutionary, had died without divulging the secret number of the fortune he had banked in Switzerland, it was said.

I went to see Alessandra's mother, Princess Aspasia of Greece, a friend of thirty years. Poor woman, all her life she had been dogged by Fate. Her husband had died tragically before their daughter was born.

On arriving at the Garden of Eden I found there ex-King Peter, "Prince Sixpenny", and Alessandra. Poor young couple, since their marriage in London in 1944 they had known nothing but deferred hopes. Their son Alexander was born in 1945, in Claridge's Hotel, London, the bedroom having been specially designated Yugoslav territory. He was a merry, dark-eyed little boy when I first knew him and he was now a goodlooking lad of eighteen. His grandmother, Princess Aspasia, had taken much care of him during his parents' travels. She never complained, smiled quietly, a soft-voiced, unpretentious woman.

In October I went on to Rome, again filled with bishops for the Second Ecumenical Council over which the new Pope Paul VI now presided. Soon after arrival I slipped in my bath, breaking two ribs, and found myself once more in the Salvator Mundi Hospital. Undaunted, receiving a letter from my friend Guido Wertheim asking me to join him in Florida, I picked up the telephone and told the Pan-American Airways to book me a flight to New York. On coming out of hospital the first letter awaiting me was from my publisher informing me that in a printer's fire stocks of five of my books had been destroyed. Two years earlier I had lost four others by flooding in the warehouse. An author gets no insurance money or compensation for this. Moreover, I was informed that it would not now be economically possible to reprint the lost volumes. They had passed through many impressions. I felt like a mother who had suddenly lost nine of her children. A cracked rib could be mended but a burnt family could not be resurrected. At the moment I was not *enceinte* and my spirit was low. So on to a New World and winter sunshine.

IX

My Australian friend Guido Wertheim, living in Florida, wrote that he had found in Palm Beach a delightful little house and asked whether I would like to share it with him for the winter. His suggestion fitted in with my plans. A young friend in Rome, Nicoletta Panni, the soprano, was going to make her debut at the Metropolitan Opera House in New York. We were making up a party to go there for this momentous occasion. Her grandfather had been the celebrated Giuseppe de Lucca who, for thirty years, was a much loved baritone there. I suggested, therefore, that Guido should find an apartment in New York for a month and that afterwards we should go to Florida for the rest of the winter.

I flew to New York on November 1st, 1963, to a city in which I had many friends. Guido had found inexpensive accommodation in an hotel between Broadway and Fifth Avenue. It was high up so that we were in sunshine most of the day. In 1929, in Venice, Bernard Shaw had introduced me to a honeymoon couple there and asked me to show them something of the city. The young man was Gene Tunney, the world's heavy-weight boxing champion, who had earned some two million dollars by twice beating the renowned Jack Dempsey in 1926 and 1927. They were a charming couple. Tunney was handsome, modest and intelligent, with a passion for Shakespeare. We founded in those days a firm friendship. He was now a very successful business man with an office on the 37th floor of the Pan-American building. He gave a lunch for me in the Sky Club, a restaurant on the 56th top floor, with all New York below us in bright November sunshine.

Nicoletta made her début, as Mimi in La Bohème, and had a good reception from a crowded house. Only that morning, I had found in a shop a gramophone record of her famous grandfather singing with Caruso in the sextette from *Lucia de Lammermoor*. I made her a present of it at supper after the début.

301

On the afternoon of November 22nd as I sat writing in our apartment Guido came in and said: "It's quite unbelievable!" I asked him what was quite unbelievable. "Haven't you heard!—President Kennedy's been assassinated in Dallas, Texas." Everything stopped in New York. All that evening we were in front of the radio as detail after detail was given out to the world.

We had tickets for a performance of *The Meistersinger* at the Opera House the next day. It was cancelled and replaced by a memorial service. In a hushed house the director, Rudolf Bing, came before the curtain, asked the audience to rise, and said that the orchestra would play Bach's *Lament*. At the end we all left the Opera house. Everyone spoke in whispers.

On December 1st Guido and I flew to Palm Beach. The little house he had found was enchanting. It stood opposite the golf links, a few hundred yards from the Breakers' Hotel, with a sandy beach available. We had a veranda and a small garden in which grew grapefruit, oranges and avocado pears. I was fascinated by a tree called a bombax. It was a grim grey-branched tree with fat buds. Overnight these would burst, revealing a large flamboyant flower like a pink silk shaving brush. No wonder it gave us the word "bombastic" for a show-off. My great delight was the mockingbird. One would come and sit on a telephone wire and pour out an unbroken song, of great volume and range. The nightingale and all the other famous songsters are a poor second compared with this prodigy. Rightly it has been chosen as the State Bird of Florida. Another attractive visitor was the humming-bird. It would hover over the flowers, its wings invisible in their speed, while it dipped its long probiscis into the stamen of the flowers. We found it liked honey-sweetened water which we hung in glass tubes on branches. It was smaller than a tit, of an iridescent blue. I took Kodachromes of them. Their wings were too rapid for my camera's lens. They appeared suspended and wingless.

Not far from us was the Indian River, running parallel with the Atlantic shore for some three hundred miles. We took a little ferryboat to cross from Palm Beach to the shopping town of West Palm Beach. There was a café down by the river wharf and here I often sat, near the tethered yachts, fascinated by the pelicans that came to pick up anything thrown out by landing fishermen.

One of them, so venerable that I called him Mr. Wordsworth, with his domed head and solemn eye, would catch bananas and oranges in his pouch. He was an exhibitionist and one day seated himself in a friend's car and rode with him to the fishmonger's shop where he knew he would be rewarded. I used to watch the pelicans' homing flight as they went, in perfect triangular form, down the coast at sunset to their nesting ground. After observing these different birds for a week I got an idea for a book. I began to write a novel, which I called *A Flight of Birds*. The characters in it were a green budgerigar, a swallow, a crimson parrot, a bluebird, a pelican, a robin and a wren. These birds changed the lives of the persons who kept them, bringing them good fortune and also disaster. To help me in my ornithological research there was an excellent subscription library, with reading room and a shady garden.

We bought bicycles and made excursions over the flat land by the riverside, and into the jungle and the ocean creeks. We bathed in the warm, blue Gulf Stream. Each evening the sun went down in flaming splendour. The day temperature was a steady seventy-five degrees. It was an earthly paradise.

I took one of my characters from life. A smartly dressed young man used to drive an old lady in a Cadillac car. He was witty and amusing, and very attentive to her. One day the old lady, having her hair done at Elizabeth Arden's, had said to the young hairdresser, "I like you. Will you marry me and look after me? Of course I shall look after you." So thirty-eight and seventy-eight had married. She had two daughters and a son. They raised no objection, for he took mamma off their hands, and her money was in a trust. The young husband gave her ceaseless attention, smiling, cheerful, indifferent to the things said about him. He was only free after 10. p.m. "Darling", as he called her, insisted that he should hold her hand until she fell asleep in bed. Then out he would go to the night-bars, and enjoy himself. He had no guarantee of a "settlement" on her death and we thought him rather foolish. "She gives me a good time and I'm fond of her," he would say. After five years she died. Then one day in Rome the widower called on me. He was on a cruise. The old lady had valuable jewellery, and had saved money. She had left him $500,000. "So now you're a playboy," I said. "Oh no, not at all," he replied, "I've gone back to Elizabeth

Arden's, I believe in work. This is just a break." "Perhaps you'll find another client," I said, jokingly. He laughed gaily. "Who knows? I was quite in love with the old girl, and I made her last years happy." He married another elderly lady later, and gained a quarter of a million dollars. *Da capo.* He had given me the opening chapter of my novel. I merged his story into that of another I heard of a man who went mad collecting humming-birds.

I began *A Flight of Birds* on December 8th. I finished the novel next year, on February 5th, 1964, utterly exhausted. Five days later I flew to Nassau over the shallow lagoons to visit my old friends, Sir Guy and Ann Henderson. He had now retired from his Chief Justiceship of the Bahamas and had created a lovely home at Lyford Cay. I do not know of a more beautiful hour's flight anywhere in the world, the emerald sea breaking on little, palm-girt atolls, the endless variety of colour in the water, azure, mauve, emerald, purple, lucent with tropical light.

I had gone for a rest but there was none. There was a party of eighty guests for me, lunches on yachts moored in the harbours, dinner with the Prime Minister in Lord Beaverbrook's former house, a dinner at the Lyford Cay Club, a lecture by Peter Scott, who had been to the breeding ground of the pink-tipped flamingoes. I had seen him, a baby in his mother's studio. Kathleen Bruce, the sculptor, was a sister-in-law of Dorothy Bruce, the daughter of Jesse Boot, who had been my tennis partner fifty years ago. Kathleen had married gallant Captain Robert Scott, of the South Pole drama. One forgets that other people grow up as well as oneself. It was a shock to see this portly, middle-aged man, now a famous ornithologist, who had once been a naked cherub rolling on a carpet.

How kind were Ann and Guy, but I was unwell, and aware of ghosts. Tod Iliffe was here no more, nor Louis Paget with whom I stayed in 1939 in a chalet surrounded by palms, bananas and eucalyptus trees. He had lived on Hog Island, later more appropriately christened Paradise Island, and had taken me "trolling" for tunny in the Gulf Stream. Now Nassau had become a wedding cake, sugared over by Canadian and American millionaires, and with raffish company promotors offering tax havens. The unavenged ghost of the murdered Sir Harry Oakes had not been laid, and there was a threatening Negro ground-swell. One day they would take over. The Whites deserted Nassau in the summer heat. I was bitten by flies that infected me and was so ill back in Palm Beach that I wondered if I could get on the plane for England. At Nassau two letters awaited me that sent my spirits to zero. Polly Monckton, who had seemed so tired in Venice, was dying of cancer. I wired her flowers. The second letter informed me that "Fay", Lady Norman, had died, aged eighty. So more doors had closed.

Guido put me on the 'plane at Miami for the night-flight to England. All that I remember of that flight is the marvel of a full moon over the ocean. First there was the scented warm air of Nassau, then the lights of Bermuda and then the dawn breaking in a splendour of turquoise and rose. As we approached Heathrow at breakfast-time I looked down on myriad toy houses and imagined all the business men shaving in bathrooms, with a whiff of bacon and eggs downstairs. I was fortunate in being met at the airport. My friend William Ballance had retired and found for himself a Sussex nest on a hill, with folds of the wooded weald in view. He put me to bed and sent for the doctor, who kept me there. I heard birds sing in an April garden and saw the flash of swallow's wings. It seemed a cool green paradise after the subtropical heat.

A letter had been held back from me. It was from Polly. ". . . those lovely freesias arrived a week ago and are scenting my room. I am still here; this long drawn-out dying is a nightmare. Why in the Prayer Book do they pray against sudden death? All my friends are marvellous. Do you know I am reading *Scissors* again? What a charmer he was, like its author! How unwise and naughty of you to make yourself ill again writing at such a pitch. Excuse this shaky handwriting but I'm in bed. Much love my dear, and thank you for your friendship." This was the last letter. She had gone. What grace and warmth had been taken from my life.

CHAPTER FOURTEEN

In England Now

I

I watched the spring from my Sussex window. While I lay in bed I corrected the proofs of *The Life of Norman Birkett*, written by my friend Montgomery Hyde. It was singular that a man so sweet in temper should have written so bitterly in his diary about some of his colleagues at the bar. One of the judges smelt, one of them was mentally sick, one libidinous. There was a note of comedy. A judge returning to the robing-room found his gold cigarette case was missing. He asked the sergeant on duty if anyone had been in the room while he was on the bench. "Only Mr. Justice H . . . sir." "But damn it, someone's stolen my cigarette case!" "I thought he was acting a bit suspicious, sir!" commented the sergeant. I prevailed on my friend to make severe cuts. Writers of diaries would often like to return to earth and censor them, which their near relations sometimes fail to do.

While I lay working a book arrived from Christina Foyle. It was an autobiography, *My Life and Fortunes* by Paul Getty, notorious as the richest man in the world. "We are giving a Foyle lunch for his book. All London will be there. Will you take the Chair? You are the best and safest chairman I have ever had," wrote Christina. My inclination was to refuse. I was still hors-de-combat. Moreover, from all I had heard of Getty I didn't like him. I read the book and my opinion of him changed completely. I told Christina, rashly, I would take the chair. Perhaps I should be well in six days. I wasn't. I had a haemorrhage. I was determined not to let Christina down, whose enterprise I had always admired. On the day, ignoring my friend's protest, I dressed, got him to help me down to the car and was motored fifty miles to Earl's Court. He was very solicitous, and more apprehensive than I was.

The whole world was there, over six hundred, all the tycoons the city could produce, all those who found millionaires irresistible, the opportunists, the publicity hounds, the Press. During the preliminary cocktails I had to sit down, wobbly. When I got to the Chair to my dismay there was a note from Christina. Would I please call on the distinguished guests, and ask them to take a bow? I did; the Israeli, Italian and Cuban ambassadors, the Duke of Bedford, Lord Brocket, John Braine, the novelist, Mr. Charles Clore, the "take-over tycoon", Sir William Coldstream, Sir Frank Francis, Sir Gerald Kelly, P.R.A., Laurie Lee, the poet, Sir John Rothenstein of the Tate Gallery, Ruskin Spear, R.A., Sir Stanley Unwin, the publisher, Sir Emrys Williams, Sir Charles Wheeler, President of the Royal Academy, Mr. Peter Wilson who, at Sotheby's, knocked down pictures for a million pounds, Sir Isaac Wolfson, who gave away millions. I went steadily through the list, with a few appropriate words for each, twenty-five all told. I omitted Sir Adrian Boult. I wrote him a note of apology. "Alas, I wasn't there, held up by a rehearsal," he replied.

Exhausted, I fell back in my chair and began a harder task, cultivating Mr. Paul Getty on my right. He was not prepossessing by reputation or appearance. He looked like a depressed bloodhound. But I had liked his book and found him therein a sympathetic character. I had stayed at his home, Sutton Place, when it was the Duke of Sutherland's. It was loudly trumpeted that he put a pay-call-box in the hall for his guests to use. Very rightly. He had had a bill of over £1,000 run up by guests who made lengthy calls from their rooms to Teheran, Kamchatka, Bombay, etc. I read that he had had five wives, Wasn't that excessive, I asked him. "No woman likes to be married to an oil-rag," he replied. There were long silences. I believed the poor man was nervous. But he made a modest, short speech, without a note. Later he wrote: "I owe you thanks for the very kind and flattering introduction you gave me." And from Christina, "How can I thank you? You made a delightful speech and were a marvellous chairman." My friend got me down into his car and took me home. The next morning when my doctor examined me he said, "I find you're much better." "Of course I am," I replied, "I went to Earl's Court yesterday and took the chair and spoke at an enormous banquet for Paul Getty." He looked horrified. "Do you know, my dear doctor, why I am much better? I drink the blood of my audience."

By the end of the month I was about again. I went to Brocket Hall. There were no servants. Ronnie brought me my breakfast on a tray. I lay in a state bed like a pasha. "I don't suppose Lord Melbourne or Lord Palmerston ever carried in a guest's breakfast on a tray!" I observed. Angela had turned a front bedroom into a kitchen and made a dining-room of the adjacent bedroom. Ronnie served and Angela cooked, and we all washed up. The food came mostly from Fortnum and Mason in Piccadilly, by car at week-ends when they came down. Nevertheless, we lived well and gaily. All those magnificent rooms were unoccupied. There were thirty bells and no one to answer them. There was only a "daily", Sundays excepted. A month after Ronnie had put in a bathroom for a lodge-keeper he and his family suddenly departed.

On Sunday Ronnie and Angela went to evening service in the village church. Unwell, I stayed behind. I wandered through all the rooms, looked at pictures, picked up books, sat at a desk in the library where two Prime Ministers had worked. The silence was so great I seemed at the bottom of the well of Time. I stood by the foot of the great staircase, and, perhaps with a touch of hysteria, I called up loudly—"Lady Caroline, won't you come down and talk a little?" My voice echoed under the high lanterned dome. Then utter silence. If only I could turn a Time-switch and bring back a summer's day in 1800 when the Devonshires with their "legits" and "illegits" were visiting here, and William Lamb had first noticed the elfin Caroline. They had romped up and down this staircase. I opened the door of the bedroom where Melbourne and Palmerston had loved, and died. The gold evening sun fell on a print of "Old Pam", princely in his State robes. I got afraid in the grand saloon, with all those dead kings and queens staring at me. I felt I was being watched by a hundred ghosts. "The evil that men do lives after them . . ." Melbourne when Home Secreatry had signed the warrant sending thirty farm labourers to life slavery in Australia. Starving with their families on twelve shillings a week, they had revolted and burned ricks, a capital offence. They were torn from their wives and children, manacled and hustled into great hulks where many of them died en route to Botany Bay. Lamb was a kind man, but he was an aristocrat, with the inseparable arrogance of his caste, terrified that the Revolution might be repeated here. Were we all now paying for those wicked times? Lamb with £150,000 a year, untaxed, how could he know what life was like on twelve shillings a week?

Lady Caroline had a passion for page-boys. She dressed eight of them in a livery of scarlet and sepia. Once she cut open the head of a boy, throwing something at him. "My lady, you've killed me!" the boy cried. She went into the hall and had hysterics; this hall with not a sound now. I tried to read, I could not, and when at long last Ronnie and Angela returned and I unbarred the great door for them, I fell upon them in near hysteria, for all the rooms had begun to shout at me.

A few days later I went with my friend Ballance to call on John Masefield at Burcote Brook. The place seemed more derelict than ever, the long pot-holed drive overgrown with trees, the lawns unmown, the house unpainted. The hinges on the hall door had given way and it shrieked over the tile floor as Masefield opened it. There was no servant. Judith, his devoted daughter, was out. She had gone into Abingdon to hunt for one. He led us into his bleak study, with its big windows looking over a wild lawn down to the brook. He sat and talked with us in his beautiful voice but I noticed that he had to keep shading his eyes from the light. There was an air of frugality about the place and I was uneasy about him. What could it be like here in the dark and cold and silence of winter?

I asked him if he was still writing. "Yes," he said. "Poets do not retire, and I hope to be able to write better some day. When I used to visit Thomas Hardy he told me that whenever he had an idea he jotted it down for further use. He raised the lid of his desk and showed me about a hundred slips. He was eighty-four then—I'm eighty-six, and I make notes," he said with a smile. I told him that I had found a photograph of Robert Browning mounting the stairs of the Palazzo Rezzonico in Venice, after his last walk. I said Browning did not die in the great bedroom they showed tourists, but in a little back room next to the kitchen because it was warmer there. "How very, very interesting," said Masefield. "You know, he was pestered by fans, especially Americans. A man who had given him some cigars asked him to write some verses in his autograph album. Taken aback, Browning wrote: 'For the cigars, Thankee,

Yankee.'" I asked Masefield to show my friend the delightful portrait, by Sir John Lavery, of him at work in his study, painting ships on the backs of chairs, his hobby. He took us into the dining-room to look at the portrait. "Lavery was over eighty when he painted me. One evening we played billiards and he easily won. He laughed, saying to me: 'I'm good at the game because I began life as a billiard marker!' So you see we had something in common for I had worked in a bar in New York and he in a billiard saloon!"

We stayed two hours, and there was no lessening of his vivacity, but I felt we should go. On the hall table as we went out I noticed three silver photo frames. One contained the scroll of the Freedom of Ledbury, his native town. In another frame was his appointment in 1930 as Poet Laureate, signed by King George V. "Rudyard Kipling should have had it," said Masefield. "King George never read poetry, but at his Naval College he had learned some of my sea shanties. 'I like his verses,' said the King to the Prime Minister. So I got it!"

The third document in a silver frame was the Order of Merit. I picked it up and said "Of all things I believe that is the one most worth having!" As I replaced the frame and turned to leave, he put his hand on my shoulder and said gently, "There are other things." I asked him what others. He smiled and answered, "Conversation like yours!" We went to the door and he waved us goodbye as we got into our car. Is it immodest of me to recount this? Well, if you get the Garter you wear it.

I went to see my brother at Nottingham. He was dying, and I felt I should not see him again. He was calm and happy. He had always been imperturbable. He thanked me for all my kindness. Our lives had been so different; we had always been strangers. He lived two more months, to the age of eighty-three despite all those operations.

II

Back in my old quarters in Rome I received a letter one day from the Town Clerk of Nottingham. Two of the City's aldermen would be in Rome, might they call on me? I replied, wondering what was the reason. They arrived, I gave them dinner and then they disclosed their mission. The City of Nottingham wished to confer its Freedom on me. I felt honoured. Previous Freemen had been General Booth of the Salvation Army, Captain Ball, V.C., the flying ace of the First World War, and Lord Trent, old Jesse Boot, the city's greatest benefactor, founder of its university.

One day while my friend and colleague H. V. Morton was dining with me, a telegram arrived. By a unanimous vote of the City Council the Freedom of Nottingham would be conferred on me next May. All this presaged the end. Well, it was gratifying. When Joseph Conrad was fifteen he had been given the Freedom of Cracow, and exempted from all taxes, in honour of his father, a patriot. And Prince Philip, receiving the Freedom of the City of London, observed that, according to the official citation, he received it as "a person of distinction within the meaning of Section 259 of the Local Government Act, 1933." "It is always comforting to be told one is a person of distinction. But it is even more comforting to know that it's by Act of Parliament!" said Prince Philip. The pleasure for me was increased by the fact that I had never received from the British Government any recognition of my services to it. America and Italy had honoured me, and now my native city. I had two visitors that week, young Aubrey Cartwright and his beautiful blonde wife, Eva. They had been married in Stockholm, her home, and had settled in Casa Estella at Cap d'Antibes and in an apartment in Paris. Health, a large fortune, good looks, they seemed to have everything. In a way, since Lucien's death, he had been my ewe lamb.

One morning in October, I had a shock, learning how time flies. That brilliant boy, Tarquin Olivier, who had delighted his grandmother at Apple Porch, had married a lovely young actress. I congratulated him. He was now twenty-eight, an experienced traveller. "Dear Cecil," he wrote, "how well I remember the days at Apple Porch and at Pilgrim Cottage! Life is bursting at the seams. We are off to Kenya for the Commonwealth Development Corporation. My first book *Eye of the Day* is now in its third impression. Heigh, ho! Yours ever, Tarquin." A friend at the wedding wrote: "They made the handsomest couple that ever came out of a church porch." At the ceremony all of the three actress-wives of Laurence Olivier were present, Jill Esmond (Tarquin's mother), Vivien Leigh and Joan Plowright.

I spent the New Year of 1965 at Luigi Rolandi Ricci's castle and there, on January 20th, I saw, on the television screen in the gunroom, the funeral procession of Winston Churchill. Luigi invited in all his staff to witness it. I was very proud of the native genius we have for arranging these public occasions. It was a flawless and moving drama. It had been my good fortune to know this prodigious man for well over forty years.

III

In May I went to England for the Freedom ceremony. My first public engagement was at a Foyle lunch given to mark the publication of a book of meditations by the late Pope, Giovanni XXIII. The various Churches, threatened by drowning in the rising tide of modernism, were now clinging together like posts in a Venetian lagoon. The Chairman on this occasion was the proselyte Earl of Longford. On his right sat Cardinal Heenan, Archbishop of Westminster. Others present, represented the Churches, diplomacy, art, literature and politics. There were the Irish, Chilean and Italian ambassadors, Earl Attlee, the Earl of Arran, the Bishop of London, Lord Iddesleigh, Mr. Douglas Woodruff and Cecil King. Where was the President of the Methodist Connection? I sat next to Mr. Charles Forte, of the Kingdom of Restaurants. What was I doing there, why had Christina invited me? It might be because I had known Giovanni XXIII since those days when he had been Patriarch of Venice. I was completely taken by surprise when a note came along asking me to reply for "The Guests", but I was glad of an opportunity to pay tribute to that warm-hearted, large-minded Pope whose smile was a benediction. Afterwards, I asked Christina why she had picked on me. "I knew you would be discreet and safe. The speeches were so trite, we had to have some relief!" Possibly my function was to de-unction.

At my publisher's I signed copies of *A Flight of Birds*, the product of my Palm Beach winter. It made me a little sad and reflective. This was my twenty-fourth novel and it would be my last. I had signed a new novel in this office for so many years, with such great hopes. It was difficult to believe I should never do so again.

I went to Lady Birkett's at Speen, and to a new place, Lamb

House at Rye, where Montgomery Hyde was now living in Henry James's old home, a red brick Georgian house with a walled garden. It was a most lovely day and we sat on the terrace, haunted by the presence of the novelist. We speculated on how, as a writer who complained that his books did not sell, and whose plays had failed, he contrived to live in such mollycoddle comfort with a butler, a cook, two parlourmaids, a gardener and a page boy. My host produced the probate of James's Will in 1916. He left £3,000. That could only produce some £150 a year. How was it possible to live in this style, with an apartment in London also? Had he been living on capital, had he an annuity? Despite "failure" as an author, he enjoyed enormous prestige. People made pilgrimages to see him and he received the O.M.

IV

The City of Nottingham had built itself a new Council House, grandiose, with an Olympian façade, a Council Chamber, and a fine banqueting hall. It had displaced a ramshackle, grim Exchange, built over a meat market, "The Shambles", with animal corpses lit by gaslight. In this den I had worked, a desperate boy of fifteen. I used to smell the banquets upstairs. Now I was going to eat at one given in my honour. As a boy I had seen General William Booth, Nottingham-born, creator of the Salvation Army, ride through the City, standing, with a flowing beard, like an Old Testament prophet, in an open carriage, on his way to receive the Honorary Freedom of the City. Forty-five years ago, a young editor, I had been in the Chamber and seen Jesse Boot, the founder of Boots the Chemist, paralysed from the feet up, receive the Freedom. And now here I was. There were moments when I did not believe it.

I had brought with me from London a dozen guests, including my publisher. I was received at a special sitting of the Council by the Lord Mayor, the Sheriff, the aldermen and councillors. The Town Clerk read out the citation. I was "a distinguished son of the City". I signed the Register. A parchment scroll was then handed to me in a large silver casket by the Lord Mayor. On it, symbolically, were engraved an inkpot and two quill pens. In response to eulogies from two aldermen, I made a short speech of thanks. Afterwards, in the great hall, came the banquet with a hundred and eighty guests, all the notabilities of the city and county. Here, following the lunch, I replied to the Lord Mayor's proposal of my health. I observed that Caesar had received divine honours from his city of Rome, by his own wish. There had been no request on my part, only a generous gesture had brought me here—and not too late. "In the year I was born Mr. Gladstone received the Freedom of Liverpool, his native city. He was much aggrieved that the honour had been so long delayed, for he was eighty-three. At the age of seventy-three I am a decade behind Mr. Gladstone. I do not know what he said on that occasion. Certainly he said it eloquently and at great length. I will not emulate him in style, or length. I am the only author on your list of Freemen. I can think of local authors more worthy, such as Lord Byron and D. H. Lawrence. Nearly sixty years ago I began my career as an employee of your Corporation. In the basement of this Council House I used the office typewriter and the office paper on which to write my poems, a preposterous office boy. Quite correctly the Press has called this occasion 'a fairy-tale story'. It is indeed, and thanks to you I am the Happy Prince in it."

V

Leaving Nottingham, somewhat fatigued by the festivities, a B.B.C. interview, much handshaking, I motored south with my friend Ballance towards Market Bosworth. I had a purpose. Early in the fifteenth century my family had come from Stanton Lacy, Salop, and settled at Sutton Cheney. They lived in the manor house there and there was a legend that the Roberts children had watched from the roof the Battle of Bosworth Field, in 1485. I had visited the house when a small boy, with my father, but my interest in its history then was slight. I wanted to check the possibility of the family having seen the battle.

The old mullion-windowed manor house was now a farm house. A gabled roof had been superimposed at some time on its original flat one. In the gable there was a window. The tenant obligingly let us go up into the attic which he used for incubating. We brushed the cobwebs off the window and there, immediately below us, beyond the church in which some of my ancestors were buried, was the battlefield, the memorial to King Richard III visible on it.*

Satisfied, we went on to Oxford, to lunch with Leslie Rowse. He had just returned to All Souls College from his winter sojourn at the Huntington Library in California. He was in wonderful form. He had written a book on the Earl of Southampton. On his table I was surprised to find the proofs of one on the battle of Bosworth Field. "What are you doing on my territory?" I asked. I told him about my ancestors having witnessed the battle.

After our visit to Leslie, as always ebullient and industrious, we went the next morning to call on Masefield. The broken-down door screamed. The garden was even more of a wilderness. We spent two hours with him. He wished to hear all about the Freedom ceremony. I showed him the silver casket. "What did they give you with it?" he asked. "Give me? Nothing." I replied, surprised. "Oh, when they gave me the Freedom of Ledbury I not only got a casket but the right to tether a cow on the village green!" He gave us autographed copies of *Old Raiger and Other Verses*, just published.

> April awaits the bold, he said,
> April's a wondrous thing,
> He who can seize the time and place
> May kiss with April face to face
> And pass into the Spring.

How different from T. S. Eliot's "April is the cruellest month." Masefield wrote that at eighty-seven.

One June day I lunched with John Betjeman at the Clermont Club in Berkeley Square. I was astonished to learn he was a member of one of the most expensive gambling clubs in London. "Do you gamble?" I asked. "No. This is one of the most beautiful houses in London, I've joined to save it," he explained. At lunch there was an official from the Mint. He and John had conferred on the minting of a Churchill commemorative five-shilling piece. After lunch we all motored to Buckingham Palace, where they were holding a conference, I going to the Royal Art Gallery. As always, John's hat was a disgrace. Next year I brought him from Rome a Borsalino felt. He could crush it as much as he liked. He loved it.

* See *The Growing Boy*, Ch. 11.

VI

In July and August I was in Bad Gastein and Salzburg, going on to Casa Vecchia where in its quiet I continued to work on something I had long contemplated, an autobiography. I had estimated that it would take me some ten years and five volumes. It would be the closing task of my life, if I lived that long, and would cover eighty years. All autobiographies tend to be exercises in egotism, staccato with "I"s. But afterwards I could sweep the desk of my voluminous papers and records, and free at last, sit like old Caspar in the sun, contemplating defeats as well as victories.

At the end of August a large station-wagon drove up into the courtyard and to my surprise and pleasure there were Polly Monckton's son, Gilbert (now Lord Monckton), and his wife, Marianne. But that was not all. He went behind and raised the wagon door and out of it came a stream of radiant children, Christopher, Rosamund, Timothy, Jonathan and Anthony the youngest, aged five, with governess. They had come from Germany where Gilbert commanded the 3rd British Army on the Rhine, a very youthful general, and father of a merry brood. They romped all over our old house and then went up to the castle. It was amusing to see the children pile in like puppy dogs when they departed.

That December in Rome the balletomanes reached a pitch of hysteria. Margot Fonteyn and Rudolf Nureyev were dancing at the Opera House in *Romeo and Juliet*. Seats fetched £25. I bought mine for £10, which was quite enough. The ballet was good but not outstanding. One had to suffer the Prokofiev version, strident and rhythmless. The principals had a delirious reception.

I was back at the Castello for my Christmas lunch, Rolandi Ricci, as ever, the perfect host. The B.B.C. had sent me a tape recording of the Nottingham Freedom ceremony, with my speech at the banquet. We played it over in the library after lunch. What a singular experience to sit there in a fifteenth-century castle in the Ligurian Alps and hear someone of my name speaking in the English city of his boyhood! I was rather shocked by my voice. It seemed so full of unction that it might have been the Archbishop of Canterbury performing. "It's your voice absolutely," said my friends when I complained, which further depressed me. I think

God spares us by not permitting us to hear our own voices as they really are. "O, wad some Pow'r the giftie gie us . . ." No thank you. By what intuition did I receive from my friend Monsignor Meehling, in faraway California, a Christmas gift of a bishop's scarlet cap? "Wear that, you H.S.H.," he wrote, with greetings.

At the Nottingham Freedom banquet I had said I would present to the City Library my bound manuscripts, some forty volumes. In the New Year, 1966, I followed up my promise by sending the Lord Mayor a cheque for an endowment fund, to enable the Library to acquire manuscripts. They did not know the significance of the date on my cheque, February 22nd. It marked the day, fifty-eight years earlier, when my father had fallen dead in the street, and I had gone, a boy of fifteen, to the mortuary to identify him. Immediately after, the Corporation had increased the wages of their office boy from eight shillings to seventeen shillings a week, a gesture I had never forgotten.

CHAPTER FIFTEEN

Turkey and Greece

I

Perhaps I should have called this last volume of my memoirs *The Galloping Years*, so swift were they in passing. The things we intend to do beckon us on so that sunset colours the horizon before we have completed the journey. On Christmas Eve, 1966, I stood at my window overlooking the ruins of the Baths of Diocletian. I opened it to let in the sound of bells across the Eternal Cty. They came, a sweet jangle from innumerable belfries. The fountain below me sparkled with lights round its three circular pools. The traffic cut a pattern of white and red lights around the Piazza.

I reviewed the past year. A brief summer visit had taken me to England. London had alarmed and bewildered me, so defaced by concrete monoliths. Did it belong to the English? A tourist mob, speaking all tongues, rushed madly about like ants. We seemed to have been turned into the landlady of Europe, in order to sheer up our home with an intake of foreigners. Another crowd, English, was rushing across the Channel by plane, boat and car to spend its earnings on the Continent. How much net profit was there in this feverish interchange of currency? The exchange rates rocked, the queues lengthened, the overdrafts grew. The American slogan "Go now. Pay later", had been generally adopted. I feared a Nemesis.

II

That year, in May, in Rome, I was awarded the city's gold medal and a diploma in recognition, as the announcement ran, "of his writings on Italy and in particular for his contribution to the greater renown of Rome". I assumed that my *And So To Rome* had inspired this gracious gesture. Nowhere else in the world could there have been a more historic and striking setting for this ceremony. One of the great sights of Rome is the magnificent Campidoglio crowning a hill overlooking the Forum. It is the seat of all that has been great in the ancient and modern history of the capital. On the site of the ancient Temple of Jove, Michelangelo's genius has endowed it with splendour. The Senate House, the noble statue-balustraded palaces flanking the marble piazza, with the famous equestrian figure of Marcus Aurelius, the great flight of steps, guarded by the statues of Castor and Pollux, all reveal the majesty of his conception.

To the right of the Senate House, stands the large Memorial Hall. Its walls are covered with tapestries and decorated with marble busts of those who are part of Roman history, Julius Caesar, Cicero, Horace, Petrarch, Cellini, Leonardo da Vinci, Michelangelo, Raphael, Rienzi, Canova, Garibaldi, a legion of great names. The wide crimson-carpeted staircase was flanked by *carabinieri* in tricorne plumed hats. Two heraldic trumpeters sounded a fanfare on the approach of the Mayor of Rome, a cardinal's red mantle added colour to a hall holding some five hundred guests. The chief recipients of the city's honours were the Belgian Ambassador, as proxy for King Baudouin, and the ambassadors of Denmark, Norway and Sweden. The Mayor introduced the Premier who made a short speech. The Belgian Ambassador received a small gold model of the Colosseum, to commemorate the King's recent visit to Rome. My medal, in a red morocco case, had a ribbon with the colours, brown and gold, of the City. With the medal I received a crimson carton holding an engraved, illuminated diploma. On one side of the gold medal was the symbolic figure of the Roman wolf, suckling Remus and Romulus; on the reverse, my name.

The ceremony lasted about an hour and at the close the guests moved out through ten great windows on to a wide terrace, brilliant with flowers in the hot May sunshine. From our eminence we looked down over the whole length of the Forum beyond the Palatine and the columns, the ruined temples, the Arch of Titus, to the great mole of the Colosseum, backed by the blue Alban Hills. What a vista down some three thousand years of Time, the whole majesty of Imperial Rome! Cocktails were served, endless introductions made, and then we departed, our cars descending the ramp from the courtyard, past the Tarpeian Rock from which Rome had cast its traitors and criminals. Well, just now, no one was throwing me from a rock. The Honorary Citizenship of Alassio in 1960, the Freedom of Nottingham in 1965; the Gold Medal of Rome in 1966; as we departed I said to my companion "I think I shall have to buy a new hat. Mine's getting too tight!"

A month later in Oxford, en route to visit Rowse and Masefield, I spoke in the Town Hall at the Maxwell Literary Lunch. The whole world seemed gyrating at Carfax. I was jostled by Afghanistan, Japan, Spain, India, France, America, Germany and Italy, led by their shepherd who held a stick with a group number, lest they might go astray. Yet who was I to be superior, who had enjoyed years of leisured travel before the world began to suffer from mass population, mass traffic, mass touring, congested capitals, a rash of automobiles and monotonous motorways?

Inside the gate of All Souls College all was tranquil. My friend Rowse was still busy with the anatomy of the Great William. With what gusto he swept down Elizabethan corridors, opening new doors on history!

I was shocked by Masefield's appearance. He had cut holes in his shoes for swollen feet, he wore mittens, his gentle voice was fainter, but he was still beautiful with his blue eyes, his pink skin and white hair. He gave me and my friend a parting gift of another new book, *Grace Before Ploughing*, "fragments of an autobiography". He was eighty-eight. He insisted, with his infallible courtesy, in escorting us to our car. On an impulse I asked my friend to take a photograph of Judith, him and me. He waved as we went down the drive. "I fear we shall not see him again," I said. The aura of Eternity was about him.

There was another memorable encounter this summer. In my youth I had spent happy months at Rempstone Rectory, near Loughborough. I used it for a setting in my first novel, *Scissors*. I had been the guest of the rector's brother, Robert Hartley, helping in the garden while the family was on holiday. I slept in the bedroom of the daughter, Dorothy, and down the years, when the author of *Scissors* was mentioned, she replied, "Yes, he often slept in my bed but I never met him!" In the subsequent years she had become an authoress which enabled me to trace her, living alone in a cottage near Llangollen in Wales. I persuaded her to make a visit to London,

The Lord Mayor of Nottingham presents the Freedom casket to
the author

Paul Hodder-Williams with the author, cutting the eightieth birthday cake at the Savoy Hotel party

The Foyle Literary Lunch for the author's eightieth birthday—the Duchess of Bedford, *left*. The Duke (chairman) is behind the author

so at last, each in our seventies, we met. Every moment had been enjoyable. Her distinguished work had won her a Civil List pension. She was still writing her country books.

I called on my old friend Seddon Cripps, Lord Parmoor, no longer the squire of Parmoor in the Chilterns, once my country neighbour. Now eighty-four, he lived alone in a London flat, with a woman " coming in, sometimes". He cooked his breakfast, made his bed, went out to lunch, and got his own supper. "If I fall down in the flat there is no one to pick me up. What our 'civilisation' has come to!" "You will have another ten years, like your father, Lord Parmoor," I said. His mother was one of ten daughters. One of these became Mrs. Sidney Webb, the brains of the Labour movement. When she first brought her Fabian husband to stay at Parmoor her brother-in-law said to his wife as the Webbs drove away, "Have you counted the spoons?" Oddly enough, both men became colleagues in the first Labour Government, one, as Lord President of the Council, the other as President of the Board of Trade.

The Crippses were descended from Milo de Crispe, who came over from Normandy with William the Conqueror. Strange that such a line should produce Stafford Cripps, Seddon's brother, the austere, disastrous Labour Chancellor of the Exchequer who boasted "The Bank of England is my minion".

Venice in September, as always, was delightful but the hordes of tourists, rushing in, rushing out, scarcely knowing what they were seeing in a forty-eight hour stop-over before swallowing Florence and Rome, were as ubiquitous as the pigeons, always under your feet. There was the old cry—"Venice is sinking under the sea!" "Yes," said a resident, "it's going down with an overload of tourists." The Brockets came out to join me. I took them to the Garden of Eden to have tea with Princess Aspasia. For almost forty years I had been going there, raising ghosts along its seawall by the lagoon: young Lucien, his sister Bevis, Derek Mond and his brother, little Alessandra, all in the beauty of their childhood, before the world had turned sour with spilt blood.

In October, at Florence on my way to Rome, I visited Queen Helen of Rumania at the Villa Sparta, on the Fiesole hillside. She had many oil portraits; one of her father, the ill-fated King Constantine, twice exiled. The beauty of the young princess Helen, with soft-grey eyes and an entrancing smile, had been caught by Laszlo. The eyes and smile had not changed. Just before I arrived there had been excitement at the villa when her sister's son, the handsome young Duke of Aosta, had married a daughter of the Count of Paris.

It was not of fallen thrones and past sorrows that we talked when we dined and walked in the gardens with their cypresses and topiary privets. It was mostly of pictures and books and music, and of the craziness of the world in general, breaking, into despairing laughter sometimes. My hostess was kind about my work. "I can't think why you haven't been knighted," she said one day. "That, Ma'am, is not a possibility. I was born benighted," I replied. We laughed merrily. As I left she said, "Now do come again, soon. You know there is always a bed for you."

III

In the spring of 1967 my thoughts turned not to love but Asia Minor. The cause of it was this. My publishers were proposing to issue a new imprint, the twenty-second, of my novel *Scissors*. It had opened my career as a novelist in 1923, and here it was, surviving after forty-four years, possibly being read by the grand-children of its first readers. Hodders suggested that I should add a preface to the new imprint. I had written the novel, intermittently, between 1917 and 1922, and when at last it sailed forth it carried all my hopes as an author. The story had opened in Asia Minor, where I had never been. Its first three chapters were set in Amasia. in Anatolia, a town of about 20,000 inhabitants situated some seventy miles south of Samsun, a port on the Black Sea. How did I come to pitch my tent there? I had always been fascinated by the story of the Argonauts. Samsun was the terminus of a caravan route that brought merchandise from Baghdad, eighty hundred miles distant. Long before Jason with his Argonauts went to Colchis to obtain the Golden Fleece, this mountainous land south of the Black Sea had been inhabited. The caravan route from Baghdad passed through the ancient town of Amasia, a natural fort above the green valley of the Yeshil Irmak, which ran between massive cliffs. The Emperor Nerva bridged the river and carried the road through Amasia to the Roman front on the Euphrates. The town had a long history but very little was known about it. It chanced that in 1917 I was sent a book to review on this part of Asia Minor where the writer had travelled on a donkey. I felt already that this was my territory. I chose it for the opening of my novel. Like most first novels, mine was partly autobiographical and I joined up young Scissors with a lively family that I placed in Rempstone Rectory, near Loughborough.

One day, forty years after it had first appeared, I had a shock. An American called on me, one of those irrepressible, enthusiastic travellers. He had read *Scissors* and he had gone to Amasia, an arduous journey, to look at the place I had written about! "I found your description very accurate, and I was shown the house down by the river where you had written the story." I jumped and then controlled myself. "You saw the house? Who told you it was the house?" "A Turk, the mayor of the village. He had worked in Detroit and had a little English. I was rather surprised to find I was not the first who had come to see Amasia because of your novel. He knew about the book and seemed to think that your mother was Turkish and had married the British agent who was killed in a local riot, as in your story." Should I tell my visitor the shattering truth? I told him. He was astonished. He could not believe I had never been to Amasia or in Asia Minor. "You must go, you'll get quite a welcome." "I should find it very embarrassing and spoil their story," I replied. He gave me some photographs he had taken, and two packets of cigarettes. They were of tobacco grown at Amasia.

So with this caller, and the new imprint, my thoughts turned to Asia Minor. Of course one went first to Constantinople. I had been there over thirty years ago but only for two days on an Hellenic Club cruise.

I had the good fortune to have a friend, George Maddocks, who was a phenomenal linguist. French, German, Italian, Greek, Hungarian, were all alike to him. During the war he had been in the B.B.C. Foreign Department. Of course he spoke Turkish. He had now retired to Corfu. I flew from Rome to Athens and we joined up.

I seem to coincide with revolutions. I had defied one in Pamplona. I now found myself in the midst of one in Athens. We stayed at a small hotel. The next morning April 21st, George came to my room to inform me that a revolution had broken out. King Constantine was a prisoner in his palace. The Prime Minister and three hundred

M.P.'s had been arrested. The city was under martial law. We were informed by radio that no one was allowed on the streets. There was no noise, no firing, but also there was no food in the hotel, no servants turned up. Happily George had a Greek friend round the corner and we sneaked our way to his apartment, where our hospitable host gave us lunch. Then we had to go back. There was a strict curfew at 6 p.m. No one knew what was happening. We heard the army had seized power and appointed a new Premier. The King's position was obscure. On the third day the curfew was lifted but everybody was jumpy. We had been living on bread and cheese. We went out, finding tanks at strategic points. I insisted on going up to the Parthenon and spent a delightful hour in the Acropolis Museum. The next morning we sailed for Constantinople.

We had booked ourselves in at the Hotel Pierre Loti. But the name had betrayed us. We went on to the Pera Palace, the oldest, most famous hotel. It was like something out of the nineties, with ghosts of Grand Dukes, Archduchesses and Princes. After the First World War it had been a refuge for fleeing Russian aristocrats. They sold their jewels and rings to a Jew in the vestibule, threw a party, and then blew out their brains. The hotel was compelled to search guests for hidden revolvers. But now all that had receded into the very dim past. The hotel was almost empty, the new Hilton having sucked away its clients. I loved it for its dusty, shabby splendour, its immense, empty rooms, above all the stupendous view from my bedroom over the Golden Horn. And the prices were ludicrous.

A boy pulled a rope and took you up in a lift. You could have held an art exhibition in my bathroom. If you waited ten minutes the hot water came through. It was wholly delightful, with quiet servants, long corridors, endless pipes everywhere. There was a grand piano in a vast salon, whose keys had stuck years ago. Princesses had played Chopin on it, while Grand Dukes smoked cigars under the glass dome. And there, appropriately, who should we find but Darius Talyarkhan, a ruling deity, who made tea in his bathroom and served it to titled derelict ladies, Turkish, French, German and Egyptian, squatting on his divan. Darius knew everybody. He had spent the whole winter there. He gave the impression that the Pera Palace had been kept open for him. What that ancient concierge with the crosskeys on his frock coat could have told us! He had been there through the Russian Revolution. He had survived régimes and lived to see Constantinople abandoned for the new capital, Ankara.

I had some letters of introduction. I took tea in a palace where Loti had written some of his novels. I was taken to lunch at a beautiful modern apartment with a magnificent view over the Bosphorus. My host was M. Yumni Sedes, a retired Turkish diplomat who had spent much time in the Orient. He had a wonderful collection of jade tear-flasks worth £250,000. I noticed on his walls a print of the two sons of the redoubtable and infamous Ali Pasha of Jannina, who ruled a Balkan territory from his castle at Tepeleni. He had once entertained Byron whom he received with great dignity, surrounded by his court and his five Ganymedes, who brought coffee, sweets and pipes. At Jannina Byron saw corpses hanging by the dozens. In old age Ali defied the Sultan and fought fiercely until struck down. The Sultan's men cut off his head and exposed it in Stamboul. A vast treasure was seized including a famous diamond. When I remarked to my host that I had seen this print in a biography of Ali, he said: "I am his descendant. I am the sixth in line. I own Ali's head." He told me that among Ali's treasures, seized by the Sultan, was "The Spoon Diamond", so called from its shape, and that it was on view in the old Topkapi palace, where later I saw it. It is eighty-six carats with forty-nine brilliants. Sedes told me that his grandfather was the Vizier of the last Sultan and always made his Will when summoned by him. He showed us much hospitality and motored us out to lunch in a restaurant overlooking the Black Sea, which I saw for the first time.

I found that the name of Florence Nightingale was still potent in Constantinople. One morning, on emerging from our hotel, ladies in the street were selling roses. It was "Florence Nightingale Day" for local charities. We went to see the Crimean Memorial Church, built to her memory, and found, not an English clergyman there, but an American, Dr. Leeming, who was giving his services to the Anglicans. He was anxious that we should call on the Patriarch Athenagoras of Constantinople. I had met him years ago in New York during the war, where he was a very commanding figure, with his height, his long beard, his gold-topped staff and heavy pectoral cross. We went to pay our respects at the Phanar, the episcopal palace, which was a large ramshackle old house in what seemed a Turkish slum. What ardours and endurances the Patriarchs at Constantinople had known down the centuries! By law the Patriarch was not allowed to appear in his vestments driving in Constantinople, so the blinds of his car had to be drawn. Ataturk had abolished all religious precedence in Turkey.

The little smiling Bishop of Nicea ushered us into the Patriarch's presence. He warmly embraced and kissed Maddocks and myself. Being six-foot-four he had to stoop to do it. He was eighty-one years of age, fluent, genial, a magnificent-looking man with his soft brown eyes and long white beard. There were two photographs on the wall behind his desk, one of Pope Paul, whom he had met in Jerusalem in 1964 during the papal pilgrimage, where, after a quarrel of five hundred years, they lifted the excommunications the two Churches had fired at each other. They had kissed, in the new ecumenical spirit. The other photograph was of President Truman, with whom the Patriarch had had friendly relations. He had spent eighteen years in the United States before his election took him to Constantinople as head of the Greek Orthodox Church.

We talked for an hour in this pleasant bright room. Doctrines and politics came into the conversation. He thought Archbishop Makarios of Cyprus a very troublesome man and did not approve of him. The Roman and the Orthodox Churches could move in the matter of doctrine, but his Church could not accept the doctrine of Papal Infallibility. "It is the Church which is infallible, not the Pope," said the Patriarch, smiling. "But we are all getting together, after too much delay." He invited us to lunch but, alas, we were already engaged. We departed with the Patriarch's kiss of peace on our cheeks, a warm embrace, and a present, in a muslin bag, of four painted eggs, it being Eastertide. What a magnificent old fellow! One was deeply moved.

The Patriarch's residence looked into a courtyard. On the opposite side, shaded by giant fig and acacia trees, was the cathedral of St. George. The little Bishop of Nicea took us in to the large dim building. Under the altar lay the body of St. Euphemia, in a bronze casket lined with blue silk. Somehow there still seemed the heavy shadow of Moslem fanaticism and oppression over this oasis of the

Christian faith where the Crescent had triumphed over the Cross. We took our leave of the little black-robed fathers, softly courteous and smiling. They were isolated, impoverished and tenaciously brave in their faith, despite long years of hostility.

There were other signs of faded prestige when we called on the British Consul-General. He was housed in the old British Embassy. Its vast rooms were empty, its garden in decay. On the grand staircase hung the State portraits of King George V and Queen Mary. It was all dead. The seat of Government had moved to Ankara and Constantinople was in a state of neglect.

After a week we crossed the Sea of Marmora to Bursa, in Asia Minor. On going ashore we had a view of the vast barracks in which Florence Nightingale had established her hospital. Bursa was beautiful, lost in a dream of the past. It had been the Turkish capital before the capture of Istanbul. The Emperor Justinian had had a palace there. There were mosques and minarets, including the exquisite Green Mausoleum. The old town was on a hill. One sat in beautiful garden cafés, shaded by giant plane trees and drank small cups of tea, with hookhas supplied if you wished. There were innumerable poor bootblacks, so wretched that I had my boots polished twice. At the hour of the muezzin one had a shock. I looked up at the beautiful, slender minaret with its balcony where the muezzin would make the call to prayer, but no muezzin came out. From a cluster of loud-speakers there came a frightful metallic voice, relayed from a hidden gramophone. I felt it was more a call to curse than to pray.

After three days at a most excellent modern hotel, the Celik Palace, we went by bus to Smyrna or Izmir, as it is now called. What an astonishing journey—a bus full of peasants and by way of entertainment terrible, relayed music, pop and jazz, imported from U.S.A., that blared and brayed. Outside on the road a donkey led a string of four camels, peasants trudged under monstrous burdens. With no window open, the bus was a Turkish bath. There were no cars on the road, only donkeys and bicycles. We were travelling over two dead civilisations, the Greek and Roman, and crossing tracks known to Alexander the Great. Presently, a man in the bus excitedly recognised my friend. Thirty years ago George had been a master in a Turkish school in Cyprus. This was one of his pupils, grown up, bristle-whiskered, ecstatically greeting his old master, in English and Turkish. The heat, the dust, the blaring radio, eight hours of this, but I would not have missed it. Here was Turkey before the Tourist Board could transform it into a semblance of any other place reached by charter plane.

Izmir (Smyrna) was beautiful, with its white houses crowded in an amphitheatre above the harbour. We made memorable excursions to Ephesus, Sardis and Pergamum. Ephesus, the Ionian capital, went back to 1400 B.C. It had been conquered by the Amazons, one of whom, Smyrna, gave a name to that town. Ephesus saw the birth of the philosophical schools. It was ruled at one time by a fabled King of Lydia, Croesus. It was conquered by Cyrus the Great in 499 B.C. With other Greek towns it staged a revolt against the Persians, in which Athens took part. The revolt failed, but later Alexander the Great liberated the city. The ruins are still magnificent. One almost heard the feet of dead Ephesians down the wide marble street. St. Paul set his mark on it, often preaching there, and it is alleged that St. John wrote his gospel there. Apart from the superb ancient ruins, the major Christian interest is the reputed last home of the Virgin Mary. The Turkish tourist authorities, ready to capitalise on this claim, are cautious and tactful. Announcements in six languages refer to the "alleged" claim. The actual house is a little squalid brick room. It is said the Virgin came with St. John and died here. Whatever the truth may be, this simple little house, now turned into a shrine and recently restored, has been a popular place of devout pilgrimage since 1950. The damaging fact is that the brickwork is sixth century A.D., and another house of the Virgin is stated to have made three repeated flights by angels from Nazareth and to have settled finally in A.D. 1294, in Loreto, Italy, where it is encased in marble and revered.

There were only a few broken columns at Sardis, and the remains of a theatre and stadium. "Rich as Croesus". He came to a sad end. He consulted the Oracle at Delphi but it availed him nothing. Cyrus took him prisoner. After an attempt to burn himself on a funeral pyre he ended by being attached to the court and given a minor governorship. Where did all the gold come from? Legend says from a local river-bed. It is more likely that Croesus was one of the early "takeover" boys; the lesson was "too much is too much". Sardis was the first city to mint gold and silver coins.

The high spot of my tour was Pergamum. Being a man of letters, Pergamum was for me a shrine. The citadel and acropolis commanded a stupendous panorama. Here King Eumenes built in 197 B.C. his monumental altar to Zeus, with its fabulous eight-foot frieze of the fight between the Gods and the Giants. Discovered in 1837 by a German archaeologist, it is now in the Pergamum Museum in Berlin, where I had seen it. The real attraction for me on the Acropolis was not the Temple, or the great amphitheatre, but the ruins of the library. It is on a plateau, a few stones and broken columns, but the imagination takes fire as you walk over it. Here was the world's greatest library after that of Alexandria.

Pergamum was a great trading centre, of enormous wealth. The King of Pergamum, Eumenes, was a man of culture, of the Attalid family, which joined up with the Romans. He built temples and theatres and created one of the most beautiful of Greek cities. He was also a bookworm. He attracted scholars and collected books, so many books from so many sources, that Alexandria, with its world-famous library, became alarmed. It tried to stop Eumenes and his book collecting. Books were written on papyrus. Egypt had a monopoly of papyrus. It put an embargo on its export. (How familiar it all is, with the Arabs and their oil embargo contra Christians sympathetic to Jews!). Eumenes was not to be defeated. He discovered a new material to write on, dressed sheep or goatskins, parchment. (*Pergamen* in Latin.) The king built a great library to house his famous collection of two hundred thousand volumes. What became of it? When Anthony conquered the capital he gave the library to Cleopatra who shipped it to Egypt. So Alexandria won in the end. Besides men of letters, many brilliant artists were found at the court of Pergamum. The father of Eumenes celebrated his victory over the Gauls with a series of bas-reliefs. The most famous figure from this frieze ended in Rome, where it is visible to-day, long famous as "The Dying Gladiator". But he was never a gladiator, and never saw a Roman arena; he was a dying Gaul soldier.

I walked alone, quietly, over the site of the ancient library. It was my seventy-fifth birthday. I had fulfilled a wish. I had seen the library at Pergamum.

On my return to our hotel at Smyrna I had a surprise. At the end of dinner a large cake with candles was brought to me. It was a gift from the proprietress, who had learned that it was my seventy-fifth birthday. The cook had gone home so she made the cake herself, writing my name on it. There were red roses on the table, and champagne. I was much moved. I sought out the lady and found she had a very remarkable history. She had been born in the harem of the last Sultan of Turkey, her mother being one of the Sultan's wives. Alas, the next day, the eve of departure for Athens, had a deep shadow over it. I received a letter informing me that John Masefield had died, twenty days short of his eighty-ninth birthday.

The Poet Laureate has two perquisites, a small stipend as an official of the Royal Household, and the right to a memorial service in Westminster Abbey. I flew to London for this. At noon, on June 20th, I took my place in a stall. The congregation waited for the Queen's representative, who proved to be the Earl of Westmorland. I recalled seeing him at the Sutherland week-end party at Sutton Court, when newly engaged. Robert Graves made an address, Cecil Day-Lewis read verses by Masefield. Afterwards we were invited by the Dean and Chapter to a gathering in the Jerusalem Chamber. It was here I spoke with Graves for the first time. In 1919, visiting Masefield at Boar's Hill, I had seen at the bottom of the garden a half-naked youth wheeling two babies in a barrow. I asked who they were. Masefield said they were the poet, young Robert Graves, and his infant son and daughter. "Yes," said Graves, when I referred to this, "I was then a student at Oxford. What a marvellous memory you have! The two babies were my son David, killed in the last war, and my daughter Jenny. Married, she lived in Rome and told me she had met you there. She died a few years ago." I recalled also from that day in 1919 another boy in the garden, Masefield's only son, whom he lost in the Second World War. I had recently returned from Denmark, where I had seen in a bookshop a display card *The Elastic Mercy* by John Masefield. (*The Everlasting Mercy*.) The table rocked at tea-time when I narrated this, and the boy fell out of his chair with laughing. And now that had all gone into the shadows, and one of the kindest and loveliest of men would no more welcome me to his home. Forty-nine years of a cherished friendship: "Grow old along with me, the best will soon be gone," to revise Browning.

Later, I went to stay with Leslie Rowse in his home at St. Austell. One day the local vicar came in to tea. "You won't remember ever seeing me," he said. "In 1927 I was at Mundella School and you came to distribute the prizes. I received one, and I've never forgotten your talk then." In the evening Rowse and I retired to our rooms. The first volumes of my autobiography *The Growing Boy* had just come out. I was now busy with the proofs of the second volume, *The Years of Promise*. What I had begun so light-heartedly was to absorb ten years of my shortening life. Had I foreseen this I don't think I would have had the courage to start. My host was, of course, busy with the Great William, and after settling the question of "Mr. W. H." he would attend to his Dark Lady friend, and disinter her from the shadows; a phenomeon in pertinacity and research.

My next call was on my gentle friend Richard Church and his wife, Dorothy. They had moved to a new abode. It was like something out of a fairy story. The Priest's House, a Tudor cottage within the fifteen acres of gardens created by the genius of Vita Sackville-West and her husband Sir Harold Nicolson, at Sissinghurst Castle, Kent. Richard was as gentle, twinkling, industrious as ever, despite a "heart". Books for review were all round him. There was always delicious food and wine. One night, dining there, we went out into the adjoining garden. It was a wholly white garden and the moonlight lying upon it turned it into a paradise of disembodied flowers, ghosts of beauty. Down a vista of yew trees one saw the high Tudor brick clock-tower of the castle.

Back in Rome in November, I found Leonide Massine staying in my hotel. He was producing his *Boutique Fantasque* at the Opera House. I had been with him in June, 1919, when he had first produced his ballet at the Alhambra in London. I was present at the rehearsals, and here we were again at the 1967 production. We were photographed together on the stage, celebrating a friendship of forty-eight years. He was busy on his autobiography and I was able to give him some help with the proofs. He asked me to write a preface for his book, which I did. Alas, it was too late. *My Life in Ballet* had gone to press. When I read my preface to him there were tears in his eyes. "Please stand up," he said, "I want to embrace you!" So I stood up and was embraced. He was in Rome for a month. What a delightful companion he was! He was not only a great choreographer and dancer, he was a scholar with a wide range of knowledge. He owned an island, "Isola dei Galli", in the Gulf of Salerno and he invited me to stay there the following summer, but, unfortunately, I was unable to do so, being elsewhere committed.

IV

In the beginning of 1968, having worked on Massine's book, I turned to my proofs of *The Years of Promise* and sent them off to my publisher. Then I sat for my portrait to a young English artist named Geoffrey. He made me think of another young artist, Joseph Severn who, some hundred and fifty years ago, had arrived in Rome, and, after nursing poor young Keats on his deathbed, stayed on for the rest of his life. "I'm afraid I'm no Joseph Severn" said Geoffrey. "You are a much better artist than ever he was. I hope you'll have as long and as happy a life," I replied, to encourage him.

In May, on my birthday, I received a noble present from my Hungarian friend, Baron Paul Bohus who suddenly arrived in Rome. Lavishly generous, puckish in spirit, despite having spent two years in a Budapest Nazi gaol, he was full of surprises. "I've brought you a present," he said, opening a small velvet box. In it there was a double-linked gold watch-chain of beautiful workmanship. "I feel you should wear it," he said. "In *The Growing Boy* you tell how one day you surprised Winston Churchill by staring at his watch-chain and you explained that it was because it reminded you of your father's. Churchill told you that his chain had also been his father's, Lord Randolph's. So that's why I think you should wear a watch-chain!"

When Winston Churchill died I asked his son Randolph if he had inherited the chain. "Yes and I'd like to think that my son will inherit if from me. Unfortunately young men don't seem to wear watch-chains these days," he said. When Randolph died I asked young Winston if he had inherited the chain. "Indeed I have, but not possessing a waistcoat I am unable to wear it!" he replied.

One day when I showed the chain to a jeweller for an insurance valuation he shook with excitement. "It's a Breguet!" he exclaimed, dropping his eyeglass. I looked blank. "Breguet was watchmaker to Louis XVI, established in the Louvre in 1751. I've never had one in my hand before. Look! There's his B stamped on the last link."

At Christmas, 1968, there arrived at my hotel another friend, a figure famous in the world of ballet, Romola Nijinsky. A dynamic personality, amazing, bizarre, of illimitable energy, I called her "Nijinsky Unlimited". She spent her whole life propagating the fame of her late husband. Had Nijinsky lived and died normally he might have lapsed into obscurity, as is the fate of so many great artists of the stage. But the tragic story of his life, his sad, clouded end, grew into a legend of ballet history. For years Romola laboured to support him. A pretty, infatuated Hungarian girl, the daughter of a famous actress and of an aristocrat, she had deliberately pursued Nijinsky on the boat taking him and his company to South America, and captured him. His protector, Diaghilev, afraid of a sea journey, was absent. The marriage rocked the Russian Ballet. It drove Diaghilev, its inspiring genius, into paroxysms of rage. Having had his Ganymede stolen from him, the Russian Zeus vengefully dismissed and ruined Nijinsky. Some held Romola guilty of the disaster but Richard Buckle in his *Nijinsky* gives a balanced view. "She had not an inkling of an idea that she was going to split up the Russian Ballet. Nor did she foresee how much she would come to love Nijinsky, or the long years of suffering which were to bring out in her qualities she did not know she possessed." And we should not overlook the fact that there was a strain of congenital insanity in Nijinsky, evoked by his rejection.

Now in her seventies, Romola was still an indefatigable promoter of her husband's fame. She had recently visited Russia, the guest of the Government, and had lectured in the Bolshoi Theatre, packed by the enticement of the magic name. "What have you there?" demanded the Russian Customs official as she descended from the plane, holding a large rolled-up paper, "My husband, Vaslav Nijinsky!" she replied, unrolling an old Russian Ballet playbill with his name emblazoned. The official saluted, overwhelmed, and waved her on. Departing, the Government gave her a fur coat.

In the New Year, before she left for London to see a film director, she asked me to examine a proposed agreement for the filming of the life story of Nijinsky. I told her I thought it was a very faulty agreement. At her request I rewrote it for her. When she departed, in gratitude, she insisted on my accepting a small gold cigarette case that had belonged to her husband. The story of it was this. In 1912 Nijinsky had attended a lunch given by Lady Cunard. There were present Lady Ottoline Morrell, Diaghilev and others. Nijinsky had spent much time at Lady Ottoline's house. Having picked up a few words of English, he said of her: "Lady Ottoline is so tall, so beautiful, like a giraffe!" Diaghilev felt very uncomfortable at the laughter this provoked and tried to correct Nijinsky, but he repeated the words. "Yes, yes! Giraffe is beautiful, tall, gracious. She look like one!" he cried, smiling at Lady Ottoline. Overwhelmed, she impulsively picked up her gold cigarette case and pressed it on her admirer. He did not smoke but he cherished the gift, which now passed to me.

In July I paid my customary visit to Lady Birkett, a happy recluse at Windyridge. The house stood high above a deep valley with a long sloping lawn bordered with pine trees. It had for me a somewhat Tyrolean character. Servantless, Billy ran the house with quiet efficiency. In vain I tried to enlist in the kitchen. No, I was there for a rest. In the dining-room a full length portrait of Norman, in the robe and wig of a Lord Justice of Appeal, looked beneficently down on us, and at the other end was the only son and heir, young Michael in shorts, now a film producer.

On Sunday evening, July 20th, after dining, we went into the long lounge-library to watch the television, of which I am not an addict. Perhaps as an author I regard this ubiquitous intrument with some prejudice. It has lured millions from reading, killed conversation and contributed to the "herd instinct", creating a universal mind and false values. Even so, it is a great blessing for the lonely, and the mentally lazy, for the visual intake calls for no effort, though in some respects it educates.

This Sunday evening, at Windyridge, as elsewhere all over the globe, the screen presented a miracle of scientific achievement, perhaps the greatest in the history of the human race. We watched Apollo 11's astronauts, to coin a new word, Armstrong and Aldrin, come down a ladder and hop across the moon's surface like kangaroos. Neil Armstrong said, as he left the ladder, "I'm going to step off now. That's one small step for a man, one great

334

leap for mankind." Perhaps it will prove a disastrous leap.

Billy and I went to bed that night overwhelmed by what we had seen and heard, as were millions of viewers around the globe. It was as if we have seen a plumbline lowered into Eternity. When I put out my light I felt that I was something pin-pointed in latitude and longitude, being carried through immeasureable time and space, an atom in the infinite universe, sustained only by a preposterous egotism that asserted one's existence. Exactly three months later Fate enabled me to meet in the Grand Hotel at Rome the three intrepid astronauts of Apollo 11, Armstrong, Aldrin and Collins. Following the utter silence of one world they were now experiencing on their tour the vociferous acclaim of another.

On Monday morning, after a week-end made perfect by Billy's care of me, she drove me to the station. There was a note of comedy in our parting. She warned me not to overwork, to take more care of myself. When I went to the ticket window she said: "Now, buy a first-class ticket!" I remonstrated. "But, Billy, this train is always empty!" "Even so," she said, "you should have the greatest comfort. You must not economise on yourself!" So I obeyed. I kissed her goodbye. As the train drew out she stood waving, her head sunny with its crown of close brown curls. I waved back until she had vanished.

v

In August I went to stay at Countess Isa Potocka's Château de L'Echelle at La Roche-sur-Foron, some fifty miles south of Geneva, in the Haute Savoie. It was an enchanting château, commanding a view of the valley toward Chamonix. It had a twefth-century machicolated round tower. I had just finished the first draft of *The Bright Twenties* which contained a description of my visit in 1929 to Lançut, the great Polish castle of Count Potocki. I was fortunate in having for a friend his widow, Isa, who gave me the greatest help in my researches. Lançut after the Second World War had been confiscated, with the family estates, by the Polish Communist Government.

In my bedroom there was an enormous seventeenth-century iron chest. What was in it? "Potocki documents, charters, seals, honours, letters," said Isa. I asked to look in it. Two gardeners had to be brought in to lift the lid. The contents kept me in a whirl of excitement. There were letters from Prince Sanguszko, the Polish patriot whom a Czar had sent to Siberia for forty years because he had fought in the 1830 Polish Revolution. He had been made to walk there, manacled, accused of treason. He came out nearly blind and stone deaf.

Joseph Conrad recalled as a small boy visiting him, and thought he must be too great to be spoken to, as all communications had to be made on a writing pad. There were letters from the Archduke Franz-Ferdinand up to a few weeks before his assassination at Sarajevo; there were honours conferred by Emperor Franz-Josef, scrolls and seals. There were Freedoms of Cities, charters, bundles of letters in French, English, German, Czech and Polish, a feast of history.

Guests arrived at the château, Prince Faucigny-Lucinge, who was awarding the Prix Faucigny-Lucinge at an Annecy literary festival; Prince Heinrich Lichtenstein, the younger brother of the reigning Prince at Vaduz, with his pretty young Polish wife; there was young Prince Giovanni de Bourbon des Deux-Siciles, with his Bourbon nose and a pedigree going back to Il Re Nasone, Queen Caroline, Lady Hamilton and Nelson at the Naples court. We became warm friends and only by accident I discovered that in 1929 at the château of Lançut I had ridden on the top of a six-in-hand with his mother, Princess Lubomirska, then unmarried, now in Brazil.

The house party looked with amusement, I think, at my passionate digging out of things in boxes in the muniment room. All these had been thrown into four train trucks a few days before the Russians swept over Poland, to annex it under the local communists. The trucks had been supplied by the German army, and taken to Lichtenstein, where Count Alfred's cousin, the Prince, held their contents for him. He had pulled wires with the German High Command, who had placed the trucks at the Count's disposal in order that the Russians should not get them. The treasures left at Lançut had fallen subsequently into the Polish communists' hands. One of the rescued treasures, a Sèvres vase from the palace at Versailles, had been sold by Count Potocki in his necessitous exile, and had found a home in Paul Getty's museum in California. A companion vase, bought by the Duke of Wellington on behalf of the Prince Regent, had gone to Carlton House, and subsequently to Windsor Castle. I found letters between Queen Mary and Countess Betka Potocka, comparing the two vases, that had followed a visit of the Countess to Windsor. I unearthed a magnificent scimitar sword, in a red leather scabbard. It had a fine jewelled hilt, but there was no clue to its history, until, one day, on an upper landing, I came across an engraving of the Hetman Potocki, the commander of the Polish army that in 1660 defeated the Moscovites before Moscow. He was eighty years of age. The engraving showed him on a hillock, surrounded by his staff officers, a panoply of banners, and a mounted band, raising the scimitar sword to give the command to charge. Its discovery caused quite a sensation. I never exhausted the treasures in that dark muniment room, all in great disorder.

One of the frequent guests at the château, until she died, was Princess Marie-Louise, Queen Victoria's granddaughter, a formidable old lady. She would arrive in June with no maid, being too poor, as she explained. She was always regal and a stickler for protocol. She annexed one of the visitors as her gentleman-in-waiting and kept him running. One morning, on leaving her bedroom, she asked him to carry some books and a bottle of whisky down into the garden. He slipped on the circular tower's stone staircase and went with a fearful crash down a flight. Her Highness, when the noise had subsided, standing at the head of the stairs, called down "Is the bottle safe?" She had an iron will. Despite an attack of diarrhoea, she insisted on keeping a lunch engagement. Stops had to be made. Village lavatories in France are apt to be crude, so Countess Potocka had to go and find out whether the seat was possible for a royal fundament. The old lady observed: "I can put up with the inconvenient seating but it's the paper that's so trying!" My hostess during these visits was turned into a maid, secretary-companion. "I was left exhausted but everyone adored her. What a character!"

After three weeks I left the château with some heartache, overwhelmed by the kindness of my hostess. Not a detail had been overlooked. She had even insisted on sending me to see the Mont Blanc Tunnel, recently opened, the longest, seven miles, in the world, between Chamonix and Courmayeur, four miles in Italy, three miles in France, eight thousand feet under ice-capped granite.

VI

My friend George Maddocks had retired from the B.B.C. and settled in Corfu. Fluent in Greek, he was *persona grata* there. In September I visited him. He lived on the first floor of a Venetian house overlooking the harbour, with the Albanian and Greek mountains visible across the Straits. The Venetians had once ruled Corfu and their stamp is still upon it. Some of the local aristocrats, though Greek, have Venetian blood in their veins. George's house was next door to the official residence of the Bishops of Corfu and when, during our visit to the Patriarch, Athenagoras, he had told him where he lived, the old man's eyes filled with tears. In early manhood he had been Bishop of Corfu. "What lovely people! What a lovely island, and what a dear house that was!" he exclaimed. He was thirty-six when he went there. He spent eighteen years in America as Archbishop of North and South America, until he was elected Ecumenical Patriarch in 1948 and flew to Constantinople in President Truman's private plane. By law he was compelled to assume Turkish citizenship. He was the 262nd successor of St. Andrew, the leader of 160 millions of Orthodox Christians. "I still think fondly of Corfu, I had such bright hopes there!" said the old Patriarch.

George's landlord lived on the top floor, Count Palatiano, descended from an old Byzantine-Venetian family. He was tall, aristocratic and English in appearance. He possessed some fine portraits and he pointed to one of them, Isabella Beauclerk. "That is my grandmother, through whom I am descended from the Dukes of St. Albans," he said. Conscious of my surprise, he turned to a table on which was opened a page of Debrett at "Duke of St. Albans". He was in it, Anthony Beauclerk, Count Palatiano. How odd to settle in Corfu and find your landlord is of Corfiote-Venetian-St. Albans descent! Count Palatiano had other portraits, one of a young count in full Corfiote costume, fustanella, etc., painted in 1826 by Delacroix, and a ten-foot oil painting of two beautiful Beauclerk girls in white flowery dresses, the Count's grandmother, Isabella, and her sister Louisa.

One day we went to lunch with Commander and Mrs. Vaughan-Hughes. He had inherited through his Greek mother a house that

338

was once a fourteenth-century Venetian fortress that stood by the harbour at Couloura. Here I settled a question that had been unanswered for over fifty years. When I visited the British Fleet at Scapa Flow in 1916 just before the battle of Jutland, I was a guest of Admiral Jellicoe on his flagship the *Iron Duke*. In his salon he had a piano. Before sailing out to the battle all inflammable furniture had been beached. I often wondered about the fate of the piano. In 1935, on going to speak at The Portsmouth Brotherhood, I was entertained on Jellicoe's old ship, still in commission. I forget to ask about the piano. Did it ever get back on board? My host was then a young officer in the *Iron Duke* in 1935. Yes, the piano was there, I now learned.

The weather during my visit was halcyon. There was still a small British colony extant on the island, foremost among them Emlyn Williams, who lingered there. The King and Queen of Greece did not visit their Royal Palace in the town, but lived in a villa elsewhere in which our Prince Philip was born. I was surprised to learn that the palace was the seat of the Order of St. Michael and St. George. The State rooms were kept locked but my host's brother, a K.C.M.G., had right of access to them. Here Gladstone had once stayed, during an unhappy period as Commissioner. The palace, which had fallen into disrepair during the war, had been restored by our ambassador. But it was a sad and lonely building, the garden weedy before its classical façade.

At the end of the month I flew to Rome and was there in time to attend a recital by Artur Rubinstein. I had known him since the Twenties when, a young Pole, he had played at a soirée in the Venetian palazzo of Princess de Polignac; and now, here was he was, aged eighty, more vibrant than ever, an extrovert romanticist in love with life and people. My stall was not six feet away from the keyboard. He played with great élan the Chopin *Concerto No. 2*. Nearly all pianists do a lot of hand and brow wiping. There was never one bead of sweat on him. He came back and gave an encore, not, as one might expect, a simple *Nocturne* or the pianissimo *Berceuse*, but the thundering *Polonaise in A Flat*, working up to a tornado in the bass, again with not a bead of perspiration. Smiling and waving, he left an audience madly applauding. On the morrow he would be playing in Milan.

On the last day of the year as I sat writing, my window open to Roman December sunshine, a telegram arrived from Michael Birkett. It informed me that his mother had died very suddenly. I was stunned by this irreparable loss, closing a friendship of nearly half a century. I could still see dear Billy standing on the long platform at Great Missenden, waving as the train bore me away. Another door had closed forever.

CHAPTER SIXTEEN

Journey's End

I

Authors retire when they run dry, not when they are old. In 1970, although seventy-eight, I was still a hard worker. In that year I had published the third volume of this autobiography, *The Bright Twenties*, and I was working on its successor, which I called *Sunshine and Shadow*. There had been plenty of both in my life and though now the shadows were lengthening I was not aware of any loss of zest. I still hoped to count some useful and pleasant hours, to find happiness in the autumn of my years. Twenty-five of my forty-five books were still in print. I had been writing for over sixty years.It was odd to think that the grandchildren of my first readers were now reading my books, but one day I had a shock. I called at a well-known bookshop and asked for a copy of my novel, *The Remarkable Young Man*. The long-haired assistant returned, after a search, saying "I regret we haven't the book—there's been no demand for his books since he died." I told him that he was "The Remarkable Young Man" for he had achieved the feat of talking to a corpse.

I was in Paris on my seventy-ninth birthday. With reference to the Potocki chapters in *The Bright Twenties*, Countess Potocka gave a party at her house in the Rue de L'Elysée. It stood, one of a row of fine houses that overlooked the President's Palais de L'Elysée, running into the Champs Elysées. De Gaulle had cast envious eyes on these mansions, wishing to demolish them and build a block of administrative offices next to his official residence but he met resolute opposition.

The staircase of the house, leading to the first-floor salon, was hung with Potocki portraits that had been retrieved from the Château de Lançut in Poland. There were ninety guests. Their names, announced, sounded like a roll-call of French history. There was a white-headed old butler who had been in the Potocki service for over fifty years. What memories he must had had of a vanished regime in the family palaces in Warsaw, Cracow and Lançut!

Some of my English colleagues were there but two whom I would like to have seen were absent. Terence Rattigan was in Bermuda, Graham Greene was in Antibes. He wrote: "I would have broken my firm resolution to avoid cocktail parties for the pleasure of celebrating your seventy-ninth birthday but I'm afraid I can't get to Paris on the eighteenth." Three months later he published a volume of autobiography, *A Sort of Life*, that gave me some concern. In 1925, a gangling youth just down from Oxford, the future novelist of genius had come as a journalist-pupil to the *Nottingham Journal*, which I had edited. I did not mind his romancing about me as a sort of Mr. Micawber, suffering from creeping paralysis and wearing an eyeglass on a ribbon, but I objected when he proceeded to state, "He was said to be the son of a local tradesman, but other rumours, which he did not seem to resent, had it that he was the illegitimate child of one of the dukes in The Dukeries." The only possible inference from this was that I was the illegitimate son of the sixth Duke of Portland who, in 1924, happened to have taken the chair in the Council Hall at Nottingham when I lectured for the Byron centenary celebrations! I made an immediate protest against this ridiculous allegation, which he had picked up, he explained, from gossip in my reporters' room. The passage was deleted from all further reprints of his book, but this did not stop a colourful legend. "I always thought you had ducal traits!" wrote a friend. If Graham Greene had been present at Countess Potocka's he might have checked his data. Alas, he did not come, and fell into error, for which he apologised.

On that day there were two parties in the Rue de L'Elysée. The French President was giving one across the way for Prime Minister Heath. There was a traffic jam of cars for both.

I stayed for a few days in Paris with my cousin Walter, surviving at eighty-two with the bullet he had received in his lung in a Greek riot sixty-five years earlier. In June I went to Nottingham to give a lecture for the Writers Club at the University. When the taxi took me from the station to my hotel I asked the driver where he was going. I could not recognise the city of my birth with its new face-lift. Some of it, concrete and glass, in the current vogue of window-punched packing cases, reminded me of a town in the Middle West, it was so brashly new and uniform.

At the lecture I received the "distinguished-old-boy-treatment", with the Lord Mayor in the chair and the audience very kind to me. On my last day in Nottingham I had a genial visitor, a stranger, Mr. Cyril Goodman. He had a car waiting outside and wanted to take me to Rempstone Rectory which he had just bought. I said I was pressed for time. He would run me out, give me lunch and get me back for my 4 p.m. London train. "After all, you wrote *Scissors* about the Rectory and in a sense it belongs to you," he said, smiling. So I went. He had spent a large sum on the old Rectory, bathrooms, radiators, a modern kitchen, paved walks. I showed him the room, Dorothy Hartley's, that I had slept in. "Then we will call it 'The Cecil Roberts Room'," he said, "and it will always be at your disposal." My host took me out to lunch. A local inn had been converted into a restaurant that would have done credit to the Bois de Boulogne. I asked who had performed this miracle. The proprietor came forward. He was a Pole. "Did you ever hear of a château called Lançut in Poland, the property of Count Potocki?" I asked. His eyes opened wide. "Heard of it! I was once employed there! You are the only person I've met in England who has ever heard of it." So we talked of that château near Cracow. "You will always have a welcome here," he said on my leaving.

In Nottingham I found that the Victoria Station, on the site of my birthplace, had in turn been demolished and in its place a twenty-storey building, with offices, shops and a supermarket had been erected.

A check to my ego came in the train going to London. A pros-perous-looking man got into my carriage. He lit an expensive cigar and started to talk to me about racehorses. I did not seem very intelligent. He then tried duck shooting in which, again, I could not shine. He turned to plastic and I learned he had three factories making a million buttons a week that went all over the world. Finally, he asked me what I did. I told him I wrote books. "Books!" he said, "I never read them!" I felt I had been put in my place. He offered me a cigar as a solace. But I did not smoke. After that he was silent for the rest of the journey.

II

When I went to lunch with William Plomer, the poet-novelist, at the Café Royal, he found me in good form. "I can tell you the reason," I explained, "This morning I came out of prison after two years hard labour, writing *Sunshine and Shadow*. It's an occasion for me to get drunk but I've no capacity for drink, as you know." To be frank, like some criminals, I had enjoyed my imprisonment. So we gossiped happily about poetry and dressing-gowns and sitting for your bust—as he had just done, in fact about everything. I apologised for talking so much. "Now tell me about yourself." "No," he said, "I would rather hear you talk. When I think of the range of your interests and your experience and your energy and curiosity and good memory, I feel decidedly dim." How modest and genuine William was!

And now to Venice, with nothing to do except correct six hundred sheets of typescript. The old haunts there never failed to enchant me; the balcony of the Robilants on the Grand Canal for the Regatta, which had known Byron, with his mistresses and private zoo in the courtyard, where Shelley had called and, playing with Byron's little daughter, Allegra, had recorded the event in the worst line, possibly, in English poetry—"We sat there rolling billiard balls about." I called on the Ashley Clarkes, not at an Embassy this time but in their little palazzo next to the garden where I had written one of my novels; and then to visit Prince Alphonse Clary at his palace on the Zattere, for whose grandfather young Chopin had played in their lost Bohemian castle at Teplitz; how rewarding all talk with him was! And, as down the years, I went to the delicious, lagoon garden of Princess Aspasia. It was the last time I would see her. The next year when I arrived in Venice she had just died. I went out to the island cemetery and found her grave. The flowers on it were still fresh, but the flowers on the adjacent grave had perished, left in tribute to Stravinski who had preceded her by only a short time. A few yards further along was the grave of Diaghilev. I had been there in 1929 when they buried him. Leaving, I learned that Frederick Rolfe, alias Baron Corvo, that tortured, unhappy author of *Hadrian VII*, who had died of starvation in Venice, was buried in a columbarium, sky-high, in "Paupers Row". (Where were the Corvites, and the "fans" of that warped genius ?)

Venice was noisy with tourists who blocked the Merceria in footsore processions. I found the antidote to this confusion born of coach-and-charter-plan. I walked about after midnight, when the great Piazza and the streets were empty, and a full moon threw its silver light upon Gothic marble windows and little bridges over dark canals, so that passing down the arcades towards St. Mark's, lace-like, pinnacled with saints and domed, I might have met the ghosts of Canaletto, Guardi, Casanova and Goldoni, who walked there while the pigeons slept and the gold-winged angel on the Campanile veered towards the east.

En route to Rome at the end of October I lunched at the Villa Sparta with Queen Helen. How beautiful, all grey and russet, lay Florence in the valley of the Arno!

Back in Rome in my old quarters I welcomed Richard and Dorothy Church. I was alarmed to see how feeble he had grown. He did not get out of the car to look at the fountains at the Villa d'Este. Orietta and her husband gave a dinner for him at the Palazzo Doria. You reached the *piano nobile* by an enormous wide flight of steps, forbidden to Richard with his heart condition, but it happened there was a lift tucked away in a corner so it was brought into use. He loved every moment, his mind as alert as ever. He carried home for me the corrected script of *Sunshine and Shadow*. We would meet next summer. On Christmas Eve, 1971, a letter came thanking me for my customary seasonal present of wine.

So once again our thanks for the vintage and the friendship that doubles the bouquet. You added, too, so much to our holiday in Rome. We cannot forget the intimacy and warmth. It was Rome with something extra to history. It gave a meaning to the pomp of the Vatican and took the poison out of the traffic! There is no object in writing novels today, so that I am at a loss what to do, other than my reviewing. Poetry is equally at a discount. No doubt you feel the same after finishing and delivering your fourth volume. We are both suffering from post-natal fatigue, aggravated by *anno domini*. God have mercy upon our fountain pens and refill them as Elijah refilled the widow's cruse!

The New Year opened ominously, with a strike. Last spring there had been an economic blizzard. The pound had been devalued twice, the dollar twice. Soaring inflation had made nonsense of thrift. There was political insanity in the air. The Trade Unions, which had abolished the appalling industrial slavery of the eighteenth and nineteenth centuries, had become the tyrants of the present century, blackmailing the public to enforce uneconomic demands. Riding in a London bus I learned from a notice that its driver was making twice what I was. He would be subsidised if he struck. and pensioned in old age. The page-boy at my club arrived in a taxi and could not be disciplined since he would walk out. It was the mode among the young to look like tramps. If you spoke good English you were suspect. I observed with despair the vogue of Beatlemania with its erotic ecstasies. In the moneyed world there was madness too. Insane prices were paid at auctions in the panic engendered by inflation. (£1,200,000 for a painting by Velasquez of his valet, which fifty years earlier had fetched £84,000; and £200,000 for a Stubbs painting of a stallion, sold a century earlier for £860.) Looking at "modern" art, architecture, sculpture, music and literature I seemed to have entered the Age of Ugliness. When the Rolls-Royce Company lowered its radiator, like a Greek Temple, it lost its grandeur, and went into bankruptcy; it seemed symbolic of the disintegration of the British Empire. I became aware that I had lived through a turbulent period of history, straddling two great wars, with another ever-threatening, and seen standards demolished by which life had been regulated by our fathers. To bolster the untenable export-import theory black and brown labour was drawn upon, creating appalling social and economical problems in a country grossly overpopulated. On the credit side we had abolished poverty, the slums and oppressive hours of labour. The young enjoyed a moneyed freedom that would have seemed a mirage in my youth.

In March came news that did not surprise me. Richard Church died quietly while making morning tea, an achievement. For me the *summum bonum* is in Keats' line in the *Ode to a Nightingale*—

"To cease upon the midnight with no pain". Dr. Matthews, a retired Dean of St. Paul's, surpassed even this. "Aged ninety-two, he died in bed reading", reported *The Times*.

III

The preparations mounted for the celebration of my 80th birthday and the publication of my book. There was to be a Foyle Literary Lunch and my publishers were giving a cocktail party at the Savoy Hotel. To save labour and the hazards in sending out invitations, I joined my party to theirs. Two days before flying to London I caught influenza. I staggered into Michael Gilliam's studio at the B.B.C. to rehearse the interview he had taped. A day later I stood with Paul Hodder-Williams in the Savoy Hotel to receive our hundred and sixty guests. Hodders had ordered a large cake, in book form, entitled *Sunshine And Shadow*. There were so many candles on it that blowing them out nearly suffocated me. Paul made a generous speech:

> I am the fourth Hodder-Williams to be chairman of Hodder and Stoughton since we started to publish Cecil. My three uncles, Ernest, Percy and Ralph, preceded me and I cannot express his publishers' verdict in truer words than those written to him by Ralph at the time of his brother Percy's death. "You know you were his favourite author. He was always excited and confident about you and, business apart he had both pride and affection for you." We have not changed.

So up went the glasses and out went the candles. Somehow I made a reply. After a small dinner party at the Ritz Hotel, given for me by my fifty-year-long friend Mrs. Boehm, I went home to bed. It had been a wonderful day.

The next morning I looked through letters and telegrams, from Noël Coward, Queen Helen of Rumania, Terence Rattigan, the Lord Mayor and City Council of Nottingham, the British Council in Rome, the Society of Authors, Compton Mackenzie, Romola Nijinsky, and many others. What greatly moved me was a telegram from former members of my *Nottingham Journal* staff in 1920: "Greetings and salutations in enduring memory of those six vital years in which 'Scissors' was the youngest editor of England's oldest newspaper." I much regretted the absence of Aubrey Cartwright, now the father of two sons. He was in Sarasota, Florida. "I am attending an important archaeological conference or I would be with you, dear Pedagogus," he cabled. "I will see you in August."

I was up and about again for the Foyle Literary Lunch. Sir John Betjeman took the chair. The Dorchester Hotel ballroom, was filled with four hundred guests. Friends had come from the United States, Italy, France, Germany, Austria, Spain, Poland and Greece. I made a reply to John's very complimentary speech. And this time it was not easy, for my heart was full. I felt I could utter the old prayer—*Nunc Dimittis.*

In the inscrutable manner of destiny it was not I who was called. I did not see Aubrey that summer. Five months later he suddenly died, aged forty-two. A month later dear Isa Potocka died. So I would go no more to Casa Estella and the Château de L'Echelle. At eighty, one has entered a time of closing doors and vanishing friends.

Epilogue

Just before my birthday celebrations a young man from a London paper came to interview me. He wanted to know what philosophy I had derived from a long experience of life. "John Betjeman has written of you 'He has done what so few of us have done, thoroughly enjoyed life.' Do you agree with that ?" he asked.

I told him I did, and was most grateful for what had been granted me. My work had been my joy. Despite the defeats and the failures, and I had known plenty, destiny had been kinder than I had anticipated. My schoolmaster had called on me to recite Shakespeare's famous lines from Hamlet: "There's a divinity that shapes our ends, rough-hew them how we will." I astonished him by saying that I thought the poet had misplaced the comma, and the line should run: "There's a divinity that shapes our ends rough,— hew them how we will." Certainly my early years were rough and took a lot of hewing. But I had rewards. All my life I had been blessed with a consuming zeal. From the age of twelve I had wanted to be an author, and I had been an author. I said to my interviewer —"I account it my good fortune that what it has pleased me to do has given pleasure to others, as my mail assures me. I have been able to work most of my life in freedom and to live in beautiful places—for how terribly grim is the environment of many. I have been blessed also with a remarkable memory, with fluent speech and good eyesight, for I've never needed glasses for reading or writing. These blessings have come from no virtue of mine but from innate endowments. Next to writing I have loved reading, travelling, and good conversation."

"You have had a long and varied experience of life—what has it taught you ?" asked my interviewer. "Very little," I replied, "We like to persuade ourselves that experience makes us wise, I doubt this. I believe that if one had the chance of starting life all over again one would commit the same follies, or others as fatal. We are terribly fallible. What has fifty thousand years of life taught the human race? Nothing. It is still organising itself for mass murder. With every step forward of science the threat of it grows worse. But the world will go on, despite disasters and atomic bombs. The sex impluse is the most powerful and ungovernable thing in the world. The young will always be in one another's arms, in ecstasy. Happily, they have no burden of recollections, no means of comparison with the past. They live in the immediate present. To know much is to foresee much, and be apprehensive. A philosopher has said that most people lead lives of quiet desperation. Today, with incessant political turmoil we lead lives of noisy desperation. Universal communication has brought us universal worries."

"Then you are a pessimist about life?" asked my visitor. "Not at all," I replied. "Having often feared the worst I have been pleasantly surprised by the better. Of course, I've been the prey of a highly-strung temperament. That goes with any artistic endowment. I've always been envious of staid, normal people—and yet I should hate to be one! That I'm alive and alert at eighty is a miracle since I have sadly abused a frail constitution with overwork. I've failed in many ways, and my ambition has not been satisfied—how many of us are satisfied? This has not embittered me. Life is far too short to wade through a morass of regrets, and accuse Fate of unkindness. Many do not get what they deserve, and many do not deserve what they get. We are pawns of Destiny and to protest is to be like a flea shouting at an elephant. All one can do is to make the most of what one is endowed with, and that is considerable. A life that gives us all a sunrise, a sunset, the moon at night, the miracle of spring, is richly endowed, in my mind. In the more personal sense, I count it good fortune to have been born English, inheriting my country's wealth of Nature, art, music, literature and language, with freedom to enjoy these, and also to have been born a man— I've never felt that women, without whom we should neither exist nor survive, have had a fair deal. Happily we are remedying this."

My interviewer asked if in my autobiography I had told everything. "Certainly not," I replied. "Of course, I've seen and heard enough to blow off the roof of our human habitation but I don't want any *succès de scandale*, I am nauseated with the strip-tease school of writers who butcher their relations and friends to make an author's holiday. It is all so easy if you feel no restraint of decency and loyalty".

"I suppose, since you have written so many books, forty I believe, you have found writing easy?" "Oh, no! Not at all," I replied, "although I have been manipulating words for over sixty years. Words are slippery things and the English language is a superlatively rich one and offers a bewildering choice. All good writing is in reality a mosaic of exact selection and form. It obsesses you. Sometimes I've got out of bed in the middle of the night to go to my desk and change an adjective that has kept me awake. Friends accuse me of being 'absent'—I've been busy with a line in my head. Fiction, of course, is easier than other forms of writing, more fluid. These five books of autobiography have cost me ten times more worry and labour over ten years than any others I have written. If I had foreseen what they involved I doubt if I should have had the courage to begin—and, you know, ten years after you are seventy are precious!"

We talked a long time. When my visitor rose to leave it was the sunset hour. We stood a while by the window of my room and looked out over Rome, the Eternal City, which had just celebrated its 2,720th year since it had emerged from the mists of legend. Its millions had come and gone, in the frailty of brief life. Standing there, my visitor asked me one last question. To sum up, what did I consider were the most important things in life? It was not an easy question to answer but after a little meditation I ventured a reply: "Health, contentment and happiness," I said.

The End of the Fifth and Final Volume of this Autobiography.

Index

compiled by Robert Urwin

A Man Arose (author's tribute to Churchill), 200, 201, 250
Abbotsford, visit to, 161–2
Aberconway, Lord, 86, 155, 166
Acapulco, visit to, 268
Acton, Harold, 100, 283
Aeschylus (*Persae*), 237
Aguilar, Senor M., 76
Alba, Duke of, 73, 105–6, 112, 211
  family history of, 74–6
  guest of, 74–5
Alessandra, Princess (later ex-Queen of Yugoslavia), 62, 81, 93, 101, 187, 197, 300
Alexander, Field Marshal Lord, 110, 112
Alexander, King of Greece, 283
Alexandra, Queen (Consort to Edward VII), 79, 80
Alexandria, visit to, 257–8
Alfonso XIII, King of Spain, 53, 76, 257, 277
Ali Pasha of Jannina, 325
All Souls College, Oxford, 217, 226, 230, 274, 315, 330
Alassio
  author's homes in, 24, 38, 43, 44, 45, 87:
    Villa Margherita, settling in at, 45–51
    Palazzo Vairo, apartment at, 115, 118–23, 132, 145, 147–50, 152–3, 158, 167–9, 176–7, 187, 194–5, 208, 228–9, 236, 275

Villino Romano, 244–5, 247
  decision to leave, 229, 230, 247
  English "colony" at, 46, 48–50, 120–2, 229
  Honorary Citizen of, 217, 232, 320
Allingham, Ann, 24
Allingham, Tony, 24
And So To America (author's), 14, 18, 41
And So To Bath (author's), 218
And So To Rome (author's), 49, 52, 54, 60, 82, 136, 280
Anderson, Sir John (later Lord Waverley), 85
Anthime, caretaker of Mrs. Cartwright's villa on Riviera, 28
Aosta, Duchess of, 229, 283, 321
Arandora Star, sinking of, 144
Arden's, Elizabeth (New York), story of hairdresser at, 303–4
Argyll, Duke of, 107
Armour, Mr. and Mrs. Norman, 209
Armstrong, Neil (Moon-landing of), 334–5
Arran, Earl of, 312
Arrau, Claudio, 160
Arthur, Sir Raymond, 209
Ashbourne, Lord (Admiral Superintendent, Gibraltar), 103
Ashcroft, Dame Peggy, 170
Aspasia, Princess, of Greece, 62, 81, 197, 233, 300, 344
Asquith, Lady Cynthia, 240
Athenaeum Club, 50, 194

Athenagoras, Patriarch of Constantinople, 325–6, 338
Attlee, 1st Lord, 118, 312
Auden, W. H., 116
Auer, "Teddy", 261–2
Aynho Park, Banbury, 136, 157

Baciocchi, Felice, 51
Balanchine, George, 241
Baldwin, Stanley (later 1st Earl Baldwin), 205
Balfour, David, 214, 232
Balfour, Sir John, 107–8
Ball, V.C., Captain, 311
Ballance, Lieutenant-Colonel William, 171, 180, 206, 305, 306, 309, 314
Bangkok, tour of, 261–2
Baruch, Bernard, 193
Basore, John, 52, 99
Bauer, Gunther, friendship with, 28–9, 91, 169–70, 183
marriage of, 187
Beale, Mrs. Truxton, 61, 62
Beatrice, Infanta (of Spain), wife of Prince Torlonia, 53, 76
Beatty, Lord and Lady, 86
Beauclerk family (in Corfu), 338
Beaverbrook, Lord, 17, 209
Bedford, Duke of, 307
Beecham, Lady (Utica), 85
Beecham, Sir Thomas, 24, 40, 85
death of, 242–3
Beerbohm, Sir Max (see also Jungmann, Elizabeth)
author's visits to and conversations with, 123–7, 129–30, 142, 152–3 158–9, 164, 174
cartoons by, 127
illness and death of, 180, 181–2
memorial plaque to, 194, 214, 232–3
Benes, President, 35
Bennett, Arnold, 126
Berners, Lord, 139, 145
Bestegui, Charles, 215
Betjeman, Sir John
friendship with author, 115, 139, 163–4, 176, 224–5, 236, 252, 291, 315, 348, 349

Collected Poems (1958), 236
Summoned By Bells, 236
Bevan, Stuart, 203
Bingham, Lady Cecil, guest of, 109–13
Birkett, Sir Norman (later Lord) and Lady (Billy)
friendship with and hosts to author, 34, 65, 86, 95–6, 113, 115, 123, 139, 153, 174, 184, 194, 201–4, 221–4, 231, 248–50, 293, 312, 334–5
Lord Birkett's TV appearance and radio talks, 222; career of, 223; George Blake spy trial and, 249
death of Lord Birkett, 258, 259, 263–4, 273–4
death of Lady Birkett, 340
Bisaccia, Duke and Duchess de, 227–8
Blake, George, spy affair, 249
Block, Senor (Spanish friend) 69, 70, 72
Blue Sisters Order, anecdote on, 162–3
Bock, Mrs. Alida, 186–7, 189, 190, 228, 244, 247, 275, 299
Boehm, Mrs. "Perry", friendship with, 31, 77, 91, 102, 105, 109, 114, 116–17, 159, 195, 347
Bohus, Baron Paul, 299, 332
Boleyn, Anne, 83
Bolshoi Theatre, 333
Bonaparte, Elisa, 51
Bonaparte, Prince Jerome, 100, 146, 246
Bonnie Prince Charlie, 160, 161
Boot, Sir Jesse (later 1st Lord Trent) 136, 252, 304, 311, 313
Booth, General William, 311, 313
Borghese, Princess Pauline (Napoleon's sister), 151
Bori, Lucrezia, 80, 100
Boult, Sir Adrian, 307
Bourbon des Deux-Siciles, Prince Giovanni de, 336
Bourbon-Parme, Prince Louis de, 179
Bouvier, Professor Arthur, 275
Bracken, Brendan (Lord Bracken), 202–3

Bradfield College, 153, 207
Braine, John, 307
Braque, Georges, 193
Brassouvie, Baron, 67
Breguet (watchmaker), 332–3
Bridport, Lord and Lady
history of dukedom of Brontë,
238–9, 240
visit to Sicilian home of, 238–9
Bright Twenties, The (author's), 335,
341
Brocket, Lord (Ronnie) and Lady
(Angela)
Brocket Hall, description and
history of, 283–91
visit to Ireland with, 293–9
visit to Venice with, 299–300
Brodie, Harry, 291
Brolio Castello, 89
Bronislava (Nijinsksy's sister), 241
Bronson, Mrs. (friend of Robert
Browning), 128
Brontë, Duke of, *see under* Bridport,
Lord and Lady, *and* Nelson,
Lord
Browning, Robert, 53, 61, 126, 128,
136, 145, 309–10, 331
Asolando, 128
Brownlow, Lord, 196
Bruce, Hon. Mrs. (Dorothy Boot),
252, 304
Bruce, Kathleen, 252, 304
Buckle, Richard (*Nijinsky*), 333
Buckner, Richard, 285
Burghesh, Lady, 140
Byron, Lord (the poet), 214–15, 286,
314, 325
death of and burial at Hucknall
Torkard, Notts., 288
statue in Rome, 212–13
Byron, Rev. Lord, 136

Cacciatore, Vera, 30
Cadogan, Sir Alexander, 18
Callas, Maria, 197–8
Campbell, Mrs. Patrick, 253
Canova cenotaph, St. Peters, 101
Cap d'Antibes
Casa Estella, Mrs. Cartwright's
guest at, 17, 27–30, 86, 94, 132,

142, 155, 166, 176
La Garoupe, Lady Norman's guest
at, 155, 164–6, 178–9, 187,
228–9, 232, 233–5
Caraccioli, Prince, 238
Caralt, Luis de, 70–1, 72
Cardenas, Donna Lucienne de, 241
Cardinal de Bernis (Marcus Cheke),
197
Carol, King of Rumania, 283
Carton, County Kildare, guest at,
293–7
Cartwright, Aubrey, 13, 24, 29, 37,
42, 43, 53, 82, 86–7, 90–1, 113,
208, 348
marriage of, 293, 311
Cartwright, Mrs. Beatrice, friendship with author, 13, 15, 17, 27,
28, 35, 37, 86, 98, 139, 140, 142,
143, 144, 145, 166, 176, 208,
209
death of, 185–6
Cartwright, Dallas, 28
Cartwright, Sir Fairfax and Lady,
89, 157
Cartwright Richard, 136
family history of, 136–7
death of, 157–8
Caruso, Mrs. Dorothy, 17
Casals, Pablo, 183
Cashel, Dean's Palace at, 298
Cassino Monte
author's visit to, 31–2
story of bombardment and battle
of, 14, 22, 31–2, 33–4, 110–11
Lord Alexander's views on,
110–11
Catherine, Princess (of Württem-
berg), 100
Cato Street conspiracy, 271
Cecil, Lord David, 175, 194
The Young Melbourne, 287
Cecil, Lord Robert, 60–1
Cellini, Benvenuto, 77
Château de la Cröe, Duke of
Windsor's Riviera home, 28, 29
Cheke, Sir Marcus and Lady, 197
Chequers, Bucks., visit to, 185,
204–5
Child, Sarah, 84

Chopin, Frederick, 180–1, 184
  concerts in England, 180
Church, Richard
  friendship with and visits to, 214,
    232, 248, 291, 334, 345
  death of, 346
Churchill, Sir Winston, 112, 135,
    185, 192, 221, 312
  author's last meeting with, 200–1
Churchill, Randolph, 332
Churchill, Mrs. Randolph, 86
Churchill, Lady Randolph (Sir
  Winston Churchill's mother),
  140
Churchill, Winston (Sir Winston's
  grandson), 86, 332
Clark, Sir Kenneth and Lady, 61,
  100, 145
Clark, General Mark, and bombard-
  ment of Monte Cassino, 110–11
Clarke, Sir Ashley and Lady, friend-
  ship with, 156, 214, 232–3, 245,
  246, 344
Clary, Prince Alphonse, 344
Clements (Czech Communist leader),
  35
Clifford, Mr. and Mrs. Bede, 209
Clifton Colliery, Nottingham, 95
Cloetta, Antoine, 186
  guest of, 230, 283
Clore, Sir Charles, 307
Coldstream, Sir William, 307
Coleridge, Lady Georgiana, 175
Collier, Constance, 125
Colquhoun, Archibald, 244
Colum, Padriac, 146
Conrad, Joseph, 126, 231, 311, 336
Constantine, King of Greece, 283,
  323
Cook, Kennedy, 145
Cooper, Alfred Duff (later Lord
  Norwich), 42, 43, 60, 62
Cooper, Lady Diana, 41, 42, 43, 60,
  62, 256
Copenhagen, visit to, 269
Corfu, visit to, 338–9
Cornell, Katherine, 102
Corvo, Baron, see also Rolfe,
  Frederick
  Hadrian VII, 344

Coward, Sir Noël, 193, 273, 347
Cowper, Earl, 289
Craig, Gordon, visits to, 123, 142–4
Crane, Mrs. Murray (Josephine),
  friendship with, 18, 34, 55, 60,
  61, 94, 146, 208, 211
Cripps, Seddon (2nd Lord Parmoor),
  friendship with and visits to,
  24, 155, 229, 321
  history of Cripps family, 321
Cripps Sir Stafford, 26, 49, 85, 86,
  155, 321
Croesus, King of Lydia, 328
Cuevas, Marques George de, 228–9
  background and career, 241–2
  death of, 240, 242
Cunard Lady (Emerald), 23–4, 334
  affair with Sir Thomas Beecham,
  242–3
  death of, 40–1

Da Falla, Manuel (The Three
  Cornered Hat), 80
Dali, Salvador, 18, 56, 212
Davenhill, Mr. (Don Guillermo),
  British Consul in Granada, 79
Day-Lewis, Cecil, 330
Denikin, General, 221
Diaghilev, Serge, 333, 334
Dickson, Dorothy, 175
Dickson, Lovat, 291
Diercks, Barry, 179
Diogène, M. and Mme., 69–70
Dior, Christian, 193
Domecq, Senorita, 78
Doria, Prince and Princess, 43–4, 152
  daughter Orietta, 43
Dromoland Castle, County Clare,
  297
Dublin, visit to, 293–9
  Horse Show at, 297; and tour of
  Ireland, 298–9
Duncannon, Lord and Lady, 83
Dunstan, Eric, 187
Duveen, Lord, 100

Eccles, Sir David (later Lord Eccles),
  63
Eden, Sir Anthony (later Lord
  Avon), 185, 187

Edinburgh Festival, 159–63
Edward VII, King, 79
Edward VIII, King, see Windsor, Duke and Duchess of
Egypt, tour of, 166–7
Eight for Eternity (author's), 14, 17, 21, 22, 30, 33, 38, 51, 110, 199
Einstein, Lewis, 211
Eisenhower, President, 187
Eliot, T. S., 315
    Poems, 126
Elizabeth, H. M. Queen, 121, 245, 246
Elizabeth, the Queen Mother, unveils Byron statue in Rome, 212–13
Esher, Lord, 85
Esmond, Jill, 311
Esterhazy, Prince(s), 57, 58, 59
Eugenie, Empress, 75

Falls, Cyril, 250
Faucigny-Lucinge, Prince, 336
Ferdinand VII, King of Spain, 113
Ferrero, Marchese, 122
Filippo, Prince, 43
Fischer-Dieskau, Dietrich, 169
Fitzgerald, Lord Edward, 294–5
Fitzwilliam, Lord, 20
Flecker, James Elroy (Poems), 108
Fleming, Sir Alexander, 192
Flight of Birds, A (author's), 303–4, 312
Florentia, Armada wreck, 107
Fonteyn, Dame Margot, 217, 316
Forster, E. M. (Passage to India), 49
Forte, Sir Charles, 312
Foyle, Christina (and Foyle Literary Luncheons), 85, 273, 306–7
    author's eightieth birthday lunch, 348
    author as chairman at Paul Getty lunch, 306–7
Frankau, Pamela, 19
Freeman, John, 222
Freyberg, General Lord, 110, 155
Fulton, Wayne, 267–8
Furtwangler, William, 193

Galleani, Count, 122
    Banca Galleani, 122–3

Garbo, Greta, meeting with, 132–3
Gates, Everard and Stella, 138, 176, 185
Gautier, Theophile, 181, 252–3
Getty, Paul, 336
    Foyle luncheon for, 306–8
Gibbs, Sir Philip, friendship with and visits to, 139, 175, 194
    death of, 264
Gibraltar, author's stay at, 102–4
Gielgud, Sir John, 170
Gilliam, Michael, 275, 347
Glasgow, author's lectures at Athenaeum Theatre, 97–8
Goddard, Lord Chief Justice, 223
Golden Ball inn, Henley, 64
Golding, Louis, 169
Goldman, M. (owner of "Burma Gem" business), 166, 188
Gone Rustic (author's), 142, 154
Gone Sunwards (author's), 210
Goodman, Cyril, 343
Gordon-Lennox, Lord Nicholas, 175, 198, 208
Gowers, Sir Ernest, and Gowers Report on preservation of historic houses, 85
    author's speech on, at Foyle luncheon, 85
Granby, Marquis of, 255
Grand Cruise, The (author's), 272, 275
Granville, Lord, 290
Graves, Robert, meetings with, 330
Gray, Effie (wife of Ruskin), 78
Greene, Graham, (A Sort of Life), 234
Greenwich Royal Naval College, 124
Grosvenor, Sir Richard, 270
Growing Boy, The (author's), 201, 252, 315, 331, 332
Gruenther, General, 111
Guadalupe, visit to, 268
Guests Arrive, The (author's), 30
Guitry, Sacha, 193

Haile Selassie, Emperor, 277
Halifax, Lord, 217

Hall, Radclyffe, and *Well of Loneliness* case, 249
Hallward, Bertrand, 136
Hanbury, Sir Thomas and Lady, 121
Mrs. Hanbury, 121
Hankey, Mr., Chargé d'Affaires, Madrid, 73, 80
Hannay, Sir James Fergusson, 85, 118, 196
death of, 251-2
Hare, Augustus (*Walks in Rome*), 129
Hart-Davis, Rupert, 233
Hartington, Marchioness of (Kathleen Kennedy), 20
Hartley, Dorothy, 320-1, 343
Hartley, Robert, 320
Haydn, Joseph, 57-9
story of "Haydn's skull", 57
Hazlerigg, Lord and Lady, 115
Headfort, Elizabeth Marchioness of, 297
Heenan, Cardinal, 312
Helen, Queen-Mother of Rumania, friendship with, 109-10, 113, 229, 285, 321-2, 345, 347
Helpmann, Sir Robert, 160
Henderson, Sir Guy and Lady, 209, 304
Heuss, President, 193
Hill, Mrs. Kathleen, 185, 204
Hilton, James, death of, 164
Hodder-Williams, Paul, 347
Hodder-Williams, Ralph, 21, 347
Hoffman, Malvinia, 107
Hong Kong, visit to, 263, 264-6
Honolulu, visit to, 267-8
Hood, Sir Alexander Nelson, 239, 240
Horsley, Cecil (Bishop of Gibraltar), friendship with author, 103-5, 145
death of, 147
Howard, Leslie, 211
Huidobra, Manuel, 54, 72, 73
Humby, Betty (Lady Beecham), 85, 242-3
Hutchinson, A. S. M., 97
If Winter Comes, 97
Hutton, Barbara, 277
Hyde, H. Montgomery, 306, 313
Life of Norman Birkett, 306

Ibn Saud, King, 193, 277
Iddesleigh, Lord, 312
Ightham Mote, near Sevenoaks, restoration of, 205-6
Iliffe, 1st Lord (Tod) and Lady (Charlotte)
friendship with and guest of, 65, 138, 153, 159, 172-3, 194, 206-7 209, 221
death of, 230
Iliffe, 2nd Lord (Langton), 236
Illingworth, Lady, 270
home of (history of), 270-1
author's birthday party at, 271-2
India and Ceylon, tour of, 259-61
Innocent X, Pope, and Velasquez portrait, 112-13
Inverchapel, Lord, 23
Ionides family, 119
"The Emperor, 119-20
Iron Duke (Jellicoe's flagship), 339

Jacobs, Naomi, 195
James, Henry, 126
visit to home at Rye, 312-13
Jekyll, Francis, 153, 155, 174
Jekyll, Gertrude, 174
Jellicoe, Admiral 1st Earl, 339
John XXIII, Pope, 212, 278, 312
death of, 279
Jowett, Benjamin, 49
Joyce, James, 23
Jungmann, Elizabeth (later Lady Beerbohm), 124, 125, 128, 130 152, 158, 180, 198
marriage to Sir Max Beerbohm, 181

Khan, Aga, 193
Kahn, Florence (Max Beerbohm's first wife), 125, 127
Karajan, Herbert von, 160
Keats, John, 136, 150-1, 173, 346-7
Kelly, Felix, 37, 54
Kelly, Sir Gerald, 135, 307
Kemsley, 1st Lady, 110
Kennedy, President John, 167
assassination of, 302
Kennedy, Mr. and Mrs. Robert, 167
Kennedy, Mrs. Rose, 167

Kersley, Nancy, 23
King, Cecil, 312
King's Story, A (Duke of Windsor), 147
Kipling, Rudyard, 125, 310
Kirby, Kenneth, 263
Kitzbuhel, visit to, 182, 195
Knole Park, Kent, visits to, 16, 96, 138
Kolchak, Admiral, 221
Küngsholm, author's world cruise in, 251, 255–69, (see also under various places visited)

La Rochefoucauld, Armand de, 17, 116, 227–8, 252, 259
Lacy, Alec, 220, 231, 274
    Greek Pottery in Bronze Age, 220
Lamb family (and Lady Caroline Lamb), see under Brocket, Lord and Lady
Lamberg, Count, 182
Lançut estate, Poland, treasures of, 336–7, 343
Lavery, Sir John, 310
Lawrence, D. H., 117, 126, 179, 240, 314
Lear, Edward, 99
L'Echelle Château de, Haute Savoie (home of Countess Potocka), 335
    guest at, 335–7
Leeming, Dr. (American clergyman in Constantinople), 325
Lehar, Franz, visit to home of, 171–2, 195
Leigh, Vivien, 311
Leinster, Dukes of, family history, 293–5
Leinster, Rafaelle Duchess of, friendship with, 176, 197, 294
Lerici, visit to Shelley's home at, 51
Leslie, Sir John, 55, 244
Leslie, Sir Shane, 146, 171
Lichtenstein, Prince Heinrich, 336
Ligonier, General Viscount, 122
Lorca, Garcia, 79
Love is Like That (author's), 184, 185, 186, 187, 194, 245
Lucca, Giuseppe de, 301

Ludwig II (King of Bavaria), 57
Lupescu, Madame, 283
Lusignon, James, and Lusignano village, 191
Lyell, V.C., Lord, 18
Lynd, Sylvia, 164
Lyon, William, 160

McCardie, Mr. Justice, story of suicide of, 203–4
McClelland, Rev. H. S., 97–8
Macdonald, Marechal, Duke of Taranto, 215
McDougal, Ian, 103, 105
McEachern, Neil, friendship with, 215–16
    "The Marshal of Flowers", 216
McGuigan, Cardinal, 32–3
Mackenzie, Sir Compton, 97, 347
MacPherson, Duncan, 142
McWilliams, Mrs., host at Coconut Grove, 210
Maddocks, George, friend and travelling companion, 188, 323–4, 326, 327, 338–9
Magie, David, (Roman Rule in Asia Minor), 99
Makarios, Archbishop, 326
Mallet, Sir Victor, friendship with, 43, 117, 145, 156, 246
Maniaces, Ancient Greek general, 238
Mann, Thomas, 193
Manos, Colonel, 233
Margaret, Princess, Countess of Snowdon, 53, 212, 213
Maria Pia, Princess, of Italy, 179
Marie-Louise, Princess, 337
Marshall Hall, Sir Edward, 222
Mary, Queen (Consort to George V,) 23, 205, 337
Masaryk, Jan, 34
    death of, 35–6
Masefield John
    friendship with and visits to, 153, 200, 231, 248, 273, 292, 309–10, 315, 320
    death of, and memorial service, 330–1

Massine, Leonide, 80, 195
  friendship with, 331–2
  My Life in Ballet, 331
Matthews, Dr., Dean of St. Paul's, 347
Maugham, W. Somerset
  friendship with and guest of, 66,
    67–8, 123, 129, 130, 135, 159,
    193, 224, 231
Maugham, Syrie (Mrs. Somerset
  Maugham), 27
Maurois, André, 231–2
Maxwell, Elsa, 198
Maxwell Literary Lunch, Oxford,
  320
Maxwell-Scott, Sir Walter, 161
Maxwell-Stuart, Colonel and Mrs.,
  160–1
May, Henry, 62
May, John, 214, 232
Mazarin, Cardinal, 252
Mdivani, Princes Alexis and Serge,
  17
Medina, Lola, 79
Meehling, Monsignor Frederick,
  257, 317
Melbourne, Lord (Queen Victoria's
  Prime Minister), and marriage
  to Caroline Lamb, 286–9, 308–9
Melchett, Lady, 62
Mellon, Andrew, 113
Mendl, Sir Charles, 134
Mendl, Lady, 133–4
  story of her gold unicorn, 133
Menuhin, Yehudi, 92, 183
Menzies, Sir Robert, 217
Mercati, Marie, 100
Methuen, Lord, 219–20
Michael, King of Rumania, 283
Michelangeli, Benedetto, 128
Michelangelo, story of his Sleeping
  Cupid, 218–19
Monckton, Major-General Gilbert
  (2nd Lord Monckton), 175,
  176
  family of, 316
Monckton, Lady "Polly"
  friendship with and visits to, 175,
    205–6, 218–19, 299
  death of, 305
Mond, Derek, 62, 321

Mont Blanc Tunnel, 337
Montalembert, Marquise de, 245
Montgomery, Field Marshal Lord,
  112
Montoro, Maria Duchess of, 105–6
Morgan, Charles, 169
Morgan, Pierpont, 277
Morrell, Lady Ottoline, 334
Morton, H. V., 311
Muggeridge, Malcolm, 130
Mundella School, 331
Muselier, Admiral, 220

Nassau, visits to, 209–10, 304–5
Nelson, Admiral Lord, and history
  of dukedom of Brontë, 238–9
Neville-Terry, Consul-General,
  Rome, 145
Nicea, Bishop of, 326
Nicholas II, Czar (and Dowager
  Empress), 57
Nichols, Beverley, 291
Nicolson, Sir Harold, 331
Niehans, Dr. Paul
  family background and career,
    191–3
  famous patients of, 192–3, 255
Nightingale, Florence, 325, 327
Nijinsky, Madame Romola, 299, 347
  story of her life with Nijinsky,
    333–4
Nijinsky, Vaslav, 333, 334
Nobili, Signora, 30
Norman, Lady "Fay"
  friendship with and visits to, 86,
    155, 165–6, 178–9, 187, 188,
    228, 233–5, 240
  death of, 305
Norman, Sir Henry, 166
Norman, Nigel, 235
Nottingham
  author given Freedom of, 310–
    11, 312, 313–14, 317
Nottingham Journal, 123, 342, 347
Nureyev, Rudolf, 316

Oakes, Sir Harry, murder sensation,
  209, 304
O'Brien, Hon. Grania, 297, 299

Olivier, Sir Laurence (later Lord), 311
Olivier, Tarquin (*Eye of the Day*), 311
One Small Candle (author's), 23, 34
Origo, Marchese and Marchesa, 117
Orlovsky, Count, 211
Osbourne, Lloyd, 27

Pachmann, Vladimir de, 180
Page, Cadness, 175, 291
Paget, Louis, 304
Paget, Miss (of Villa Garibondy), 179
Palatiano, Count, 338 (*see also* Beauclerk family)
Pallanza, Villa Taranto, guest at, 215, 216
Palma, *see under* Spain, Majorca
Palmerston, Lord, 285, 287, 289–91
Pamphili, Prince Fillipo Doria, 199
Panni, Nicoletta, 301
Paris, Comte de, 18
Parker, Lord Chief Justice, 249
Parmoor, 1st Lord, 24
Parmoor, 2nd Lord, *see* Cripps, Seddon
Paston-Bedingfield, Sir Edward and Lady, 83
Pastor, Don Antonio, 75
  his definition of a Grandee of Spain, 75–6
Patterson, Charles Jerome Bonaparte, 100
Patterson, Elizabeth, 100, 146
Paul VI, Pope, 300, 326
Pearson, Sir Neville, 175
P.E.N. International conferences, 61, 169, 184
Percy, Robert Heber, 145
Pergamum, Turkey, visit to, 329
Pergamum Museum, Berlin, 329
Perkins, Ward, 214
Peter, ex-King of Yugoslavia
  meetings and friendship with author, 80–1, 93, 100, 187, 197, 299–300
  death of, 101
  son Alexander, 98, 300

Philip, Prince, Duke of Edinburgh, 245, 246, 311, 339
Philip II, King, of Spain, 77
Pietramella (Futa Pass, N. Italy), 60
Pilgrim Cottage (author's), 129, 130, 142, 154
  sale and disposal of, 142, 153–5
  story of conversion of adjacent cottages, 39, 55, 64–5
"Pilgrims, The", Lord Birkett as president of, 250
Pius IX, Pope, 278
Pius XII, Pope, 94–5
  treatment by Dr. Niehans, 191, 192, 193
Plater, Mr. and Mrs., 155
Plomer, William, 244, 344
Plowright, Joan, 311
Podhajsky, Colonel, 170
Pogson, Mr. and Mrs. Frank (Orietta Doria), 252, 280
Portal to Paradise (author's), 156, 159, 170, 172, 190, 232
Potocka, Countess Betka, 337
Potocka, Countess Isa, guest of, at L'Echelle, 335–7; and in Paris, 341–2
Potocki, Count Alfred, 336, 343
Potocki, Hetman (Polish general), 337
Potter, Mary, founder of Blue Sisters Nursing Order, 163
Pound, Ezra, 23, 126
Praslin-Choiseul, Duc de, 245
Prokosch, Frederick, 129
Proust, Marcel, 66
Pryce-Jones, Alan, 164, 194

Quarrell, Chance, 204
Quick, Dorothy, 208, 268–9
  friendship with Mark Twain, 269
Quiller-Couch, Sir Arthur, 225

Rapallo, Villino Chiaro (Sir Max Beerbohm's home), 123–4, 129, 131, 158
  memorial plaque to Sir Max, 232–3
Rattigan, Terence, 347

Razor's Edge, The (Somerset Maugham), 62

Reid, Beryl (Lucien's and Bevis's mother), visit to, 247–8

Reid, Bevis, 93, 321

Reid, Lucien, 24, 30, 62, 93, 247, 272, 299, 311, 321

Remarkable Young Man, The (author's), 152, 155, 159, 173

Rempstone Rectory, Loughborough, 320, 323, 343

Renault, Mary (*The Last of the Wine*), 238

Ribblesdale, Lady, 146, 161

Ricasoli, Baron, author's host at Castello Brolio, 89

Rolando Ricci, Luigi (Marchese del Carretto), friendship with author, 190–1, 201, 216, 229, 236, 238, 239, 276, 283, 312, 316
family homes of, 246–7, 275

Richmond, Duke and Duchess of, 198

Rieu, Dr. E. V., 50, 291

Rieu, Sir Louis and Lady, 49–50, 229

Roberts, Cecil, *see also under various names, place names (visits to etc.)*
in U.S., post-war reflections and frustrations, 13–14, 17–19; return to England, 19–20
friendship with Duke and Duchess of Windsor, 16, 28, 36, 38, 101 (*see also under* Windsor, Duke and Duchess of)
methods and preparations for constructing novels, 22–3, 174, decision to emigrate, 24–7, 52, 141–2, 153
meeting with Jan Masaryk, 34–5
brother's illness in Venice, 40–2
fight for conversion of Henley cottages, 39, 55, 64–5
tour of Spain, 69–81 (*see also under* Spain)
tour of North Italy to Salzburg, 86–93; back to Rome, via Venice, 93–5
Atlantic crossing in tornado, 101–2

involved in riot in Pamplona, 108–9
disposes of Pilgrim Cottage, 142, 153–5
tour of Greece, 156–8
tour of Egypt, 166–7
attends Edinburgh festival, 159–63
donates travel prize to old school, 176
last meeting with Sir Winston Churchill, 200–1
assists in release of Baron Wolfner, 188
B.B.C. broadcast by: *Young but not Angry*, 205
created Honorary Citizen of Alassio, 217, 232, 233
move from Alassio to Rome, 230, 247, 276–82 (*see also under* Alassio *and* Rome)
world cruise in *Küngsholm*, 251, 255–69
seventieth birthday party, reflections on, 270–2
visit to Dublin and tour of Ireland, 293–9
awarded Freedom of Nottingham, 310–11, 312, 313–14, 316, 317, 320
awarded Rome Gold Medal, 318–20
tour of Greece and Turkey, 322–30
eightieth birthday celebrations, 347–51

Roberts, Charles, 115

Roberts, Sir Richard, 115

Roberts, Walter, author's cousin, 226, 231, 342

Robilants, the, 61, 93, 344

Rockefeller, John D., 241

Rodd, Peter, 86

Rodriguez, Francisco, Triana stables of, 106

Rogeri, Count, 245

Rolfe, Frederick (Baron Corvo), 344–5

Rome
award of city's Gold Medal to author, 318–20

Rome—*cont.*
English College:
author's lecture at, 198–9
history of, 199
Ecumenical Councils in, 279–80,
300
Salvatore Mundi Hospital, 244,
255, 300
Grand Hotel, 276–82, 310, 331–3,
335, 345–6, 351
Roosevelt, Mrs. Eleanor, 211
Roosevelt, President Franklin, 211,
270
Rothenstein, Sir John, 307
Rothermere, 1st Lord, 209
Rothschild, Baron Eugene de, 16
18, 183, 195
Rothschild, Baron Maurice de, 42
Rowse, Dr. A. L., friendship with
and guest of, 217–18, 225–6,
230, 250, 274, 282, 291, 315,
320, 331
Rubinstein, Artur, 160, 339
Rucellai, Countess, 128
Rumbold, Richard, 243–4
A Message in Code (diary of), 244
death of, 244
Ruskin, John, 78, 151

Sackville, Lord and Lady, author's
hosts at Knole, 16, 65, 96, 138,
153, 194
death of Lady Sackville, 221
Sackville-West, Vita, 73, 331
Salzburg
tour of Northern Italy to, 86–93
other visits to, 195, 316
San Lucar, Duke of, 69
Sand, George, 180–1
Sandoz, Maurice, 61, 191
author as guest of, 56–8
death of, 59–60
stigmata experiences of, 55–6
Sandys, Mrs. Duncan (and daughter
Celia), 153
Sanguszko, Prince (Polish patriot),
336
Santa Margherita villa, author's
home in Alassio
Santayana, George, 145

Santayana, Pardo de, 140
Santos Domingo, Marques de, 108
Sarasate Museum, Pamplona, 108–9
Sawyer, Eric, 179
Schlegel, Lieutenant-Colonel, 31–2
Schwarzenberg, Prince, 117
Schwarzenberg, Dr. Felix, 183
Schwarzkopf, Elizabeth, 116
Scissors (author's), 123, 291, 305,
320, 343
story of writing of, 322–3
Scott, Sir Peter, 252, 304
Searle, Alan, 193
Sedes, M. Yumni, 325
Selected Poems (author's), 231
Sermoneta, Duchess of, 139–40
Severn, Rev. Henry, 173–4
Severn, Joseph, 150–2, 173, 174, 332
inspiration for *The Remarkable
Young Man*, 150–1
Sharp, William ("Fiona Macleod"),
239
Shaw, George Bernard, 27, 232, 288,
301
"Shaw's Corner", Ayot St. Law-
rence, 288
Shaw, Marcelli, 158
Shearer, Moira, 160
Sheen, Monsignor Fulton, 17
Sheldon, Edward, visit to, 253–4
Sidney, Mrs. Albert (later Countess
Potocka), 62
Sissinghurst Castle, Kent, 331
Sitwell, Edith, 146
Sitwell, Sir Osbert, 146
Smyth, Sir John, 93
So Immortal a Flower (author's), 22,
156, 209
Sommer, Rudi, 170, 183
Spain
author's visits to and tours of, 54,
66–7, 69–81, 105–9:
Barcelona, 70–2, 180
Granada, 79–80
Huelva, 107
Madrid, 72–7, 80–1, 108
broadcast in Spanish from,
72–3
Majorca (Palma), 180–1
Pamplona, 108–9

Spain—*cont.*
Salamanca, 108
Seville, 77–9, 105–7
Torremolinos, 105
Spear, Ruskin, 307
Spears Against Us (author's), 22, 90, 182
Spry, Constance, 175
Stanley, Lord, 86
Starkie, Professor and Mrs. Walter, 73, 211
Stevenson, Robert Louis, 27
Stewart, Lady Margaret, 244
Strachey, Lytton, 126
Stravinsky, Igor, 344
première of *The Rake's Progress*, 116
Strong, Austin (*Seventh Heaven*), 253
Stuart, Hon. Simon, 82, 89, 90–1
Suez crisis (1956), 185, 187
Sunshine and Shadow (author's), 14, 24, 62, 244, 288, 341, 344, 345
publishing of, and eightieth birthday celebrations, 347–8
Sutherland, Duke and Duchess of, guest of, 82–4, 209
Sutherland, Graham, 135

Talyarkhan, Darius, 128
Tensing, Sherpa, 260
Terrace In The Sun, A (author's), 95, 102, 117, 140
Terry, Ellen, 142
Teyte, Maggie, 18
Thompson, Dorothy, 35
Thorwaldsen, sculptor, 212
Three-Cornered Hat, The (Da Falla), 80
Tickle, Monsignor, 199
Tissier, Louis, 24, 252, 272
Tito, President, 277
Tomlinson, H. M., 153
Torlonia, Prince, 53
Toumanoff, Prince, 55
Training Our Airmen (author's), 137
Traquair, ancestral home of Earls of Traquair, author guest at, 160–1
Trent, 1st Lord, *see* Boot, Sir Jesse
Trevelyan, Sir George, 82
Trevelyan, Dr. George Macaulay, 82

Trinity College, Cambridge, 82, 89
Turkey, visit to, 324–30
Pera Palace hotel, 324–5
Pergamum, 329
Tunney, Gene, 301
Twain, Mark, 269

Unwin, Sir Stanley, 307

Vanderbilt, Mrs. Grace, 18, 36, 37, 101
Varé, Daniele, (*The Laughing Diplomat; The Maker of Heavenly Trousers*), 92
Vaughan-Hughes, Commander and Mrs., 338–9
Venice
visits to, 30, 41–2, 60–3, 93, 115–16, 299–300, 321, 344–5
Giardino Eden, 62, 93, 300
Gritti Hotel, 60
Palazzo Labia, 215
Victoria Four-Thirty (author's), 21, 80, 93, 237
censorship of, 140–1
Vienna, visits to:
P.E.N. conference at, 169
Schönbrunn Palace, 169, 171
other visits, 169–72, 182–4, 195–6
Villa Mauresque, W. S. Maugham's home at Cap Ferrat, 67
Vitelleschi, Marchesa Stella, friendship with author and career of, 252–4
Vittorio Emanuele III, King, 257
Vulcania, S.S., 31, 32
voyage through tornado, 101–2

Walker, Mr., Director of National Gallery, Washington, 112–13
Warwick, Earl of, 85
Waugh, Alec, 169, 281
Waugh, Arthur, 281
Waugh, Evelyn, 280–2
Weir, Lord, 137, 157
Wellington, 1st Duke of, 108, 270, 271, 286
Wellington, 6th Duke of, 80
Wells, H. G., 66

Wertheim, Guido, friendship with, 43, 66, 67, 69, 208, 209, 300, 301, 302, 305
Westmorland, Earl of, 83, 84
Wheeler, Sir Charles, 307
Wide Is The Horizon (author's), 245, 250, 265
Williams, Emlyn, 339
Williams, Sir Emrys, 307
Williams, Guy (of Humbert and Williams company), 78
Williamson, Brigadier, and wife, Leila ("Eve Orme"), friendship with and visits to, 169, 175, 198, 220–1, 231
  daughter Mary, 175, 198
Farewell to the Don (Brigadier Williamson), 221
Willkie, Wendell, 200, 253
Wilson, Peter, 307
Wind, Edgar, 94
Windsor, Duke and Duchess of, 23,
  28, 37–8, 62, 101, 147, 182, 195–6, 209
  author as guest of, 16, 36
  Duke's comment on Bonnie Prince Charlie, 101
A King's Story (Duke of Windsor), 147
Winkler, Kurt, 144–5
Wolfe, Humbert, 20
Wolfner, Baron Jancsi, 188, 193–4
Wolfson, Sir Isaac, 307
Women's Press Club, 175
Woodruff, Douglas, 312
Wrangel, General, 221

Yattendon Court, Berks. (home of the Iliffes), 138, 172, 221
Years of Promise, The (author's), 331, 332
Yeats, W. B., 292–3
Young, Mrs. Hilda, 244

Zweig, Stefan, tragedy of, 91